THE
HOMICIDAL
EARL

Also by Saul David

Mutiny at Salerno:
An Injustice Exposed

Churchill's Sacrifice of the Highland Division:
France 1940

THE HOMICIDAL EARL
The Life of Lord Cardigan

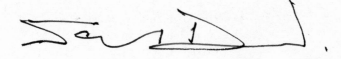

Saul David

LITTLE, BROWN AND COMPANY

A *Little, Brown* Book

First published in Great Britain
by Little, Brown and Company 1997

Copyright © Saul David 1997

A CIP catalogue record for this book
is available from the British Library.

ISBN 0 316 64165 0

Typeset in Bembo by M Rules
Printed and bound in Great Britain by
Clays Ltd, St Ives plc

Little, Brown and Company (UK)
Brettenham House
Lancaster Place
London WC2E 7EN

To Juliet

Contents

Acknowledgements

First and foremost, I must thank Mr Edmund Brudenell and the Honourable Mrs Marian Brudenell of Deene Park for their kind hospitality and permission both to reproduce family paintings and to quote from the family papers in the Northampton Record Office. Without their cooperation, this book could not have been written.

I would also like to thank Her Majesty Queen Elizabeth II for permission to quote from the Royal Archives; the Trustees of the National Library of Scotland for permission to quote from the Brown Papers; the Trustees of the British Library for permission to quote from the Peel Papers; the Trustees of the National Army Museum for permission to quote from the Blunt, Forrest, Harrowby and Raglan Papers; and Wiltshire Record Office for permission to quote from the Ailesbury Papers.

During the course of my research I wrote to and visited many institutions. The following individuals were particularly helpful and I am grateful; Lady de Bellaigue, Registrar of the Royal Archives; Dr Peter Boyden, Head of the Department of Archives, Photographs, Film and Sound at the National Army Museum; Judith Curthoys, Assistant Archivist, Christ Church, Oxford; Alasdair Hawkyard, Archivist, and Mr P.D. Hunter, Librarian, at Harrow School; Mrs J.M. Johnston, Archivist, Wiltshire Record Office; Julian Russell, Research Assistant at the National Library of Scotland; Colonel Robin Merton, Regimental Secretary of the King's Royal Hussars; Rachel Watson, County Archivist,

Northamptonshire Record Office; Dr C.M. Woolgar, Archivist and Head of Special Collections, University of Southampton.

I must also acknowledge the help given to me by the Marquess of Anglesey, Viscount Colville, and the staffs of the British Library, the Cardiff Central Library and Monmouth Library.

Finally, I would like to thank three people who have been behind this project (almost!) every step of the way. Julian Alexander, my literary agent, for convincing me that it would sell; Richard Beswick, my editor at Little, Brown, for proving Julian right and for much useful advice besides; Louise, my wife, for indulging my choice of a somewhat precarious career.

Map 1: The Route to the Crimea: April to September 1854

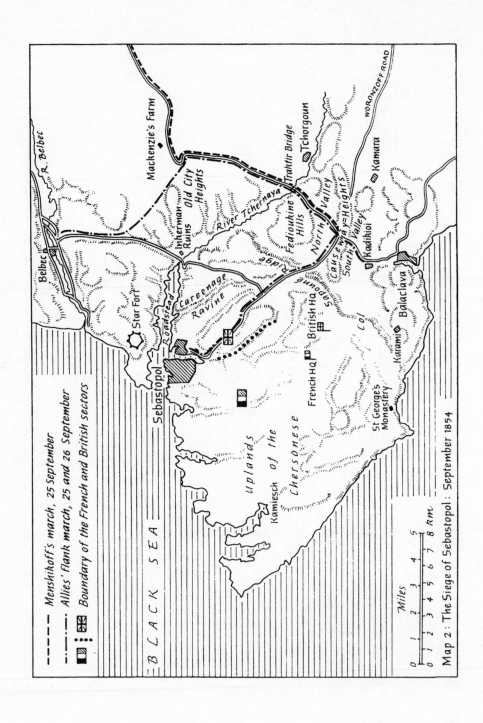

Map 2: The Siege of Sebastopol: September 1854

Menshikoff's march, 25 September
Allies' flank march, 25 and 26 September
Boundary of the French and British sectors

BLACK SEA

R. Belbec
Belbec
Star Fort
Mackenzie's Farm
Inkerman Ruins
Old City Heights
River Tchernaya
Fedioukine Hills
Traktir Bridge
Tchorgoun
North Valley
Kamara
Causeway Heights
South Valley
Kadikioi
Karani
Balaclava
Karami
Col
St George's Monastery
Sapouné Ridge
British HQ
French HQ
Carepnage Ravine
Roadstead
Sebastopol
Kamiesch
uplands of the Chersonese
WORONZOFF ROAD

Miles
0 1 2 3 4 5
0 1 2 3 4 5 6 7 8 km

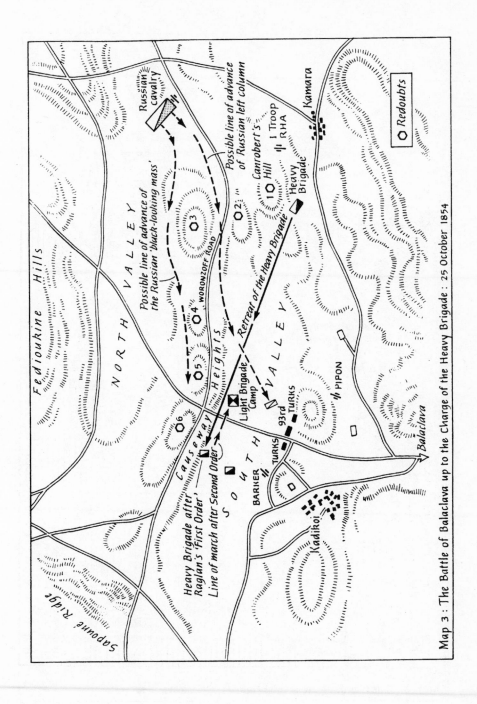

Fedioukine Hills

Sapouné Ridge

NORTH VALLEY

Russian cavalry

Possible line of advance of
the Russian 'black-looking mass'

Possible line of advance
of Russian left column

Kamara

Canrobert's
Hill

1 Troop
RHA

Heavy
Brigade

○3

○2

1○

WORONZOFF ROAD

Causeway Heights

○4

Retreat of the Heavy Brigade

○5

SOUTH VALLEY

PIPON

○6

Light Brigade
Camp

TURKS

93rd

TURKS

Heavy Brigade after
Raglan's 'First Order'

Line of march after Second Order

BARKER

TURKS

Balaclava

Kadikoi

○ Redoubts

Map 3 : The Battle of Balaclava up to the Charge of the Heavy Brigade : 25 October 1854

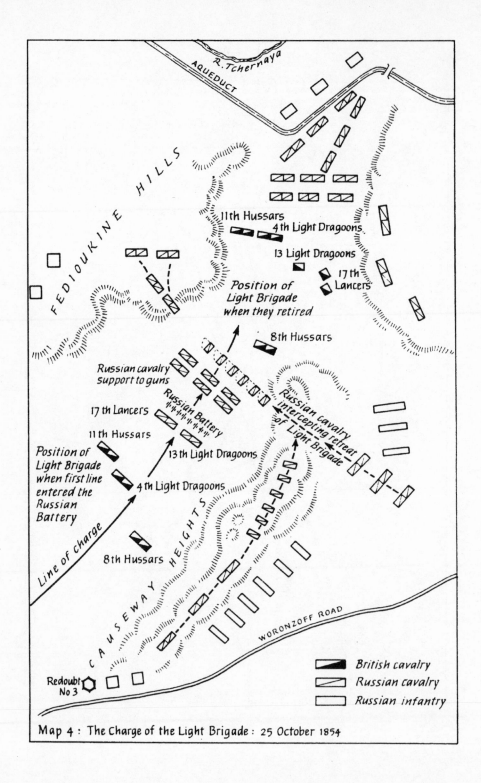

R. Tchernaya

AQUEDUCT

FEDIOUKINE HILLS

11th Hussars
4th Light Dragoons
13 Light Dragoons
17th Lancers

Position of
Light Brigade
when they retired

8th Hussars

Russian cavalry
support to guns

Russian cavalry
intercepting retreat
of Light Brigade

17th Lancers

Russian Battery

11th Hussars

13th Light Dragoons

Position of
Light Brigade
when first line
entered the
Russian
Battery

4th Light Dragoons

Line of charge

8th Hussars

CAUSEWAY HEIGHTS

WORONZOFF ROAD

Redoubt
No 3

British cavalry
Russian cavalry
Russian infantry

Map 4 : The Charge of the Light Brigade : 25 October 1854

THE
HOMICIDAL
EARL

Prologue

The morning of 25 October 1854 did not begin well for the 7th Earl of Cardigan. Asleep aboard his yacht in the harbour of Balaclava, he missed the opening of the Russian dawn assault on the outer defences of the port. When he did arrive to take command of his Light Brigade of cavalry, it was watching helplessly as a huge force of Russian infantry gradually over-whelmed the four Turkish-held redoubts armed with British naval guns on the Causeway Heights to the north of the town.

By 7.30 a.m., after a fierce struggle, the strongest redoubt had fallen, and the remaining three soon capitulated, their inadequate garrisons fleeing in disorder. Forced by this reverse to withdraw out of artillery range to the west, the men of the Light Brigade were again frustrated onlookers when a 'Thin Red Line' of Highlanders and a glorious uphill charge by the Heavy Brigade successively repulsed an attempt by a horde of Russian cav-alry to cross the valley south of the Heights and pierce Balaclava's inner defences. There had been an opportunity to share the Heavy Brigade's glory by charging the Russian cavalry in the flank, as one of the Light Brigade's most experienced officers had urged, but Cardigan had chosen to interpret his orders to mean to stand fast unless directly attacked, and he did nothing.

Lord Raglan, the British commander, perched high above the battlefield on the Sapouné Ridge to the west, then tried to press home his temporary advantage by ordering the cavalry, supported by infantry reinforcements, to advance 'and take any opportunity to recover the Heights'. But the

1

infantry had not yet appeared in sufficient strength and Lord Lucan, the cavalry commander, was unwilling to move his horsemen against pre-pared enemy positions until they had done so. Instead he sent Cardigan's brigade to the head of the valley north of the Heights, to enable them to execute one arm of a pincer attack when the infantry did arrive.

With Cardigan and his men languishing inactive in the plain below, anxious for an opportunity to prove their worth, Lord Raglan became increasingly impatient. More than thirty minutes had ticked by when a member of his staff shouted: 'By Jove, they're going to take away the guns!' Through field-glasses, the Russians could be seen bringing forward horses with lasso tackle to remove the captured naval 12-pounders. The great Duke of Wellington had reputedly never lost an artillery piece, and Raglan, his devoted lieutenant, was anxious to retain the same proud record. Turning to Airey, his Quartermaster-General, he dictated an urgent order to Lucan:

> Lord Raglan wishes the cavalry to advance rapidly to the front –
> follow the enemy and try to prevent the enemy carrying away the
> guns – Troop Horse Artillery may accompany – French cavalry is
> on your left. Immediate.

Captain Nolan, Airey's aide-de-camp and the best horseman on the staff, was detailed to carry the pencil-written order. It was an unfortunate choice given that Nolan had been loud in his criticism of the performance of Lucan and Cardigan thus far in the campaign. 'Tell Lord Lucan the cav-alry is to attack immediately,' Raglan called after him, as Nolan spurred down the precipitous slope.

Within five minutes he had located the cavalry commander – mounted with his staff between the two brigades – and handed him the order, which Lucan carefully read with growing alarm. Now he was being asked to advance to recover the guns without even infantry support. It was mad-ness. Hesitating, he impressed upon Nolan the 'uselessness' and 'dangers' of such an attack.

'Lord Raglan's orders are that the cavalry should attack immediately,' Nolan retorted.

Seven hundred feet lower than Raglan, his view obscured by rising ground, Lucan could not see the captured naval guns being towed away. Did Lord Raglan have a different objective in mind? 'Attack, sir! Attack what? What guns, sir?' he demanded.

Waving his hand vaguely westwards, in the direction he remembered the redoubts were located, Nolan exclaimed: 'There, my lord, is your enemy! There are your guns!'

Looking in the direction of Nolan's gesture, the only guns visible were nine Russian 6-pounders – the sun glinting off their polished brass barrels – one and a half miles distant at the opposite end of the north valley, protected by a vast array of cavalry and infantry. However suicidal, this must be the objective, he reasoned, unwilling to question the insolent staff officer further. Instead, he trotted the short distance round to where Cardigan and his knot of staff officers were waiting, and said: 'Lord Cardigan, you will attack the Russians in the valley.'

'Certainly, my lord,' Cardigan replied, 'but allow me to point out to you that there is a battery in front, a battery on each flank, and the ground is covered with Russian riflemen.'

'I cannot help that,' was the retort, 'it is Lord Raglan's positive order that the Light Brigade is to attack the enemy.'

Resigned to his fate, Cardigan rode over to Lord George Paget commanding the second line, and reminded him that he expected his 'best support'. He then returned to his position at the head of the brigade. A few yards behind him were his staff officers – instantly recognisable in their blue tunics and cocked hats – themselves a little way ahead of the commanding officers of the leading regiments, the 17th Lancers and 13th Light Dragoons, deployed side by side in two lines. In these final seconds before the brigade hurtled to its fate, as an ominous silence fell upon the valley, disturbed only by the creak of leather and the jingle of harness, Cardigan cut an impressive figure. Sitting ramrod-straight in the saddle of his magnificent chestnut charger, Ronald, he stared straight down the valley. Tall and remarkably handsome for his 57 years, with flashing blue eyes and luxuriant moustache and whiskers, his splendid form was perfectly set off by the cherry, blue and gold-embroidered uniform and fur busby of his regiment, the 11th Hussars.

'Here goes the last of the Brudenells,' Cardigan muttered as he turned to his trumpeter. 'Sound the advance!'

Breaking from a walk into a trot, the 673 riders had gone no more than 100 yards when Captain Nolan, shouting and waving his sword, appeared from the left of the brigade, riding diagonally across its front in the direction of the Causeway Heights. Suddenly aware that the brigade was not going to wheel to the right to attack the Heights, Nolan had taken it upon himself to correct the awful error. To an infuriated Cardigan, however, it appeared as if the eccentric Nolan was hurrying the brigade along. A junior staff officer, with no business taking part in the charge, was daring to precede him at the head of the brigade! 'No, no!' Cardigan bellowed. 'Get back into line!'

But Nolan continued his gallop past Cardigan towards the Heights, turning in his saddle to shout: 'Come on!'

At that moment, with less than 50 yards separating Nolan and Cardigan, the Russian artillery to the north of the valley opened up and a shell burst between them. As a fragment of shrapnel hit Nolan square in the chest, piercing his heart, he gave an unearthly shriek. The sword dropped from his raised arm, which remained erect as the rest of his body contorted inwards in spasm. It was this convulsive twitch of the bridle-hand that caused his horse to wheel and disappear between the advancing squadrons of the 13th Light Dragoons. The last hope of averting the terrible tragedy had gone.

As the ever-diminishing Light Brigade thundered towards the Russian guns amidst a hail of bullets, shrapnel and round-shot, Cardigan's thoughts were a mixture of fear and anger: fearful that he would be maimed or killed; angry that Nolan had tried to usurp his authority.

What did not occur to him was what he had to gain by surviving the charge. That simply by virtue of having led it he would return home a hero, decorated by the Queen, lionised by society and cheered in the streets. That by emerging from twenty minutes of hell, he would all but wipe out the disgrace and scandal that had dogged his career: two courts-martial, two court appearances for adultery, a near-fatal duel, a state trial for intent to murder, dismissal from the command of a crack cavalry regiment, blackballed by the leading military club, debates in Parliament about his conduct – all would be conveniently forgotten in the light of his valour at Balaclava. But was Lord Cardigan a hero? Or was the long-drawn-out criticism of his conduct in the Crimea by fellow officers – that he was incompetent, petty-minded, incapable of tactical flexibility and, worst of all, an implicit coward for leaving his men in the lurch when needed most during the famous charge – justified, and in keeping with his reprehensible past?

1

A Chequered History

The sleepy village of Hambleden, Buckinghamshire, perched between the Chiltern hills and an outside bend of the River Thames, was an unlikely venue for the birth of a future Earl of Cardigan. Yet there, on 16 October 1797, in the modest Jacobean manor house, was born James Thomas Brudenell, the 7th and last of his line.

Traditionally, heirs to the earldom arrived at Deene Park, the Brudenells' Northamptonshire country seat. An imposing mansion with strong Tudor and Georgian influences, it had expanded over the centuries from a quadrangular medieval manor house that pre-dated the Norman Conquest. For many years it had been owned by Westminster Abbey and used as a hunting lodge; then from around 1215, the time of the Magna Carta, it was leased to local squires with an obligation to provide hospitality once a year for the abbot and his entourage. This arrangement continued after it first came into Brudenell hands in 1514.

Brudenells of any significance can be traced back to the fourteenth century, when they were freeholders on the border of Oxfordshire and Northamptonshire. The first to rise to prominence was William Brudenell, son of a minor landlord, who – during the reign of Edward III – married a Buckinghamshire heiress and acquired estates in the counties of Buckingham, Hertford and Oxford. His son, Edmund, trained as a lawyer and became Richard II's Attorney and Coroner in the Court of Common Pleas for life. When Richard was usurped by Henry Bolingbroke, Duke of Lancaster, in 1399, he resigned, later becoming a Member of Parliament for Buckingham.

5

Edmund's great-nephew, Robert, a younger son with little inheritance, also took up law and in 1510, a year after Henry VIII had become King, he was made a justice of the Court of Common Pleas. A knighthood followed in 1517, and four years later he became the Court of Common Pleas' Chief Justice. With the proceeds of his lucrative legal career, Robert had been investing in land since the turn of the century; in 1508 he bought the family estates from his impecunious cousins, and six years later acquired Deene from the Lytton family. By the time of his death in 1531, Sir Robert had property in seven counties and had laid the foundations of the Brudenell fortune.

The man responsible for the family's elevation to the aristocracy was Thomas Brudenell, Sir Robert's great-great-nephew who, on the death of his childless uncle in 1606, inherited the family estates. At first, he did not appear to be a strong candidate for royal favour. In the summer of 1605 he had married Mary Tresham, the daughter of Sir Thomas, a leading Catholic, and sister of Francis, a conspirator in the Gunpowder Plot who died in prison. Yet, despite embracing his wife's outlawed religion, Thomas was able to use his wealth to take advantage of the Stuart predilection for selling titles. When James I created the Order of Baronets in 1611, to raise money for the colonisation of Ulster, Thomas was one of the first to pay the fee of £1,000. Seventeen years later, with Parliament refusing to grant the new King, Charles I, any more money to fund his disastrous war with France and Spain, Sir Thomas was ennobled as Baron Brudenell for the consideration of £6,000. Owing, however, to his allegiance to Catholicism and his earlier conviction for recusancy (refusal to attend his parish church), he was not able to take his seat in the House of Lords until 1640.

Given his religion and his close links with the Court, particularly Charles I's Catholic Queen, Henrietta Maria, it was inevitable that Lord Brudenell would support the royalist cause in the Civil War against the Puritan-dominated Parliament. But the raising of a troop of horse for the King was to cost him dear: two years in the Tower, the forfeiture of his estate, the sacking of Deene, the expenditure of the bulk of his fortune. Despite all this, when Charles I – imprisoned in Carisbrooke Castle on the Isle of Wight and desperate for money to fund an escape attempt – wrote to him in September 1648, promising him an earldom in exchange for £1,000 in cash, he did not hesitate to comply. It was all in vain, however, for within five months Charles I had been tried and executed by the radical 'Rump' Parliament. But in 1661, following the death of Cromwell and the restoration of the monarchy, Lord Brudenell got his reward when

Charles II honoured his father's promise and made him the 1st Earl of Cardigan. He was 83, and destined to enjoy his high rank for just two years.

During the next fifty years the Brudenells consolidated their power and wealth by marrying into some of the greatest families in the realm, including the Constables, Saviles, Talbots and Bruces. Such alliances refined still further their renowned good looks, made them increasingly proud and arrogant, and undoubtedly contributed to the woe that befell the more headstrong of them. One such was Anna Maria, daughter of the 2nd Earl and married at 18 to the Earl of Shrewsbury. An outstanding beauty, notorious for the laxity of her morals, she went too far when she openly flaunted her affair with the Duke of Buckingham. In his diary, Samuel Pepys described the bloody duel that ensued in 1668 between Shrewsbury, Sir John Talbot and Bernard Howard on one side, Buckingham and two cronies – Holmes and Jenkins – on the other:

> [They] met yesterday in a close near Barn Elms, and there fought.
> And my Lord Shrewsbury is run through the body, from the right
> breast through the shoulder, and Sir John Talbot all along up one
> of his arms, and Jenkins killed upon the place and the rest – all in
> a little measure – wounded. This will make the world think that
> the King hath good councillors about him, when the Duke of
> Buckingham, the greatest man about him, is a fellow of no more
> sobriety than to fight about a whore.[1]

Anna Maria is said to have disguised herself as a page, held her lover's horse during the fight, and that night made love to him as he wore the shirt stained with his own and her dead husband's blood. As punishment the adulterers were bound over by the House of Lords 'not to converse or cohabit for the future', while Anna Maria's son was handed over to the care of his grandfather, Lord Cardigan. After serving more than a year of penance in a Paris convent, Lady Shrewsbury was forgiven by Charles II and returned to Court. There she met and married a member of the King's household, and quietly lived out the remaining twenty or so years of her life.[2]

The 2nd Earl was given little respite, however. In the reign of William and Mary, his son and heir, Francis, was convicted of high treason for supporting the Jacobite cause and spent four years in the Tower. Fortunately, the Earl managed to outlive his errant son and was succeeded in 1703 by his grandson, George. Quick to realise that adherence to Catholicism

7

would bring him and his family into perennial conflict with the monarch, the 3rd Earl publically abjured his religion in 1708 and became a committed supporter of the Established Church and Protestant monarchy. When Lady Cardigan, the wife of the 3rd Earl, became Woman of the Bedchamber to Queen Caroline, wife of George II, in 1731, there began a period of close association with Hanoverian sovereigns that lasted for more than a century. Eschewing high political office – some said because of a lack of intellect – they were content to accumulate, by intermarriage and royal favour, ever more power in the form of appointments, land and titles.

All four of the 3rd Earl's sons held positions in the royal household, and three became peers in their own right. The exception was Robert, the third eldest and grandfather of the 7th Earl. Born in 1726, and educated at Winchester and Oriel College, Oxford (where he took his degree), he followed the traditional route of a younger son into the Army. At 33, he married Anne, daughter of Sir Cecil Bisshopp, much to the annoyance of Horace Walpole who wrote: 'So the pretty Miss Bisshopp, instead of being my niece, is to be Mrs Bob Brudenell. What foolish birds are turtles, when they have scarce a hole to roost in.'[3]

Both Robert and his wife were honoured by royal appointments: he was Groom of the Bedchamber to George III's brother, the Duke of York, and later aide-de-camp to the King; she was one of the four Women of the Bedchamber to Queen Charlotte. Then in 1768, whilst in command of the 4th Regiment of Foot, Robert died suddenly. His widow was three months pregnant and a son was born posthumously, also named Robert; without a father, a title or a fortune, his future looked bleak.

All this changed two years later with the premature death of the 35-year-old son and heir of George, the 4th Earl of Cardigan. When the old Earl died in 1790, therefore, the title passed to his eldest brother James. Since he was a 65-year-old widower with no children, it was taken for granted that he would eventually be succeeded by his young nephew Robert. This calculation was thrown into some doubt the following year when the young-again 5th Earl became engaged to a woman half his age – Lady Elizabeth Waldegrave, the Princess Royal's Lady of the Bedchamber. Society was much amused by the apparent mismatch, comparing it with the ill-starred union of January and May in Chaucer's *Merchant's Tale*. Not so Robert who, fearing the loss of his inheritance, dissolved into tears on hearing the news. He need not have worried for, despite a long and happy marriage, the couple had no children.

Though strikingly handsome, in every other sense Robert was an unexceptional man, modest and kind, with little of the traditional Brudenell love of finery and pomp. He had been brought up with the expectation of succeeding to one of the richest earldoms in the realm, but by a single parent with a modest income. Joining the majority of his kin in the service of the royal family, he became an equerry to Queen Charlotte in 1791. His politics were conservative, and his ambition little more than to lead the life of a country gentleman.

It was not entirely out of character, therefore, when he chose as his bride a young lady who, while beautiful, could not have been acceptable to his uncles. Yet Penelope Cooke, the woman in question, was hardly of humble birth. Her father, George Cooke of Harefield Park, Middlesex, was a respectable landed gentleman, while her mother was the daughter of a baronet. In addition her brother, Henry Cooke, a notorious military dandy nicknamed 'Kangaroo' on account of his long legs, was to end up with a knighthood and a colonelcy after a long career as secretary and confidential aide-de-camp to the Duke of York, Commander-in-Chief of the Army. But she was not an aristocrat, had no dowry worth mentioning, and was never likely to be seen by his uncles as suitable material for a future Countess of Cardigan.

Knowing all this, Robert took the unprecedented step of proposing, and being accepted, before consulting with the heads of his family. When, towards the end of 1793, he summoned up enough courage to inform his uncles, the Earl of Ailesbury was at first supportive, taking it for granted that Robert's 'prudence in other things' would 'show' in his choice. However, he was quickly disabused of this notion once he learnt the identity of the prospective wife, and immediately sent his elder brother, the Earl of Cardigan, to talk some sense into their lovesick nephew. Within days, Cardigan reported back on the outcome of the interview: Robert had accepted that there was 'a great deal of good sense' in their arguments opposing the alliance, and that he was 'very much obliged' for their 'advice'; he had agreed to pass on their objections to his fiancée, and would write as soon as he had received an answer; he had 'cried very much and seemed very unhappy'.[4]

But the 22-year-old Miss Cooke was never likely to back out of such a favourable match while the man she loved was willing to go ahead regardless. There was the danger of disinheritance, of course, but only an unlikely last-minute heir could prevent the earldom from devolving upon her future husband, since to split the estates from the title would be unthinkable.

9

Consequently, the couple stood firm, and early in 1794 Robert wrote to inform Lord Ailesbury of the forthcoming marriage. 'I hope most sincerely the step I am going to take will meet with your approbation,' he concluded, 'as nothing could make me so miserable as to forfeit your good opinion.'[5]

The reply was ambivalent. While Ailesbury considered the marriage imprudent, and 'therefore I never have, nor can I now, express my approbation of the step you are going to take', he had 'heard nothing but what is favourable of Miss Cooke's character and person, and my best wishes will attend you in all situations'. While hardly a blessing, it nonetheless implied that he was not prepared to sever all links with his nephew over this issue. Indeed, within a year of the marriage at St George's Church, Hanover Square, on 8 March 1794, Robert was writing to Ailesbury to inform him of the birth of his first child – christened Elizabeth. The warm tone of the letter – 'My Dear Uncle' and 'Your Affectionate Nephew' – indicate that Ailesbury had let bygones be bygones, which is confirmed by the fact that by 1797 Robert was sitting as a Member of Parliament for his uncle's 'pocket' borough of Marlborough.[6]

Towards the end of 1797, there occurred an event that could not fail to unite the whole family. In the rented manor house at Hambleden, where the young couple had been living since 1796, Penelope gave birth to a healthy son, christened James Thomas in honour of his two surviving uncles; an earlier son, born the year before, had not long survived childbirth. The significance of this new arrival was that he was destined to be the first Earl of Cardigan to succeed his father for three generations.

Despite the high station that awaited him, the young heir's early years were more like those experienced by the sons of minor landed gentry. His parents lived quietly and modestly, undertaking charitable works for the parish as befitted a couple of their station. Writing in retrospect, the parish rector, Henry Colborne Ridley, described Robert Brudenell as a man 'who has ever been a great friend to Hambleden', and who used to rent land close to the village and offer it at a nominal rate to the poorest families to grow vegetables. Ridley was more candid in contemporary correspondence, noting that Mr Brudenell 'has his failings but some good qualities', while his wife was 'indeed a sweet woman, possessing a temper, both mild and engaging'.[7]

Early Promise

It was, perhaps, unfortunate that young Brudenell was destined to spend his formative years almost exclusively in the company of women. The sons of gentlemen, particularly aristocrats, had limited contact with their fathers and spent most of their time with siblings, supervised by nurses and other – usually female – household servants. This was fine if they had brothers, but Brudenell remained an only son since six children subsequently born to his parents were all girls. Only during the time spent with his tutor and, occasionally, his male cousins did he escape this feminine influence.

Without the natural challenge of another male, and amidst a coterie of adoring and respectful females, he was over-indulged and developed a despotic, domineering nature towards his supposed inferiors. This attitude did not, however, extend to the fairer sex; on the contrary, he was at ease with them, enjoyed their company and treated them – the prettier the better – with an almost medieval chivalric respect.

Men were a different proposition. With no experience of the spirit of compromise which brothers often need to get along, he tended later in life – by his rude manner and overweening pride – to create crises out of relatively insignificant dramas. At the same time, he was deferential to those he saw as his superiors and always retained a keen respect for authority and the natural order of things. By both nature and nurture a conservative, content with his station in life and anxious to retain the status quo in church, state and society, only at the very end of his life did he come to understand the necessity for change if a semblance of the old order was to remain in a century of upheaval.

Perhaps one of the greatest myths expounded about the future 7th Earl of Cardigan is that he lacked brains – that he was, in the words of Cecil Woodham-Smith, his best-known biographer, 'unusually stupid', and that 'his glorious golden head had nothing in it'. His academic record, however, provides solid evidence to the contrary. After arriving at Harrow on 6 September 1809, a month short of his twelfth birthday, he did well in the basic examination of his Greek and Latin and was placed in the Third Form Head Remove.[1]

Founded in 1571 as an endowed grammar school to educate 40 local boys free of charge, Harrow had become by the turn of the nineteenth century – thanks to the gradual exploitation of a clause in its charter allowing the admittance of fee-paying pupils from further afield – one of the five great 'public' schools patronised by the sons of nobility and gentry (the others were Winchester, Eton, Westminster and Rugby). The trend, however, was only recent; prior to 1750, most had been educated at home and then went on to university or to travel in Europe.

During the Head Mastership of the popular Dr Joseph Drury, Harrow became the most fashionable public school of them all; in 1803, for example, more than 10 per cent of the 345 boys were either peers or the sons of peers. It was also one of the most academic, and among its pupils were some of the foremost intellects of the century including Henry Temple (the future Viscount Palmerston), Robert Peel and Lord Byron. The carved names of all three can still be seen in the dark panelling of the original Elizabethan School House.[2]

When Dr Drury announced his retirement in the spring of 1805, Byron led a campaign to have him replaced by his brother, Mark, the Under Master. But the governors were divided 3:3 over the issue and the deciding vote, cast by the Archbishop of Canterbury, went to his only rival, Dr George Butler, a Cambridge don. Outraged, Byron devoted his remaining months at the school to organising opposition to the new regime. After refusing the traditional invitation to dine with the Head Master at the end of the half-year, he is said to have taken a prominent role in the notorious three-day summer rebellion, the highlight of which was to have been the firing of a train of gunpowder in a corridor through which Dr Butler used to pass on his regular nightly rounds. Butler escaped without injury, however, and Byron later claimed that he had 'saved the schoolroom from being burnt, by pointing out to the boys the names of their fathers and grandfathers on the walls'. A second, even more serious rebellion in 1808 indicates that time had not endeared Butler to all his pupils. Undoubtedly, his proclivity for personally flogging his boys, both junior and senior, did not help. After some fluctuation, the school roll rapidly diminished in the latter years of Butler's rule, falling to just 115 in 1829, the year of his retirement.[3]

It was into this somewhat volatile atmosphere that James Brudenell arrived in the autumn of 1809. Among his contemporaries were Henry Perceval, son of the future Prime Minister; Charles Yorke, later Earl of Hardwicke; and the Honourable Arthur Calthorpe, uncle of a man who, many years later, would implicitly accuse him of cowardice in the face of the enemy.

Assigned to the Head Master's House, Brudenell joined upwards of 70 boys, all paying four guineas for entry, four guineas for annual fees and up to £100 a year for board, lodging and extra tuition. Most of this money went directly into the pocket of the Head Master who, even allowing for expenses, could make more than £4,000 a year (roughly £160,000 today, forty times as much), although his official salary was only £30. And this at a time when the average peer's income was £8,000, a substantial merchant's £2,500, and a comfortable shopkeeper's only £100 a year. The other masters, too, made a handsome profit out of offering board and lodging to pupils in their own Houses. In addition, many boys boarded at the Dames' Houses, two establishments run by Mrs Leith and Mrs Armstrong. Here, fees were lower but conditions were more chaotic and food notoriously poor.[4]

Despite securing a place in the relatively ordered atmosphere of the Head Master's House, Brudenell found his first few days particularly traumatic. Torn from the bosom of an adoring family, he was forced to undergo the gratuitously brutal initiation ceremony of running the gauntlet between two rows of boys armed with knotted handkerchiefs. He also had to come to terms with being made to 'fag' for a senior, a system compulsory for boys below the fourth form. A fag's duties included the upkeep of his fagmaster's clothes, fetching hot water (and hot rum punch from the local public house in cold weather), and fielding when the seniors were playing cricket. Rank was no exemption and everyone from the Duke of Dorset down had to go through this servile experience, frequently enforced by violence. At the same time, it was a tradition for mothers of new boys to put them under the care of seniors, either cousins or the sons of friends. This afforded Brudenell a modicum of personal protection and the opportunity to breakfast with his guardian once a quarter.

The school day in Brudenell's time was split into four periods: First

School from 7 to 9 a.m., followed by breakfast; Second School from 11 a.m. to noon; Third School from 3 to 4 p.m.; Fourth School from 5 to 6 p.m. Lock-up was at 6 p.m. in winter and 8.30 p.m. in summer. Every Tuesday was a whole holiday, and every Thursday and Saturday a half-holiday (no periods Three and Four). All lessons were taught in the old School House, forms having to share whatever room was available. The curriculum was classical – based on Latin, although unusual in the prominence it gave to Greek. The mainstays were Horace, Virgil and Homer, although pupils would be made familiar with the Greek tragedies. So much time was spent construing verse that the more exceptional boys, like Peel, could almost think in the ancient languages. Harrow also offered a good grounding in writing, public speaking, mathematics, history, geography and modern languages. In addition, Dr Butler had a keen personal interest in science, and occasionally lectured on the subject to his class pupils or members of his House like Brudenell. William Henry Fox Talbot, the 'father' of photography who was at Harrow during 1811–15, was allowed to conduct chemistry experiments in the Head Master's House until an attempt to 'gild steel' caused an explosion; all potentially dangerous experiments in the future were undertaken on the premises of a 'good-natured blacksmith, who lets him explode as much as he pleases'.[5]

Food during Brudenell's spell at Harrow was reasonable, if less varied than many were accustomed to at home. Fox Talbot, who also boarded in the Head Master's House, wrote in 1812 that 'our general dinner is roast mutton and rice pudding, but sometimes veal on Sunday, roast or boiled beef, pork or beef pie or soup, with perhaps plum pudding, apple pie, dumplings, so that we fare well here.' The diet could also be supplemented by food parcels from home.

Of the sports played at Harrow, football, cricket and rackets were the most popular. The former took place on the gravel court which surrounded the old School House on three sides, so that the ball had to be kicked round the building to reach the opposite goal. Such games bore little resemblance to the modern game, quickly degenerating into a violent struggle for the ball – called a 'squash' – in which hands, knees and faces were badly cut by the sharp pitch. Beagling was also popular and, given Brudenell's later love of fox-hunting, it is likely that he was one of a dozen or so boys who subscribed to a pack, and who crossed the farmland around Harrow in pursuit of rabbits and hares.

For more than a year, Brudenell kept a relatively low profile. But after

24 February 1811, it was no longer possible for him to remain anonymous, for on that day his great-uncle, James, the 5th Earl of Cardigan, died at home in Upper Grosvenor Street aged 85. He was succeeded by his nephew Robert who became the 6th Earl and inherited Deene, a town house in Portman Square and 15,000 acres of land in Northamptonshire, Leicestershire and the West Riding of Yorkshire worth a reputed £40,000 a year in rents. Young James consequently succeeded to the courtesy title of Lord Brudenell. Charles Torlese, a fellow pupil, later recalled that Brudenell was nicknamed 'The Astronomer' on account of his habit of walking with his head and eyes 'raised upwards as if he did not condescend to look on any around him'. As Torlese only arrived at Harrow in the summer of 1810, it is possible that Brudenell's proud bearing coincided with this sudden elevation to the fantastically rich aristocratic élite.[6]

Contrary to popular belief, it may also have been the young lord's excellent academic progress that set him apart. By 1812 he had moved up to the Fourth Form Head Remove, and in the Trials (or exams) during the first term he came top of the class, resulting in his elevation to Under Shell. Such a move was accompanied by the initiatory ordeal of being 'tossed in a shell': after evening prayers, the new arrival would be taken into a low room and tossed from a blanket until he had struck the ceiling the requisite number of times. Of course, the 'tossers' were not always accurate in their aim, and initiates often missed the blanket on their downward plunge and crashed into the wooden floor.[7]

It was another violent activity, then in vogue at Harrow, that may indirectly have led to Brudenell's premature departure. In the same way that gentlemen would indulge in duels, or 'affairs of honour', on the least pretext, public schoolboys were much given to pugilism. 'Hardly a day passing,' according to William Gladstone, an Old Etonian, 'without one, two, three, or even four more or less mortal combats.' Prize-fighting was highly popular among all classes at the time, and fist-fighting at school was organised on the same lines. There was no time limit as such, and intermediate halts were only called when one or other of the protagonists was knocked down. The combatant's seconds were then given a minute to revive him, and only if they failed would the fight be considered over. Seen as the ultimate test of that combination of courage and endurance which in the eighteenth century was known as 'bottom', yet it could also be highly dangerous and in some cases fatal. At Eton in 1825, after an insignificant quarrel, Francis Ashley Cooper, the 13-year-old son of the Earl of Shaftesbury, fought Charles Wood, a year older and considerably bigger.

After a brutal combat lasting more than two and a half hours and 60 rounds, both collapsed and had to be assisted from the field. Ashley Cooper fell into a coma and died that night.[8]

Brudenell's own experience of the 'noble art' was – according to Charles Torlese, a witness – indisputable evidence of his 'physical courage'. Years later, Torlese wrote:

> He had a quarrel with a Scotch boy, Munro, which could not be settled without a fight in the ground set apart for pugilism in a field behind the School. These fights were very attractive, and the ground was always crowded. In the first round Lord Brudenell broke the bone in the back of his right hand, and was disabled from striking another blow. Yet he would not give up to meet his opponent, defending himself as well as he could with his left arm. At last, by the order of Dr Butler, . . . [he] was compelled to leave the ground. The injury to his hand was so great that he was immediately placed in a post-chaise and sent up to London to have the broken bone set by a surgeon.[9]

Torlese does not give a date for Brudenell's fight, but a separate source hints at a link between it and Brudenell's sudden departure from Harrow in early May 1812. On the 7th of that month, William Fox Talbot wrote to his mother:

> You must know that Lord Brudenell had obtained leave on last Saturday evening to go home & return on Monday morning: he happened to sprain his hand, & as the surgeon did not come to see him, till 3 o'clock on Monday afternoon, he did not think it worth while to return to Harrow that evening; & supposing Tuesday to be an holiday, he staid till Wednesday morning & brought an excuse about his hand, which Doctor Butler not choosing to receive, set him two eclogues of Virgil, (160 lines) to learn by heart; by return of the chaise he came in, he sent a letter to his father, telling him of his punishment – *the same evening the same chaise returned with a letter to Doctor Butler saying that as he did not choose to receive the excuse*, Lord Brudenell *must leave the School*!!! & accordingly in an hour & a half he left Harrow never to return. Doctor Butler forgot the character of a gentleman, & could not master his passions, but even insulted him. This example will most

likely be soon followed; & there could not be a more deadly blow
to Doctor Butler's interests.

. . . It was too hasty of Lord Cardigan, for he should have
written desiring that his son should be excused *at most*, on the
other hand Doctor Butler seems to have a *sort of pleasure* in pun-
ishing – as we have lately had, I am sorry to say, too many
examples . . .

It is just possible that these two injuries to Brudenell's hand occurred at
separate times; but if Fox Talbot's 'sprain' and Torlese's broken bone were
one and the same, then the reason for Brudenell's removal from Harrow
becomes more explicable. An injury caused by fighting would have provoked little sympathy from Dr Butler, and would not have been seen by
him as a justifiable excuse for Brudenell extending his leave by two days –
hence the harsh punishment. In any case, whether the injury was sustained
by fighting or other means, Butler seems to have reacted in a typically dra-
conian manner and, as Fox Talbot predicted, such an incident may well
have contributed to the steady decline in pupils during the latter years of
his Head Mastership. Notwithstanding Brudenell's supercilious bearing,
though, not every Harrovian was glad to see the back of him. Fox Talbot
noted: 'I have lost a friend in Lord Brudenell, & I shall feel it some time –
one never knows the value of a thing till one possesses it no longer.'[10]

Within days, however, Fox Talbot was mourning an even greater loss.
On 11 May, Spencer Perceval, the Prime Minister, was assassinated in the
lobby of the House of Commons by John Bellingham, a deranged
Liverpool merchant who blamed the government for the failure of his
business (he was hanged in Newgate a week later). Two of Perceval's three
sons at Harrow were close friends of Fox Talbot.

Also during that momentous year, the tide of war turned against
Napoleon with disastrous defeats in Russia and Spain; the steamship *Comet*
managed seven knots on the Clyde; the waltz was first danced in London's
ballrooms, and gaslights appeared in the capital's streets.

Until late 1815, Lord Brudenell lived at home. His education was catered
for by a tutor, but he missed the competition provided by a class of equals.
This may have had the effect of both arresting his academic development
and, paradoxically, of actually *reinforcing* his already over-developed sense of
self-importance. While he had shown signs of arrogance during his time at

Harrow, it is just possible that a few more years amidst such rough and tumble might have mellowed him. Instead, he returned to the familiar adoration of his sisters and was gainsaid by no one, bar his parents.

The fact that his education might have suffered, however, was of little importance. Brudenells did not traditionally become intellectuals or politicians, and in the circles in which he moved it was often a disadvantage to be 'over-educated'. For this reason, many rich aristocrats up at Oxford or Cambridge did not bother to take their final exams – and Brudenell was to be one of those. But he was far from stupid, as his record at Harrow amply demonstrates, and it is important to bear this in mind when considering the controversies that lay ahead.

It was during these years at Deene – between the ages of 14 and 18 – that he developed into a first-class rider and shot. Situated in north-east Northamptonshire on the fringe of ancient Rockingham Forest, the great house was on land that teemed with pheasants, partridges and hares. Brudenell would wander the estate with two pointer dogs, shooting game on the ground and out of trees; it was only later in the century that the custom of driving thousands of hand-reared pheasants over a party of guns became fashionable.

But fox-hunting was his real passion and for this, also, Deene could hardly have been better placed, with three of the smartest and best hunts in the country close at hand. The Pytchley, his local county hunt – noted for its wooded runs – sometimes drew from Brudenell coverts, while to the north and north-east, in Rutlandshire and High Leicestershire respectively, were the Cottesmore and the Quorn. The latter hunt, renowned for its long, open runs, had been at the forefront of the revolution in fox-hunting in the eighteenth century. Before then, the sport had been conducted in a very leisurely way, with landed gentlemen pooling their hounds and pursuing virtually anything that would run; but in the second half of the century, during the long mastership of the great Hugo Meynell, there developed the 'Leicestershire style' of galloping thoroughbreds right up to fast hounds. Thus the modern hunt was born.

Young Brudenell took to the sport as if he were born to it; even among the finest riders in England, he stood out as an exceptional talent. 'His style of riding was peculiarly easy and graceful,' wrote W.H. Whyte-Melville, the author who became a close friend, many years later, 'his spare well-shaped figure and length of limb giving him every advantage in the saddle; while in that essential quality for which we can find no better word than pluck, it is hardly necessary to say he was unrivalled.' The secret of his success, according to Whyte-Melville, was his willingness to leave his horses 'very much to their own sagacity, never pulling them about', with the result that 'they seldom failed him at his need, facing and getting over extraordinarily large fences with apparent ease and safety'. Falls, however, were inevitable, and he had a 'considerable number, some of a truly serious nature'. The worst came at the end of a long run when his tiring horse failed to clear a huge gate and he was thrown into the Uppingham Road beyond. For 24 hours he lay unconscious, hovering close to death, and it was many weeks before he had fully recovered. If anything, though, the experience height-ened his appetite for a sport he pursued with vigour for the rest of his life.

He seemed to approach hunting with the same courage and fortitude that he had displayed when fighting an opponent for upwards of an hour with one hand disabled. Possibly it awakened the competitive instinct that had been dampened by his premature removal from Harrow – the follow-ing episode would seem to suggest so. Wilbrahim Tollemache, the younger brother of his future wife, also had the reputation of being a superb horse-man, so the two wagered on who would return first at the end of a run. When the hounds plunged into the Welland, the river that divided the counties of Northampton and Rutland, Brudenell (despite being a poor swimmer) forced his horse in after them. Tollemache did likewise and both quickly became separated from their mounts. As Brudenell struggled vainly for the opposite bank and Tollemache, doing a passable impression of an otter, passed him in mid-stream, he still managed to call out, 'Mind, Wilbrahim, I was in first.'[11]

On 1 March 1815, seven months before Lord Brudenell's eighteenth birth-day, Napoleon escaped from exile on the Isle of Elba and set in chain a sequence of events that were to have a profound effect on the young noble's choice of career. Within three weeks the royal army had changed sides and Napoleon entered Paris on the day the restored King, Louis XVIII, hurriedly left. As Napoleon remobilised his troops, the Allies decided on a four-pronged advance to bring him, once again, to heel.

Faced by three times as many troops, Napoleon's only hope was to defeat the Allied armies one by one. At first everything went to plan and, on 16 June, he surprised the Prussians at Ligny in Belgium and forced them to retire. Two days later, he met the Duke of Wellington's army – half British, the rest Dutch, German and Belgian – near the village of Waterloo on the main road to Brussels.

By early afternoon, having failed to capture the fortified farmhouse of Hougoumont, Napoleon sent four huge columns of French infantry, 16,000 strong, against Wellington's centre, which was weakened by an intense bombardment. Two key outworks were taken with hardly a pause and, as the massed ranks neared the crest of the ridge, a Dutch-Belgian brigade fell back in disorder. Now, with only a single British infantry brigade standing in the way of the French, it seemed inevitable that Wellington's army would be split in two. But led on by Sir Thomas Picton, who was mortally wounded, the Gordon Highlanders counter-attacked, taking the French by surprise and checking the advance.

At this critical moment, the cream of the British cavalry was let off the leash by the Earl of Uxbridge (later Marquess of Anglesey). They tore into the French infantry and their escorting cuirassiers, sending them reeling back. Unfortunately, wild with excitement and drunk with success, much of the Union Brigade failed to check its charge, continuing on towards the heart of the French army. Despite putting 15 guns out of action, the remnants were intercepted by French cavalry and cut down as they belatedly tried to withdraw. Of 300 Scots Greys who rode into action, only 21 returned.

The outcome remained in the balance until Marshal Blücher's Prussians arrived on the field in early evening. In desperation, Napoleon sent forward the élite infantry of the Imperial Guard but, met by musket fire from front and flank, they turned and fled. The battle was as good as won, and Wellington now ordered a general advance.

According to the divisional commander Sir George Cooke, who spoke to Captain Rees Gronow, the Regency dandy, a few days after the battle, 'it was lucky for Lord Uxbridge that the field had been won' or 'he would have got into an awkward scrape for having engaged the cavalry without orders from the Duke'. In Cooke's opinion, it was Wellington's intention to 'keep the cavalry in hand . . . so that they might have charged the French squadrons when the latter had exhausted themselves in their attacks on our squares'. From his experience in the Peninsular War, Wellington was mistrustful of cavalry officers 'who hurled their men at full gallop on the enemy, without supports, and without any actual plan or intimation beyond the ardour of a sportsman going at a five-barred gate'. Uxbridge seemed to have done just this with the unnecessary loss of the Union Brigade, and if the Prussians had not arrived when they did the overall result might have been very different.[12]

Wellington's assessment of the battle – 'the nearest run thing you ever saw in your life!' – was no exaggeration. The crucial contribution of the Prussians, however, was soon conveniently forgotten. The British public were told, and wanted to believe, that Waterloo had been won *solely* because of the stoic bravery of their infantry and the reckless heroism of their cavalry. In particular, the charge of the Union Brigade took on mythical proportions: here, people said, was a perfect example of how a sudden strike by horsemen could turn a battle.

For a fine young rider like Lord Brudenell who, as he later wrote, 'always had an inclination for the service from early youth, but was prevented from going into the Army by my parents – being an only son of a family of 8 children', the frustration of having missed such a glorious occasion must have been almost unbearable. Particularly galling was the fact that contemporaries from Harrow had been present on the field of battle, having purchased their commissions as young as 16 years of age. For the moment, however, dynastic considerations were uppermost in the mind of his father, who still held the purse-strings. Brudenell was forced to bide his time and accede to his father's demand that he spend some time at Oxford University before entering Parliament. Accordingly, on 21 November 1815, shortly after his eighteenth birthday, Brudenell arrived at Christ Church to begin a Bachelor of Arts' degree.[13]

Life for an undergraduate at Oxford during the Regency period depended very much upon station and wealth. Every student's status – from nobleman, gentleman- or fellow-commoner, foundationer, scholar or exhibitioner, commoner, batteler, servitor and bible-clerk, down to a college servant – was differentiated by his clothes, his privileges and the level of his fees. As a nobleman – a peer who could vote in the House of Lords, his eldest son or the younger son of a duke or a marquess – Lord Brudenell was entitled to wear a silk gown laced with gold and a cap with a golden tassel. At Christ Church, the most popular college for noblemen, he dined at the high table and had access to the senior common room. He did not have to submit to tutorial supervision or college exercises, and was not even obliged to take a degree, though he could do so a year earlier than a commoner. In return, he had to pay the highest fees; added to his expenses – board and lodging for himself, his servants and his horses – he was unlikely to have cost his father much less than £500 a year.[14]

While at Christ Church, Lord Brudenell was the contemporary of a number of other future peers, among them Lords Wilton and Godolphin who years later would sit in judgement of him on a charge of intent to murder. According to college records, he studied the 'usual course of the period which included texts like Cicero, Livy, Herodotus, Horace and Virgil, along with mathematics, logic and theology'. Less usual was that at a time when noblemen rarely remained at Oxford for longer than two years – a period which enabled the few who were so inclined to sit their finals – he stayed for his third year and 'was submitted for examination in the Easter term of 1818'. Admittedly, he was absent during Michaelmas term 1817 – possibly as a result of his serious fall while hunting – but this does not explain why he began a third year at all. Given his academic prowess at school, it is just possible that he did so because he was enjoying his studies as much as his rowdy social life. In the event, he did not take his exams and so never received his B.A., but the very fact that he was even submitted is proof that he was taking his studies more seriously than was normal for men of his station. Again, the popular image of a frivolous, empty-headed young man does not ring true.[15]

It seems likely that Brudenell's father was responsible for him leaving Oxford without a degree, much as he had earlier been responsible for cutting short his promising academic progress at Harrow. He may have felt that at the age of 20, it was high time his son left his books behind and began to assume the position of responsibility that would be expected of a future Earl of Cardigan. Later, as a matter of course, his son would sit in the House of Lords; in the meantime, there was much to be learnt from a spell in the lower House. It was particularly convenient that his cousin, Charles Brudenell-Bruce, the 2nd Earl of Ailesbury, still controlled the 'pocket' borough of Marlborough and was happy to let his young kinsman represent him in the House of Commons. So on 18 February 1818, in the middle of his final term at Oxford, he went through the formality of being elected a Member of Parliament.

Before undertaking the sobering duty of legislating for the nation, he was sent to broaden his horizons on a Grand Tour of Europe, visiting France, Italy, Russia and Sweden. No details exist of this trip, but he was almost certainly accompanied by one or more young men and would have had ample opportunity, like Lord Byron before him, to sample both the culture and the young women of the countries that he visited. Later in life he demonstrated a voracious sexual appetite, and there is good reason to speculate that he was well out of the starting-blocks by the age of 20 years.

The Britain that Lord Brudenell returned to in 1818 was in the process of rapid and dynamic change. The agricultural revolution had left it the most enclosed and best cultivated country in Europe, and much of the nineteenth century was taken up with draining, sweetening and fertilising the sour, waterlogged enclosures.

The industrial revolution, too, was gaining momentum. Manchester was awash with cotton mills, Sheffield with iron furnaces. From South Wales to County Durham, coal was being hauled out of the ground by steam-engines – which marvels of the industrial age were also being used to drive locomotives, propel steamships, lift weights, operate lathes and heat factories. While the passenger train was not introduced until 1830, Britain already had the best transport network in the world. A huge accessible coastline, slow navigable rivers and a great canal system provided water transport throughout the country. Road traffic in England and Wales moved along 19,000 miles of paved streets and turnpikes and 95,000 miles of public highway; by 1830 the turnpikes had extended to 25,000 miles, including 3,600 miles in Scotland.

At the same time, the population of Britain was expanding at an unprecedented rate. Between 1811 and 1821 it rose from 12½ million to 14½ million, at 16 per cent the highest proportionate decennial increase ever recorded. By 1851 it had climbed to 21 million, thus almost doubling since the turn of the century. Yet, while fatalities from bubonic plague, leprosy and scurvy were negligible, and those from rickets, smallpox and typhus were much reduced, the overall death rate was still very high. Britain had an essentially young society, with half the population under the age of 20 and little more than one-tenth over 50 years. 'This characteristic youthfulness of 19th Century British society,' wrote Norman Gash, the great social historian, 'may help to explain . . . its emotionalism, its idealism, its naïvety, and, as far as crowds were concerned, its tendency to riot and disorder together with its timidity in the face of authority.'[16]

Large towns were growing the fastest. In the first fifty years of the century their population increased by 189 per cent, compared with a growth rate of 71 per cent in rural areas and small towns. London was easily the biggest with a population of more than 1 million in 1811 and 2.3 million in 1851 – more than half that of the rest of the 70 biggest towns put together. And although industrial and commercial centres like Manchester (cotton), Liverpool (commerce), Birmingham (small craftsmen), Bristol (colonial trade) and Leeds (wool) were next in rank, the fastest growing centres at this time were seaside holiday towns like Brighton, Margate and Weymouth.

London – with its mix of industries, trades and professions – had no single marked identity. It was the centre of commerce, politics and society, and dominated the rest of the nation. Ruling over it was the Prince Regent, the eldest son of George III, who had assumed the executive role in 1811 when his father, afflicted with the rare and then unknown metabolic disease of porphyria, went insane.

The prince was not popular, however, having led a particularly dissolute life. In 1785, aged 23, he had secretly married his mistress Maria Fitzherbert, a Roman Catholic widow six years his senior. However, the union was invalid under the terms of the Royal Marriage Act of 1772 – which stated that the sovereign had to give his consent – and ten years later the handsome but flabby prince married his cousin Princess Caroline of Brunswick-Wolfenbüttel, the daughter of George III's eldest sister. In return, the government agreed to pay off his huge debts of £630,000. A jolly, plain-looking woman, not noted for her personal cleanliness, Caroline had little appeal for the prince; he only managed to get through the ceremony under the influence of drink and spent his wedding night collapsed in the grate. Next morning, the prince performed his conjugal duty for the one and only time, and in the process conceived their only child, Charlotte, who married Prince Leopold of Saxe-Coburg in 1816 and died giving birth to a stillborn son the following year.

Married in name only, the prince returned to the arms of Mrs Fitzherbert; but his embittered and increasingly eccentric wife was not to be outdone, particularly after her return to Brunswick in 1814. Night after night she attended balls and masquerades, supper and gambling parties, often scantily and bizarrely clad. According to Lord Redesdale, she appeared at a hunting party in Baden 'with a half pumpkin on her head', telling the bemused Grand Duke that it was the 'coolest sort of coiffure'. At Genoa she proceeded through the streets in a gold phaeton, dressed in pink and white, showing a large chunk of her ample bosom and two fat legs in pink top-boots; at Naples, on a visit in defiance of her government, she is said to have seduced the King, Joachim Murat, Napoleon's brother-in-law.

But Caroline's worst excesses, for which she was eventually tried, were alleged to have been conducted with Bartolommeo Pergami, her swarthy young Chamberlain. According to Guiseppe Sacchi, a former equerry, the two were often seen walking arm in arm and kissing, and balls given at Pergami's villa near Milan were 'quite brothels' attended by women of 'very low condition'. He had frequently seen Pergami enter the Princess's room late at night, and they often travelled in the same carriage where 'two or three times' Sacchi found them in the morning 'both asleep and having their respective hands upon one another . . . Once Pergami had his breeches loosened and the Princess's hand was upon that part.' In July 1819, after 85 witnesses had been interviewed, an official government inquiry reported that overwhelming evidence 'established the fact of a continued adulterous intercourse' between the Princess and Pergami.[17]

With his errant wife out of the country, however, the Prince Regent could ignore her indiscretions and concentrate on his own enjoyment. He held court at Carlton House, his palatial London residence in Pall Mall which had been reconstructed by Henry Holland at enormous cost. Its gaudy screen of columns was not to everyone's taste, though: 'One of the meanest and most ugly edifices that ever disfigured London,' wrote Captain Rees Gronow. Canova, the sculptor, condemned it by saying that Rome contained 'a thousand buildings more beautiful . . . any one of which would be more suitable for a princely residence than an ugly barn'.[18]

A frequent visitor over the years was George 'Beau' Brummell, the wit and arbiter of Regency fashion. The son of a valet, his father had risen to become private secretary to the Prime Minister, Lord North, enabling him to acquire various profitable appointments and to leave a fortune of £65,000. Brummell was sent to Eton, where he distinguished himself as the foremost scholar and sportsman. Noted for his exquisite manners and impeccable appearance, he quickly came to the attention of the Prince of Wales who gave him a commission in his own regiment, the 10th Light Dragoons. So began a long friendship that only soured when Brummell got too big for his top-boots and began to exercise his wit at the expense of the prince and his mistress Mrs Fitzherbert, while supporting the cause of the latter's rival, the Countess of Jersey. The breach was made irreparable, according to Captain Gronow, when Brummell turned towards the prince at a ball and said to Lady Worcester: 'Who is your fat friend?'[19]

Oddly, Brummell seemed in no hurry to heal the rift and was reputed to have remarked to a Colonel Macmahon, 'I made him what he is, and I can unmake him.' In the end, Brummell's gambling was his downfall; despite once winning £10,000 from George Drummond of the banking family, playing whist at White's, he squandered his fortune and in 1816 was forced to flee his debtors to the Continent. He died twenty-four years later, impoverished and insane in a Caen asylum.[20]

But in his heyday, which continued long after his alienation from the prince and into the halcyon early years of the Regency, Brummel's taste in clothes, art and furnishings reigned supreme. Where he led, the country –

including the prince – followed; tradesmen vied for his custom, knowing his patronage was a licence to print money. It was he who made popular the dandy's dress of tall hat, muslin cravat, waistcoat and pantaloons; when riding he would favour a blue coat with brass buttons, leather breeches, top-boots, and a cravat so stiff and broad that he had difficulty seeing his feet.

In such outfits, the swells of the day would ride in Hyde Park between 5 and 6 p.m., while society beauties drove in gorgeous two-seater *vis-à-vis* carriages, attended by powdered footmen and wigged coachmen. The park marked the limit of fashionable London, and was charmingly rural in appearance with cows and deer grazing beneath its plentiful trees. Most people of rank lived in large town houses in the Georgian squares of Mayfair to the east and Belgravia to the south, or in the fine Nash terraces that fringed Regent's Park to the north. They were all well placed for the shops of Bond and Regent Streets, the theatres and fleshpots of Haymarket, and the clubs of St James's and Pall Mall.

Entering Parliament in 1818, Lord Brudenell joined the majority Tories, the party of his family and political patron. Supporters of the status quo in Church, Crown and Constitution, and therefore essentially conservative, the Tories were at the same time prepared to accept change which did not affect their own privileged position within the state. They had the support of the Church, the universities, the services, the unreformed municipal corporations in the towns, many of the great landed families, and nearly all country gentry. They had been in power since 1807, and would remain so until 1830.

Part of the reason for their success was the disunity of the main opposition party, the Whigs. Fractured since 1815 into three main groups, each dominated by powerful aristocratic families, they were only marginally more progressive than the Tories. United on the subject of Catholic emancipation – allowing Catholics to sit in Parliament – they could not agree on the issue of parliamentary reform. But in many other respects they were like the Tories, and there is much truth in Hazlitt's remark that the two parties were like competing stage-coaches which splashed each other with mud, but travelled by the same road to the same destination.

Brudenell's impact on politics at this time was virtually non-existent, and his fellow M.P.s had to wait almost thirteen years to hear his maiden speech. In part this can be attributed to his young age and the fact that he was overawed by the quality of intellects then ruling the lower House – among them George Canning, Robert Peel, and Viscount Castlereagh. But the main reason was that he found Parliament boring and longed to emulate his grandfather's career as an Army officer.

It was the tense political atmosphere of the post-war years that gave Brudenell an opportunity to slake, in part, his thirst for military experience. With the end of war, the booming wartime economy had collapsed as demand fell away and exports suffered. Agriculture was particularly badly hit: the price of livestock, wool and grain tumbled, while foreign competition added to the misery. To counter this, Parliament passed a law prohibiting the importation of foreign corn when the domestic price fell below 80s a quarter. But this gave no relief to graziers, hard-pressed by the minimum agricultural wage and the poor rate. Thousands of small farmers, and even some lesser gentry, were ruined.

When Lord Liverpool's government abolished income tax in 1816 – thereby relieving the rich of a larger share of the post-war economic burden – the rural poor rioted. Hampden Clubs sprang up throughout the country, calling for political reform, and William Cobbett sold single-page pamphlets for 2d with the same message. Circulation of his 'Twopenny Trash' had reached 50,000 in February 1817 when it was outlawed by the 'gag' laws – which proscribed seditious meetings and literature – and Cobbett was forced to flee to the United States.

While trade picked up in 1818, the harvest was bad and discontent returned with a vengeance the following year. On 16 August 1819, a political reform meeting was held at St Peter's Field, Manchester. Up to 80,000 men, women and children of the cotton districts of Lancashire were intently listening to an address by the main speaker, Henry 'Orator' Hunt, when the young chief magistrate, William Hulton, lost his nerve, read the Riot Act and ordered Hunt's arrest. The Manchester Yeomanry, with drawn swords, rode forward but were soon swamped by the huge crowd. Over-reacting, Hulton ordered the 15th Hussars to rescue the Yeomanry by dispersing the meeting, and troops that had served so heroically at Waterloo went into action against their own countrymen. When the clamour died down and the dust had settled, bodies and personal belongings were strewn across the blood-soaked turf. The 'Peterloo Massacre' left 11 dead and more than 500 wounded. For his part, Hunt was sentenced to two years in prison.

Many Whigs were outraged, and supported the fund set up for the victims, but Tory Cabinet ministers like Viscount Sidmouth, the Home

Secretary, and the Duke of Wellington, Master-General of the Ordnance, saw revolution around the corner and applauded Hulton's actions. On 1 November 1819, egged on by Sidmouth and Wellington, Lord Liverpool's government passed the Six Acts, emergency devices to keep order: three were directed against seditious publications and meetings, two against the unlawful stockpiling and use of arms, and one made it easier to punish misdemeanours.[21]

In the days before an organised police force, public order was the responsibility of the regular Army. But it had duties abroad and could not hope to safeguard the whole country; therefore, to supplement it, the government encouraged the expansion of volunteer regiments which had sprung up since 1794 to guard against a French invasion. The 22-year-old Lord Brudenell was anxious to comply and shortly after the introduction of the Six Acts, he wrote to William 'Squire' Cartright of Aynhoe, the commander of the Northamptonshire Yeomanry and his local M.P., offering to raise a troop of horse from amongst his tenants.

On 10 November, Cartright replied, saying that he took it for granted that 'His Majesty's Government will be extremely glad to accept the offer' and that 'all loyal subjects ought to feel much indebted to your Lordship for so praiseworthy a step, at so critical a moment'. He wrote again two days later, with news that Lord Sidmouth approved the undertaking and that Lord Brudenell should 'lose no time in taking the preliminary steps towards accomplishing your object'.[22]

Brudenell then set about organising his new command with an eagerness and efficiency that would later become his trademark. By the end of December he had received his commission and the 58 N.C.O.s and privates of the 12th (Deene) Troop of Northamptonshire Yeomanry had been kitted out with gold-laced jackets, overalls and cloaks, funded by a country subscription to which the young noble had contributed £100. Made up of local tenants and freeholders who provided their own horses, the troop was armed with sabres and pistols from the regular military stores at Weedon. Hours were spent drilling in the great park around Deene but – much to its young officer's regret – the new troop was never called into action. Nevertheless, Brudenell's martial appetite had been well and truly whetted and it would not be long before he had exchanged this 'week-end' soldiering for the real thing.

3

———•———

Mrs Johnstone

With Parliament due to reopen on 15 February 1820, and no sign of disturbances in Northamptonshire, Lord Brudenell left his hunting and soldiering for the capital. But it was soon obvious that the country as a whole was anything but quiet.

In December an *agent provocateur* had informed the Cabinet that a group of fanatics led by Arthur Thistlewood, a former estate agent, were planning to assassinate them at a dinner to be given by Lord Harrowby, Lord President of the Council, at his home in Grosvenor Square on 23 February. As more gory details filtered through – that the plotters intended to sever the heads of Lords Sidmouth and Castlereagh and take them away in a bag – the government was divided on how to respond. Wellington and Castlereagh, the most bellicose, wanted the Cabinet to conceal pistols in their dispatch boxes, so that they and their servants could hold up the assassins until the army had surrounded the house. Their more timorous colleagues refused and, while preparations for the dinner went ahead, soldiers and police descended on the plotters' hideout in a stable-loft in Cato Street. Nine were arrested, but in the confusion Thistlewood and thirteen others escaped. Rounded up soon afterwards, they were convicted of treason, and Thistlewood and four other ringleaders were hanged and their heads displayed in the City.

The trouble was far from over, however. Hard on the heels of the Cato Street Conspiracy was a series of disturbances in the north as armed insurrectionists were reported at Barnsley, Sheffield and Huddersfield, and artillery was ordered to Wakefield. But with the economic situation improving and the moderate reformers distancing themselves from the extremists, the public clamour for reform died away.

During this period, Lord Brudenell did little more than go through the motions of representing Marlborough, attending the House erratically and with little effect. While he bided his time, waiting for a favourable opportunity to convince his father that the choice of a military career was not so injudicious, he concentrated on enjoying himself. As well as making frequent trips back home to hunt, he spent much time in the clubs of St James's. A founder member of the Traveller's Club, where candidates for membership had to have journeyed more than 500 miles from England, he was also elected to White's in 1820 (as his father and grandfather had been before him).

The oldest and grandest of gentlemen's clubs, White's had been founded at the turn of the eighteenth century at White's Chocolate House. A member since 1798, 'Beau' Brummell had been in the habit of standing in the famous Bow Window with his impeccably turned-out cronies – among them Lord Robert Manners and Lord Alvanley – laying down the law of fashion or offering another example of his cutting wit. Once, when asked for the settlement of a debt of £500, Brummell replied, 'I paid you when I was standing at the window of White's and said as you passed, "How do you do?"'[1]

Unlike Brummell and the more irresponsible dandies of the day – chief among them the Earl of Sefton, who was said to have lost £200,000 at Crockfords, the gaming club – Brudenell was not an inveterate gambler. He did not mind the occasional wager, however, and White's betting book contains thirteen of his entries spanning the period from 1822 to 1850. The early ones indicate his optimism that Britain would soon be involved in a major war and, consequently, that military glory for him was just around the corner. In December 1822, he bet Mr Cornewall 10 guineas that England 'will be at war with some European power by this day three years'.

This was a reaction to the crisis in Spain where, in 1820, a rebellion by liberal army officers had forced the absolutist King Ferdinand VII to cede real power to an elected parliament. But since then the country had fallen into a state of semi-anarchy and the ailing French King, Louis XVIII, was threatening to restore his fellow Bourbon monarch's authority by force. Seeking a compromise, the British government sent Lord Fitzroy Somerset to Madrid in January 1823 to ask the liberals to install Ferdinand as a constitutional monarch.

Brudenell was not keen on Somerset's chances of success, however, and on 29 January bet his uncle, Colonel Sir Henry 'Kangaroo' Cooke, 20 guineas that 'in the event of the occupation of Madrid by the French army they . . . will not have evacuated Spain within four months.' He proved right on both counts, for shortly after Somerset's mission ended in failure in early April, French troops marched into Spain and did not leave until the last pocket of liberal resistance in Cadiz had been neutralised towards the end of the year. By November 1823, Brudenell was still more convinced that Spain (or another incident) might be a *casus belli*, and he bet Mr Greville 50 guineas that England would be at war with a major power within a year. But Britain did not go to war with France or any other power in the time scale allowed by the original bet, and he showed a net loss of 40 guineas on the three wagers.[2]

But while the young lord could not afford to fritter away his allowance, he was even less prudent with his good name. During the early 1820s, and possibly before, he became infatuated with Elizabeth Johnstone, the beautiful wife of Captain Frederick Johnstone, a close friend since childhood. Born on 8 December 1797, the eldest daughter of John Halliday and Lady Elizabeth Stratford, the young Mrs Johnstone was impeccably connected. Her maternal grandfather was the 3rd Earl of Aldborough, her paternal grandmother was Lady Jane Tollemache, the daughter of the 4th Earl of Dysart. When the childless 6th Earl died in 1821, her father inherited the bulk of the Dysart estates in Cheshire, Northamptonshire and Suffolk and assumed the name of Tollemache.

Captain Johnstone, in contrast, came from a respectable gentry family of comparatively modest means. An officer in the 19th Lancers at the time of his marriage in August 1817, Johnstone did not have enough money to provide a home of his own and the newlyweds were forced to move in with his mother, where they remained for two years. This disparity between Mrs Johnstone's married and premarried standard of living was a cause of friction between the young couple from the start. A second, and perhaps more important, irritant was the birth of a daughter in 1818. The exact date is not recorded and it is just possible – when subsequent events are taken into account – that the child was conceived out of wedlock and so necessitated the union. This would explain the low-key wedding, with only parents and close friends attending. It would also explain why, after just three months of marriage, Johnstone told his father-in-law of the 'unhappiness that existed between them', and that his wife had 'proposed a separation' (a suggestion she was to repeat after the birth of her daughter).

According to her father, while nothing came of these incidents the couple 'continued to live very unhappily together'.[3]

Captain Johnstone's mother, who was in the best position to know, later testified that her son's wife appeared to be 'much attached to him' when they were married, but that she noticed 'a material change afterwards'. It was no coincidence, she felt, that during this period her daughter-in-law first came into contact with Lord Brudenell, first at society events and then when the Johnstones were invited to Deene. So keen had Brudenell's interest in the young Mrs Johnstone become that he was even in the habit of turning up at her mother-in-law's house to inquire after her. This would have posed little threat to most recently married young mothers, but Elizabeth Johnstone was far from typical. Not only was she patently unhappy with her new state, she also had the temperament to ensure that she did something about it. A more spoilt, wilful, single-minded young woman it would have been hard to find – and in this sense she was the mirror image of Brudenell.

Much of her formidable temper was inherited from her impulsive father, an admiral in the Royal Navy. Famous for saving a British brig by engaging a French squadron of eight ships of the line and four frigates with his one ship of the line off Toulon in 1810, he was also reputed to have thrown a Frenchman out of a window for nudging him during a game of billiards in Calais. At home his punishment could be equally summary. He once put his 16-year-old sister-in-law, Lady Emily Stratford, across his knee and spanked her for making fun of him during dinner; when his mother-in-law, Lady Aldborough, complained he threatened to thrash her too.[4]

It was perhaps inevitable that, set such examples, the vivacious and headstrong Mrs Johnstone would eventually seek to escape from an unhappy marriage by reciprocating Lord Brudenell's attention. Not only was he heir to an earldom and one of the richest fortunes in the kingdom, he was also strikingly handsome – tall and blond, his nose straight and Roman, his eyes piercingly blue. Such a man was irresistible, and it may have been the break-up of her parents' marriage during the early 1820s that signalled the death knell for her own.

The opportunity arose in early 1823. The Johnstones had been living at Englefield Green, Surrey, in a house provided by Mrs Johnstone's father – Admiral Tollemache since he came into his inheritance – but when Mrs Johnstone fell ill towards the latter end of 1822 she was moved to her father's nearby home to convalesce. On 7 January 1823, Captain Johnstone went to stay at the Dorset home of Henry Sturt and his wife Lady Charlotte, the younger sister of Lord Brudenell. Mrs Johnstone, who had recently recovered from her illness, did not go, and her father later stated that he was not aware that she had been invited. After just one week in Dorset, Captain Johnstone received a letter from his father-in-law informing him that his wife had left her daughter in London and gone to live with her grandmother, the dowager Lady Aldborough, in Paris.[5]

It was not a coincidence that Mrs Johnstone fled to the sanctuary of her maternal grandmother, whose eccentricities made even Admiral Tollemache seem conventional. While the mistress of Lord Westmorland, the Lord Lieutenant of Ireland, she had given the Honourable Arthur Wellesley (the future Duke of Wellington) a lift in her coach to a party outside Dublin; but finding his company so dull, she left the party without him and he was forced to return to Dublin in the cart carrying the band. Years later, meeting Wellington in Paris, she remarked: 'I little thought when I left you to find your way back with the fiddlers that some day you were going to play the first fiddle in Europe yourself.'[6]

A resident in Paris since the first fall of Napoleon in 1814, Lady Aldborough was notorious for her acid wit and unconventional lifestyle. According to Captain Gronow, who met her after Waterloo, 'she kept open house, and gave agreeable dinners, made up of pleasant men and good-looking women, not remarkable for any false modesty or affected prudery'. During such evenings, 'hardened men of the world' were known 'to blush and look aghast when this free-spoken old lady' posed 'sundry searching questions respecting their tastes and habits'. Her appearance, he later recalled, was equally outlandish: 'She wore habitually, when going out in the evening, a long white veil, which was fastened to her wig, and hung down to her feet; white satin shoes with diamond buckles, very short sleeves and petticoats, and an extremely *décolleté* gown.'[7]

Protected by such a woman, who seems to have wholeheartedly approved of her grand-daughter's actions, Mrs Johnstone was free to cock a snook at her husband. When he arrived in Paris to fetch her, she refused to see him and he was forced to return home empty-handed. Soon after, the eager Lord Brudenell arrived in the French capital. No doors were closed to this most eligible young bachelor, and before the summer was out he was living openly with Mrs Johnstone in Versailles. In the autumn they returned to London and brazenly moved into a Bond Street hotel together.

The following spring Brudenell fought his first duel – but not, oddly enough, with Captain Johnstone. The man with whom he exchanged ineffective shots was Sir Gilbert Heathcote, owner of Cottesmore House in Rutlandshire and a second cousin of Mrs Johnstone. It was not on behalf of her honour that the two did battle; rather on account of Brudenell's sister whom Heathcote had somehow mistreated. The irony was not lost on Lady Derby who observed that, after receiving Brudenell's shot, Heathcote should have said: 'Now, my lord, I must beg you to receive my shot for your conduct to my cousin!'[8]

The cuckolded husband preferred to take the safer and more lucrative recourse of legal action and, on 23 June 1824, at the Sheriff's Court in Holborn, Brudenell was charged with having debauched another man's wife. Although none of the principals appeared in court, and only two witnesses were called on behalf of the plaintiff – Admiral Tollemache and Captain Johnstone's mother – London was still captivated by the society scandal and hungrily consumed the comprehensive report that appeared the following day in *The Times*.

Seeking damage limitation, Lord Brudenell chose not to contest the charge – so avoiding lurid evidence of his 'debauchery'. Instead, he instructed his counsel to try to keep the award of damages as low as possible. Johnstone's counsel, Mr Brougham, had the opposite aim, and the impression given to the jury after his opening speech and the evidence of Johnstone's mother was of a tender and affectionate husband doing his best with a fickle wife who could not adjust to her reduced circumstances. They made the mistake, however, of trying to reinforce this point by calling Admiral Tollemache. While much of his brief evidence supported their thesis, his insistence that the marriage was in trouble from the start, that 'upon the whole, they lived very unhappily together', and that they had agreed to a separation before the flight to Paris, undercut the impression that Lord Brudenell had broken up a difficult but by no means doomed union.

Brudenell's counsel immediately sought to exploit this unexpected assistance by hammering home the idea that the marriage was over even before his client became involved. No man 'respected more the relationship between man and wife' than Lord Brudenell, he began, but sometimes 'unhappy differences of temper or habits may arise, which would render the marriage life unhappy, and occasionally place the husband in such a situation, as to render the loss of a wife a circumstance of no very great injury'. Nonetheless, his client 'was a nobleman of the strictest honour, who approached the consideration of this painful subject with every sentiment of regret', but who 'felt that he had a reparation to make' and 'would willingly submit to such damages as the jury . . . might think proper to award'.

However, it was worth bearing in mind, he said, that 'whatever occurred between Mrs Johnstone and Lord Brudenell, did not take place till long after the lady had quitted her husband's protection' and that, accordingly, his client had not 'had recourse to the ordinary arts of the seducer'. While he would not deny that Lord Brudenell had 'formed a very violent and irresistible attraction for this lady – for she was . . . a lady of great beauty and accomplishments', he could not help observing that although his 'learned friend had talked of the affectionate manner in which this couple had lived together', 'not a single servant . . . had been called to support this statement'. Admiral Tollemache's evidence, no less, 'went distinctly to prove the reverse'. The jury were at least partly convinced because their award of £1,000 to Captain Johnstone, while hardly insignificant, was much smaller than it might have been.[9]

Immediately following the trial, Brudenell made a further gesture of reparation by offering to give Captain Johnstone the 'satisfaction' of a duel. He had already received another man's fire without injury, and was warming to the drastic method by which gentlemen settled questions of honour. But while a handy shot himself, he was up against an experienced military man who might well have made him regret his youthful impetuosity. Fortunately, Johnstone declined, reputedly telling Brudenell's messenger that he had already been given 'the satisfaction of having removed the most damned bad-tempered and extravagant bitch in the kingdom'. It was a line that would be echoed by Brudenell himself twenty years later.[10]

Thus far, society may have revelled in such a public scandal but it would hardly have been outraged. Under the mores of the time, when high-born gentlemen from King George IV down had mistresses and bastards as a matter of course, Lord Brudenell had done little to offend. What made the affair extraordinary was that Brudenell was determined to solemnise it by marriage. If Mrs Johnstone had been a low-born courtesan like Dorothy Jordan, the long-time mistress of the Duke of Clarence (later William IV), wedlock would have been out of the question. But she was high-born, descended from earls on both sides of the family, and would have been an ideal choice as the future Countess of Cardigan if she had not already been married. She was also beautiful and spirited – with raven hair and large flashing eyes set in an exquisite oval face – and represented the type of challenge that was missing in the predictable life of a rich young aristocrat.

Inevitably, Lord Brudenell's parents opposed the match. A married woman of such reputation, whatever her antecedents, was hardly an ideal choice for their only daughter-in-law. But divorce was a long-drawn-out process in the 1820s and this gave Brudenell the opportunity to try to overcome his parents' objections. Until the Matrimonial Causes Act of 1857, marriages were the remit of the Ecclesiastical Courts and every divorce required a separate Act of Parliament. In the Johnstones' case, this was not enacted until early 1826, by which time neither of Brudenell's parents was in a position to oppose the match.

A hint as to the coming tragedy is contained in a letter from Brudenell to his political patron and kinsman, the Marquess of Ailesbury, dated 21 September 1825. In response to Ailesbury's solicitous enquiries as to the health of his parents, Brudenell states that his father 'is making gradual progress towards recovery', although he 'has not yet regained the use of the Side affected'. The symptoms described suggest a stroke. His mother, too, has been ill but 'has made more rapid progress towards recovery, tho' the utmost vigilance and care are necessary to prevent a recurrence of the attack to which there is an evident tendency'. Brudenell was right to warn of a further relapse, because within five months his 55-year-old mother was dead. This left his father neither physically nor emotionally strong enough to oppose the wedding, which took place on 19 June 1826 at the parish church of St Nicholas with St Mary Magdalene, Chiswick, near to the Tollemache mansion of Ham House.[11]

If, as his second wife confirms in her memoirs, Brudenell was made painfully aware of the 'ungovernable temper' of his first wife during the two years when he lived with her in sin, why did he go ahead with the marriage? It may be that he felt he could tame her, but the more likely explanation is that he appreciated that Mrs Johnstone had divorced her husband and abandoned her daughter on his account, and that his honour would not let him leave her high and dry. As his second wife put it, 'he chivalrously married her'. This was, perhaps, the greatest mistake of his young life. To soften his own excesses of character he needed a loving, down-to-earth and above all loyal companion; instead, he got a selfish, profligate and duplicitous vixen who brought out the worst in his own high-handed nature.[12]

The one positive result of his relationship with Mrs Johnstone was that it almost certainly caused his parents to withdraw their opposition to his wish to join the Army. Writing years later, he describes the reason as 'certain family events' and the date as 1823. As Brudenell spent much of this year living openly with Mrs Johnstone, it is easy to see how his parents must have hoped that the distraction of an Army career would cause him to forget his infatuation; they might even have made it a condition. Either way, they were to be disappointed, and it is ironic to consider that if they had removed their veto earlier, he would have had less opportunity to go gadding about the Continent after another man's wife.[13]

Once the decision had been taken, the family connections were put to good use. Colonel Cooke, Lady Cardigan's brother, put in a good word at the Horse Guards (the London headquarters of the British Army) and on 6 May 1824, barely six weeks before his trial for debauchery, Brudenell was gazetted as a cornet in the 8th (King's Royal Irish) Hussars. He was 26 and, while old for such a junior rank, had the inestimable advantage of limitless money and influence. As he later wrote, no less a personage than the Duke of York had 'promised that if I would pay attention to my duties, he would push me on in the service'.[14]

The Duke was no stranger to exercising his authority on behalf of favourites. Appointed Commander-in-Chief by his father, King George III, in 1795, he was forced to resign thirteen years later after it was discovered that his mistress, Mary Anne Clarke, had been using her influence over him in the disposal of commissions, for which she received bribes. Nominally cleared of involvement by a House of Commons inquiry (with a majority of 84), he was reappointed as Commander-in-Chief when his brother became Prince Regent in 1811. But the Duke of York also did much good for the Army, ending the custom of commissioning juveniles and simplifying the fancy dress that served as a uniform by doing away with powder, pomatum, long tails and cumbrous equipment. He also authorised a Code of Regulations to be drawn up and the adoption of a volume of Instructions for Field Exercise. Sadly for Lord Brudenell, the Duke of York had only two and a half years to live, a short time in which to be pushed up the ladder of command.

The 8th Hussars, the regiment to which the mature cornet had been appointed, had begun their existence as dragoons, or heavy cavalry, raised in 1693 from Irish Protestants pledged to defend the throne of King William III against the supporters of the deposed Catholic James II. At the outset of the American War of Independence in 1776 they were reclassified as light dragoons and in May 1823, after their return from twenty years' service in India, they were renamed as hussars and ordered to replace their light blue and silver tunics with tunics of royal blue and gold, topped by red and white plumed helmets. Added to battle honours won with Marlborough in Spain, the Duke of York in Flanders, and against the

French in Egypt, their colours proudly bore the names of 'Leswaree' and 'Agra', successful engagements fought under General Lake during the Second Mahratta War.

However, the state of the 8th Hussars hardly mirrored its reputation when Lord Brudenell joined it in 1824. Major-General Lord Edward Somerset, the Inspector-General of Cavalry, carried out a review of the regiment at Romford on 26 June and wrote in his report that 'discipline does not seem to be very well regulated; and as yet the training and instruction of the officers and men in the Field Exercise have made but little progress.' Furthermore, the new recruits since the return from India had 'made little progress in their drill' while their 'conduct in quarters has not been perfectly orderly' and many men had been found 'out of Barracks at night'. The scapegoat was Lieutenant-Colonel the Honourable Henry Westenra, an experienced officer who had been given command only six weeks before. In his report, General Somerset noted that Westenra did 'not appear to possess much energy or activity', and few were surprised when he was relieved of his command after just five months at the helm.

Lord George Russell, his replacement, could not have been more different. The second son of the Duke of Bedford, he possessed much of the energy if less of the intellect of his illustrious younger brother, Lord John Russell, the parliamentary reformer and future Prime Minister. A hard-bitten soldier who had fought in the battles of Talavera and Barossa, and served on Wellington's staff at Vittoria and Toulouse, in 1826 he proposed the reorganisation of the cavalry formation along French lines and received a more than enthusiastic response from his former chief. That he had already put his own house in order was recognised by Sir Hussey Vivian, who inspected the 8th Hussars at Hounslow in the summer of 1825 and reported: 'I owe it to Lieutenant Colonel Lord William Russell and the Officers and [N.C.O.s] . . . to state that the great improvement that must have taken place in every respect is such as to assure me of the utmost Attention having on their part been paid to their Duties.' Twelve months later, Vivian wrote: 'The improvement that has taken place within the last six months is very great indeed, and . . . this Regiment will, I have no doubt, in another year be one of the most efficient in His Majesty's Service.'[15]

Making up for lost time, Lord Brudenell was foremost among the zealous young officers helping Colonel Russell to make the 8th Hussars a byword for smartness and efficiency. 'I was a member of Parliament all this time,' he later wrote, 'and neglected much of my Parliamentary duties for the purpose of doing orderly duty as a Subaltern officer . . .' But life even for a dutiful cavalry officer was none too taxing. A regiment of hussars was usually made up of around 330 men, divided into six troops. The day began with morning stables, at which only troop commanders had to be present to inspect the men's grooming of their horses. All would then attend riding school, skirmishing drill or, occasionally, full-dress field days – in which the whole regiment would practise field manoeuvres. At 11 a.m., administrative business would be conducted in the regimental office by the commanding officer and the orderly officer, followed by lunch in the officers' mess at midday. For the men, foot drill took up part of the afternoon, but most junior officers considered their work over by noon as only troop commanders and the orderly officer had to attend evening stables when horses were again groomed and bedded down.[16]

Yet duty was one of the least disparities between officers and men. The former had to purchase their commissions for considerable sums (the smarter the regiment, the higher the price) and so necessarily came from the highest echelons of society. A cavalry officer had to provide his own horses and uniforms, and was expected to lead the type of social life consistent with his station as an officer and a gentleman. This usually meant hunting in the shires, attending the dinners and balls of the London Season, and yachting at Cowes, in addition to being able to afford a share of a mess bill that often reached exorbitant proportions with the amount of fine wines and choice delicacies consumed. Furthermore, officers did not have to live in barracks and many incurred the additional expense of staying in smart hotels or leasing grand houses.

Paid just a shilling a day before stoppages, and subject to the harshest discipline, the men came from the opposite end of the social spectrum. Mostly illiterate members of the labouring classes, they often joined up as a last resort, to avoid the workhouse, prison or worse. Famously described by Wellington as 'the scum of the earth', they were treated as such with brutal floggings for even minor breaches of military discipline. Originally lodged with resentful citizens, since the Napoleonic Wars they had been housed in crowded barracks with 20 men often sharing a room little more than 20 feet square. Rations were adequate but monotonous, with each man receiving 1 lb of meat, 1.5 lb of bread and one-third of a pint of rum a day. For variety, the meat was sometimes accompanied by 1 lb of hard biscuit and a pint of wine was issued instead of rum. Occasionally a man who had attained the rank of sergeant-major was commissioned – free of charge – as an officer, but this was officially discouraged because of the financial burdens that life as an officer placed on the recipient. It was also felt – rightly to some extent – that soldiers were less willing to be officered by men from the same social background as themselves.

Lord Brudenell, of course, came from the *right* family, and this, as much as his zealous attention to duties, meant that he was able rapidly to scale the ladder of rank. After just eight months he was a lieutenant, and in June 1826 (shortly before his wedding) he became a captain and troop commander. He may have neglected his parliamentary duties – such as they were – during his early years in the Army, but he still had time for more leisurely pursuits, particularly fox-hunting. He was present, for example, at a famous run of the Quorn in February 1826 when, during Squire Osbaldeston's second term as Master, a huge field of more than 200 rode in pursuit for over an hour with just two brief checks. According to Charles Apperley, better known as 'Nimrod', the hunting correspondent for the *Sporting Magazine*, Lord Brudenell was one of only ten riders who kept up with the pace and even had the sang-froid to inquire after the identity of a rider who had been unhorsed at some particularly treacherous rails. 'Can't tell, my Lord,' replied the nearest horseman, 'but I thought it was a queerish place when I came o'er it before him.'[17]

This smooth early phase of Lord Brudenell's military career was abruptly halted in January 1827 when his patron, the Duke of York, died and was succeeded by the Duke of Wellington. Two months later, a Catholic Emancipation Bill sponsored by the Radical M.P., Sir Francis Burdett – which would have enabled Papists to sit in Parliament – was defeated by just four votes in the House of Commons, and Ireland was in danger of exploding over the issue. Troops were needed to ensure order and the 8th Hussars, after an absence of twenty-five years, were posted to Dundalk. That winter, with the regiment partially dispersed around the outlying district, the commanding officer absent and his second-in-command ill, Brudenell found himself the senior rank. With an opportunity to demonstrate his keenness for efficiency, and ignoring the cold damp weather, he ordered a field day. Inevitably, the horses and men suffered from such senseless exposure to the elements and many were unfit for duty when the irate Colonel Russell returned. Some time after this, Brudenell began a two-year placement in Dublin on the staff of Sir Charles Dalbaic, the commander in Ireland, and it may well have been this incident that hastened his departure.

When Brudenell returned to the regiment at Longford in 1830, it had a new commander – Russell having sold out more than a year before to the Honourable George Molyneux, the younger son of Earl Sefton. The remarkable thing about Molyneux was that he was just 28, much younger than the majority of his officers, and younger even than Brudenell. It may well have been the arrival of this upstart colonel that caused Brudenell, an upstart himself, to leave the regiment. In May 1830 he bought the rank of major, enabling him to purchase the next available lieutenant-colonelcy. But Molyneux was hardly likely to want to sell his, and as no other commanding officers of cavalry seemed willing to retire, the only option was to buy the rank of a lieutenant-colonel on half-pay and wait for a vacancy. This he did in December 1830, marking his progress in six and a half short years from cornet to lieutenant-colonel. To many this exemplified the absurdity of a purchase system that could place an untried officer, by virtue of his connections and money, in command of others more experienced and suited to command. Theoretically, the system was proof against such an abuse; in practice it was all too vulnerable.

The origins of the system dated back to Charles II's reign in the late seventeenth century, when money was paid for the procurement of commissions in the burgeoning standing army in the same way as it was for any other public appointment. Legal recognition came in 1702 when the High Court ordered Lieutenant Ive to pay £600 to Captain Ash for procuring him a commission in the Royal Marines. Ive had tried to pull out at the last minute and the commission was given to another officer, but the court, satisfied that Ash had kept his side of the bargain, ruled that Ive must pay. The House of Lords confirmed the decision on appeal. But it was not until George I issued a royal warrant in 1720 that the institution was formalised and regulated. The main conditions were as follows: outgoing ranks were not to recommend their successors; commissions could only be sold to those holding the preceding rank; the price of each rank, depending on the regiment, was fixed.

While commissions could no longer be sold to non-military persons hoping to make a quick profit, they could still be bought by young officers eager for rapid promotion and willing, unofficially, to pay over the odds. This abuse was only partially ended in 1798 by an Act of Parliament which declared null and void all purchases made through unofficial Army agents. By the 1820s, the principle of the system had changed little since George I's day. Commissions could be purchased up to the rank of lieutenant-colonel – generals were appointed on merit. Promotion could only come about if there was a vacancy – usually through retirement – and was strictly by seniority. When a major retired, for example, the senior captain would be given the opportunity to buy his commission. If he did so, the other captains would move a step nearer the head of their rank, which in turn would create a vacant junior captaincy and enable the senior lieu-tenant to purchase it, and so on through all the ranks. If the senior officer at any given rank chose not to buy (for whatever reason), his immediate subordinate could do so.

This was fine in theory, but in practice money talked. An officer like Lord Brudenell could never have attained the rank of lieutenant-colonel in just over six years if he had played by the rules; it would have taken him much longer to reach a position of seniority in each rank from where he was eligible to purchase the next. He short-circuited it – like so many other rich officers – by bribing senior officers of the same rank to waive their right to purchase, so that it devolved upon him. In addition, he offered way over the official cost of a given rank, so encouraging more senior officers to retire. Such sharp practice caused a huge inflation in the unofficial price of commissions. A cornetcy in a regiment of hussars had been set at £840 in 1821, but the recipient could expect to pay at least double that. Lieutenant-colonelcies were much harder to come by and therefore more inflated, with officers prepared to pay up to five times the official price of £6,175. Later in his career, Brudenell was reputed to have exceeded even this exorbitant sum.

Not all officers had to purchase their commissions. About a quarter of the total vacancies came about as the result of death, brevet promotion and augmentation of the Army; such commissions were generally conferred upon the sons of distinguished officers, widows and poorer clergymen, meritorious non-commissioned officers and promising cadets at military seminaries. While financially strapped, and often leapfrogged by junior officers able to pay for the next rank, these officers obtained promotion in the same circumstances under which they had been commissioned in the first place, and for free. Although dependent upon variables, the process was accelerated by the speed with which other officers purchased promo-tion, so moving them one step up the ladder of seniority.

Senior military commanders were all too aware that the system had its drawbacks, not least the rapid promotion of rich but inexperienced officers like Brudenell, but they felt that its benefits were far more significant. In a memorandum submitted to a House of Commons committee considering the abolition of the system in 1833, the Duke of Wellington wrote:

> The permission to sell their Commissions to younger, more active, healthy, and energetic and better qualified men, relieves the service from a burthen, at the same time that it throws none upon the

State in the shape of remuneration, reward, or provision for men worn out by length and arduous nature of the services required from all British Officers. It is the promotion by purchase which brings into the service men of fortune and education, men who have some connection with the interests and fortunes of the country, besides the Commissions which they hold from His Majesty. It is this circumstance which exempts the British Army from the character of being a 'mercenary army', and has rendered its employment for nearly a century and a half not only not inconsistent with the constitutional privileges of the country, but safe and beneficial.[18]

It would not be until 1871 – during the Liberal ministry of William Gladstone – that such powerful voices were muted and the purchase system was abolished in favour of promotion solely on merit. The architect was the great Army reformer Edward Cardwell, the Secretary of State for War, who had been put in control of the Commander-in-Chief, the Duke of Cambridge, the previous year and so was in a position to ignore his opposition.

It was not only Lord Brudenell's military ambition that had suffered a setback, for a year earlier his political career had temporarily stalled over the issue of Catholic emancipation. As a Tory and a staunch defender of Church, State and Monarchy – like his patron, the Marquess of Ailesbury, and his father, the Earl of Cardigan – his initial stance had been one of vehement opposition to the removal of Catholic civil disabilities. Accordingly, he had voted against Sir Francis Burdett's Emancipation Bills of 1825 (passed by the Commons but rejected by the Lords), 1827 (rejected by the Commons by just four votes), and 1828 (passed by the Commons by six votes and rejected by the Lords). What made the introduction of a fourth Bill in 1829 so different was that it was sponsored by a Tory government headed by the Duke of Wellington and his deputy, Sir Robert Peel.

The 'Iron Duke' had become Prime Minister in January 1828 after the dissolution of Lord Goderich's government. When Burdett's Bill arrived in the House of Lords in June, he was opposed to it – fearing that it would fuel Irish independence – and his uncompromising speech ensured that it was defeated by 44 votes.

By August, however, Wellington was beginning to see emancipation in a more favourable light, telling George IV that a 'rebellion' was 'impending' and asking for his permission to consider a solution to the Irish problem. The catalyst for this was the overwhelming victory by Daniel O'Connell, the leader of the Catholic Association, over Vesey Fitzgerald, a Cabinet minister, in the County Clare by-election in July. As a Catholic, O'Connell was unable to take up his seat, but the symbolism of his victory was obvious and before the end of the year, Wellington had decided that emancipation was the only way to avoid an explosion in Ireland. His cause was helped immeasurably in January 1829 when both Sir Robert Peel, the Home Secretary and Leader of the Commons, and George IV agreed to put previous misgivings behind them and support him.

As a prerequisite to emancipation (and partly as a concession to 'Ultra' Protestant Tories set against *any* concessions to Catholics), Wellington introduced a Bill suppressing the Catholic Association in February 1829 and by the end of the month it had been passed by both Houses. But when he drove to Windsor to discuss the next step, emancipation, the King told him that he had changed his mind, having been influenced by his favourite brother, the 'Ultra' Duke of Cumberland. It needed immense pressure from the government to force the King to give in, however. After Wellington, Peel and Lord Chancellor Lyndhurst had threatened to resign during a torturous five-hour interview at Windsor on 4 March, a tearful George IV told them that he would look for alternative ministers; but when the Duke arrived home, a letter from the King was awaiting him.

> My dear friend,
>
> As I have found the country would be left without an Administration, I have decided to yield my opinions to *that* which is considered by the Cabinet to be for the immediate interests of the country. Let them proceed as proposed with their measure. God knows what pain it costs me to write these words.
>
> G.R.[19]

Two days later, the House of Commons passed Peel's motion that it 'resolve itself into a Committee' to consider the 'Laws imposing Civil Disabilities on His Majesty's Roman Catholic Subjects' by 160 votes. Lord Brudenell did not vote, despite the fact that his patron, Lord Ailesbury, had instructed him to oppose the motion. On 10 March, Peel introduced the Roman Catholic Relief Bill – enabling members of that religion to vote in elections for M.P.s and to sit in Parliament without having to renounce their faith –

and eight days later the House of Commons passed it for a second reading by a majority of 180. *Hansard's* record of parliamentary proceedings only includes the names of those who voted against the Bill, and as Brudenell was not one of them it is possible that he voted for it. Although on military duty in Ireland, he had returned to vote against Burdett's Bill of 1828, and could easily have done so again with the reverse purpose. On 30 March the Bill was passed for a third reading by a similar majority and sent up to the House of Lords. Once again, Brudenell's name does not appear in the voting lists, despite the fact that this time *Hansard's* listed all those who voted for and against. Within ten days the House of Lords had also passed the Bill for a third reading by more than 100 votes.

But even if Brudenell did not vote for Catholic emancipation on 18 March, he certainly did not vote against it – either then, or during the other two crucial divisions in March. Such an abstention was tantamount to tacit support, and explains why the Marquess of Ailesbury – a vehement opponent of emancipation to the bitter end – turned him out of his seat soon after. Years later, in an attempt to secure the Lord-Lieutenantcy of Northamptonshire, Brudenell reminded Sir Robert Peel of his earlier sacrifice: 'I was obliged to vacate my seat (Marlborough) in consequence of my determination to support you and the Duke of Wellington's administration upon the Catholic Question.'[20]

Brudenell always insisted that his 'support' for Catholic emancipation was consistent with his undeviating loyalty to the Tory party, but surely there were other factors at work. After all, by not opposing the measure as he had done the previous year, he was both betraying his Protestant principles and defying his political patron and kinsman. There has to be an explanation more compelling than loyalty to the Tory administration; not least because Brudenell would later vote against Peel on another issue of fundamental importance – the Corn Laws.

The answer seems to lie in the fact that the measure was sponsored by the Duke of Wellington, a staunch Tory who hitherto had also opposed it. Speaking in the House of Lords seventeen years later, Brudenell cited Catholic emancipation as one of the few examples of his voting 'inconsistency', and said it had come about because of his 'high opinion' and 'profound respect' for Wellington. To a military man like Brudenell, the 'Iron Duke' was a god; if he was prepared to sacrifice his principles, then there had to be a good reason. Certainly, Wellington's warnings of an explosion in Ireland would have struck a chord with Brudenell who, from his service there, was well placed to gauge the mood of the people. But even if Wellington was the determining factor, Brudenell's stand still indicates a mental flexibility at odds with the traditional portrayal of him as an unthinking reactionary.[21]

The cost for Brudenell was his seat; Wellington, on the other hand, almost forfeited his life. On 16 March, two days before the first vote on the Bill in the Commons, a letter appeared in the *Standard* from the Earl of Winchilsea, a leading 'Ultra' peer, announcing that he had cancelled his £50 subscription to King's College, London, because the Duke of Wellington, a founder, had used it as a smoke-screen behind which he could 'carry on his insidious designs, for the infringement of our liberties, and the introduction of Popery into every department of the State'. Twice Wellington demanded a retraction, twice Winchilsea refused. So serious a threat to the smooth passage of Catholic emancipation did the Duke consider Winchilsea's letter that he was forced to challenge him to a duel. A notoriously bad shot, Wellington's intention was to maim Winchilsea by aiming for his legs, thereby affirming his honourable support of emancipation in language that the extremists could understand. They met at Battersea Fields in the early morning of 21 March, accompanied by their seconds and Wellington's physician, Doctor Hume.

It was to be Wellington's first and last duel, but he showed little sign of nerves as Sir Henry Hardinge, his second and fellow Cabinet minister, marked out his firing position and then measured the regulation twelve paces towards a ditch near to where Winchilsea was waiting. 'Damn it! Don't stick him up so near the ditch,' the Duke called out. 'If I hit him he will tumble in.'

It just remained for Hardinge to read out a prepared statement, chastising Winchilsea for his unforgivable behaviour and laying the blame for the duel firmly at his door. The two men then stepped up to their marks, both facing side-on – so as to reduce the target area – with their pistols held down by their sides. 'Fire!' signalled Hardinge, but as the Duke brought up his pistol to the horizontal he noticed that Winchilsea had not moved his arm. Deliberately moving his aim a few degrees to the side, Wellington fired wide. His opponent then raised his pistol and fired into the air; Lord Falmouth, Winchilsea's second, believing his principal had gone too far by writing the letter to the *Standard*, had made him promise that if he survived the Duke's shot he would not shoot back. Believing that honour had been satisfied, Falmouth produced a written statement by Winchilsea regretting his actions. But still the Duke was not satisfied, and for a moment it seemed as if a second shot was inevitable. Dr Hume came to the rescue by

inserting into the statement, with a pencil, the words 'in apology'. The Duke accepted it, pausing only to wish the two relieved lords good morning before cantering off the field.[22]

Learning of the fight the following day, the editor of the *Morning Herald* was horrified, noting in an editorial:

> Yes, reader, the Duke of Wellington, the conqueror of a greater conqueror than either Alexander or Caesar, the first warrior of his day, the victor of a hundred battles, the Prime Minister of Great Britain, and the author of a measure which, he says, is necessary, absolutely necessary, for the welfare of the Empire, setting all these things at nought, placed himself in a situation where it was probable that he might have become a murderer; he might have committed a deadly crime, which would have brought him to the bar of his country to plead for his life as a felon of the blackest dye. And all this risk was run, forsooth – all this wickedness was to be perpetrated – merely because a noble lord, in a fit of anger, wrote a pettish letter, which even his best friends and warmest admirers laughed at. Truly it is no wonder that the multitude should break the laws when we see the law-makers themselves, the great, the powerful, and the renowned, setting them at open defiance.[23]

4

The Arch-Conservative

George IV's nineteen-year reign – nine as Regent, ten as King – came to an end in the early hours of 26 June 1830. The immediate cause was a ruptured blood vessel in the stomach, but the post-mortem also indicated that the corpulent monarch, long afflicted by dropsy, had been suffering from a general hardening of the arteries and a weakening of vital organs. Years of debauched living had finally taken their toll.

The Duke of Clarence, his 64-year-old brother, succeeded as William IV. The father of ten illegitimate children by the actress Dorothy Jordan, Clarence had joined the race to provide an heir to the throne after the death of the Prince Regent's daughter, Charlotte, in 1817. The following year he married Princess Adelaide of Saxe-Meiningen, a plain but practical woman 27 years his junior. But no children resulted, leaving his niece Princess Victoria, the only daughter of the late Duke of Kent, as his successor. A tall, hard-drinking jolly fellow who had joined the Navy as a boy and risen to the rank of Lord High Admiral, he was immediately dubbed the 'Sailor King'.

His *faux pas* were legendary: during a speech hailing the disparity of social rank among senior Army officers, he said of two generals present: 'You my Lord, are descended from the Plantagenets, and you are descended from the very dregs of the people.' His first act as King was to confirm Wellington's government in office; but all new reigns required a General Election, and Parliament was dissolved the following month. This gave Lord Brudenell the opportunity to return from the political wilderness in which he had languished since the previous year.[1]

The political system had changed little since the reign of Charles II. In 1827, John Croker estimated that 276 out of 658 seats in Parliament were at the disposal of landed patrons, the majority of whom were Tories. Eight peers alone controlled 57 seats. Many represented 'rotten' or 'pocket' boroughs, where the votes of a handful of dependent voters returned two members. One of the most notorious was High Wycombe, whose 34 voters were all tenants of Sir John Dashwood. Men like Dashwood could either bestow these seats on protégés and relations, and rely on their votes in the House of Commons, or they could sell them to the highest bidder.

By failing to oppose Catholic emancipation, Brudenell could no longer expect a seat under the former arrangement; his only option now was to buy one. But demand for such seats was high during the election of 1830, and he was forced to travel the long distance to Fowey in Cornwall to secure one. There is no record of exactly how much he paid for this 'rotten' borough, whose electorate of 300 was controlled by the powerful Lacy family, but it could not have been less than £5,000 and was probably more.

How much value Brudenell was likely to get from his investment was left open to doubt by the Whig/Radical opposition's choice of parliamentary reform as its main election battle-cry. Lord John Russell's February Bill had been heavily defeated in the Commons, but the ousting of the tyrannical French King, Charles X, in the July Revolution had fired a popular demand for reform. It was a call eagerly taken up by a hungry populace, now 16 million in number, suffering from the effects of economic depression and the severest winter in almost a century. Their plight had not been helped by the despised Poor Law, which set a poor rate that kept people only marginally above starvation level while preventing them from moving to other parishes to look for work.

But with fewer than one in ten men eligible to vote, popular pressure had a negligible effect on the General Election, with the result that Wellington's administration ended up with slightly more support in the Commons than hitherto. The response was a series of riots, particularly in Kent, aimed at landowners. Amidst this backdrop of discontent, Parliament opened on 2 November. Earl Grey, the Whig leader, made a speech suggesting to the government that some form of parliamentary reform was necessary given the volatile nature of the people. Wellington's dismissive response – which was representative of most Tory members at that time – did more to make reform inevitable than Grey's moderate suggestion ever could have done:

... I never read or heard of any measure ... which in any degree satisfies my mind that the state of representation can be improved ... [If] at the present moment I had imposed upon me the duty of forming a Legislature for any country, and particularly for a country like this, in possession of great property of various descriptions, – I do not mean to assert that I could form such a Legislature as we possess now, for the nature of man is incapable of reaching such *excellence* at once, – but my great endeavor would be, to form some description of legislature which would produce the same results. Under these circumstances, I am not prepared to bring forward any measure of the description alluded to by the noble Lord.[3]

Such was the strength of public feeling against this statement, particularly in London, that Wellington felt it necessary to advise the King to cancel his state visit to the City on Lord Mayor's Day, 9 November, in case of a riot. Six days later, the 'Ultra' Tories gained revenge for Catholic emancipation by voting with the opposition on a motion to investigate Civil List Accounts. The government was defeated by 29 votes, and the following day Wellington resigned; whereupon William IV invited Grey to replace him, so bringing to an end more than twenty-three years of uninterrupted Tory rule.

Although a rainbow coalition of Whigs, Radicals and Canningite former Tories, the new ministry was agreed on at least one issue: the need for parliamentary reform. There was a short delay as Parliament was adjourned until February 1831, but on the first day of March Lord John Russell introduced his second Reform Bill. It planned to abolish more than 100 'rotten' borough seats, redistribute many of them to the big towns and counties, and increase the number of voters by about half a million. As both of Fowey's seats were earmarked for abolition, Lord Brudenell had a vested interest in taking an active part in parliamentary business. He also had the opportunity, being back in London since going on half-pay the previous December.

But even his vote could not prevent the House of Commons from passing Russell's Bill for a second reading by a majority of just one on 22 March. Committee stage was next, and it was there that the reform suffered defeat. Realising that the government was unlikely to be able to get the Bill through the Commons, let alone the Lords, Earl Grey asked William IV to dissolve Parliament and let the electors have their say. At first the King refused, but he changed his mind on 22 April after learning that a Tory peer, Lord Wharncliffe, intended to introduce a motion challenging the royal prerogative of dissolution.

Most of London's inhabitants were overjoyed, and the Lord Mayor ordered illuminations throughout the capital. Many wealthy Tories who signalled their opposition to reform by shrouding their houses in darkness had their windows smashed by an unruly mob that marched up Piccadilly. The most prominent victim was the Duke of Wellington, who lost most of the new plate-glass on the ground floor of his London residence, Apsley House – in darkness by pure coincidence because of the recent death of Kitty, Duchess of Wellington, whose corpse lay within. The Duke himself was out of town, however, and it was left to his servant to prevent further damage to the house by dispersing the crowd with a blunderbuss. The Brudenell mansion in Portman Square was also blacked out, but escaped damage because the mob never ventured beyond Mayfair.

While Lord Brudenell and most other members of 'rotten' boroughs came through the General Election unscathed, it was a disaster for the Tories. Almost all the big town and county seats fell to the Whigs and the Radicals, which, added to a number of boroughs under the control of Whig patrons, gave the new government a sizeable majority in the Commons; this was swelled to an estimated 140 seats by the support of Irish and Scottish M.P.s who approved reform, not least because it planned to increase their representation.

It was now that the term 'conservative' was used to categorise those Tories determined to defend the constitution. In January 1831, the *Quarterly Review* had defined the struggle as between 'the conservative and subversive principles'. Three months later, Wellington spoke of the 'conservators of the constitution' in a letter to Lord Wharncliffe, and in May he received a letter from Lord Wilton pleading with him to lead 'a party of Conservatives'. The name stuck.[4]

With a healthy majority to ensure passage through the Commons, the government pressed on with Russell's Reform Bill. On 6 July it passed for a third reading by 136 votes. A week later, facing the abolition of his seat if the Bill became law, Lord Brudenell finally broke his 13-year silence in the lower chamber when – during a futile Tory attempt to hold the Bill back from committee stage in the early hours of the morning – he supported the call for an adjournment. Assuring ministers that the opposition 'were not to be browbeaten' by the kind of 'uproar and confusion' that had greeted the previous request for an adjournment until the following day, he suggested one of his own until 5 p.m. It was defeated by 170 votes.

In no way discouraged, indeed warming to the unfamiliar sensation of being listened to by the legislators of the nation, he spoke again soon after. 'Were they to go, at four o'clock in the morning, into a Committee on a Bill, the discussions on which would last five weeks, merely because His Majesty's Government thought it a point of dignity to persevere?' he asked. They should be resisted, and he was one of those 'determined not to withdraw the Motion for adjournment' while he could get 'one single Member to join him'. Unfortunately for this stoic defender of principle, exhaustion was driving ever more Tories to their beds and only 25 of them, including Brudenell, supported the final lost vote for an adjournment. Finally, at 7 a.m., the government carried the day and the House resolved itself into a committee and adjourned.[5]

Having at last broken his duck, Brudenell was anxious to use his new-found oratorical powers to save his constituency from abolition, and the chance came during a debate in committee stage on 21 July. The borough of Fowey, he told the House, was 'situated in two parishes' with a population in 1821 of 2,400 and more than 300 voters. Yet the government 'had laid down the rule, that where a borough contained more than 2,000 inhabitants, having at the same time more than 300 voters, its franchise should not be interfered with'. Consequently, he was 'at a loss to conceive why this borough was to be disenfranchised', particularly as it 'had of late much increased in commerce, wealth and prosperity'.

Russell replied for the government, pointing out that the House had already agreed not to admit adjoining parishes to a borough in order to enable it to muster the population necessary for representation. Without it, Fowey had fewer than 2,000 inhabitants and could not be an exception to the rule. Put to a vote, the government easily carried the day and Fowey remained one of the constituencies due for extinction.[6]

So confident had Brudenell now become on the floor of the House that he did not confine his contribution to parliamentary reform alone, and on 12 August he spoke in a debate on the subject of Holland's invasion of the newly created Kingdom of Belgium. In 1814, after the ejection of Napoleon by the Allies, the Low Countries had been reunited for the first time since the sixteenth century into the Kingdom of the Netherlands. But the two halves of the country were very different: the former United Provinces (or Holland) in the north was Protestant and based on commerce; the former Austrian Netherlands (or Belgium) in the south was

Catholic and heavily industrialised. It did not help that the ruling family of Orange came from the minority north, which also received a disproportionate share of representation in the national parliament.

Religious, economic and political tensions were finally released in riots in Brussels sparked by the July Revolution of 1830 in France. Within six weeks the Dutch had been expelled from the city and a provisional government had declared Belgian independence. The great powers, including Britain, then reversed their earlier support for a united Netherlands by warning Holland not to use force to put down the rebellion. The following January, at a conference in London, these same powers recognised Belgium as an independent state whose neutrality they would guarantee. As their new King the Belgians chose Leopold of Saxe-Coburg, former husband of George IV's deceased daughter, Princess Charlotte, and uncle of the future Queen Victoria. It was this dynastic connection as much as the guarantee they had given that caused the British government to condemn Holland when it defied the international community by invading Belgium in August 1831.

To Lord Brudenell and others, the pro-Belgian policy smacked of currying favour with Catholic France. He, for one, expressed his 'regret that the bias of the minds of Ministers was clearly against the King of Holland'. As an 'ancient ally', the 'first shot fired by the British forces, on land or water', would be 'an indelible disgrace to the country'. Noting that the government had also allowed the French to intimidate Portugal, another 'old and faithful' ally, and the Russians to mete out punishment to the Poles, he came to the conclusion that 'the tendency of our foreign policy now was to oppress the weak, and truckle to the strong'. 'If this system were continued,' he concluded, 'the English name would be a by-word for all that was base and dishonourable.'[7]

His powerful rhetoric was in vain, however. A second London Conference sanctioned intervention by France, and within weeks its troops had forced the Dutch to withdraw. Belgian independence was assured.

But parliamentary reform was the issue that really mattered to Brudenell, and he was given ample cause for celebration on 8 October when the Duke of Wellington and the majority of Tory peers (including the Marquess of Ailesbury and the Earl of Cardigan) defeated the Reform Bill in the House of Lords by 41 votes. The following day the pro-reform *Morning Chronicle* was published with black borders, while Wellington's effigy was burned at Tyburn (now Marble Arch). Four days later, Apsley House was attacked by the mob for a second time, one stone narrowly missing the Duke's head as he sat at his writing-table. Riots also broke out in Derby, Nottingham and, most seriously, in Bristol – where the defeat of the Reform Bill coincided with the appointment of the unpopular Wetherell as City Recorder. During bitter fighting between demonstrators and the Army, half the city centre was razed and the casualties numbered several hundred.

Spurred on by the ugly mood of the country, Russell introduced his third Reform Bill to the House of Commons in December. Once again Brudenell diligently attended the exhaustive debates that took place over the next three months, but his vote could not prevent the Bill from being passed with comfortable majorities of 162 and 116. The country then waited with bated breath as the Bill was sent up to the House of Lords. On Friday, 13 April, it was passed for a second reading by nine votes, and it seemed as if the peers were bowing to public pressure. But the 'Conservatives' were just biding their time, and in early May they ambushed the Bill in Committee stage by approving an amendment to postpone the consideration of the first clause.

The following day, Lord Grey went to see William IV to demand the creation of fifty Whig peers to ensure the passage of the Bill. The King refused, Grey resigned, and Wellington was asked to form a government on the condition that he introduced a limited form of parliamentary reform. Grudgingly he agreed, but Peel and other leading Tories refused to join him under such a proviso. Meanwhile, the country was reacting angrily to Grey's fall: the Liverpool Stock Exchange closed in protest, and barricades began to go up in Birmingham and Manchester. Revolution seemed close at hand, and cavalry regiments were ordered to sharpen their sabres. Parliament met on the 14th, but Alexander Baring, Wellington's Chancellor of the Exchequer, was bayed down each time he tried to speak. One M.P. after another rose to denounce Wellington for deposing Grey and then resurrecting the very reform he had formerly opposed.

The game was up. Unable to raise support in the House of Commons, Wellington resigned and Grey was recalled. He presented William IV with an ultimatum: either promise to create enough peers to pass the Reform Bill or face a revolution. On the 18th, with the *Morning Chronicle* proclaiming 'the eve of the barricades', the King gave his written guarantee, but Wellington and more than 100 Tory peers made it unnecessary by agreeing to abstain. Even parliamentary reform was preferable to a permanent Whig majority in the House of Lords. The Bill was finally passed on 4 June by 106 votes to 22.

The widely held belief of conservatives like Lord Brudenell was that the Reform Act itself was little short of revolution. They feared that the disfranchisement of 111 small borough seats, the addition of 63 big town seats and 62 county seats, and the increase in the electorate to one in seven of the total male population (one in five in England and Wales), would give the balance of power to the rising commercial and merchant middle classes. They could not have been more wrong.

The effect of parliamentary reform was to increase the influence of the House of Commons over the executive, which in turn weakened that of the monarch. But the traditional social élite – the aristocracy and greater gentry – still held sway in both Houses, and the period between the Reform Acts of 1832 and 1867 was for them a political golden age. The worst of the 'rotten' boroughs had been abolished, but many remained in which local 'influence' was still decisive. Furthermore, money still talked at election time, ensuring either uncontested seats or ballots in which the most 'generous' candidate prevailed. Centrally organised political parties began to develop to take account of the expanded electorate, but it was not until after the Reform Act of 1867 had increased it still further that they were able to exert discipline over their members. The post-1832 House of Commons was composed of aristocratic factions who were all too willing to vote against their party on individual issues. In five out of the six parliaments between 1841 and 1868, the indiscipline of lower House members brought about the resignation of at least one administration.

Captain Gronow's recollection of the first post-reform General Election in December 1832 is confirmation that politics were far from becoming the democratic process so feared by the ruling élite. Having tried and failed to gain election from Grimsby the previous year after assuring Lord Yarborough, his chief supporter, that he would not use bribes, he was determined not to repeat the mistake. This time, standing as a Whig candidate at Stafford, he left a crowd of electors in no doubts as to his intentions. 'I made them a speech of some length,' he wrote, 'setting forth the principles upon which I presented myself to their notice, and solicited their suffrages, concluding by significantly assuring them that they should all have reason to be satisfied with me.'

This meant setting to work 'to bribe every man, woman and child in the ancient borough of Stafford . . . I engaged numerous agents, opened all the public houses which were not already taken by my opponents, gave suppers every night to my supporters, kissed all their wives and children, drank their health in every sort of abominable mixture, and secured my return against great local interest.' Even then the voters were not happy and forwarded a petition to the House of Commons recommending that Gronow be unseated because, in his own words, 'I had not bribed the electors sufficiently.' The document produced much merriment in the House when it was read out by the clerk and, not surprisingly, the Speaker ruled that it could not be received.[8]

Lord Brudenell, meanwhile, had decided to stand for his local seat, the newly created two-member constituency of Northamptonshire North. Traditionally, the county had been Tory with 'Squire' Cartright sitting uncontested for 34 years. But in the General Election of 1831, with reform the key issue, Cartright had been defeated by the Whig Lord Milton. Brudenell was determined to win back at least one seat for the Conservatives. On 21 July, with the prospective election still months away, he took out an advert in the pro-reform *Northampton Mercury* so as to avail the electors of his intentions. 'Should I be so fortunate as to meet with your favourable support,' he announced, 'at the same time that I shall always be found to advocate those measures which may tend to the stability of our Constitution in the Church and State, I shall ever support such as may conduce to the general interests and welfare of all orders of society, without reference to the quarters from which they emanate.'[9]

Of course, some of those given the vote by the recent extension of the franchise were hardly likely to agree that Brudenell's opposition to parliamentary reform was conducive to the 'welfare of all orders of society'. Similarly, his championing of the Corn Laws – the system of protective tariffs against foreign corn – would not appeal to town-dwellers who had to pay more for bread. On the other hand, Northamptonshire North was a largely rural county with a powerful farming interest, and to be known as the 'Farmer's Friend' was no bad thing.

The other candidate early to declare himself was Lord Milton, heir to the influential Earl Fitzwilliam and incumbent of the former single-member constituency. His reformist zeal – manifesting itself primarily in support for parliamentary reform, repeal of the Corn Laws and abolition of slavery in the Empire – was in direct contrast to Brudenell's conservatism. For a while these differences seemed irrelevant, as no other candidates came forward and it looked as if the election would be uncontested. All this changed when Brudenell coaxed his neighbour, Squire Tryon of Bulwick, to stand as a second Tory or Conservative candidate. Milton responded by persuading another Whig, William Hanbury of Kelmarsh, to take part.

So why, given the 'first two past the post' system, did Brudenell put his own election in doubt? The answer is probably that he felt his wealth and standing in the county would make his selection certain, while there was just a possibility that he could haul Tryon into Parliament on his coat-tails. Even so, it indicates a deeply held conviction for Tory or Conservative principles that went beyond mere self-interest.

That many of the shire's inhabitants did not share these principles was brought home to Lord Brudenell during electioneering in the market town of Wellingborough in September. He and a small band of mounted supporters were in the process of riding into town when they found their passage blocked by a jeering crowd. Dismounting to be less conspicuous, they tried to force their way through; but Milton's 'rent-a-rabble' was warming to the task now, and a shower of stones and filth rained down on the small knot of men and horses. Brudenell was hit on the back of the head by a stone, and before long had received 'considerable personal injury', while his friends suffered a similar battering. The riot soon spread to nearby streets, probably the result of Tory townsfolk joining in, and troops had to be called from nearby Weedon Barracks before order could be restored. Brudenell and his party eventually extricated themselves and, 'soiled by Whig excrement, and covered by Whig spittle', hastily left the town.[10]

Determined to prevent a repeat performance of this humiliation, Brudenell now rode everywhere accompanied by a huge retinue of horsemen, many of them Deene tenants. While this precluded further injury, his lukewarm stance on the question of reform continued to produce as many jeers as cheers wherever he spoke. Forced to respond to Milton's vocal denouncement of slavery, he said that he was 'most anxious to see the slave emancipated', but 'in his present and uneducated and ignorant state [he] is unfit for freedom'. The solution was to cause 'his condition to be improved, so as to qualify him for emancipation'.[11]

But as in Stafford, it was money rather than slogans which really made the difference. According to *The Times,* one of the few non-partisan newspapers, Brudenell had already distributed £10,000 in 'election expenses' a full month before polling. A similar amount, at the very least, would be disbursed over the next 30 days. Today, such a total expenditure would be equivalent to roughly £600,000.[12]

Nomination of the candidates took place at Kettering on Saturday, 15 December. Despite the pouring rain, the town had been crowded since dawn. Shortly before 10 a.m., Lord Brudenell and Squire Tryon rode in at

the head of an immense body of horsemen – many of them local yeomanry – with a band playing and blue Conservative party pennants flying.
Making straight for the White Hart Inn, they joined their opponents to
hear the High Sheriff read out the King's writ. The whole party then
moved on foot to the 'hustings', a platform erected in the market place. By
now the rain had stopped and a huge crowd had gathered. Many of those
nearest the platform were pro-Milton Whig supporters, but hemming
them in from behind was Brudenell's private army of horsemen. If there
was to be any trouble, he had made sure that the Conservatives would not
come off the worst.

A loud cheer greeted the arrival of the candidates. After each of the four
had been proposed and seconded, Lord Milton was the first to speak.
Addressing the assembled throng as 'Men of Kettering, and Gentlemen',
he began by reiterating exactly what he stood for. He was not in favour of
the Corn Laws because he believed that they had 'seduced' the farmer
'into offering a larger rent than he would give' if they 'were not in existence'. Consequently, the farmer 'would be far better off' without them.
As 'an ardent supporter of the Reform Bill, and an earnest lover of liberty
in all its varieties', he 'felt confident' that the electors 'would not desert the
colours which they had exhibited at the last election'. On the question of
negro slavery, he stated that 'his endeavour would be to assist and co-oper-
ate with those whose object it was to make the last fetter drop from the
hand of the last slave'.

Loud cheers greeted this last remark and, emboldened, Milton closed
his speech with a personal attack on the election methods of his primary
opponent, Lord Brudenell. He thought 'it much more respectable and
more English that a candidate should openly state his opinions and objects
to the electors, than that he should go creeping up the back stairs of every
house to explain them in private'. This was a thinly veiled reference to
Brudenell's practice of using a combination of bribes and threats to win
votes. The crowd responded with cheers and hisses as Milton ploughed on,
stating that 'he did not think that such conduct would obtain a single vote
from men of independent character'.

Lord Brudenell was next, and he began by refuting Milton's allegation.
He could 'assure the Noble Lord that he never crept up the back stairs of
the house of any elector'. The 'Noble Lord' must have been thinking of
the 'back-stairs way in which he got into Parliament last time'. More
cheers and hisses greeted this sally, before Brudenell continued. He did not
see why, because he thought 'it his duty to pay his respects to the electors

in person', he 'should be charged with back-stair proceedings'. He was a 'strict conservative' and 'earnestly opposed to the policy of His Majesty's present Government'.

The charge that he was an opponent of the Reform Bill 'was true', and he 'had yet to learn what benefit the people of England had derived from that measure'. Half drowned-out by the clamour that greeted these words, he raised his voice to say that if the Bill led to a 'parliament prepared to vote for the repeal of the Corn Laws', he would 'have been proved right in his opposition'. For the 'Noble Lord' had failed to explain 'what was to become of agriculturalists during the interval between the repeal of the Corn Laws and the golden period at which both parties are to be prosperous and happy'. Brudenell ended by mentioning an issue particularly dear to his heart, the recent conflict with Holland. The Whig government had 'commenced a war against our old ally, a Protestant people, to whom we were bound by every tie calculated to command respect'. The only object had been 'to suppress a loyal and gallant people'.[13]

Whether these speeches swayed any last-minute voters is doubtful. Over the next week polling took place, and it was reported first that Milton and Hanbury were leading, then Brudenell and Tryon. But come the announcement of the victors at 2 o'clock on Friday, 21 December, Lords Milton and Brudenell had predictably edged ahead, a combination of money and local 'influence' having ensured that honours were shared between these two great aristocratic families. The fact that one was Conservative, the other Whig, was almost an irrelevance. But for those who had refused to be pressurised into voting the 'right way', the punishment was swift and merciless. Mr Smith, a farmer, was said to have been evicted from his property because 'notwithstanding his being Lord Cardigan's tenant, he had voted against Lord Brudenell . . . he being the landlord's son'.[14]

———•—

Court-Martial

Lord Brudenell had little time in which to savour the fruits of victory. The previous March, just six days before the Reform Bill was passed for the last time by the House of Commons, he had exchanged commissions with Lieutenant-Colonel Joseph Thackwell of the 15th (King's) Hussars. Now, shortly after the election, he and his new regiment were posted to Ireland.

Raised in London as light dragoons by Colonel George Elliot during the Seven Years' War, the regiment had fought in most of the glorious battles of the Napoleonic Wars, including Vittoria, Corunna – and Toulouse, where it had routed Marshal Soult's cavalry. At Waterloo, too, it had served with distinction. At one stage of the battle, when engaged with French cuirassiers, the command had devolved upon the then senior Captain Thackwell, after the colonel had been wounded and the major killed. But soon after, Thackwell was disabled by a musket bullet through the bridle-hand and another officer had to take charge. When the Prince Regent was crowned George IV in 1821, the regiment was chosen to provide his escort to the coronation. From here on it was known as the King's Hussars.

Replacing an officer like Colonel Thackwell, who had served in the 15th for 31 years, 12 of them as commander, was never going to be easy for Lord Brudenell. Aged 34, he was younger than many of his captains, a number of whom had seen service at Waterloo. Such officers were bound to resent a wet-behind-the-ears aristocrat who had never been in action and had only assumed command by virtue of his wealth and connections – particularly as the officer he was succeeding was both efficient and popular. Thackwell's cool and decisive action had contained the reform riot in Nottingham the previous October and had drawn praise from local magistrates, General Bouverie, the district commander, and General Hill, the Commander-in-Chief. In gratitude, the inhabitants of Nottingham had raised a subscription and with the proceeds presented Thackwell with a silver soup-tureen and books to establish a regimental library.

Busy lobbying in Parliament against the Reform Bill, Brudenell did not join his new regiment at Hulme Barracks, Manchester, until May 1832. He was welcomed by a letter from Thackwell, congratulating him 'most sincerely on succeeding to the command of one of the best Regiments in His Majesty's service'. The former commander should also have been congratulating himself for having relieved his successor of around £20,000 for the honour of leading such an illustrious regiment. His misgivings would come later when he realised that the excellent relationship he had built up between commander and officers had been destroyed by his vain and overbearing replacement.[1]

Despite the 15th Hussars' reputation as one of the finest cavalry regiments in the British Army, Lord Brudenell was not satisfied. He wanted it to be *the* smartest and *the* most efficient, and nothing – least of all previous practice – was going to stand in his way. From now on his officers would be expected to follow regulations to the letter. Field days and reviews would be stepped up; horses and men turned out at all times as if they were on parade. And as the quality of hospitality would reflect on the regiment, only French cuisine, fine wines and champagne were acceptable.

It was not long before the new regime was arousing, in the words of the regimental history, 'a good deal of discontent'. The chief cause appears to have been an order by Lord Brudenell confining the men to barracks which – intended as a means of protecting them from an outbreak of cholera in the Lancashire area – backfired. The end result was 'reprehensible proceedings on the part of certain of the men in the ranks', and it took a visit by the local district commander, Major-General Sir John Colquhoun Grant, to placate the irate troopers. Brudenell's talent for mismanaging men would be seen to more explosive effect before too long.[2]

In May 1833, the 15th Hussars arrived in Newbridge, Ireland, and Lord Brudenell at once set to work to bring his regiment to the peak of efficiency. For the first five weeks he ordered field days at least four times a week, with squadron skirmishing drill on the remaining weekday. When not galloping, the troops would be kept at a continuous trot of eight miles an hour, and such manoeuvres would last up to five hours. If the horses were still warm when they returned to stables, they would remain saddled for a further two hours to protect them against colds.

Faced with such unrelenting duty – Brudenell's predecessor, Thackwell, had rarely exceeded three drill exercises a week – the horses developed sore backs. The more they were worked, the thinner they got, and the thinner they got the more their saddles rubbed. To alleviate the problem, Brudenell reduced the drill days by one for the remaining two weeks at Newbridge, and ordered the saddles to be repositioned. Neither expedient made much difference, and when the regiment left for outposts in Kilkenny and Carlow it was a shadow of its former self. 'No regiment ever marched into Newbridge in better condition,' said Major Sir Walter Scott, son of the recently deceased novelist and Brudenell's second-in-command. But, 'I never saw such a squadron as I had the command of when I left Newbridge, in regard to their low condition, and number of sore backs.'[3]

After his squadron had arrived at Carlow, Major Courtney Philipps informed Lord Brudenell of the 'unusual number' of horses with sore backs, adding that he had not ordered punishment drill because it was 'not the fault of the men'. This did not satisfy Brudenell, who heaped most of his criticism upon the troop commander with the most horses unfit for duty, Captain Augustus Wathen. It did not help that the men of Wathen's troop had the worse disciplinary record in the regiment, or that some of their horses had the misfortune to have naturally long coats, and so often attracted Brudenell's criticism for their dishevelled appearance during Saturday watering parades.[4]

And so it was that an officer of 20 years' service – eight of them with the 15th Hussars – who had served at Waterloo, was identified by his inexperienced commander, junior in age, as the epitome of inefficiency and indiscipline. Naturally, Wathen balked at being continually criticised, causing Brudenell in turn to see this as a challenge to his lawful authority. Other officers incurred the displeasure of the new colonel – particularly those who harked back with nostalgia to Thackwell's firm but fair helmsmanship – but none to the same extent as Wathen. Gradually, the officers' mess divided into pro- and anti-Brudenell factions, an unsavoury process that was to be repeated throughout his career as a commanding officer.

According to the *New Weekly Despatch*, a Dublin newspaper, it was the treatment of Lady Brudenell by the other officers' wives that caused her husband to behave with such 'petty envy, and vindictive spleen' towards

Captain Wathen. Notorious since her well-publicised divorce, Lady Brudenell had apparently been less than faithful to her husband and was described as 'the wife of a gallant Major – the friend of another – the attaché of a third – and, at last, the lady of the Lieutenant-Colonel'.

Because of this reputation, the wives of the regimental officers are said to have snubbed Lady Brudenell, and none more so than Wathen's spouse, the daughter of the Earl of Rothes and a 'lady' in her own right. Of course, any insult to his wife was bound to have infuriated Brudenell and may well have resulted in him making, as the *New Weekly Despatch* claimed, 'the military duties of the officers, irksome, onerous, and oppressive'. On the other hand, he had ever been a military martinet, a stickler for drill and discipline, and may simply have been insisting on the rigorous methods he felt necessary to obtain maximum smartness and efficiency. Whatever the motive, it led to an atmosphere of disharmony among the officers that was bound to reach an impasse sooner or later.[5]

The first major confrontation was precipitated by the receipt of an order on 10 August for the 15th Hussars to move without delay to Cork, there to be held in readiness for foreign service. The cause was the civil war in Portugal between the forces of the absolutist usurper Don Miguel and his liberal elder brother, the former King Don Pedro, fighting on behalf of his 14-year-old daughter, Maria de Glória. Predictably, Britain supported the constitutionalists and a Royal Navy officer, Captain (later Admiral Sir) Charles Napier, was in command of Don Pedro's fleet when it landed liberal reinforcements in the Algarve in June. The following month they took Lisbon. As these successes continued, the need for British assistance waned, and Miguel finally capitulated in May 1834.

But Lord Brudenell could not see into the future, and for a time it seemed as if he was about to be presented with a heaven-sent opportunity to test himself and his regiment in action. If so, he was determined to ensure that his men would do him credit. To enable the horses with sore backs to recover, he suspended field days for the first two weeks the regiment was in the Cork area. But thereafter, and before all the horses were fully fit, they took place three times a week, with skirmishing drill in the intervals. Even more unpopular was his decision to order new clothing and equipment for many of the men without first consulting their officers.

Clothing was the responsibility of the colonel, who was given a fixed sum, called 'off-reckonings', with which he paid for each man's uniform, including dress and stable-jackets, overalls (trousers) and busby. As the less elaborate stable-jackets and undress overalls were worn at all times bar field exercise and ceremonial occasions, they received the most wear and tear, and sometimes had to be repaired or replaced within their regulation lifetime of two years. When this happened, the hussar in question would be stopped the cost out of his own pay.

With previous commanding officers, it had been the responsibility of the troop commander or his sergeant-major to decide when new or repaired stable-jackets were necessary. Brudenell, typically, made it his own business, usually during dismounted parades when he would inspect the troops in open column. The hussars with clothing declared unsatisfactory would then report to the regimental office where they would be told the cost of repair − if feasible − and asked if they preferred to pay for new articles. Many did, fearing that repair would be only a temporary solution. The problem with this new system was that it bypassed the troop commanders and depended upon the arbitrary decision of the colonel.

Fanatical about the smart appearance of his men, Lord Brudenell now instructed that many cloth overalls would have to be replaced, despite the fact that he had ordered a general issue while the regiment was in Manchester. In addition, he insisted on 60 new stable-jackets during the months of September and October. By comparison, only 21 extra jackets had been ordered during the four years prior to his arrival. Inevitably, Captain Wathen's troop was hit the hardest. According to his sergeant-major, James Thom, there was an 'unusual issue and charge' for ten stable-jackets and a number of cloth overalls during these two months. As there were insufficient stoppages to pay for these articles, the troop debt ultimately rose to more than £28, well above the regulation maximum of £10, giving Brudenell another opportunity to find fault with his irksome subordinate.[6]

On 25 September, Wathen failed to appear on parade and when Brudenell demanded an explanation, he insisted that he had been given a different time by Lieutenant Hecker, the adjutant. The truth later emerged that the adjutant had indeed changed the time of the parade but had failed to inform Wathen; in any event, Brudenell refused to accept Wathen's explanation and in the ensuing row he ordered his arrest. For more than six weeks the unfortunate captain was confined to barracks while Lord Hill, the Commander-in-Chief at the Horse Guards, adjudicated on Brudenell's request for a court-martial.

One of Wellington's leading generals in the Peninsula, Hill had succeeded his old chief when the latter became Prime Minister in 1828. As General Sir Rowland Hill, his kind manner and preoccupation with his men's well-being while campaigning had acquired him the sobriquet

'Daddy'. Tough when he needed to be, he was more often merciful, particularly when he considered that errors were the result of temper or inadvertence rather than deliberate dereliction of duty. So it was that he viewed Brudenell's 'turn-up' with Captain Wathen as an insignificant spat that in no way warranted a military tribunal. Wathen was to be released forthwith.

Brudenell received the unpalatable news on Sunday, 20 October, at the house of Major-General Sir Thomas Arbuthnot, commanding the southern district of Ireland. Lord Hill's letter dismissed the charges against Wathen, pointing out that the accused's absence was due to the Adjutant Hecker's 'mistake as to there having been two parades'. In response, Brudenell insisted that Hecker 'had corrected his error in good time', and that he should be allowed to 'say something to the adjutant as to the major-general's good opinion of him in the presence of the other officers'. Receiving permission to tell Hecker that Arbuthnot was 'fully aware of his zeal', Brudenell returned to barracks mollified. At 5 p.m. the regimental officers, including Wathen, assembled in the mess-room to hear Lord Hill's judgement. Major Sir Walter Scott later testified that after reading out Hill's letter, Brudenell made the following observations:

> This letter, which must be considered decisive upon what Lord
> Hill is pleased to term my differences with Captain Wathen,
> admits of no comment; but I must say, Lord Hill has been misled
> in his opinion with regard to the adjutant, as it is my opinion that
> the adjutant fully and adequately performed his duty.

He went on to say that 'at the approaching inspection' he would 'write such a letter to the major-general, as would induce him, in his confidential report, to make such representations, as would do away with any impression at headquarters of the adjutant's want of zeal', and that 'he was certain Captain Wathen had had half an hour's notice' before the actual parade, 'or at least twenty minutes'. Then, with a supercilious wave of his hand and in a manner that Major Scott felt was 'most ungracious', he said: 'In consequence of this decision of Lord Hill's, release that officer from arrest.'

Needless to say, Captain Wathen was disturbed by Lord Brudenell's interpretation of Hill's decision, and hardly optimistic for the days ahead: 'From what I had just witnessed, and from previous occurrences which had taken place, I had reason to fear, that for the future it would be both difficult and dangerous for me to serve under his Lordship's command.' Back in his quarters, Wathen wrote to Brudenell, requesting immediate leave of absence so that he could return to England on urgent private affairs. Asked, via Adjutant Hecker, what these private affairs were, Wathen replied that they were 'matters immediately affecting my future prospects' and that it was 'of the utmost importance' to 'see a relation, before he quitted London for the winter'. Clearly, Wathen intended to leave the regiment by either exchanging or selling his commission, but Brudenell was in no mood to allow him to do either.

Back came a second note from Hecker, informing Wathen that Brudenell 'will not consent to apply for leave of absence for you' because he 'does not think the day on which an officer's conduct is animadverted on in strong terms, by order of the general commanding-in-chief, is the proper moment for him to apply for the indulgence of leave of absence'. Adding insult to injury, Hecker pointed out that the colonel 'does not consider your troop in good order, although the attention of the troop officers within the last month has effected considerable improvement in it', and that, consequently, it 'requires the constant care and attention of all its officers'. This last point was particularly rich given that, shortly after, one of Wathen's lieutenants, Wood, obtained promotion in the regiment and the other, Hickman, was immediately granted leave, thus leaving the troop commander with no subalterns. Furthermore, although Wathen was next in line for furlough, two other troop captains, Macqueen and Ives, were informed that they could go after the half-yearly inspection in November.[7]

By now, of course, Wathen's card had been well and truly marked and Brudenell was set on a course that was bound to end in further collision. Ample opportunity for criticism was afforded at field exercise, and many had been the time when Brudenell, in full hearing of the troops, had commented on Wathen's poor riding posture and method of holding the reins. On the first field day after his release, it was Wathen's sword-handling that was under scrutiny. 'Carry your sword, sir,' Brudenell demanded, 'can't you carry your sword properly?'

Matters began to come to a head on 4 November. Again at field exercise, as the regiment trotted past in open column of troops, Wathen was positioned in front of the centre of his troop rather than to one side. He later claimed that he absent-mindedly took up this position, the correct one before a recent change in cavalry drill, because he had not gone through the parade movements since his arrest. Brudenell, however, was convinced it was deliberate and halted the regiment. Riding up to Wathen, he said loudly, so 'that every one in the field might hear', that if a captain of six years could not command his troop he would 'bring up the junior cornet in the regiment to take command of it'.[8]

That afternoon Wathen was ordered to accompany a member of his troop, Private Surret, to the regimental office. As well as being recently charged for a new stable-jacket *and* overalls, Surret had also been accused of not taking proper care of his horse and so causing its sore back. This entailed punishment drill, the wearing of marks of disgrace and a fine. But Surret had refused to sign his account, insisting that he was not to blame for his horse's infirmity.

After a heated exchange, Brudenell lost his temper, calling Surret 'one of those lazy, idle fellows of this troop' and that if he had 'done his duty' he 'should have reported it as inefficient at head quarters'.

'Do you choose to sign your account, sir?' asked a furious Brudenell. 'Now, I'll have you out before all the regiment; I won't wait for you to complain to the general, but I'll have you out. You shall complain, I'll force you, I'll oblige you to do so. If you were to go back for fifty years, such a troop could not be found throughout the service.'

Shocked by Brudenell's brutal comments, Wathen waited for Surret to be dismissed before he responded. 'Your Lordship has made very severe animadversions upon my troop. After what you have said, and that in the presence of a private, I think it will be but justice to me that you should bring the state of it under the notice of the General at the inspection, and then make good the assertions you have put forth.'

'I shall do as I please; you are not to dictate to me, sir,' Brudenell responded coldly.

Wathen, in turn, was dismissed, then shortly after recalled.

'You addressed me in an improper manner, sir, when you were here just now,' said Brudenell imperiously. 'Now, sir, what do you mean by what you said?'

'My lord, I am not aware I said anything improper.'

'Yes, you did; do you *dare* to doubt my word, sir? This is what you said,' uttered Brudenell, holding up a written paper.

Despite all that had gone before, Wathen was severely shaken by this latest revelation. Could Lord Brudenell, an officer and a gentleman, really have stooped so low as to authorise the secret recording of a private conversation with a fellow officer? Yet there was the proof before him. Outraged, he refused to read the paper.

'Do you doubt my word?' Brudenell demanded.

'I was not aware that my words had been taken down in writing,'

Wathen replied with as much calmness as his thumping heart would allow.

'I dare say not, sir! but I find it very convenient!! Do you mean to deny that these were your words?'

Noticing that the adjutant was still making notes of the conversation, Wathen said: 'Under these circumstances, I think it better not to say any thing further, than that I am not aware of having said any thing improper.'

'Then, sir, I tell you that you did; and I now reprimand you for it. I desire you to be more careful for the future. I can tell you, that in regard to your troop, I shall adopt any course I think fit; I shall not, in order to *gratify your feelings*, report it to the general. I shan't do any such thing, but you may adopt any course you please.'

Assuming the interview was over, Wathen turned and moved towards the door.

'Come back, sir!' yelled Brudenell, pointing to the floor between his feet.

Wathen complied, before asking, 'Has your Lordship any further commands?'

'No, you may retire.'[9]

Three days later, Captain Wathen was once again bidden to the regimental office. As he entered, Lord Brudenell was at his desk scrutinising the troop ledgers. He looked up.

'Your troop debt is very great, greater than that of any other troop in the regiment, and you shall have to account for it to the major-general during the inspection tomorrow.'

'I am aware it is great,' Wathen replied, 'but I have reason to believe that it is not in reality greater than that of other troops.'

'But I tell you it is,' said Brudenell, mentioning a troop debt that was considerably lower.

'I am responsible only for my own debt,' stated Wathen, 'but I am sure that if you mention the matter to the other captains they will tell you that their real debts are not shown. I have *charged* the stable-jackets, which perhaps they have not done.'

'Your troop is the worst in the regiment,' sneered Brudenell. 'It must be your bad management.'

'There has been no neglect on my part. It has been impossible to keep my troop out of debt.'

'For what reason?' asked Brudenell.

'The number of flannels, shirts, boots and shoes that have been issued to the men with a view to going on foreign service is one reason,' responded Wathen. 'But the chief cause is the number of stable-jackets and cloth overalls which have been issued, particularly during the last month. I have been charged £12 in the month's abstract for these articles alone, and I have at the same time advanced the tailor £22 from my own purse, as most of the men are under stoppages and there is no fund from which to pay him.'

'That is not a sufficient reason,' Brudenell replied. 'Less stable-jackets and overalls have been issued in my time than at any former period. You are dismissed.'[10]

The following day, 8 November, General Arbuthnot arrived for the half-yearly review. The morning was taken up with an inspection of the regiment in the field, followed by a tour of the barrack-rooms and cooking facilities. After lunch, Arbuthnot dealt with the financial state of the 15th Hussars, when one by one the troop captains were ordered to attend the regimental office to have their books inspected. Captain Wathen had been told by the adjutant that they would be called in order of seniority, so he was both perplexed and alarmed when captains junior to him were called. Finally, the only one left, his turn came.

As well as Arbuthnot and Brudenell, there were two officers in the orderly room when Wathen entered: the adjutant, Lieutenant Hecker, and Arbuthnot's aide-de-camp, Captain Charles Corkran. Arbuthnot began the discussion by asking Wathen if he was in the habit of settling with the men himself at the end of each month.

'Yes, sir, I settle my own accounts.'

That, apparently, was enough for Arbuthnot. With a slight bow of his head as if to indicate the interview was at an end, he said: 'Captain Wathen, your books are made out quite correct, and I am satisfied with them in all respects.'

But Wathen was not finished. Convinced that Brudenell must have carried out his threat of the previous day, he wanted to put his side of the story. 'General, I understand Lord Brudenell has made a complaint to you respecting the amount of debt in my troop, and I wish to offer some explanation on the subject.'

'Captain Wathen,' came the perplexed reply, 'Lord Brudenell has made no such complaint to me. I have not yet examined the returns of the regiment, and I know nothing of the matter; and I must say that it does appear strange to me, that you should, on surmise, state such a thing of your commanding officers; but, Captain Wathen, as you have expressed a wish to enter into an explanation on the subject, I am ready to hear what you have to say.'

The debt, Wathen told him, had been created by an 'unusual' supply of stable-jackets which had been sent to him from the tailor's shop on whose 'orders' and 'for what purpose' he 'did not know'.

'Surely you must know that these jackets were sent to you by orders of your commanding officer,' said Arbuthnot. 'But has the supply of them been an unusual one?'

'Sir, in the seven years I have been captain of a troop I cannot recall ever having been issued so large a proportion of articles. With regard to the stable-jackets, the colonel's clothing has, in former years, generally sufficed, with the exception of two or three jackets a year. Also, a much greater number of cloth overalls have been issued than I have ever known to be the case.'

'Pray, Captain Wathen,' rejoined Arbuthnot, 'have you heard any thing said about this?'

'Yes, sir.'

'What, have there been complaints about this? Did the men come to you to complain?'

'No, sir, they did not.'

'How have you heard it then?'

'From my sergeant, my sergeant-major,' Wathen replied, adding that he had already mentioned this to Lord Brudenell.

'I positively deny that Captain Wathen has ever made such a report to me,' interjected Brudenell.

Arbuthnot then asked Wathen to confirm that he had reported the matter to his commanding officer. 'Yes, sir, I did.'

'Sir, it is fal—' shouted Brudenell.

'Lord Brudenell, stop!' commanded Arbuthnot, motioning with his hand for silence and cutting Brudenell's sentence short in the process. Realising that Brudenell had come close to accusing a fellow officer of lying, Arbuthnot then asked Wathen to leave the room.

'Lord Brudenell, what an expression you were very near making use of to Captain Wathen! I request you will not interrupt me again when I am speaking to an officer.'

Wathen was told to re-enter. 'Were those jackets ordered without your knowledge?' asked the general.

'Lord Brudenell did not speak to me on the subject.'

Again Brudenell interrupted: 'It's not true, sir, he knew it perfectly well. There have been less jackets in my time than in any former period. I'll call the quartermaster. The captain talks about the custom of the regiment, the quartermaster will tell you.'

'I have said nothing that cannot be seen from an examination of my ledgers,' said Wathen.

'This officer is making complaints against me,' said Brudenell, his voice rising. 'Now, sir, you allow him to go on in the same way you did the men in the field in the morning; this is the most gross case of *mutiny* I ever knew.'

Once again Arbuthnot told Brudenell to control himself before asking Wathen if he had not said his men had complained.

'To be sure he did, and now he wants to deny it,' Brudenell interjected.

Wathen insisted that he had not said what the general supposed, pointing out that the general had asked him if they had complained and he had said they had not. He had only wished to account for the cause of his debt and to exculpate himself from blame. But while he was on the subject he wished to state that since he had been released from arrest he had daily been subject to Brudenell's censure; the lieutenant-colonel was perpetually telling him that it was his bad management that caused his troop to be in such a state, and that it was not only the worst troop in the regiment but in the service.

'Well, sir, and is it not so?' Brudenell asked.

Shortly after, word arrived that the parade was ready for inspection and Arbuthnot, grateful for the interruption, terminated the conversation. After the parade, which lasted barely twenty minutes, the officers returned to the regimental office, accompanied by the quartermaster, George Chettle, and the remaining troop captains. Chettle stated, with little basis in fact, that the issue of stable-jackets was not an unusual one as a third of the men had had new ones during the last two years of Thackwell's colonelcy. One by one the troop captains agreed, adding that the issue had not created discontent among the men.

'Captain Wathen,' said Arbuthnot, 'it does appear to me extremely strange that the men of your troop alone should be discontented.'

'Sir, I did not say so.'

'Surely, Captain Wathen, you cannot deny it,' responded Arbuthnot, appealing to those present for confirmation.

'Sir, you have misunderstood me; I did not refer to discontent, I said I had heard it from my sergeant – my sergeant-major, he is clerk to me, and it was natural he should point out the reason of my debt being so heavy.'

Appealed to by Arbuthnot, Captain Corkran remarked that he had inferred, from what had been said, that Wathen had heard from his sergeant

71

that the men had complained. Again, Wathen rejected this, stating that the general had asked if the men had complained and he had said no. Appearing to concur with this, Arbuthnot brought the interview to a close.[11]

On Monday, 11 November, when General Arbuthnot returned to continue his inspection, he spoke privately with Captain Wathen in the regimental office before commencing. In his, the general's, opinion, Wathen had said there had been complaints about the issue of clothing. He wanted, therefore, to speak to the sergeant who had 'informed' Wathen. Again Wathen was forced vehemently to deny that he had said this; apparently satisfied, the general dismissed him.

During the inspection of the equipment of Wathen's troop, Lord Brudenell exacted his revenge. Calling for a stable-jacket belonging to Private William Hopkins, he showed it to Arbuthnot, saying: 'This fellow came to complain of a new stable-jacket being ordered for him, and he seemed to consider that it was a violent grievance that I should order him a new one. Now look at it.'

Complying, the general remarked that as the pay of the cavalry soldier was so good, the man ought to have a new jacket. With that, Brudenell tossed the jacket towards its owner, saying, 'There, sir.'

Then he turned to Captain Wathen, and in a low voice said: 'I can tell you, sir, you shall have plenty more new jackets in your troop.'[12]

The following day, shortly after lunch, Wathen was ordered to attend the regimental office where he found Lord Brudenell and Adjutant Hecker. Had he, Brudenell asked, received an order conveyed through the adjutant to him the previous Friday?

'Yes, and I spoke to the men accordingly,' Wathen replied.

At this point, Brudenell instructed Hecker to make a note of all questions and answers. 'Was it on Friday night that you spoke to the men of your troop?' he continued.

'It was.'

'Did you speak to your men on Saturday night?'

'No, I did not.'

'On Sunday night?'

'No.'

'What did you say to them when you spoke to them on Friday night?'

'I said that I had received orders to express to them that the major-general had been highly gratified at their appearance and steadiness in the field, and their excellent conduct in quarters, since they had been under his command.'

'Was nothing else said to them?'

'No.'

'Did you express your own individual approbation to them?'

'I did not.'

'It's very extraordinary; you may go, sir, and I'll send for you again,' said Brudenell.

Fifteen minutes later, Wathen was recalled and questioned again along the same lines. Flustered, he asked: 'Pray, my lord, may I inquire on what account these questions are put to me?'

'Yes, I'll tell you,' replied Brudenell triumphantly. 'It has been reported to me, from three different sources in the regiment, that on Saturday night you assembled your men, that you addressed them, that you told them you were very much pleased with them, that the left troop of the line had been particularly admired, that you made some allusion about going on service, and had said your heart was with them.'

Wathen replied that he had indeed spoken to his men, not on Saturday night but after midday stables, but that the report of his words was inaccurate. He then repeated what he had said, while Hecker made a written note.

'Have you got all that down?' said Brudenell to Hecker, when he had finished cross-examining Wathen's account.

'No, I cannot follow Captain Wathen, he speaks too fast for me to follow him in writing.'

Turning to Wathen, Brudenell instructed him to repeat again what he had said.

'As my words are to be taken down, had I not better give it to your lordship in writing?' Wathen asked.

'I am not to be dictated to, the way I am to command *my* regiment,' said Brudenell firmly. 'I choose to have it verbally, and you'll state it all over again.'

Wathen refused, offering again to put it in writing.

Brudenell exploded. 'Now, sir, do you disobey my *commands*? I here most solemnly declare, that as I am commanding officer of this regiment, if you don't comply with my orders, you shall be placed under arrest.'

Once more Wathen offered to give a written account and finally Brudenell assented. As Wathen made to leave the room, Brudenell roared, '*Come here, sir, you shan't go away!* Now sit down here and write it.'

Two and a half pages into his account, Wathen was informed by Brudenell that it was time to attend a punishment parade and that he would have to hand over what he had written. 'Excuse me, my lord,' replied Wathen, 'I cannot give you an unfinished letter.'

'Then you can finish it after parade,' said Brudenell.

'Very well, sir,' said Wathen, putting it in his pocket and moving towards the door.

'You shall not take it out of the office; give it to me, sir!' commanded Brudenell. 'Do you dare to disobey my commands?'

'My lord, I cannot give up an unfinished document.'

'Then put it in that box till you come back from parade, *I* shan't read it; *the adjutant* will be upon parade with you, *all* the officers will be there together, you will all leave parade together, so you can have no objection.'

'My lord, I decline leaving my letter.'

'Then, sir, you disobey my positive commands,' said Brudenell. 'Mr Hecker, bring in some witnesses.'

The adjutant returned with the two senior officers already on parade, Captain Wood and Lieutenant Wakefield. Brudenell repeated to them what had taken place and once again asked Wathen to leave his statement in the box. Wathen refused. Major Sir Walter Scott was called and again, in his presence, Wathen rejected Brudenell's command. Asked by Brudenell if he could see any reason why Wathen should not comply, Scott said he could not. Satisfied, Brudenell ordered Wathen to be put under arrest.

'My lord,' responded an astounded Scott, 'I am sure Captain Wathen, on consideration, and under these circumstances, will see the propriety of giving up the statement.'

'No, no, it is too late. Mr Hecker, you will place Captain Wathen in arrest,' said Brudenell. 'I appeal to any honest man if I have not had ample forbearance or sufficient temper.'

Realising Brudenell was serious, Scott turned to Wathen. 'You had better give up the statement.'

'No, sir, as it is now too late.'

Back in his room under arrest, Wathen completed the written statement and forwarded it to Lord Brudenell. It repeated his earlier assertions that the previous Friday he had assembled his troop 'after evening stables, and stated to them the entire approbation their appearance and steadiness in the field had called forth from the major-general, as well as their excellent conduct in quarters'. The following day he had spoken to the men 'after midday stables' because some of the horses had not been as well turned-out at the watering parade as he could have wished. He expressed his displeasure with this state of affairs, 'particularly so after the commendations which had been passed upon them by the major-general'. He went on to say that 'some officers, who were present in the field', had 'remarked upon the cleanliness and soldierlike appearance of the troop as it filed past'. That the troop was 'still under orders for foreign service' and if it did go he, Wathen, 'had no doubt but that they would continue to do credit both to themselves and the regiment'.[13]

The morning prior to Captain Wathen's arrest, General Arbuthnot had compiled a special report 'describing in the *strongest possible* terms the extreme impropriety of that officer's conduct on the preceding Friday and Monday'. That he expected this to result in charges against Wathen is unlikely; his intention was probably a severe reprimand from Horse Guards. But taken in conjunction with Brudenell's account of events on 12 November, it persuaded headquarters that a court-martial was necessary. Accordingly, Dublin ordered Brudenell to prefer charges; there were six in total.

The first three related to the interview with General Arbuthnot on Friday, 8 November. Wathen was charged with stating 'in an invidious and improper manner . . . that an unusual supply of stable-jackets had been issued . . . without his knowledge, thereby imputing improper conduct' to Lord Brudenell; with stating 'that he had been informed by the sergeants of his troop that the men were discontented at having new stable-jackets'; and with stating, 'contrary to truth and fact', that 'he had reported or mentioned' to Lord Brudenell 'that the men of his troop had expressed discontent'. All three charges were, according to Brudenell, revised and approved by General Arbuthnot.

The fourth charge was for making a false statement 'that in compliance with instructions . . . on 8th of November . . . he had assembled his troop after evening stables to convey to them the Major-General's approbation. The fifth was for addressing his men in an 'irregular and unofficer-like manner' by saying that 'some strangers or civilians had particularly remarked the soldier-like appearance of his troop' and 'that he had no doubt that had they gone on service, they would have done their duty as well as any other troop, notwithstanding any unpleasant circumstances which had occurred in the troop'. The last charge was for refusing to obey Lord Brudenell's order 'to repeat verbally what he had said to his men on the said Saturday' and then 'repeatedly' refusing to 'leave his written statement locked up in the regimental office, during his absence at parade'. Charges two, three, four and six described 'conduct unbecoming the character of an officer and a gentleman'.[14]

Found guilty on any one of these charges, Wathen was liable to be cashiered. This was clearly Lord Brudenell's way of ending the feud between them and signalling to the rest of his officers that opposition to his will, in whatever form, was not to be tolerated. But instead of just one solid charge, that of disobeying a lawful order, he made the mistake of preferring a number of weaker ones relating to previous events, giving the impression of a persecutor not a prosecutor.

The trial began on Monday, 23 December 1833, in an improvised court-room at Cork barracks. Sitting at a long table at the top of the room in full dress uniform were the members of the court: Major-General Sir John Buchan, the president, and 14 other officers, including the colonels of the 4th Dragoon Guards, 89th and 91st Regiments of Foot. With them sat a civilian lawyer, David Walker, acting Deputy Judge-Advocate-General and legal adviser to the court. At right-angles to them, behind a small table, sat Captain Wathen. A solitary figure, he had chosen to defend himself. Directly opposite, behind a similar table, was Lord Brudenell, the prosecutor. These two handsome protagonists were dressed identically in scarlet tunics trimmed with ermine, scarlet and gold pelisses, and royal blue overalls. The only difference was that Wathen had been deprived of his sword and, temporarily at least, his honour.

Brudenell opened proceedings by stating that it was 'with feelings of deep regret' that he was 'compelled to appear' as the prosecutor of one of his own officers, but that he would not be 'furthering the good of the service' were he to 'hesitate in coming forward'. The case required 'calm and dispassionate consideration', particularly in light of the 'unprecedented manner in which all the circumstances of the case have been misrepresented and prejudged by the public press'. The example he gave was the detailed account in Cork's newspapers of the incident resulting in Wathen's arrest on 12 November, 'but so garbled, and perverted, as to give the most favourable impression' of Wathen.

Commenting on the first charge, Brudenell said that Wathen's comments to the general on the 'unusual' supply of stable-jackets could never be justified because he was 'not bound to follow precisely in the steps' of his 'predecessor'. Charges two, three and four were 'for making statements contrary to truth and fact' and so required 'no comment'. Regarding the fifth charge, 'Wathen was not justified in saying anything to his troop with regard to the approbations of civilians', and it was 'unnecessary to talk to his troop about their bravery on foreign service . . . because there never . . . could be any doubt as to the good conduct of any troop of the 15th Hussars . . .' Finally, on the sixth charge, that of disobeying orders on the 12th, Brudenell stated that he had treated Wathen 'with every forbearance, and showed every reluctance to place him in arrest'.

Major-General Arbuthnot was called first, in support of charges one to three, and for a time everything went well for the prosecution. He told the court that, during their interview of 8 November, Wathen had stated that his debt 'had been created by an unusual supply of stable-jackets' which had 'created much discontent amongst the men'. Yet, when asked, both the quartermaster and the other troop officers had stated that the issue was not unusual. To top everything, Wathen had then denied, 'in a very abrupt and disrespectful manner', that he had said the men were discontented.[15]

During cross-examination, however, details of Brudenell's victimisation of Wathen and his troop began to emerge. Lord Brudenell had noted on the return of Wathen's troop debt that the 'issues in question' did not justify such a large figure, so implying mismanagement on Wathen's behalf. Yet, Arbuthnot said, Brudenell had failed to note that other troop debts would have been even greater than Wathen's if the recent issues of stable-jackets and overalls had been charged. Arbuthnot did not say as much, but the implication was that, contrary to standard practice, the charge for stable-jackets in other troops had been deferred by at least a month to give the appearance that their debt was lower than it was, so putting Wathen in the worst light. He also said, in response to a question from the court, that he had 'cause to believe that Lord Brudenell's feelings towards Captain Wathen were not amicable'.[16]

Arbuthnot's lengthy testimony was spread over the first three days of the trial: the 23rd, 24th and, with an adjournment for Christmas Day, the 26th. He was followed to the stand on the latter day by his aide-de-camp, Captain Corkran, who in turn was succeeded on the 27th by the other staff officer, Colonel Charles Turner. These two simply confirmed Arbuthnot's version of events, with Corkran adding that Wathen had stated the issue of stable-jackets was 'unnecessary' and that his manner had been 'disrespectful' towards the general, while Turner said that Wathen had 'forgot himself as a gentleman'.[17]

The fourth witness for the prosecution was Lieutenant Hecker, the adjutant. In the wake of Turner, he took the stand on Saturday, the 28th. But what should have been a routine bolstering of the case for the prosecution turned into a personal disaster for Lord Brudenell. Under cross-examination by Wathen, Hecker caused a sensation by admitting that immediately after being appointed to the adjutancy on 17 August 1832, he had been ordered by Brudenell 'to commit to paper the nature of conversations which might occur in the regimental office'.

In all, he told the court, he had secretly taken down in writing the conversations between his commanding officer and at least four other officers, including Captain Wathen. He also said that the excess of Wathen's troop debt over regulations was due 'in a great measure' to the recent issue of stable-jackets and overalls, and that Brudenell had 'found fault' with the horses of Wathen's troop at 'most watering parades'.[18]

Next to be questioned were three of Wathen's N.C.O.s, Sergeant-Major Thom, Sergeant Clarkson and Corporal Denby, and for a time things went badly for the defendant. Examined by Brudenell, all three said that they had 'not' reported to Captain Wathen that the men had expressed discontent at the issue of new stable-jackets. But as before, cross-examination by Wathen and the court weakened the prosecution case. Thom agreed that there had been 'an unusual issue and charge for stable-jackets and cloth overalls within the last twelve months', that this had made it impossible to keep the troop debt within regulation, that he had mentioned this fact to Wathen, and that he had 'overheard words which tended to show that [the men] were dissatisfied'.

Clarkson, also, had heard the men 'express their dissatisfaction' although they had not complained to him directly. Only Denby rejected suggestions that the men were dissatisfied, but his evidence was brought into question when he admitted that he had once told Sergeant-Major Thom that Wathen intended to stop his promotion. In other words, he had a grievance against Wathen and a reason for being less than truthful.[19]

On the sixth day of the trial – New Year's Day, 1834 – Captain Augustus Blythe was questioned. No, he did not consider the issue of nine stable-jackets immediately prior to 8 November as unusual, he told Brudenell. In cross-examination, however, he admitted that only two jackets had been issued to his troop between 1827 and 1831, while a further five were issued during November 1833, making 14 for the year. As to the noting down of conversations between the commanding officer and his subordinates, he confirmed that it had not been the custom when he was adjutant.

Next up was Quartermaster Chettle. He too, did not think the issue of stable-jackets to the regiment, 60 in number, was unusual. But when Wathen confronted him with his own return for the years 1827 to 1831, giving a total of 21 jackets, he countered lamely that the regimental tailor might not have been aware of some. He also admitted that his estimate of a third of the men usually having to pay for replacement stable-jackets was based on written statements by Colonel Thackwell in 1825 and 1828. The court was not impressed.

Private Chester, the regimental tailor, managed to repair some of the damage when, in response to a question from Brudenell, he estimated that, over the previous 6–8 years, each troop had required between 15 and 20 extra stable-jackets during their two-year lifetime. But this verbal evidence could not compete with Chettle's written return for the years 1827 to 1831 which gave a regimental *total* of just 21.[20]

Finally, also on New Year's Day, Lord Brudenell himself took the stand. Under cross-examination, he confirmed that he had, on 7 November, asked Captain Wathen the reason for his troop debt being the biggest. He had, he admitted, received the debt and credit lists from the troops for the month of September, but he had not been aware that some troops were more in debt than Wathen's. He only realised this later, he said, on reconsulting the lists. If this was difficult for the court to swallow, they realised why when he responded a little too honestly to the court's inquiry as to whether he had been 'in any instance actuated by a hostile feeling towards Captain Wathen?'

'After an officer has systematically thwarted and opposed me for two or three months together,' Brudenell replied, his anger getting the better of his judgement, 'I will not pretend to say that my feelings towards that officer are the same as towards one who has conducted himself regularly.' Even so, he added unconvincingly, he had always treated Wathen 'fairly'.[21]

Hecker, the adjutant, came next. Questioned by the court on the fourth charge, he said that he believed that Wathen had complied with the verbal order to speak to his men on the 8th because he had heard so from Sergeant-Major Thom and Sergeant Clarkson, both of whom had originally made statements to the contrary. When Thom's turn came, he explained this seeming contradiction:

> The question put to me by Lord Brudenell was, 'Did Captain Wathen assemble his troop on that evening, to communicate to the men an order delivered to him?' My answer was, that he did not do so. Lord Brudenell again sent for me, and asked me if Captain Wathen had not addressed his men in the stables on the

evening of the 8th, and my answer was, he did, mentioning at the same time I was only certain of one stable.

Thom went on to say that he had since heard from Sergeant Clarkson that Wathen spoke in two other stables, making a minimum of three out of six. Thom's testimony ended at 3 p.m., and with Major Mitchell – a member of the court – unwell, the case was adjourned until the following Monday, 6 January.[22]

Corporal Denby, Wathen's *bête noire*, was the next witness for the prosecution, and he insisted that his troop captain had not spoken to his men on 8 November. 'I have heard from Sergeant-Major Thom that he did address some part of the men,' he told the court. 'I do not believe it.' Unfortunately for Brudenell, Denby's integrity was destroyed when Sergeant Clarkson testified that he had heard Denby say to a group of N.C.O.s 'that as Captain Wathen had stopped his promotion, he would stop Captain Wathen's'.

Captain Rose, yet another prosecution witness, added to his commanding officer's woes when he confirmed, under cross-examination, that it had 'long been the practice' for troop captains 'to communicate orders . . . to the men as you find them assembled in their respective stables'.[23]

The case was again adjourned for a few days, to give Major Mitchell time to recover from his illness. He had not done so by Thursday, 9 January, so the trial resumed regardless with Major Sir Walter Scott giving evidence as a prosecution witness for the sixth charge, that of disobeying orders on 12 November. Under cross-examination, Scott created the second major sensation of the trial. Asked by Wathen if he considered Brudenell's order to leave the unfinished statement in the regimental office on 12 November a 'lawful command', 'as expressed by the articles of war', Scott replied: 'I did not at the moment consider whether it was lawful or unlawful; but the same day I thought that the command was not a lawful one.'

There was more. 'Was I not placed in arrest before I had time to benefit by your advice,' Wathen asked, 'and did it appear, from his Lordship's hasty manner, as if he willingly seized upon an opportunity to place me under arrest?'

Scott answered 'Yes' to both questions; he added that he was not aware that Wathen had 'ever opposed or thwarted Lord Brudenell', rather that Wathen had 'always paid due deference to him'. He also related how Brudenell had told him on 9 November that he would have to serve on a regimental court-martial the following Monday because 'he could not trust' Wathen 'after his conduct the night before in the presence of the major-general'.

'Do you not consider,' asked Wathen, 'that the discovery lately made of the conversations being taken down in the orderly-room has been most painful and revolting to the feelings of the officers?'

'There can be no doubt but that it has been both,' replied Scott.

There remained one final blow for his commanding officer. 'Has Lord Brudenell been in the habit of communicating to you, or consulting you as senior major of the regiment, on all matters relative to the discipline of the corps, and the conduct of the officers?' asked the court.

'No,' said Scott, 'I can recollect no occasion upon which I have been consulted.'

So ended the disastrous case for the prosecution, which had backfired so badly upon its architect Lord Brudenell.[24]

After yet another adjournment to give him time to prepare, Captain Wathen began his defence on Monday, 13 January. Reading for two hours from a prepared speech, his voice low and dignified, he detailed his deteriorating relations with Lord Brudenell since his release from arrest on 20 October. Under the circumstances, he told the court, he might have been excused for feeling 'vindictive'.

'But I must now declare,' he said, 'that notwithstanding the injuries and persecutions I may have received, I neither am, or ever have been, actuated by such motives. In vindicating my own character, it is not my wish to misrepresent or colour facts, but to observe a strict regard to truth.'

One by one, he denied the charges against him, skilfully referring to testimony by Brudenell's own witnesses that supported his arguments. Finally, he referred to his own record of service, knowing that it would contrast starkly with that of his commanding officer. The holder of 'his Majesty's commission for twenty years', he had served in 'two active campaigns' and 'was present at Waterloo'. He also referred to glowing testimonials from three senior officers – Lieutenant-General Sir Colquhoun Grant, Colonel of the 15th Hussars, Major-General Sir John Browne, commandant of the cavalry depot, and Lieutenant-Colonel Joseph Thackwell, former commander of the 15th – saying that 'they had reason to be perfectly satisfied with my conduct during a period of many years'.

'Lieutenant-Colonel Lord Brudenell has been in command of the regiment not quite two years,' he said, 'and this is the second occasion within a month on which he has preferred charges against me. I cannot, there-fore, but feel that I have met with much unkindness, where I might naturally have looked for protection and support; but I have endeav-oured, throughout the transactions which have taken place, to conduct myself with temperance and forbearance, and I now entertain a confident hope, that it will appear to the Court that I am not guilty upon any of the charges.'[25]

So as not to leave the court in any doubt, Wathen then called his first defence witness, Major Sir Walter Scott. Among other things, Scott stated that on 7 November Wathen had told him that Brudenell had 'found much fault' with him 'on account of the excess' of his troop debt and that he would 'have to account for it to the major-general'. In addi-tion, Scott agreed that the recent issue of stable-jackets had been unusual and that Wathen was incapable of 'wilfully making any assertion or state-ment contrary to truth and fact'. He also outlined Brudenell's system of drill that had, particularly at Newbridge, so lowered the condition of the horses.[26]

The following day the remaining defence witnesses were called. Major Courtney Philipps testified that he was 'perfectly satisfied with the groom-ing of Captain Wathen's troop' when under his command at Carlow. 'I always found him, when there, most zealous and attentive to his duty.' Philipps, too, had 'never observed Captain Wathen disrespectful to his superior officers' and considered 'him incapable of wilfully making a mis-representation'. Contrary to what Corporal Denby had previously testified, Private Robert Young of Denby's squad confirmed that Captain Wathen had indeed spoken to the men at stables on 8 November.

Finally, and tellingly, Wathen called Lieutenant-Colonel Chatterton of the 4th Dragoon Guards, a member of the court. 'I have known Captain Wathen nine years,' said Chatterton, 'and have always heard he was partic-ularly zealous, active, intelligent, and fond of his profession; and I am convinced from my personal knowledge of him, he would not in any way derogate from the character of an officer and a man of honour.'[27]

Adjourned for a day to give Brudenell time to prepare his closing address, the court met for the tenth and final time on Thursday, 16 January. Brudenell began by stating that he had 'received directions from Dublin to frame charges', that General Arbuthnot had 'entirely approved of the first three' and that all six were vetted by Horse Guards. He then gave his own version of events since 20 October, inevitably differing in parts not only from Wathen's but from other witnesses such as Major Scott.

His second-in-command's testimony had particularly hurt him. 'I cannot,' he said, 'but express my extreme surprise that Sir Walter Scott should be so unacquainted with his duty as senior major of this regiment, as to suppose that conversations between him and myself relative to other officers on points of regimental duty, should not be considered confidential, whatever may be his own private feelings of hostility towards me, and of which, until that day, I was totally unaware.'

He concluded: 'I beg to assure this honourable Court, that I have not been actuated by any vindictive or personal feelings in bringing forward these charges. I can conscientiously state that the good of the service, and the welfare of the regiment which I have the honour to command, have been the only motives which have actuated me in the performance of this painful duty.'[28]

While few realised it at the time, these words unwittingly exposed the essence of Lord Brudenell's nature. He was, indeed, passionately and unwaveringly motivated by 'the welfare of the regiment' and the 'good of the service'. But instead of consulting his more experienced subordinates as to the best way to achieve both, he had decided for himself that only a rigid adherence to regulation, drill and discipline would suffice. A clash with the commander of the least efficient troop was inevitable.

The findings of the court were not announced for two weeks. In the meantime the press, which had faithfully reported every word, left its readers in little doubt as to the likely verdict and the lesson to be learnt. Taking it for granted that 'Captain Wathen has had a most honourable acquittal and that Lord Brudenell has been reprimanded', *The Times* asked how the latter ever could have reached such a position.

> How came Lord Brudenell, – an officer of no experience or pretensions compared to those of a hundred other gentlemen who *had* seen and beaten a foreign enemy –, how came such an unripe gallant as that to be put over the heads of so many worthier candidates, and to be forced into a command for which, we may now say, he had proved himself so utterly incompetent? Through whose interest and at whose instigation was it that the King's service suffered so severe a wrong? We trust such practices will never be repeated.[29]

A week earlier, the *United Service Gazette* had explored the same theme:

Feeling all the enormity of the tyranny of Lord Brudenell's persecution of Captain Wathen, we are willing to give him the
benefit of negative exoneration, which his infirmity of temper
and incompetency to command may be supposed to afford. We
look beyond him for the legitimate objects of blame. We refer all
the inconveniences and disagreeables which have recently
occurred to the men in office at the Horse Guards, who, suffering their private feelings to interfere with the public good, placed
an inexperienced individual in command of a regiment of
Hussars. Had Lieutenant Colonel Lord Brudenell been an unti-
tled soldier of fortune, where had the Cornet of four and twenty
now been? Assuredly not in the command of a regiment of
Hussars! The thing is monstrous, and we hope may prove a
warning to men in office for the future; as they must now be
pretty well convinced that their *friends* are in some cases enemies
to the service.[30]

The result of a relatively petty episode, the Wathen trial had become an
instant *cause célèbre* because its exposure of Lord Brudenell's alleged tyranny
provided ready ammunition for the growing number of people in and out
of Parliament who wanted to reform the Army – in particular to abolish
the purchase system. Only the previous year, amidst the progressive atmosphere of the first post-Reform Parliament, a House of Commons'
committee had debated the future of the system. Now many M.P.s, particularly the Radicals, saw Brudenell's behaviour as proof that a system that
favoured rank and fortune ahead of experience and merit was fundamen-
tally flawed.

To such men, Brudenell was symbolic of a social and political status quo
that, notwithstanding the Reform Act, still jealously guarded its privileges
and opposed real change. On the other hand, few Conservatives leapt to
his defence, with most Army officers of the opinion that his over-zealous
and injudicious actions deserved some form of censure. No one could have
predicted its severity, however.

A Change of Fortune

Lord Brudenell and his officers were dining in the mess when the findings of the court-martial arrived in the form of a General Order from the Commander-in-Chief, dated 1 February 1834. As Brudenell read the document, it was obvious from his set expression that it was not to his liking. Captain Wathen, it stated, 'is Not Guilty of any of the Charges preferred against him. The Court, therefore, honourably acquits him of each and of all the Charges.'

There was more. 'Bearing in mind the whole process and tendency of this Trial,' it continued, 'the Court cannot refrain from animadverting on the peculiar and extraordinary measures which have been resorted to by the Prosecutor.' It went on to state that Brudenell's motives for laying charges could not be ascribed *solely* to a wish to uphold the honour and interests of the Army', and that 'his conduct has been reprehensible in advancing such various and weighty assertions . . . without some sure ground of establishing the facts'. A junior officer had been 'listened to, and Non-commissioned Officers and soldiers examined with the view of finding out from them, how in particular instances the Officers had respected their respective duties'. This, the court pronounced, was 'a practice in every respect most dangerous to the Discipline and the Subordination of the Corps, and highly detrimental to that harmony and good feeling which ought to exist between officers'. In addition, Brudenell had introduced a 'system of having the Conversations of Officers taken down in the Orderly-room without their knowledge, – a practice which cannot be considered otherwise than revolting to every proper and honourable feeling of a Gentleman, and as being certain to create disunion, and to be most injurious to his Majesty's Service'.

The King had approved the findings and, although 'some parts of the Evidence might reasonably bear a construction less unfavourable to the Prosecutor than that which the Court have thought it their duty to place upon them, yet, upon a full consideration of the circumstances of the Case, His Majesty has been pleased to order, that Lieutenant-Colonel Lord Brudenell shall be removed from the command of the 15th Hussars'. To complete Brudenell's humiliation, Lord Hill had added that the General Order was to be 'read at the head of every Regiment in his Majesty's Service'.[1]

Outraged by the decision, Brudenell left at once for the mainland, riding more than 60 miles in the darkness and rain to Clonmel to catch the stage-coach to Dublin. Within 36 hours he had rejoined his wife, who had preceded him by a couple of days, at their town house in Carlton Gardens, a stone's throw from the Horse Guards and Whitehall. He was dismayed to discover that newspapers on both sides of the Irish Sea were applauding the verdict. Dublin's *New Weekly Despatch* stated: 'The Persecution of Captain Wathen: the mode, the time, the whole arrangement of the proceedings before the Court Martial – has, very properly, met with the disapproval of the Horse Guards – the indignation of the whole army – and the animadversions of the highest person in the realm.' Brudenell's conduct had been 'disgraceful and dishonourable – replete with petty envy and vindictive spleen; conduct which we sincerely hope will never be tolerated in the British army'.[2]

Such virulent criticism was largely unwarranted given the fact that his conduct, however ill-advised, had been motivated by a genuine desire to produce an efficient regiment. He was convinced, rightly it would seem, that he had been made a political scapegoat. 'There being at that time a Conservative Horse Guards and a Whig Government,' he later wrote, 'Lord Hill was forced through prudence to remove me from the command of the Regt.' He immediately set about changing the minds of both.

Interviews were arranged with Hill, Lord Melbourne, the Home Secretary and Lord John Russell – but all to no avail. On St Valentine's Day, 1834, in a desperate effort to clear his name, he sent (via Horse Guards) a Memorial to the King requesting his own court-martial. He repeated the request in a covering letter to Lord Fitzroy Somerset, the Military Secretary, rightly asking him to point out to Lord Hill that he had

been 'pronounced guilty, by a tribunal which was not by the usage of the
service competent to try me, of charges upon which I was never arraigned;
on evidence which I had not sufficient opportunity of meeting'.

The Memorial itself stated that the two practices condemned in the
finding of the court were not general and had been undertaken sparingly:
the first 'in only one instance', the second 'only in reference to certain officers' and in the form of questions and answers. If he had 'erred in any
thing', he wrote, 'his error has consisted in a single indiscretion, not in a
systematic misconduct, that it has been the result of mistaken judgment,
not of perverse intention'.

Over the next five days, Somerset received two more letters from
Brudenell, both requesting a Court of Inquiry if a court-martial could not
be sanctioned. The first pointed out that 'some measure of this nature is of
the utmost importance for the vindication of my character; as in consequence of the animadversions . . ., an opinion is generally entertained that
I have been in the habit of having the private conversations of the officers . . ., in the mess-room and elsewhere, taken down and afterwards
reported to me'. The second noted that any such court 'would abstain
from alluding to any part of Captain Wathen's conduct, or from criminat-
ing any other officer in the regiment'.

On 22 February, Somerset replied, giving William IV's response to the
Memorial. The King was 'pleased to signify his satisfaction at the temper-
ate and judicious manner' in which Brudenell had written his
'explanations', and they 'tended to confirm' his already stated opinion
'that some parts of the evidence . . . might reasonably bear a construction
less unfavourable to your Lordship than that which the Court have thought
it their duty to place upon them'. It was for this reason, Somerset wrote,
that the King had decided not to cashier Brudenell, merely to remove him
from command on to half-pay . Yet the King was also of the opinion 'that
to assemble a Court Martial, or to institute any other proceeding . . .,
would be to depart from long established practice . . . and to set a precedent of most inconvenient and injurious example'. Somerset added that
Lord Hill expressed his 'own regret' and that it had 'not been in his power,
consistently with his duty, to recommend to His Majesty to comply with
your Lordship's application'.

Brudenell responded three days later, imploring Lord Hill to reconsider.
'I pray to be allowed . . . to prove that I have uniformly done my duty in
the command of the regiment,' he wrote. As evidence, he quoted three
major-generals who had inspected the 15th Hussars within the previous 12

months. At Newbridge, Sir Edward Blakeney had said 'he had never seen a regiment in a higher state of order'; Sir Thomas Arbuthnot, after the 'most minute inspection' at Cork, had said 'he could not find a single fault'; and even Sir John Buchan, the president of the court-martial, had expressed 'his highest approbation of its appearance'. Somerset replied on 1 March that 'there is nothing in what you have now brought under his Lordship's notice which would justify him in reopening the question'. Officially, the matter was closed.

But Somerset knew Brudenell socially, had stayed at Deene Park, and was anxious to reassure him that his career was not over. If he behaved 'in a restrained manner', Somerset told him unofficially, it might later be possible to reappoint him as a commanding officer. Much the same advice was given by the Duke of Wellington, no longer in office but still with immense influence in matters military. Brudenell was given to understand that if he 'remained quiet' for at least a year, a new command might be possible.[3]

That Brudenell took the advice seriously can be seen by his self-control in the face of near-hysterical press censure. John Drakard, the Radical publisher of *Drakard's Stamford News*, wrote that Brudenell's 'system of espionage' – in which he had concealed a soldier 'to write down the conversation that passed between the officers in the orderly room' – had 'created universal disgust'. Such antipathy had been heightened 'by the fact that it was instituted by a mere apprentice – nay almost a baby in the service, – one probably as deficient in military valour as he is in the celebrity of his military career, – upon men who have reaped the laurels of victory in numerous actions, and deserved the gratitude of their country'.

Admittedly, Drakard had more reason for hostility than most. Upon publishing earlier criticisms of the young colonel, he had been sought out by an irate Brudenell and publicly horse-whipped. Now, with Brudenell so firmly in the glare of publicity, there was little chance that it would happen again. 'We could say more upon the meanness of demeanour which has characterized Lord Brudenell,' wrote Drakard, alluding to their previous confrontation, 'but we are averse to mix up private injury with public matters.'[4]

With his enforced retirement from active service, Brudenell had time to devote to his other interests: politics and sport. But while he hunted regularly, his attendance at the House was sporadic and he spoke in none of the great debates of 1834. In July, Lord Grey's Cabinet finally disintegrated over Ireland. The Prime Minister had proposed a double-edged policy:

Irish Church reform as a concession on the one hand, and a Coercion Bill to restore law and order on the other. But the hardline members of his government had already resigned over the transfer of tithes for the Protestant Church of Ireland to lay purposes, and in July the 'left' also went over the issue of coercion. Still with a large majority in the House of Commons, a Whig administration was the only option, and in Grey's place William IV chose Lord Melbourne.

The former Home Secretary's first ministry was brief. Shortly after the summer recess, the Houses of Parliament were badly damaged when used Exchequer tallies set fire to a chimney. Opponents of the Climbing Boys' Bill of 1834, which had prohibited sweeps under the age of 10, shouted 'Sweep!' as the fire raged. The first reformed Parliament would never sit again. On 10 November, Earl Spencer died, elevating his heir Lord Althorp to the House of Lords. Melbourne named Lord John Russell as Althorp's successor as leader of the Commons, but William IV was not in agreement and dismissed the ministry. The minority Conservatives then took over, with Wellington taking the reins until the nominated Prime Minister, Sir Robert Peel, could return from Europe in December. The inevitable General Election took place in January 1835.

Trumpeting Peel's battle-cry of moderate reform, the Conservatives made gains but still ended up with a seven-seat minority in the Commons. There was no change in Northamptonshire North, however, as prospective candidates realised the futility of opposing the scions of two such great families and Lords Brudenell and Milton were re-elected without a contest. It may now have seemed to Brudenell that Peel's Conservative ministry – albeit still in a minority – would provide the best opportunity for a return to active service. But it was still too soon and, besides, Peel had more important matters on his mind, not least his plan to introduce the commutation of Church tithes in Ireland without the bugbear of transferring rents and church property to lay purposes. However, the opposition refused to accept church reform without lay appropriation, repeatedly defeated the Bill and in April Peel resigned. Once again, Lord Melbourne was asked to form a government – it would last six years.

With the political outlook so bleak, it was fortunate for Lord Brudenell that his family still had close connections with the Hanoverian Court. The old 6th Earl of Cardigan had been Equerry to King George III's wife, Queen Charlotte, for 20 years, while his Countess had become a Lady of the Bedchamber in 1818. Harriet, the cleverest and most beautiful of Brudenell's sisters, had carried on the tradition by marrying Earl Howe who in 1830, at the age of 35, had been appointed Queen Adelaide's Lord Chamberlain. An Ultra-Tory and staunch opponent of parliamentary reform, Howe was forced to resign by Lord Grey in early 1832 for scheming against the Whig government. But the outraged Queen refused to appoint a replacement, and for a time Howe continued as *de facto* Chamberlain.

Many suspected the two of having an affair, although Charles Greville – who had little time for the Queen – was convinced that the relationship was platonic, if injudicious. 'Howe,' he noted in Brighton in December 1832, 'conducts himself towards her like a young ardent lover; he is never out of the Pavilion, dines there almost every day, or goes every evening, rides with her, never quitting her side, and never takes his eyes off her. She does nothing, but she admits his attentions and acquiesces in his devotion; at the same time there is not the smallest evidence that she treats him as a lover.'[5]

Lady Howe was both mystified and outraged. Tall and vivacious, an excellent rider like her brother, she could not understand how her handsome, courteous husband could be so romantically attached to the Queen. But while 'vexed to death at the whole thing', she was anxious to avoid scandal, as was the Court. To nullify gossip, Lord Denbigh was appointed Adelaide's Chamberlain in early 1833, but Howe remained a close confidant.

Naturally, Lord Brudenell appealed to his sister to use her husband's influence at Court to seek royal approval for his reappointment to command. The initial response from Queen Adelaide was encouraging but non-committal:

> The King begg'd me to say that he feels most deeply with his family, laments the Events which have taken place, but cannot do anything for Ld. B. *at present*. But I am certain he is *most* anxious to serve him. Tell Lady H. from me to *entreat* her brother to bear his trials patiently at present and things may become better for him but any violent act of his might make his case much worse than it is and could do no good.[6]

But Brudenell had another ally at Court – he was a close friend and hunting companion of Lord Adolphus Fitzclarence, the seventh of William IV's ten illegitimate children by Dorothy Jordan, and could count on him to put in a good word. This twin-pronged assault seemed to be bearing dividends when, in early 1835, Brudenell was invited to hunt with the

King's staghounds in the New Forest. The actual day was doubly satisfying for him when he comprehensively outrode Thomas Assheton-Smith, a former Master of the Quorn and universally recognised as the 'straightest man across country that ever rode to hounds'.[7]

In June, there was more good news, when the conservative *Naval and Military Gazette* reported a rumour that Lord Brudenell was about to be given command of the 90th Regiment of Foot. 'We shall be glad to find it well founded,' noted the *Gazette*. 'We have repeatedly alluded to the harsh proceedings adopted towards this gallant and talented nobleman, and we should rejoice in his restoration to the service.' Of course Brudenell would have preferred a cavalry appointment, but if the rumour was accurate it meant a commitment by Horse Guards to return him to some form of command.[8]

As events proved, the report was not without some foundation. By September 1835, having remained 'quiet' for more than 18 months, no word had come from the Horse Guards so Brudenell twice went to see Lord Fitzroy Somerset. Reporting the interviews to Lord Hill, Somerset noted: 'They did not have any satisfactory results . . . On the first occasion, he hardly gave me the opportunity to speak . . . But on the last I distinctly told him that your Lordship considered that you must not recommend him for employment at the present moment, assuring him however that you had every disposition to meet his wishes when it might be practicable.'

Somerset also revealed that Brudenell claimed to have the support of Lord Howick, the Secretary-at-War, but wondered how he had come by that opinion. Meanwhile, in accordance with Hill's wishes, Somerset had seen Lord Melbourne and told him 'as I had previously told Lord Brudenell that the question was one upon which there should be a complete understanding between the [Commander-in-Chief] and [Government]'. Melbourne, in response, had agreed to write to Howick asking him if he was 'ready to fight the battle in the House of Commons'.[9]

Encouraged by his conversations with Somerset, Brudenell wrote to Wellington, telling him that there was the prospect of a lieutenant-colonelcy in a regiment then serving in India. Would he, the Duke, 'induce' Lord Hill to obtain the government's approval? The colonel of the 11th Light Dragoons was, indeed, looking to exchange on to half-pay but, as Somerset's letter to Hill makes clear, no promises had been made. On the other hand, Hill had already begun to sound out the government's opinion on the subject of Brudenell's reappointment. But Wellington was unaware of this, and sent a sharp reply:

I must . . . tell you that you entirely misunderstood me if you supposed that I ever fixed, in my own mind, much less stated to
another a period after which you should be recalled . . . I cannot
but think you are mistaken respecting the feelings and sentiments
of the Ministers in your case . . . Lord Hill knows well that if he
should consult my opinion on any matter it will be communicated
to him frankly . . .[10]

Undeterred, Brudenell kept pestering Somerset. 'Lord Brudenell favoured
me with another of his disagreeable visits yesterday,' he reported to Lord
Hill on 14 October. 'I confined myself to telling him that you could not
recommend his appointment to the 11th Light Dragoons.' Previous to this,
Brudenell had written to Somerset while he was on holiday with his
family at Dover, enclosing a copy of a letter sympathetic to his case from
General Sir Hussey Vivian, Master-General of the Ordnance, to General
Sir Henry Hardinge. But as Vivian's letter contained no mention of
Melbourne's and Hill's views, Somerset considered it 'quite useless'.[11]

By the turn of 1836, however, events were moving inexorably in Lord
Brudenell's favour. Generals Lord Stafford and Sir Frederick Ponsonby
backed Vivian by supporting Brudenell's rehabilitation. It was generally felt
in military circles that Brudenell had been too harshly treated and it was
now time to welcome him back into the fold. Lord Hill was already of that
opinion; Melbourne and Howick were the final obstacles, and before long
they too had been cleared. On 25 March 1836, the Horse Guards
announced that Lord Brudenell was to exchange with Lieutenant-Colonel
Michael Childers of the 11th Light Dragoons, stationed in Meerut,
India.[12]

Court intervention is said to have proved decisive. Years later, an anonymous letter describing the sequence of events appeared in the *Morning
Chronicle*. 'The blow struck at the Cardigan family, by the disgrace of the
heir of that noble house, vibrated sensibly through every branch of it,'
stated the letter. On behalf of Lady Howe, the Queen broached the matter
with the King, but he 'refused to interfere with what he emphatically
called Lord Hill's righteous judgment'. And so matters would have rested
if Brudenell and his sister had not 'induced the old Lord Cardigan to beg
a private audience with the King, at which his grey hairs and infirmities
more moved the good monarch than all the petticoats put together'. Lord
Hill was called and, 'in spite of his declared opinion that Lord Brudenell
was constitutionally unfit for command, the reappointment took place'.[13]

If there was any truth in this account, Brudenell owed much to his sister and father – and to the King. Within 18 months all three were dead.

But Brudenell was not out of the woods yet. Radical M.P.s were anxious to make capital out of his rehabilitation by asserting the right of Parliament to veto unsuitable military appointments. In late March, Sir William Molesworth, the young and wealthy Radical M.P. for East Cornwall, gave notice of a motion censuring Lord Hill's decision. This was going too far for much of the moderate press who felt, in any case, that Brudenell had suffered enough. On April Fool's Day, *The Times* warned that 'the official responsibility of the Commander-in-Chief, in the distribution of military employment, ought not to be lightly tampered with by the House of Commons'. Though 'never tried by any military tribunal, nor convicted of any crime', Brudenell had been 'severely punished' for his indiscretions. 'The next consideration was, ought such a punishment to be aggravated into everlasting exclusion from the service? It would, we think, be harsh to say so.'[14]

The conservative *Morning Post* agreed: 'For a moment suppose this officer a Radical – thus deprived of his command upon charges not only not proved but not even formally preferred against him . . . How would Sir William Molesworth have denounced the atrocious tyranny of the Horse Guards!' He was not a Radical and had suffered 'for two years the penalty of faults which, at the worst, could have proceeded but from an injudicious zeal in the enforcement of military discipline'. Now, 'restored to the career from which it was never intended permanently to remove him, the malice of half-a-dozen spiteful individuals is exerted to prevent his Majesty from receiving into his favour a loyal subject, a gallant officer, and an honourable man!'[15]

Even the normally critical *Morning Chronicle* was prepared to concede that it was 'the opinion of several distinguished officers, that Lord Brudenell had been hardly used'. But unlike *The Times,* its overall opinion had not changed. '[We] are quite certain his Lordship, with the best intentions in the world, can never obtain that authority in a regiment which its colonel ought to possess; we, therefore, must regard Lord Brudenell's appointment as indicative of anything but sound discretion.' The system – by which Lord Hill, 'the irresponsible head of the army', could make such a decision without political control – was to blame. 'It is quite clear that Ministers would never have given a regiment to Lord Brudenell,' the *Chronicle* declared, ignorant of Somerset's close consultation with Lords Melbourne and Howick.[16]

On the evening of 3 May, Sir William Molesworth introduced his motion demanding a select committee to 'inquire into the conduct of the Commander of the Forces in appointing . . . Lord Brudenell to the lieutenant-colonelcy of the 11th Light Dragoons'. Despite the late hour, there were more than 360 M.P.s in the large committee room that had served as the lower chamber since the destruction of the Houses of Parliament by fire in 1834.

Molesworth spoke first, contending at length that the Commons had 'a distinct right to demand an explanation with reference to any appointment in the army which may seem to them objectionable'. Brudenell's reappointment was 'improper' because he had formerly been 'censured in terms so strong, that if that censure be a just one, he is, in every way, unfit to command a regiment'. If, on the other hand, 'that censure be an improper one, it cannot fail to be highly injurious to the army to place in a station of important trust an officer against whom that censure stands recorded and uncancelled in the order-books of the army'.

He did not, Molesworth told the House, 'seek to censure, again, that noble Lord' but 'to censure him who has appointed the noble Lord'. After all, it would not be unreasonable for the officers of the 11th Light Dragoons to ask, 'is the harmony – is the good feeling, which so long existed amongst us, of so little consequence in the eyes of the Commander-in-Chief, that he should appoint to command us, one who has been solemnly declared to have introduced into his previous regiment a practice 'highly detrimental to that harmony and good feeling which ought to exist between officers?' Molesworth continued:

> A more gallant regiment does not exist in his Majesty's service, nor one that has better served its country . . .: some of the officers have been nearly as many years in the army as the noble Lord has lived years in this world. The two majors have served with this regiment since the years 1806 and 1811. With what feelings will they view the advancement over their heads of this young officer, who has never heard the sound of a musket, except in the mimic combats of a review, who entered the army in 1824, with unexampled rapidity obtained an unattached lieutenant-colonelcy in 1830 – in 1832 the command of a regiment – in 1834, two years afterwards, was removed from that command for alleged misconduct – and now, in 1836, two years more, is deemed the fittest and most proper person to command their regiment? They . . . will say that

94

courtly influence, courtly favour, and courtly intrigue, have biassed
the otherwise sound judgment of the Commander-in-Chief, and
compelled that distinguished and otherwise irreproachable officer,
to make . . . an appointment which cannot fail to produce the
painful belief in the minds of all connected with the British army
that provided an officer possesses wealth and influence, it matters
not what his past conduct may have been – it matters not that the
solemn decision of a court-martial may have been against him . . .
This belief, if it were to become general, in my opinion, is one
highly injurious to the honour, to the discipline, and to the subordination of the British army, and thus fully justifies me in
demanding from the House a Committee to inquire into the conduct of the Commander-in-Chief.

Despite making a number of highly relevant points, Molesworth sat down
to faint applause because the House had hardened against a speech that
seemed to be asserting political control over the administration of the
Army. It had ever been one of the cornerstones of the British Constitution
to exclude the Army from politics and vice-versa. Delivered by a Radical
who had championed secret ballots in elections, colonial self-government
and the abolition of both flogging and transportation for convicts, it was
doubly unacceptable.

Joseph Hume, the veteran Scots Radical, seconded the motion and
then Lord Brudenell spoke. He would, he told the House, neither 'impugn
the decision of the court-martial' nor say anything which 'might appear
disrespectful with reference to the exercise of the King's prerogative' which
had deprived him of his regiment. Instead, he explained how, before taking
any action against Wathen, he had 'consulted the general officer commanding the district upon every point, and so entirely did he concur with
me . . . that he transmitted to the Commander-in-Chief a special report on
the subject, in which, after stating that the officer had conducted himself
so improperly in his presence, that it was unfit and inexpedient that he
should remain any longer in the 15th Hussars'. When he was subsequently
'ordered to prefer charges' against Wathen, he submitted them to
Arbuthnot who 'revised and approved of them'.

Arbuthnot had even given the principal evidence, and still Wathen was
'honourably acquitted of all and every one of the charges'. There were,
Brudenell said, 'numberless cases upon record of officers having been
brought to trial and honourably acquitted', but in none of them had 'any

commanding officer, after having acted as prosecutor', been 'deprived of his command'.

Brudenell then listed a number of such cases in which the commanding officer had been criticised but not removed, and followed this up by reading out letters of support for his reappointment from Generals Vivian, Strafford, Bouverie, Ponsonby and Blakeney. Vivian had stated that when Brudenell was removed from the 15th Hussars he reported to Horse Guards that he 'never saw a regiment in finer order . . . or an officer more zealous in the discharge of his duty'; Blakeney went so far as to describe Brudenell as 'one of the most intelligent officers who ever served under my command'.

Announcing that he would now withdraw so as not to inhibit the subsequent debate, Brudenell concluded by thanking the House for the 'kindness and attention' with which they had listened to his 'statement of details' – details that were 'intimately connected' with his 'honour and character', which were as 'dear' to him 'as life itself'. Loud cheers from both sides of the chamber greeted his departure, and it was clear that the battle was as good as won.

After Lord Howick and Lord George Lennox had both spoken against the motion – with Lennox arguing that the court had been wrong to acquit Wathen and censure his commanding officer – Hume effectively acknowledged the strength of feeling in the House by saying that Lord Brudenell 'had made out a case of great grievance' and that his complaint was 'against Lord Hill, for having, as Commander-in-Chief, sanctioned the verdict of the court-martial, and proclaimed its sentence . . . and now coming forward and re-appointing the noble Lord, without any explanation to satisfy the minds either of officers or men that that sentence was a harsh and unjust one'.

But the tide of opinion was against Hume, as member after member rose to defend Brudenell and, to a lesser extent, Hill. Even Daniel O'Connell admitted that he had 'a deep and strong conviction that Lord Brudenell was an injured man' and that the court had erred 'most grossly . . . in censuring a man who had not been heard upon the point which incurred their censure'. He would vote for the motion, he said, but only 'to express his abhorrence of a practice which condemned a man unheard'.

Well aware that his motion had no chance of succeeding, Molesworth tried to withdraw it before a division; but Brudenell's supporters were keen to inflict a humiliating defeat and loudly demanded a vote. Only 42

members were for the motion, an overwhelming 322 against, including Sir
Robert Peel, William Gladstone, Lord Palmerston, Lord John Russell and
Sir Henry Hardinge.[17]

Peel, in particular, was greatly impressed with Brudenell's conduct in the
House and wrote soon after to congratulate him on his moderate and sensible speech. Brudenell replied, thanking Peel for his 'very handsome and
complimentary letter' and emphasising how 'flattered' he felt 'by the
approbation of one for whose authority and opinion I entertain a profound
respect'. The ground had been laid, at least in Brudenell's eyes, for some
form of future preferment. [18]

With the satisfactory conclusion of the Commons' debate, Lord Brudenell
was at liberty to set sail for India. That he did not leave with his wife until
September was probably due to the attractions of the London Season over
the dullness of garrison life on the dusty plains of the Ganges. He may also
have been mindful of the *United Service Gazette*'s warning that India's 'climate is even more fatal to Europeans than the chances of war, and more
feared than the dangers of the battlefield'. With the regiment due to return
to Britain in early 1838, after a 19-year stint in the subcontinent, it must
have occurred to Brudenell that the less service he saw in India the
better.[19]

His leisurely progress would seem to suggest so. Travelling through
France, Brudenell and his wife paid a courtesy call on the young Duc
d'Orléans, the eldest son of King Louis Philippe, at Compiègne near Paris,
and were guests at a grand review of 2,300 troops. From there they proceeded to Italy, and across the Mediterranean to Alexandria via Malta. The
Suez Canal had yet to be dug, but steamships were just beginning to operate between the top of the Red Sea and India. To reach them, the 50 miles
of the isthmus had to be crossed in a bone-shaking conveyance that resembled a horse-drawn omnibus. Unfortunately, no steamers were in port
when the Brudenells arrived, so they hired a recently unloaded coal-ship
instead. There was ample time to regret this choice of sail, for the 3,000-
mile journey to Bombay, on the west coast of India, took 73 seemingly
endless days – at an average speed of under two miles an hour.

Dominating the subcontinent then was the Honourable East India
Company, a trading house that had been granted its charter by Elizabeth I
and had established a permanent station on the coast north of Bombay in
1613. When the great Moghul empire – which ruled central and north

India – began to disintegrate in the early eighteenth century, the East India Company was forced to enlist soldiers to defend its valuable trade. So began a long period of territorial expansion, as obdurate rulers were defeated and the more pliant were formally recognised as 'clients'.

In 1773, alarmed by this growth, Parliament passed a Regulating Act making the Company responsible for civil government in its territories. It also gave the Governor-General of Bengal, the biggest and richest of the three presidencies ruled by the Company, supervisory control of the other two, Bombay and Madras. A year later, the India Act brought the Company's board of directors under the authority of a newly created Cabinet minister, the President of the Board of Control. In effect, the Company became the Indian agent of the British government. In 1833, the contradiction between trading and ruling was ended when the Company was instructed to cease all commercial business in return for an annuity of £630,000 from the territorial revenues of India.

When the Brudenells arrived at Bombay, the governor, Sir Robert Grant, was absent in the Mallemista Hills but had left instructions for them to be accommodated in the magnificent Porrell Palace, five miles from the city. During a pampered stay of several weeks, they visited the inland stations of Kirkee and Poonah, and were received with 'great hospitality' by Sir John Keane, Commander-in-Chief of the presidency army. Continuing their journey, they took a coastal vessel round the lower tip of Ceylon to Madras harbour, where they had to be assisted over the treacherous sand bar 'in great danger, several boats having the same day been upset, and lives lost'.

This time the governor, Lord Elphinstone, was in residence and insisted on taking them on a guided tour of the presidency, including a visit to the ruined fort at Seringapatam which Wellington, as a young colonel, had helped to storm in 1799. From Madras, another vessel took the Brudenells up to Calcutta where they stayed with the governor-general, Lord Auckland, in Fort William. The last leg of the journey was by steamer up the Ganges, pausing at Allahabad. For two weeks they enjoyed being the centre of attention in this bustling station, with its imposing fort and 'smartly turned-out people driving in the cool hours, and going to parties in the evening'. But duty called and finally, on 10 September 1837, almost a year after setting out, the Brudenells arrived at Cawnpore, home to the 11th Light Dragoons since their move from Meerut earlier in the year.[20]

The city of Cawnpore – the second largest in the fabulously rich state of Oudh – was impressive enough with its jewel-encrusted mosques, marble palaces and cool gardens full of flowers, orange trees and screeching parakeets. Prime among the sights was the *Thug* prison, full to bursting since Captain William Sleeman, the chief agent of the governor-general, had successfully infiltrated the murderous cult of *Thugee* a couple of years earlier. Regular exhibitions were arranged by the prison governor, Captain Patten, to illustrate how these worshippers of *Kali*, the Hindu goddess of destruction, carried out their ritual killings by befriending fellow-travellers and then strangling them with a piece of sacred cloth.

British and East India Company troops, however, were quartered in a tented garrison on the plain outside the city, with little shelter from the heat of the day and the cold of the night. Fanny Eden, the sister of the governor-general, who visited Cawnpore in December 1837, described it as the 'ugliest' station in India. Dead flat, with 'not a single blade of even brown grass to be seen; nothing but loose brown dust which rose in clouds on the slightest provocation'.[21]

In the summer of 1715, with the Jacobite threat at its height, the regiment that became the 11th Light Dragoons was raised by Brigadier Philip Honeywood. It was still being formed when the Earl of Mar raised the Pretender's standard in Scotland, and so missed the decisive battles north of the border. But when a number of rebels slipped south and captured Preston, 'Honeywood's Dragoons' – resplendent in three-cornered cocked hats, scarlet coats, buff waistcoats and breeches – were part of the force that retook the town. At the battle of Culloden, 31 years later, the regiment helped to destroy the Jacobite threat once and for all by taking part in the final advance on Bonnie Prince Charlie's position, ruthlessly cutting down the fleeing Highlanders.

In 1783, the 11th was reconstituted as light dragoons, with smaller recruits and lighter arms. A year later the coats were changed from scarlet to blue, and it was in this garb that the regiment saw distinguished service in the Napoleonic Wars, notably in Egypt and the Peninsula. The one exception was in operations near the besieged fortress of Badojoz, when a force of French cavalry broke through a neighbouring picquet of the King's German Legion and came up behind an outpost of the 11th. Realising too late that they were foes, four men were killed, 22 wounded and 77 captured. Honour was regained at Waterloo, however, under the command of Lieutenant-Colonel James Sleigh. After covering the withdrawal of the remnants of the Union Brigade, the 11th took part in the final advance and captured two artillery batteries.

Three years were then spent with the Army of Occupation in France; and then in February 1819, after just one year back in Britain, the regiment left for India. The high point of its service there came during the siege of Bhurtpore in 1825. The rajah had died earlier that year and his son, the rightful ruler, had been usurped by his cousin, Doorjan-Saul. An army under Lord Combermere was despatched to bring Doorjan to heel, and in December the investment of the capital began. One hundred dismounted troopers of the 11th, under Lieutenant Tuckett and Cornet Bambrick, helped to create a breach in the walls, and more volunteered to join the storming party. In the event they were not needed, as another British infantry regiment arrived to take part in the successful capture of the fortress on 18 January 1826.

After Bhurtpore, the 11th returned to Cawnpore and garrison duty. The wearing of scarlet coats was resumed in 1830, and two years later the regiment was moved north to the larger station of Meerut, in the neighbouring state of Rohilkhand. When George Loy Smith, a 19-year-old private from Yorkshire, joined the 11th in 1836 it was still at Meerut. Entries in his diary give a fascinating glimpse of life as a cavalryman in India at this time. During the hot, windy season from May to the middle of August, the troopers were confined to barracks from 9 o'clock in the morning until 5 in the evening. Barrack windows on the windward side were covered with grass shutters – 'having the appearance of large doormats' – which were kept constantly wet by native water-bearers so that 'the hot wind, after passing through them, became quite cool'. With the windows and doors on the other side kept shut, little light entered the barracks and the men were forced to entertain themselves by reading and playing cards in half-darkness. Stable hour, as in Britain, was at 6 a.m., but the advantage was that the men did not have to groom their horses, 'there being a native to every troop horse in the regiment' – paid four rupees a month, half by the East India Company and half by the horse's rider.

Officers usually had ten or more servants, including a butler, a bearer, a groom, a sweeper, a water-carrier and a gardener. But even they suffered from the physical discomfort and boredom of the hot summer months when the climate made normal regimental duties impossible and flies were a constant torment. Quartered in bungalows, or tents in the less-established stations like Cawnpore, they would rise early and take a stroll or ride before the short morning parade. Breakfast was substantial and could be anything from eggs to beef-chops, fried fish and curried fowl. Between noon and 2 p.m., calls would be made on local society, both military and civil, followed by tiffin (lunch) and a siesta. Because of the heat, beer – in the form of pale ale or dark, bitter porter – was drunk in great quantities, much to the surprise of the griffin (officer just arrived from Britain). After 5 p.m., the evening walk or ride was taken in the company of the garrison's ladies. Dinner was at 7, after which the officers might dance, read English papers or play billiards in the mess.

The heat in June was the worst, when many men, including Loy Smith, succumbed to fever. It was during his time in hospital, with deaths a daily occurrence, that he first learnt about the change of colonel in a newspaper clipping from England which read: 'What have the 11th Light Dragoons done that they should have Lord Brudenell to command them, an officer that was dismissed from the 15th Hussars for tyranny.'

The rainy season was from mid-August to October, but in 1836 little rain fell. Even so, insects were everywhere, including giant cockroaches and red ants so numerous that saucers of water had to be placed under table legs. The cold season began in November, with a drop in temperature that at last enabled the men to drill. 'We now had field days,' wrote Loy Smith, 'sometimes under the Colonel, at other times the Adjutant, when the N.C. Officers commanded the troops, and sword drill on foot occasionally under the Regt Segt Major in the afternoons.' The cold season also allowed outdoor sports, with 'Long Balls' – a competition to throw an 18 oz ball the furthest – the 'favourite game'. Hunting and snake-fighting were also popular:

> During breakfast [wrote Loy Smith], natives often brought in baskets of jackalls, wild cats, hares and other animals, which we bought for a few annahs each, to hunt across the plain, as many of the men kept dogs. Other natives brought snakes which they carried in bags; for a few pice they would put one on the ground and then let loose a mongoose . . . Then they would fight, which always ended in the mongoose being the conqueror by killing the snake.

On 28 January 1837, the regiment began the march back to Cawnpore. It was accompanied, according to the recently promoted Lance-Corporal Loy Smith, by 'five to seven thousand followers, besides elephants, camels and bullocks, to carry the tents, bedding, baggage, and all the merchandise belonging to the regimental bazaar'. Soon after arriving at a new camp ground, 'a native town springs up as if by magic, where almost anything can be purchased from a sweetmeat to a coffin'. It was during one of these halts, at Jhurtpore on the 31st, that the 11th was reviewed by General Sir Henry Fane, Commander-in-Chief in India, who expressed in orders his 'perfect approbation of the soldierlike appearance of the regiment, and of the fine condition of the horses'.

Back in quarters at Cawnpore – which Loy Smith described as 'not so nice and pleasant as Meerut' – the soldiers of the 11th had to endure one of the longest and most oppressive hot seasons ever known. The burning winds began in the middle of April and, despite pauses, did not cease until the middle of August when the rainy season began. As with the previous two years, there was little rain but much sickness, particularly cholera. At one time, wrote Loy Smith, 'we had about two hundred men in hospital and in a few weeks lost 35 men, 7 women and 30 children'. The natives were even harder hit, with the drought resulting in famine. 'They died around us by hundreds, and numbers could at all times be seen floating down the Ganges. It was piteous to see these poor wretches, some begging, others picking up bones or any offal they could find round the barracks. Although tens of thousands died from sheer starvation, little was known of it in England.'[22]

When Lord Brudenell finally reached Cawnpore on 10 September 1837, he was horrified at the condition of his new regiment. Months of inactivity and sickness had debilitated the health and spirits of formerly fit men; discipline was lax. Worse still, he was not due to take command until 23 October – the retirement date of the temporary colonel, Brutton – and was therefore unable to take immediate steps to rectify matters.

Two days before the changeover, the regiment appeared in Review Order with white trousers on the General Parade Ground, along with the 16th Regiment of Foot, two regiments of Native Cavalry, four regiments of Native Infantry and two batteries of artillery. A resounding three cheers greeted the proclamation by the general commanding the garrison that 18-year-old Queen Victoria had ascended the throne. William IV had died in the early hours of 20 June, but the news had only just reached Cawnpore.

On 23 October, Colonel Brutton handed over the regiment to Brudenell and retired after 43 years' service. Writing about this day years later, Brudenell rather unfairly dismissed the roles played by Somerset and

Hill: 'I thus gained my object without the slightest assistance from the Horse Guards, and I here had the command of a Brigade in the field – the 11th, and two native regiments.'[23]

In regimental orders, Brutton declared that he could not 'find words to express his sense of obligation to the officers and men for the support he has invariably received from them', and that it was 'a source of pride and satisfaction for him to know he leaves unsullied the high character the Eleventh has ever maintained by their exemplary conduct in the field and in quarters'.

The following day, when presenting Brutton with a piece of silver plate on behalf of the officers, Brudenell was effusive in his compliments. 'I beg, my lord,' Brutton responded, 'to return thanks for the handsome terms in which you have conveyed to me the sentiments of my brother officers, as well as for the personal expressions of regard with which you have honoured me.'

The pleasantries were continued in Brudenell's regimental orders of 24 October, although they contained more than a hint that things were about to change. After expressing his 'strong feelings of pride and satisfaction' at assuming command of a regiment 'whose distinguished services in the field have only been equalled by its exemplary conduct in quarters on all occasions', he said he was confident 'that by their zeal and co-operation, both the officers and non-commissioned officers will afford him that support which, by enabling him to maintain its order, discipline and efficiency, will conduce to the welfare and credit of the distinguished regiment to which they all belong'.[24]

Twenty-four hours later, the harsh realities of the new regime were underlined when Lord Brudenell ordered the first field day of the season. 'It was a dreadfully hard one, after so many months of inaction,' commented Loy Smith, 'the men were all completely prostrated.' As the temperature fell, field days were stepped up, and occasionally the regiment drilled as a brigade with the two Indian cavalry regiments, the 5th and the 7th, and the horse artillery. Rumours of a return to England abounded, and on 18 November they were confirmed; the 3rd Light Dragoons had landed at Calcutta and were on their way to take the place of the 11th. Volunteers who wished to stay in India and join the 3rd, or the 16th Lancers at Meerut, had three days to make up their minds, beginning 22 November.

With most men looking forward to seeing their families after an 18-year separation, there was understandable excitement and merriment, accompanied by inevitable breaches of discipline. In the evening of the first day of volunteering, Loy Smith came to blows with a man who had insulted him; next morning he was reduced to the ranks by his new colonel. As if this was not enough, 'on the third day of volunteering a circumstance occurred for which I could never quite forgive Lord Brudenell,' wrote Loy Smith.

John Dowling, an old sweat who 'had completed his service, and was going home to be discharged, was confined a few days for being drunk on picquet'. Normally, he would have been given 'eight days Congee house' (confinement in the guard house), but Brudenell insisted on a court-martial. The regiment paraded in the riding-school and was horrified to hear that Dowling had been sentenced to be flogged. 'No one present supposed for a moment that Lord Brudenell could be hard-hearted enough to carry it out,' Loy Smith wrote, 'particularly when the old man turned round to him, and in an imploring tone said: "My lord, I hope you won't flog me. I am an old man, and just going home to my friends. I should be sorry for such a disgrace to come on me now."'

'Tie him up,' was Brudenell's heartless reply, and the farriers then commenced their brutal work.

'My heart heaved and I had great difficulty in restraining myself from bursting into a flood of tears,' recorded Loy Smith. 'After the parade, loud were the denunciations against him, all, both officers and men, feeling the change that had come over us.'

An extra day's volunteering took place the next morning and, according to Loy Smith, 'numbers that had made up their mind to return to England volunteered in consequence of this exhibition', preferring to stay in India rather than serve under such a commanding officer. In all, 158 men chose to remain: 110 with the 3rd Light Dragoons and 48 with the 16th Lancers. All 609 horses would also be left behind.

But even with departure near, Brudenell would not let up. A couple of days before the first half of the regiment was due to leave, with their saddles already crated for the journey, he ordered a field day for the following morning. 'We were up half the night unpacking and preparing for it,' wrote Loy Smith. Finally, on 4 December, the Left Wing of the regiment under Major Jenkins embarked in sailing ships for the trip down the Ganges to Calcutta. The Right Wing followed a week later. Compared with the long journey up the Ganges in 1819, when 25 men died, the trip down with the current was 'very pleasant', with the loss of just two men, one of whom jumped into the water to swim and was taken by crocodiles.[25]

Brudenell, meanwhile, was enjoying himself. After seeing the last of his regiment embark on the 11th, he and his wife set out on another sightseeing trip, staying first with General Fane at his headquarters near Delhi. It was during their brief time here that Brudenell received word that his father had died at Deene on 14 August. His grief was tempered by euphoria. Now the 7th Earl of Cardigan, he was master of Deene, a mansion in Portman Square and extensive estates in three counties, and would receive an annual income of £40,000. No longer would he need to ask his father for handouts, no longer would the unseemly business of winning a seat in Parliament be necessary. To celebrate, he went tiger shooting with Colonel Arnold of the 16th Lancers at Meerut.

About this time, Cardigan was infuriated to learn that an anonymous account of his allegedly harsh treatment of his men had appeared in a Bombay newspaper. The regiment had had few offenders before his arrival, the letter stated, now 'not one' cell 'was left unoccupied and most had two tenants'. In less than a month, he had had 'eight courts-martial and more than a hundred men on the defaulters list'. But the verdicts were not severe enough for him, and on the morning of Private Dowling's trial he had told the officers that if the sentence was 'not satisfactory' he would 'report them to Sir Henry Fane, the Commander-in-Chief in India, and to Lord Hill, the Commander-in-Chief in England'. That evening 'a soldier of twenty years service was flogged'.[26]

Only later did Cardigan discover that the author of this account was Lieutenant Harvey Tuckett, the hero of Bhurtpore. 'He made several slanders and calumnies against me whilst the Regiment descended [the Ganges] to embark for England,' wrote Cardigan.[27]

Tuckett's motives for writing the letter were probably mixed: like the officers of the 15th Hussars, he had preferred the firm but fair regime of the outgoing colonel, particularly as Cardigan had made little effort to hide his contempt for 'Indian' officers – gentlemen of modest means who chose to serve in the subcontinent because it was cheaper and offered the possibility of active service. Rich and well-connected officers, on the other hand, preferred to exchange out of a regiment rather than serve in the discomfort of India. There may also have been an element of jealousy in Tuckett's antipathy: he had seen distinguished service, but had little money and was still a lieutenant 14 years on. Cardigan had joined the Army later, seen no action and was already a lieutenant-colonel.

The Cardigans left Meerut by *dak* – a covered litter borne in relays by horses and, if necessary, men – and arrived in Calcutta in time to supervise the departure of the Right Wing of the regiment under Major Rotton in the transport *Repulse* on 2 February 1838. The Left Wing, under Major Jenkins, had set sail in the *Thames*, an old East India merchantman, on 21 January.

Before embarking on the *Thames*, the men had been forced to endure the misery of three days and two nights on huge barges. 'No rations were issued,' wrote Loy Smith, 'in fact there was no place to cook them if there had. No place to lie down (the deck by day being too hot, and the dew at night was so heavy that we should have been wet through), so the only place to get rest was the hold amongst the ballast, which consisted of huge stones, so large and irregular that it was impossible to find a place anywhere to lie down. What with hunger and the misery of being unable to lie down to sleep, [this] surpassed anything I ever met with in all my career.'

The *Thames* would have been a great improvement if the authorities had not forgotten to provide hammocks or bedding. 'Consequently, both men, women and children had to sleep on the decks until we arrived at Madras on 26th January,' Loy Smith recorded.[28]

Needless to say, the Cardigans had in mind a more comfortable mode of transport. The original plan was to take the overland route to Bombay – and 500 bearers were engaged for the task – but this was cancelled when they decided to spend another week in Calcutta. Invited to a musical concert, Cardigan managed to alienate local society by telling the star performer, English-born Mrs Goodall Atkinson, that he had just come from England and could not 'be supposed to relish the performances of an Indian actress or singer'.[29]

They finally left by private ship to Madras where, again, they were guests of Lord Elphinstone. From there they crossed the subcontinent by *dak*, catching the Suez steamer at Bombay. England was reached in June in time for Cardigan to supervise the disembarkation of the *Thames* at Gravesend on the 8th and the *Repulse* at Herne Bay on the 25th. More importantly, the Cardigans had arrived in time to attend the Queen's Coronation at Westminster Abbey on 28 June. With London's population of a million and a half swelled by 400,000 visitors, Charles Greville graphically described the crush in his diary entry for 27 June:

> There never was anything like the state of this town; it is as if the population had been on a sudden quintupled; the uproar, the confusion, the crowd, the noise, are indescribable. Horsemen, footmen, carriages squeezed, jammed, intermingled, the pavement

blocked up with timbers, hammering and knocking, and falling fragments stunning the ears and threatening the head; not a mob here and there, but the town all mob, thronging, bustling, gaping, and gazing at everything, at anything, or at nothing; the park one vast encampment, with banners floating at the tops of the tents, and still the roads are covered, the railroads loaded with arriving multitudes. From one end of the route of the Royal procession to the other, from the top of Piccadilly to Westminster Abbey, there is a vast line of scaffolding.

The Coronation itself was a five-hour ordeal made more difficult, in the young Queen's words, by 'remarkably maladroit' bishops who did not always seem to know what they were doing. At one point she was handed the heavy golden Orb by the Bishop of Durham, but it should have been given by the Archbishop of Canterbury and had to be reclaimed. At last her small, childlike figure was dressed in a robe of cloth of gold, and she was offered the Sceptre, ruby ring and Crown of State. The ring was too small, having been measured for her little finger, and had to be jammed on by the archbishop while she winced in pain. As the crown was placed on her head, the Cardigans and their fellow peers and peeresses donned their coronets, causing shafts of light from the candles to criss-cross in the gloom. Trumpets and drums sounded, and outside cannon fired as the crowds roared 'God Save the Queen'.[30]

The 'Black Bottle Affair'

The regiment's new home was the picturesque garrison town of Canterbury. Surrounded by the lush meadows and hayfields of fertile Kent, it was a welcome relief from the arid plains of Cawnpore. Or at least it was so for the 200 or so men left after more than 100 old-timers and invalids had been discharged – particularly as, with little to do until new horses and recruits arrived from the depot to bring the strength up to the home establishment of 333, they had been given two weeks' leave. So while they frittered a fortune in saved pay on drink and women, the 7th Earl of Cardigan returned to Deene as its new master, a position under-lined by a banquet given in his honour by 450 local Conservative gentlemen.

Once back at Canterbury, Cardigan set about knocking the regiment into shape in double-quick time – with predictable results. According to Loy Smith, he 'drew the reins with too tight a hand, giving most severe punishments for trivial offences (there being no code to guide command-ing officers)'. The result was that the men 'became reckless', with some preferring a court-martial and jail to the punishment Cardigan had pre-scribed. 'Many a man in consequence,' wrote Loy Smith, 'that would have made a moderately good soldier, never did any good afterwards.'

One trooper was sentenced to be 'discharged with ignominy from the Service'. With the whole regiment in attendance, the 'regimental sergeant-major cut the facings and buttons off his jacket and the stripes off his overalls'. The men then 'formed a street, the front rank facing to the rear, down which the prisoner was marched . . . between a file of the guard and . . . the band in front playing "The Rogue's March". He was then turned out of the barrack gate.'[1]

Officers, too, were leaving. In mid-August 1838, the *Morning Herald* reported that in a regiment 'lately returned from India' a 'system of annoyance is carried into effect towards old officers (evidently with a view to disgust them and oblige them to retire)'. The commanding officer 'would do well to bear in remembrance the court-martial held some years since on Captain Wathen', the paper warned, adding that if the 'system' was continued the regiment would be named. White with rage, Cardigan challenged the *Herald's* military correspondent to a duel. Needless to say, he was refused, the paper noting with satisfaction that its remarks had already been 'so far productive of good as to have provoked the ire of the principal offender'. That November, Lieutenant Tuckett – the likely source of the story – exchanged with Lieutenant Forrest and went on half-pay.[2]

With the men occupied by drilling new recruits and breaking-in horses, Cardigan spent much of the year in London and Northamptonshire, enjoying the respective pleasures of society and hunting. The new Master of the Pytchley was the high-living Earl of Chesterfield, whose policy of 'late to bed, late to rise' meant that the hunt was often kept waiting upwards of an hour. When it was discovered that the cause was invariably the late arrival of his mistress, Nelly Holmes (later Lady Rivers), 'at no time an ornament to the social *morale*', according to the hunt historian, 'the burden was no longer to be endured'. But before his demise in 1840, Chesterfield led an enthusiastic field 'in which hard riding was much the fashion', and Cardigan was one of a trio of noble lords – the others were Maidstone and Macdonald – 'hard to catch and bad to beat'.[3]

This was a time when country gentlemen, however keen on racing, wore the coat known as the 'Newmarket cutaway' over an embroidered silk or velvet waistcoat, and changed into a blue coat with brass buttons and velvet collar for dinner. Communications between town and shire had improved but, with trains still in their infancy and the London to Birmingham line yet to be built, a coach-and-four was still the typical method of travel.

At Canterbury the reorganisation was going well. In October, the *Naval and Military Gazette* reported that 100 young horses had already been broken-in, and that given Cardigan's 'well-known zeal and ability' and the 'very splendid state of the men' it would not be surprising if the regiment was not 'the first corps for Queen's duty'. Relations among the officers also seemed to be improving. According to the same report, a large party of them – including Majors Rotton and Browne, Captain Richard Reynolds and Lieutenant Forrest – 'spent some time at the seat of the gallant and noble Colonel, enjoying the sports of the field, and the magnificent hospitality of Drewe [sic] Park'.[4]

By the spring of 1839 the 11th was not quite ready for Queen's duty, but it did enjoy the minor distinction of becoming the first regiment to be issued with the new Victoria percussion carbine. Field days were begun and Cardigan was increasingly occupied, although not to the extent that he was oblivious to the opportunities provided by the apparent fall of the Whig government in the early hours of 7 May. Having won a motion to suspend the unruly constitution of Jamaica by just five votes, Melbourne decided to resign (although still possessing a theoretical, if unreliable, majority). Having lost her mentor, the distraught Queen sent for Wellington, but he declined on health grounds. Finally Sir Robert Peel, the acknowledged leader of the Conservatives, was approached; put out by not being asked first, he was stiff and formal at the interview, telling the Queen that she would have to agree to the replacement of her Whig ladies-in-waiting. By custom, these were political appointments which reflected the balance of power in Parliament, and represented a valuable form of patronage for the Prime Minister. But the Queen was determined to keep 'her ladies', possibly seeing the impasse as a means of preventing a Tory government and so ensuring the return of Melbourne.

Back at Deene, Cardigan was unaware of Peel's difficulties, knowing only that he had been offered the post of Prime Minister on the 8th. Two days later, he wrote to Peel, asking to be considered for the 'situation of Lord-Lieutenant of Northamptonshire' in the event of a vacancy which could not be 'very far distant' (the incumbent, Lord Westmorland, being old and unwell). His claim was based 'upon being one of the highest in rank, and one of the largest landed proprietors in the county'; someone who had 'supported' Peel and the Duke of Wellington's administrations 'under *all circumstances*', and who had established the Conservative cause in the Northern Division of Northamptonshire at his 'own expense'. In other words, it would be a reward for his political loyalty.

When Peel replied on 12 May, he was no longer Prime Minister. He had told the Queen that he could not survive in the Commons if her ladies were not replaced, and she had responded by sending for Melbourne. But even if he had been Prime Minister, he told Cardigan, his answer would have been the same: that he 'would enter into no Engagement, express or implied, which could prevent the full and unfettered consideration of the Claims that might be preferred (in the event of a vacancy)'.[5]

Cardigan's disappointment was forgotten on 11 June when the regiment was reviewed for the first time since its return by Major-General James Sleigh, its former commanding officer who was now Inspector-General of Cavalry. So impressed was Sleigh with the appearance of the troops and every department in barracks that he told Cardigan that he would recommend that Lord Hill himself came to inspect the regiment. In regimental orders, Cardigan expressed his own 'satisfaction at the progress which has been made in the re-organisation of the corps', thanking the officers and N.C.O.s for their assistance 'in establishing a system of duties, to many of which the greater portion of the troops were entirely unaccustomed, after so long an absence in a distant climate'.[6]

One of the duties that Cardigan was referring to was the proper cleaning of the horses' white sheepskins. While in India they had been washed by the natives with something that, according to Loy Smith, 'had turned them a very bad colour which all the cleaning we could give them would not alter'. Cardigan, of course, insisted that they should be snow-white and those with the poorest colour 'were perpetually at extra drill and extra parades'. Sometimes the 'whole regiment had to parade in the afternoon, each man with his sheepskin, all the officers attending'. One simpleton who could not get his sheepskin white, and was sick of the continual punishment he received, was told in jest to try soot and grease. Much to the amusement of his comrades, he was arrested at the next parade and ordered by Cardigan to buy a new one. The merriment continued soon after when a waggon arrived from London laden with bales of new sheepskins – black instead of white.[7]

But Cardigan's fastidiousness was obviously working because in five further inspections that year – by H.R.H. the Duke of Cambridge, Lord Hill, the Duke of Wellington and Generals Sir Hussey Vivian and Lord Charles Manners – the regiment received nothing but praise. Cambridge, William IV's younger brother, who visited Canterbury just twelve days after Sleigh, expressed 'in the strongest terms, his approbation of the appearance and steadiness of the troops in the field and on parade'. Wellington, who honoured Cardigan by arriving on the day of his 42nd birthday, was impressed with the 'rapid completion of the efficiency of the regiment in so short a space of time since its return from the East Indies', and was also pleased to refer with satisfaction to the services of 'his old friends the Eleventh Light Dragoons in the Peninsula'. That evening the Duke was guest of honour at Cardigan's extravagant birthday dinner. The generals, it seemed, had been right to support Cardigan's reinstatement.

However, not everyone felt so generous towards the regiment during 1839. On 5 July, a petty incident occurred which once again brought Lord Cardigan to the unfavourable attention of the press. Captain Richard Reynolds and five subalterns had been out riding near Canterbury, and were returning through a hayfield when they were accosted by a gentleman called John Brent, a Radical magistrate and father of the landowner.

Brent's version of events – which appeared in the *Morning Chronicle* on 12 August – was that he 'civilly remonstrated' with the officers for 'damaging the crop, and breaking the hedges', and 'was met by an insulting laugh in reply'. On asking their names, one replied 'Snooks!', then shouted to the others to 'come on!' At this, one rode at Brent who was 'obliged to seize his horse by the curb-rein' until he 'could get out of his way'. But the officer continued to spur his horse, forcing Brent 'towards a brick wall'. Wriggling free, Brent announced that he was a magistrate and a gentleman, and demanded the officers' names. When they refused to give them, Brent called them 'blackguards' and threatened to report them to their commanding officer.[8]

The version given to the same newspaper by Cornet Brotherton, one of the officers, is significantly different. He had come out of the field and 'was actually in the road' when Mr Brent came up to him 'in the most insolent manner' and snatched his reins. Addressing them all as 'blackguards', Brent then demanded their names.

'As I had not at the time either whip or stick in my hands with which to administer to Mr Brent the chastisement which his brutal assault would have warranted,' Brotherton wrote, 'I spurred my horse and rode at him, as he himself describes, till I got him up against a wall, when he let go my bridle.'[9]

Brent's account is that he then followed the officers to the barracks 'but, on arriving at the gate, one of them called out to the sentinel – "Don't let that man enter."' Trying another gate, Brent was again refused entry despite saying he 'was going to the commanding officer'. He therefore had no option but to write to Lord Cardigan 'detailing the transaction'. Receiving no answer by 9 July, he sent a complaint to Lord Hill, enclosing a copy of his earlier letter.

Hill replied, regretting that any 'irregularity should have taken place' and informing Brent that Lord Cardigan 'had assured him that he had taken such steps as would prevent a recurrence' of the trespass. Under the circumstances, Hill 'felt that any further interference on his part was unnecessary'. He also enclosed a copy of a written statement by one of the officers involved that had been sent to him by Cardigan. Assuming that Lord Hill had based his judgement on this account which was, in his opinion, 'wholly incorrect', Brent wrote again. 'I called upon his lordship to afford me the opportunity of tendering direct evidence,' recorded Brent, 'as would disprove the statement made by the officer.' Hill refused.[10]

In the same edition that Brent's letter – headlined 'OUTRAGE BY SIX OFFICERS OF THE ELEVENTH LIGHT DRAGOONS' – was printed, a leading article came to the conclusion that the colonel of the regiment had 'a very imperfect idea of what is due from one gentleman to another'. Cardigan was on his way to Scotland to shoot grouse when he saw the paper, but this did not prevent him from immediately penning a furious response. Referring to Brent's claim that he had told the officers he was 'a magistrate and a gentleman', Cardigan commented: 'That he is a magistrate there can be no doubt – that he is a gentleman is quite another question.' He had reason to doubt it because Brent had 'suppressed, in his garbled statement' the circumstance of Cardigan having written to him to say that he had never received the first letter. Brent had also forgotten to mention that Cardigan had then visited him to express his 'regret that any trespass should have occurred on his property' and to assure him that he had 'taken measures to prevent a recurrence'.

That regret, he was convinced, would have been 'equally expressed by the officers at the time, had Mr Brent addressed them in a more moderate tone, instead of commencing by telling them they were "blackguards"'. In Cardigan's opinion, 'great credit' was due to the officers 'for their for-bearance'. Cardigan went on to explain how, when he refused to supply the names of the officers, Brent had 'expressed much dissatisfaction, stat-ing that it prevented him demanding "that satisfaction from any one of them which one gentleman usually requires of another"'. Cardigan's swift response, upon returning to barracks, was to send an officer to say that the commanding officer was 'perfectly ready' to offer satisfaction 'on behalf of the officers of the corps'. Not bothering to record Brent's reply, which was undoubtedly to decline, Cardigan ended his letter with a personal attack on the Editor of the *Morning Chronicle*:

> With regard to the opinion which you have so unwarrantably
> published to the world in the leading article of your journal, viz.,
> 'that I have a very imperfect idea of what is due from one gentle-
> man to another,' I have only to reply that such an assertion is an
> *infamous* and *scandalous falsehood*, and that it is fortunate for you that
> you are the anonymous editor of a newspaper.

Responding in the same edition to 'so unbecoming a threat', the Editor
warned Cardigan that were he 'to forget himself further, we should have
no hesitation in handing him over, with the least possible ceremony, to a
police officer'.[11]

Wisely, Cardigan refrained from further correspondence, leaving the
officers to put their case. On 22 August, the *Morning Chronicle* published
Cornet Brotherton's brief account of the incident. But unlike Lord Hill,
not every member of the Army was convinced. The following day a letter
appeared from 'An officer of Rank, of more than 40 years' standing', in
whose opinion Brent had 'not received the treatment which, as a gentleman, he ought to have experienced from soldiers and gentlemen'. To any
'impartial person', the explanations afforded by the 'Earl of Cardigan, and
the officers who have been alluded to, have been altogether inconclusive as
to their defence'. For him this was proof 'that it would have been better for
discipline and the interests of the army, that his lordship had not been
restored to command'.

A separate correspondent attacked Cardigan's distinction between his
gentlemanly officers and Brent's lack of breeding, pointing out that Major
Rotton was 'the nephew of the late Mr Wroughton, a respectable tragic
actor at Drury-lane theatre'. Brent was, in conclusion, 'far superior to
many of the officers of the 11th Light Dragoons, many of whose fathers
were low, vulgar, though rich tradesmen'. Others, rightly, considered the
whole affair a farce. On the same page as Brotherton's account was a
letter, purporting to come from Lord Fitzroy Somerset, which drew attention to a notice in the *London Gazette* that the Queen had granted the 11th
Light Dragoons the right to bear 'SNOOKS' on their standards. The only
person who did not see the funny side was Thomas Snooks, a Canterbury
greengrocer; in a letter that appeared the following day, he denied any connection with the officers, pointing out that what was 'fun to the military
may be death to me'.[12]

Most papers generally had more sense than to devote so much space to
an issue that should have been settled by Cardigan's personal apology.

Even the *Morning Herald*, which had previously warned Cardigan about his 'system of annoyance', took a remarkably sensible editorial line on 21 August:

> To us the matter appeared to lie in a nutshell. Some young officers, exercising their horses, rode over a hay-field, and, suddenly inter-rupted in their (possible) trespass, replied jocularly in terms that appear to have offended the full-blown dignity of the lord of the soil – a gentleman of radical politics – 'and, what is more,' a mag-istrate 'possessing authority.' Ample satisfaction for the trespass appears to have been offered and refused, but the cause of the refusal, indeed the gist of the whole affair, has its origin in the fact of its offering a means to the whig party of vilyfying a conserva-tive nobleman. Had it been a lady's reputation instead of a hay-field, the 11th dragoons might have ridden over it rough-shod with impunity.[13]

The so-called 'Brent Affair' was put into perspective the following year by a series of notorious incidents perpetrated by officers from other regiments. Captain Clark of the 9th Lancers was the most persistent and outrageous performer. Driving his four-in-hand through Hammersmith gate, he was asked for the toll and responded by horse-whipping the unfortunate col-lector. Another time, he and a rowdy party of fellow officers went on the rampage after being thrown out of a Hounslow whorehouse on a Sunday night. Ringing handbells, they charged through the streets, pulling down barbers' poles and tearing off door-knockers to throw through their owners' windows – one landed on the pillow of the baker's wife, missing her head by inches. Even more lawless was the riot organised by the Honourable E.S. Plunkett of the 86th Regiment to rescue his friend, the Honourable Adolphus Fraser, who had been arrested for debt.[14]

In comparison, the 'Brent Affair' was exaggerated out of all proportion, with Cardigan deserving little of the opprobrium he received. For until provoked by Brent's insistence on receiving 'satisfaction', he seems to have displayed, for him, remarkable moderation and good sense. He also showed, by his willingness to fight a duel on their behalf, a marked loyalty to his six officers, although three of them would later turn against him.

In February 1840, Cardigan was given, in his own words, 'the honour of escorting with the Regiment Prince Albert of Saxe-Coburg on his landing in this country to marry the Queen'. A first cousin of Victoria's – his father was her mother's brother – they had become engaged the previous October after she, as etiquette demanded, had proposed. She described the moment in her journal:

> I said to him that I thought he must be aware *why* I wished them to come here, and that it would make me *too happy* if he would consent to what I wished (to marry me); we embraced each other over and over again, and he was *so* kind, *so* affectionate; Oh! to *feel* I was, and am, loved by such an *Angel* as Albert was *too great a delight* to *describe!* he is *perfection*; perfection in every way – in beauty – in everything! I told him I was quite unworthy of him and kissed his dear hand – he said he would be very happy *'das Leben mit dir zu zubringen'* and was so kind and seemed so happy, that I really felt it was the happiest brightest moment of my life, which made up for all I had suffered and endured.[15]

On 7 February, sea-sick from a stormy five-hour crossing, Prince Albert and his elder brother, Prince Ernest, landed at Dover where a huge cheering crowd had gathered on the quay. They were met by Major Rotton and an escort of 100 light dragoons, among them the recently promoted Corporal Loy Smith whose greatest memory is not of the honour but the discomfort:

> It was a most wretched march, the weather being very cold and a drizzling rain falling nearly the whole way. We were wet through, not being allowed to cloak. On arriving at Dover about 11 am, we dismounted on the beach. Here we waited over two hours, till the Prince was ready to start, during which time we fed our horses but nothing was provided for us, nor were we allowed to leave our horses to get anything. We then escorted the Prince through Dover and as far as the windmill on Barham Downs; another escort of the 11th was here waiting that escorted the Royal Party to the Fountain Hotel, Canterbury . . . The rain now came down faster, and we cloaked and proceeded on our march back. It was quite dark before we arrived at Canterbury; we were completely saturated. What with hunger, cold and being wet through, this without exception was the most wretched day I ever spent during

the 26 years I was in the regiment. Major Rotton, in preventing us from having any refreshment, was only carrying out Lord Cardigan's orders.[16]

Despite the weather, Prince Albert was delighted with his escort's turn-out and told Lord Cardigan so when he and his brother dined with the officers of the regiment in Canterbury that evening. The following morning, another escort from the 11th Light Dragoons took the princes as far as Sittingbourne, where a detachment of Life Guards took over.

Two days later, the wedding took place in the Chapel Royal at St James's Palace. Cardigan was not invited, mainly on the strength of his politics. Devoted to the Whig Prime Minister, Lord Melbourne, the Queen had packed her court with nobles of a similar disposition. Out of a total of 300 guests, Greville counted just five Tories, including the Duke of Wellington who had only been invited at Melbourne's insistence.

Mollified by the fact that most of the greatest Tory nobles in the land had not been asked, and anxious to build on his good relations with the Queen's new husband, Cardigan applied to the Horse Guards for his regiment to be accorded the honour of being renamed the 11th (Prince Albert's Own) Hussars. The matter was settled during dinner at Windsor Castle on 7 March, when Lord Melbourne told the Queen that neither he nor Lord Hill could 'see any objection' to the request, and that Prince Albert might 'at some future time' be given command of the regiment. 'Talked of Lord Cardigan having a hot temper,' the Queen noted in her journal, 'but having got the regiment into excellent order.' Melbourne added that Cardigan had the advantage of being 'not very violent against us in politics' and that he 'did nothing but speak good of Albert'.[17]

Cardigan was notified of the decision by a letter from John Macdonald, the Adjutant-General, dated 12 March 1840. 'Her Majesty,' it read, 'has been graciously pleased to direct that the Eleventh Regiment of Light Dragoons shall be armed, clothed, and equipped as Hussars, and styled the "Eleventh", or "Prince Albert's Own Hussars".' This meant the replacement of the old uniform – shako (peaked, cylindrical hat), scarlet light dragoon jacket and blue overalls – with one said to have been designed by Prince Albert himself. It comprised a busby (nine-inch fur cap, topped by a crimson bag and a white plume), a single-breasted blue jacket profusely laced with yellow worsted cord and braid (gold for the officers), blue pelisses (mantles usually worn over one shoulder) similarly decorated and trimmed with imitation lambswool (fur for the officers), and crimson overalls with twin yellow stripes on the outside seam (gold for the officers). It was these dazzling trousers that gave birth to the regimental nickname: 'Cherry-bums'.[18]

Given that the new uniform was made by a Bond Street tailor, it is easy to believe the rumour that Cardigan contributed the enormous sum of £10,000 a year towards the cost of clothing and mounting his regiment. So intricate was the uniform's design that it was not ready to wear until midsummer; this gave the men enough time to grow that other symbol of hussar (and Life Guard) privilege: a moustache.

A further indication of royal favour was given when Prince Albert's brother, Ernest, heir to the dukedom of Saxe-Coburg, accepted an invitation to stay at Deene Park. Accompanied by, among others, the Barons de Grubin and de Lowenfels, Colonel Anson and Lord Alfred Paget, the Queen's equerry, the prince arrived in Northampton on Wednesday 18 March, to a 'very cordial' reception and the ringing of church bells. As the guests of Lord Chesterfield, they breakfasted at the George Hotel before enjoying a day out with the Pytchley.

That evening the royal party was welcomed at Deene by Lord Cardigan and the 'splendid band' of the 11th Hussars. Among the fashionable guests already there were Lord Adolphus Fitzclarence, Lord and Lady Ernest Brudenell-Bruce, Lady George Lennox and Maria, the beautiful Marchioness of Ailesbury. Lady Cardigan's cousin, Maria had married a man three times her age and was destined to become, if she was not already, Cardigan's lover.[19]

For the remainder of the week Deene Park was the 'scene of magnificent hospitality'. On Thursday, Cardigan and his guests hunted with Lord Lonsdale's Cottesmore, enjoying runs of 55 and 80 minutes and two kills, after the first of which the prince was presented with the brush. The following day they made the long journey to Rolleston, east Leicestershire, to ride with Thomas Assheton-Smith's celebrated foxhounds. According to the *Northampton Herald*, the scene 'was one of the gayest, and most animated ever witnessed in the county', with 'upwards of 2,000 horsemen, and about four-and twenty carriages, several with four horses, in one of which was the beautiful Lady Ailesbury'.

Yet this huge field, including the Duke of Leeds and at least fifty other noblemen, was kept waiting for more than an hour by the late arrival of Cardigan and his royal party, during which time one 'fine fox went scampering off' unpursued. Eventually a second was found, leading to a fine run over beautiful country that came to a premature end when the scent was lost. Under the circumstances, Assheton-Smith's hounds had 'hunted magnificently, showing what they could have done' had the scent 'been good'.[20]

Then on 30 April, to cap a perfect two months, the Horse Guards announced that Prince Albert would replace Major-General Philpot as honorary Colonel of the 11th Hussars.

But beneath the surface all was far from well with Lord Cardigan's regiment. Despite Lieutenant Tuckett's departure, the officers' mess was still displaying signs of disharmony. The main reason was said to be Cardigan's insulting behaviour towards officers who had served in India. 'I have learnt to know', stated one such officer, Captain John Reynolds, 'that the expression "Indian Officer" is meant as a term of reproach by his lordship. That it is so, the number of times his lordship has used it to various Officers sufficiently prove . . . [It] is subversive of good feeling and unanimity, to reproach men with having served in any country where they were ordered, and in this manner to create a distinction between officers of the same regiment.'[21]

There is little doubt that Cardigan identified officers who had seen long service in India as being often lax in their duty and possessed of ungentlemanly habits such as the drinking of porter. Undoubtedly, there was also an element of snobbery in that rich, well-connected officers tended to avoid foreign service. But not all who did go were impecunious, and while Cardigan undoubtedly used the term 'Indian' as a reproach he could just as easily treat the recipient with favour on another occasion. The two men who became his most bitter protagonists – Captains Richard and John Reynolds – came from rich gentry backgrounds and were part of the group of six officers whom he had so stoically defended over the 'Brent Affair'. Richard Reynolds, the senior captain, had been included in the party of officers invited to Deene in October 1838, while his cousin John Reynolds, 24, had become a troop captain on Cardigan's recommendation after just five years' service.

Even so, between Cardigan's assumption of command in October 1837 and the summer of 1840, an unprecedented 19 officers either sold out or exchanged into other regiments. Some, like Lieutenant Tuckett and Major Morse Cooper, would give the reason as an unwillingness to serve under Cardigan; most of the others remained silent as to their motives for leaving. However, the social status of the replacement officers did seem to be on the rise. Men of high station like John Douglas, Inigo Jones and the future Sir Charles Jenkinson of Hawkesbury had already joined; the Honourable Gerard Noël, son of Lord Gainsborough, and the future Lord Colville were among the later recruits. But as Cardigan's command of the 15th Hussars had proved, an officer did not have to have served in the sub-continent to be singled out for persecution; nor, in the future, would good breeding necessarily make him immune.[22]

The showdown with the so-called 'Indian' faction came on 18 May 1840, during a mess dinner in honour of General Sleigh, Inspector-General of Cavalry. Earlier that day Sleigh had carried out his half-yearly review of the regiment and had expressed himself thoroughly satisfied with all he had seen. The dinner, therefore, was something of a celebra-tion, comprising the choicest 'delicacies of the season'; to wash them down, General Sleigh had requested that only the 'mess ordinary wines' be placed on the table in crystal decanters. During the meal, however, cham-pagne was called for and offered 'to one or two foreign gentlemen, guests of Lord Cardigan, who partook of it'. Seeing the champagne, and assum-ing that it was all right to call for an alternative drink, Captain John Reynolds asked for Moselle and a mess-waiter provided it, as usual, in a black bottle. But instead of charging the glasses and taking the bottle away, at Reynolds' request he placed it on the table.

Spotting the black bottle amidst the gleaming silver and glittering crys-tal, Cardigan assumed it was porter and was beside himself with rage. Once again 'Indian' habits had invaded the mess and disgraced the regi-ment – and in front of the Inspector-General of all people! But anxious not to spoil the dinner, he decided to wait until the following day to deal with the perpetrator. Even when informed that the bottle contained Moselle, not porter, he would not be appeased; only decanted wines were fit to grace such a dinner.

Next morning, on Cardigan's instructions, Captain Inigo Jones spoke to Reynolds: 'The Colonel has desired me, as president of the mess commit-tee, to tell you that you were very wrong in having a black bottle placed on the table at a great dinner like last night, as the mess should be con-ducted like a gentleman's table, and not like a tavern or pot-house.'

Astonished at this rebuke, Reynolds made no reply but immediately went to see Cardigan and 'received no satisfactory answer' to his com-plaint. He then confronted Captain Jones in the mess-room, in the presence of Captain Forrest and a guest, Captain Carmichael Smyth of the 93rd Highlanders.

'Captain Jones,' said Reynolds, 'I wish to speak to you about the message you brought to me this morning. In the first place, I do not think you were justified in giving it at all; as a brother Captain, having no possible control over me, it would have been better taste if you had declined to deliver it.'

'I received it from the commanding officer, and as such I gave it, and if you refuse to receive it from me, I will report it,' replied Jones defensively.

'Do not misunderstand me, Captain Jones,' came the cold response, 'I have received, and do receive it, but the message was an offensive one; and I tell you, once for all, that in future I will not allow you or any man to bring me offensive messages.'

'If I am ordered to give a message, I shall give it.'

'Well, you may do as you please, but if you bring me improper messages you must take the consequences,' said Reynolds.

The threat of a duel was implicit, but Jones was equal to the challenge, saying he 'should certainly do so' before leaving the room to report the matter to Cardigan. Soon after, Reynolds was summoned to the orderly room; already there were Cardigan, Jones, Major Jenkins and the adjutant, Lieutenant Knowles. Cardigan was literally foaming at the mouth.

'If you cannot behave quietly, sir, why don't you leave the regiment,' he shouted. 'This is just the way with you "Indian" officers, you think you know everything. But I tell you, sir, that you neither know your duty nor discipline. Oh yes! You do know your duty, I believe, but you have no idea whatever of discipline, and do not at all justify my recommendation.'

Reynolds did not reply, making Cardigan even angrier. 'Well, I put you in arrest,' he declared.

Realising that the matter had got way out of hand, Jones tried to calm the situation by offering Reynolds his hand.

'No, Captain Jones, I will not shake hands with you,' said Reynolds. 'Nothing has passed which renders it necessary; I have no quarrel with you, and deny having insulted you, and see no reason why I should shake hands with you, or the contrary.'

'But I say you have insulted Captain Jones,' interrupted Cardigan.

'I have not, my lord.'

'Well, I put you under arrest, and shall report the matter to Horse Guards.'

'I am sorry for it,' replied Reynolds, before taking his leave.

Next day, under close arrest in his room, Reynolds was told that he would face two charges: for 'telling Captain Jones in an insulting and threatening manner, that, if he brought any more such messages from

Lord Cardigan, he would hold him personally responsible, or words to that effect'; and 'for refusing to accept' Captain Jones's hand.

On 21 May, Cardigan sent for Captain Forrest to confirm Jones's version of events. But Forrest was an 'Indian' officer and a friend of Reynolds, and was unlikely to say anything to implicate him. Asked if Reynolds' manner to Jones had been insulting, Forrest replied: 'Certainly not!'

'Good God! Captain Forrest,' exclaimed Cardigan, 'is it possible that your view of the subject can be so different from Captain Jones's?'

There was no reply. The following day, Reynolds was allowed two hours' exercise in the barrack yard, the first since his arrest on the 19th. Next morning, Cardigan travelled to the Horse Guards and reported the incident to Adjutant-General Macdonald. The response, in the form of a memorandum, was read out to Reynolds by Cardigan on Monday, 25 May. Lord Hill had been informed of the details and 'was pleased . . . to afford Captain Reynolds an opportunity of acknowledging his error, before the case should be officially reported in writing by his Commanding Officer'. Lord Cardigan, in the presence of Majors Rotton and Jenkins, was to express to Reynolds 'Lord Hill's hope, that':

> . . . upon mature reflection, he will be sensible of the great impropriety of his conduct throughout the discussion which led to his being placed in arrest, towards both Lord Cardigan . . . and Captain Jones; that he will promptly and cordially acknowledge that impropriety towards the former . . . and that he will, at the same time, declare his readiness to resume his friendly intercourse with Captain Jones, towards whom he has behaved in a most insubordinate and unbecoming manner, more particularly in holding out a threat of personal responsibility to his Senior Officer; conduct, which Lord Hill will think himself bound to meet with the strongest censure, if brought officially before him.

In his written reply, Reynolds stated that while he had 'no possible hesitation in at once most fully and willingly complying with Lord Hill's wishes', he also wished to state his case. He had not refused to receive Cardigan's original message, nor had he threatened Jones for bringing it 'however annoying the imputation of having made the mess a tavern' was to his 'feelings as a gentleman'. It was Jones saying in 'an offensive manner' that 'he always would bring me any message he was ordered' that had caused him to reply 'you will take the consequences if you do'. Reynolds then referred to the slur of being called 'an Indian Officer' and the suggestion that he leave the regiment, as well as the fact that he had been confined without exercise for three days. But, he concluded, he was prepared 'to waive consideration of all these points, as Lord Hill had so clearly pointed out the line of conduct' he ought to pursue:

> I, therefore, beg to express my sense of the insubordination of my conduct in having threatened my superior Officer, and my regret to . . . the Earl of Cardigan . . . for having done so. I also beg to say that I am perfectly ready and willing to remain on the same terms of friendly intercourse with Captain Jones as I was before this occurrence.

The letter was a masterpiece of ambiguity. While undoubtedly an apology, it contained so many qualifications as to make the resumption of normal relations between the officers involved impossible. It contained criticisms of both Cardigan and Jones, and ended by implying that he had never been on friendly terms with the latter anyway, and was happy for their relations to remain in this state. Naturally, Cardigan was outraged, and told Reynolds so in a stormy private interview that lasted two hours. Finally, in exasperation, Cardigan asked if he was prepared to shake hands with Jones. Reynolds refused.

'Will you drink wine with him?'

'Certainly, my lord.'

Would he do so a second time, asked Cardigan. Certainly, Reynolds replied. 'If a gentleman asks me to drink with him, I shall ask him again.'

Cardigan then tried to pin him down to a time: today? in a week?

'I will ask him in no specified time.'

With Reynolds stubbornly refusing to make a gesture of friendship towards Jones – as Lord Hill had surely intended that he would – Cardigan closed the interview, telling Reynolds that he was releasing him from close arrest but that he would still be under 'arrest at large'. A report was immediately despatched to Horse Guards, quickly followed by a protest from Reynolds. On 27 June, Cardigan received Lord Hill's response in the form of a letter from Adjutant-General Macdonald. The Commander-in-Chief had read both letters and much regretted 'that Captain Reynolds should have persisted in so qualifying his concessions upon this occasion, as to render it incumbent upon you to continue that officer in arrest'.

However, Reynolds was to be given 'a sufficient opportunity of explaining his conduct'.

That same day, Reynolds composed his explanation. He had, he wrote, 'made an unqualified concession to the wishes of Lord Hill, with perfect integrity of purpose, and without the slightest mental reservation'. He had told Lord Cardigan that he was 'perfectly prepared to meet Captain Jones', tell him he 'had no quarrel with him', and that he was 'ready and willing to remain on the same terms of friendly intercourse with him' as he had been 'previous to this occurrence'. He had refused to shake hands with Jones because it would be tantamount to 'allowing' he had had a quarrel with him, which he had not. Furthermore, he had never 'been on such terms of intimacy with Captain Jones as to warrant . . . shaking hands with him'. By keeping him under arrest for nine days, and by pressing him 'to extremity', Cardigan had treated him 'unkindly and harshly'. In conclusion, he was throwing himself 'on the clemency and the protection' of the Commander-in-Chief.

Hill was unimpressed and, while he ordered Reynolds' release on 29 May, it was 'with a censure upon his conduct'. Here the affair might have ended if Henry Harvey, guardian of the orphaned Reynolds, had not encouraged his ward to appeal to Lord Hill a second time on 4 June. Hill responded to Reynolds' claim that Cardigan's conduct throughout had been 'arbitrary, unjust, and offensive to the feelings of a gentleman' by despatching General Sleigh to Canterbury. In front of the assembled officers, Sleigh read out a letter from Hill, 'condemning Captain Reynolds' conduct in very strong language, approving of Lord Cardigan's throughout, in every particular, and stigmatising Captain Reynolds' *motives* as *pernicious and vindictive*, and refusing a Court Martial, because many things would be brought to light which would not be for the good of the service'. Sleigh added, on his own behalf, that Reynolds had 'forfeited the sympathy of every officer of rank in the service'.

Henry Harvey was outraged and wrote in turn to Hill, Thomas Macaulay, Secretary-at-War, Lord Melbourne and Prince Albert, requesting a court-martial or an inquiry to give his ward an opportunity of clearing his name. From each came a dusty response: Hill would not 'enter into correspondence' with a civilian on a matter of 'military discipline' which had 'now been finally disposed of'. Macaulay and the prince pointed out that discipline was the responsibility of the Commander-in-Chief, while Melbourne merely acknowledged receipt of Harvey's letter.

For the moment, at least, Captain Reynolds would have to suffer Hill's censure in silence.[23]

It was not until the autumn of 1840, in the wake of two further scandals involving Lord Cardigan, that a detailed account of the 'Black Bottle Affair', including all the correspondence, was first published in *The Globe* newspaper. Harvey was almost certainly the source, though he later denied this. The *Morning Chronicle* copied the heavily anti-Cardigan article word for word, provoking a series of letters less than complimentary to both Cardigan and Sleigh. One, signed 'An Officer of Rank' and sent from the United Service Club, rejected Sleigh's comment on 9 June that Reynolds had 'forfeited the sympathy of every officer of rank in the service', adding that the 'sympathies of *fifteen hundred veteran officers* in this Club are decidedly on the side of Captain Reynolds'.

Another, signed 'An Officer of the 11th Hussars', noted that had Sleigh 'done his duty faithfully and impartially' when sent down to inquire into quarrels between Cardigan and his officers, 'instead of abetting and encouraging him in his tyrannical proceedings', Cardigan 'might, perhaps, have been checked' and the 'present deplorable state of this corps averted'.

A third, signed 'A Civilian', denounced 'young men of family and fortune' who entered the Army not to share its 'dangers and honours in the field', but 'because their parents and guardians think it more respectable that they should belong to some profession than to none'. The postscript added that he 'always' had 'such wines as Moselle, Hock, Sauterne' in 'black bottles' at his table, and that he had seen them '*at* the tables of noblemen equal to Lord Cardigan both in rank and fortune, in their *native* bottles'.[24]

A letter slightly more favourable to Cardigan appeared in the *United Service Gazette*. The correspondent, 'AZ', noted that there was 'not a mess in the service where, on a public occasion, such as an inspection dinner, it would not have been an act of gross irregularity and in defiance of all rule, that an individual should call for private wine'. So 'in reproving Captain Reynolds, Lord Cardigan was strictly doing what it would have been gross neglect to have omitted'. The fact that an 'officer of experience' would probably 'have done it better' was indicative of the failings of the purchase system 'which had placed two men in situations which should have been better filled'.[25]

Perhaps the most damaging letter came from Harvey himself, and was printed in *The Times* on 6 October. It explained how Reynolds and Cardigan had first fallen out:

> A regimental court-martial having taken place, of which my ward, Captain John Reynolds was a member, the sentence on revision was not in accordance with his lordship's wishes. Soon afterwards Captain (then Lieutenant) Reynolds applied for leave of absence, when Lord Cardigan answered, 'No, sir, I will not give you leave; how can you expect me to do so when you oppose me?' And on being asked in what manner Lt. Reynolds opposed him, Lord Cardigan said, 'You were a member of the court-martial, which would not revise its sentence according to my wishes.'[26]

Many people could not take the affair so seriously, however, preferring to ridicule members of the regiment, but they did so at their peril. A drunk who, on passing two privates in the high road at Kensington-Gore, shouted 'Prince Albert's Black Bottles!', was set upon by them and given a sound thrashing. Charged with assault, one of the privates got off with a three-shilling fine after his corporal had testified to his 'most excellent character' and the fact that 'soldiers of the regiment were subject to daily annoyance by being called after whenever they appeared in public streets and roads: "There goes one of Cardigan's black bottles," or "There goes Prince Albert's cherry bums".' Their tormentor, on the other hand, was fined five shillings for drunkenness.

No event in Cardigan's military career better illustrates his extraordinary ability to provoke confrontation, to turn a petty incident into a major issue, than the 'Black Bottle Affair'. For this his injudicious language bears much of the responsibility. On the other hand, Reynolds was undoubtedly guilty of provocation, knowing as he did that Cardigan did not approve of undecanted wine at the mess table, particularly during a grand dinner. Furthermore, Reynolds could have brought the matter to a close before it got out of hand by agreeing to shake hands with Captain Jones, but he petulantly chose not to do so.

The majority of the press, and most commentators, took Reynolds' part because they saw Cardigan's behaviour as confirmation that he should never have been reappointed to command a regiment. A legacy of the over-reaction to the 'Wathen Affair', such a viewpoint was grossly one-sided, ignoring as it did Reynolds' part in the quarrel.

★

On 23 June, the 11th Hussars marched to new barracks in Brighton and Chichester. Notwithstanding the 'Brent Affair', the residents of Canterbury were sad to see them go. In an address to Lord Cardigan, the town corporation paid 'humble tribute' to his and his officers' 'noble, courteous, and gentlemanly bearing', and to 'the meritorious and respect-ful deportment of the men'. 'Deeply' did it regret their departure, 'indelibly' would the 'gratifying recollection' of their residence be impressed upon the minds of the citizens.

In his response, Cardigan could not resist a dig at Brent and his like. By their good conduct, his men had 'given another proof of their being worthy of those high honours which have recently been conferred on the regiment by Her Most Gracious Majesty the Queen, and that they are not unmindful of that very important duty of living upon terms of harmony and good fellowship with the *respectable* citizens among whom they may be ordered to be stationed'.[27]

But the 11th Hussars had no regrets because, agreeable as Canterbury had been, it offered few of the diversions of Brighton, the provincial cap-ital of society. Formerly, the spa town of Bath had reigned supreme, but by the turn of the century its greatest days were over. The writing was on the wall as early as 1783, when the Prince of Wales chose Brighton as his summer residence. He found that bathing in its sea-water, noted for its healing properties, gave him relief from swollen throat glands. The fact that he was both the heir to the throne and the leader of taste and fashion meant that society flocked to join him. By 1818, 51 coaches a day ran between London and Brighton, at a cost of just six shillings a person and a journey time of five hours. Between 1801 and 1831, the size of the town increased sixfold to almost 8,000 houses. A lull followed the death of George IV, but the opening of the London-to-Brighton railway in 1841 gave the expansion fresh impetus.

When Cardigan and his regiment arrived in Brighton in the summer of 1840, the town was nearing its zenith of popularity. Although the official Season had shifted from the summer to the autumn and winter, and people came generally to take the air rather than to bathe, society still flocked to Brighton in droves. Every afternoon they would indulge in 'carriage airing' by driving up and down the front from Kemp Town to Brunswick Terrace, acknowledging their friends and cutting those outside society. It was a world in which Cardigan and his officers, staying in the Royal York Hotel, felt instantly at home. But to be able to entertain on a scale expected of an earl and a commanding officer, Cardigan needed more spacious premises, and he and his wife soon took a town house in fashionable Brunswick Square.

They had a number of notable neighbours there. In nearby Brunswick Terrace was a house owned by the Earl of Munster, the eldest son of William IV and Dorothy Jordan, and the brother of Lord Adolphus Fitzclarence. Unable to come to terms with his illegitimacy, he shot himself in 1842. Living in Brunswick Square itself were Admiral Sir George Westphal, a midshipman on board the *Victory* at the battle of Trafalgar who had witnessed Nelson's death; George Basevi, Disraeli's uncle; and Captain Richard Heaviside, a local magistrate and director of the London-to-Brighton Railway.

In March 1840, Heaviside's wife of sixteen years had abandoned her three children and eloped to Paris with the Reverend Dionysius Lardner, the well-known scientist and author. Traced to an apartment in rue Tronchet, the lovers were confronted at breakfast by Heaviside and his father-in-law, Colonel Spicer. A powerful man standing 6ft 6ins, Heaviside hauled Lardner out of his chair and administered a thrashing so severe that his victim was forced to escape by crawling under a piano. Pausing only to throw Lardner's wig on the fire, Heaviside then left with his wife. In August, at the Lewes Assizes, he brought an action against Lardner for 'criminal conversation' and was awarded the huge sum of £8,000 in damages. The marriage was dissolved in 1845, and four years later the former Mrs Heaviside married her lover.[28]

Unwelcome comparisons with Lord Cardigan's own betrothal were soon forgotten in the wake of a second 'Indian' officer scandal. This time it involved Captain Richard Reynolds, a cousin of John Reynolds (whom he called 'Jack'). Thirty-four years old, a veteran of 15 years' service who had witnessed the fall of Bhurtpore, he too had been the object of what he later described as Cardigan's 'very irritating and offensive' conduct. Not long after the regiment arrived in Brighton, he conveyed his disillusionment in a letter to a fellow officer and sympathiser, Henry Moysey:

> I am tired of soldiering under this mad man. Cardigan has grown very much more mad than he ever was and I do assure you that on Friday last at field day he ought to have been confined. He has got a notion into his head that the officers of the regiment are insubordinate and the way he tries to put a stop to this supposed insubordination is really ridiculous . . . I will not exchange for the present, but I am quite determined to quit the service, and cannot put up with the uncomfort of serving under Cardigan much

longer . . . Jack is very much out of spirits, and my going does not improve his.[29]

Matters came to a head over a comment made by Lord Cardigan during a party at his Brighton town house on Tuesday, 25 August. The guests included some fashionable ladies and a number of his officers, but not the Captains Reynolds. After dinner, more guests arrived to dance to the music of the regimental band, and Cardigan fell into conversation with a young lady, Miss Cunynghame. 'I do not see the Captains Reynolds present. Why is that?' she asked.

'Because I have not invited them,' came the gruff reply.

'Why did you not invite them?'

'Because I do not happen to be on good terms with them,' said Cardigan, pausing before adding, 'I am afraid that, if you are very anxious to see the Captains Reynolds, you are not likely to meet them in this house.'

What was said next is disputed. Cardigan's version is that Miss Cunynghame then asked why he was not on good terms with them, to which he replied: 'Oh, that is a very long story, and I do not wish to go into it all.'

A third-hand account, given to Captain Richard Reynolds, was that Cardigan closed the conversation with the words: 'They shall not come into my house as long as they live!'

The following day, Lieutenant John Cunningham of the 11th Hussars was listening to the regimental band in Sussex Square when he was approached by a lady who had been at the party the night before. 'What a very curious woman Mrs Cunynghame is,' she said.

'Why?' asked Cunningham.

'I heard her ask Lord Cardigan several times why the Captains Reynolds were not at the ball. He gave her no answer for some time. At last, he said, "They shall not come into my house as long as they live." I thought Mrs Cunynghame must have known that Lord Cardigan and the Captains Reynolds were not on good terms.'[30]

Although the identity of the questioner was wrong – it was *Miss* Cunynghame, not *Mrs* Cunynghame – the essence of the report was accurate. Whether Cardigan actually uttered the fateful words, 'They shall not come into my house as long as they live,' is unproven, although such a remark would hardly have been out of character. In any case, that is what was reported to Captain Richard Reynolds when he paid a chance visit to Lieutenant Cunningham's room that afternoon. According to Cunningham, Reynolds responded by laughing.

Later, however, when he mentioned the report to his cousin, Captain John Reynolds, he 'appeared to be in the strongest indignation', repeatedly expressing his opinion that it was calculated to 'injure' him. The following day he wrote privately to Lord Cardigan, neither addressing him by his military rank nor signing with his own:

> My Lord – A report has reached me that on Tuesday last, at a large party given by Your Lordship, when asked why the Captains Reynolds were not present, Your Lordship replied, 'As long as I live they shall never enter my house.' I cannot but consider this report highly objectionable, as it is calculated to convey an impression prejudicial to my character, and I therefore trust Your Lordship will be good enough to authorise me to contradict it.

That Reynolds was willing to write such a letter on the basis of a third-hand report is indicative of how bad relations were between himself and Cardigan. He said later that he had had no option, 'that such report, uncontradicted, was calculated to rob me of my good name, and that it would injure me in my station in society'. But in his letter to Moysey, he had stated that he could 'not put up with the uncomfort of serving under Cardigan much longer', and it may be that the letter was a deliberate attempt to goad Cardigan into an injudicious response that would result in one or other of them being cashiered. Either way, they would no longer have to serve together. Cardigan certainly suspected that Reynolds was trying to provoke a duel and so made no written reply, affairs of honour between a commanding officer and his subordinate being strictly forbidden.

Next morning – Friday, 28 August – Cardigan confronted Captain Reynolds during field exercise on Brighton racecourse. Bidding Reynolds, Captain Inigo Jones and Adjutant Knowles to follow him, Cardigan rode 150 yards ahead of the regiment before saying: 'Captain Reynolds, I have received your communication of yesterday, to which I shall give no reply, as I consider your letter an improper one to write to me; and further, I desire that, when you do, your letters will be strictly official and addressed to me as the Commanding Officer, affixing your rank to the letter.'

Knowing full well the practice of Lord Cardigan 'to compel the silence of officers upon any observation made by him to them when called out of the ranks in front of the regiment', Reynolds held his tongue; but he was boiling inside as Cardigan dismissed the officers with a wave of his hand. Early that afternoon, when Reynolds bumped into Captain Jones outside the Pavilion stables, Jones told him that he had seen his first letter and that it was 'not', in his opinion, 'a proper letter to write'. Advising him not to write any more, 'for if he did he would lose his commission', he 'begged' him 'to sleep over it before he did a desperate thing'.

Reynolds thanked him but said that Cardigan 'had, by his conduct, grossly insulted' him, and that he had 'made up his mind' on what action to take. That afternoon he wrote a second letter to Cardigan, ignoring the latter's request to be addressed officially and with military rank:

> My Lord – Having in my letter to your Lordship of yesterday stated to your Lordship that a report had reached me that your Lordship had spoken of me in such a manner as I deemed prejudicial to me, considering the position in which I am placed, and having in the most respectful manner requested your Lordship to allow me to contradict such report, and your Lordship having this morning positively refused to give me any answer, I must beg to tell your Lordship that you are in no wise justified in speaking of me at all at a public party given by your Lordship, and more particularly in such a manner as to make it appear that my conduct has been such as to exclude me from your Lordship's house. Such assertion is calculated to injure me. Your Lordship's reputation as a professed duellist, founded on having sent Major Jenkins to offer satisfaction to Mr. Brent, the miller, at Canterbury, and your having sent Capt. Forrest to London to call out an attorney's clerk, does not admit of your privately offering insult to me, and then screening yourself under the cloak of Commanding-Officer; and I must be allowed to tell your Lordship, that it would far better become you to select a man whose hands are untied for the object of your Lordship's vindictive reproaches; or to act as many a more gallant fellow than yourself has done, and waive that rank which your wealth and Earldom alone entitle you to hold.

Amazingly, Cardigan did not rise to the bait and accept the implicit offer of a duel. Instead he calmly ordered Reynolds' arrest and despatched a report to the Horse Guards. Lord Hill responded immediately: Reynolds would face a court-martial and Cardigan would prosecute. The charge was conduct 'unbecoming an officer and a gentleman, prejudicial to the interests of the service, subversive of good order and military discipline'.[31]

8

Intent to Murder

On 4 September 1840, a particularly venomous letter attacking Cardigan appeared in the *Morning Chronicle*. Addressed to 'The Officers of the Army' and signed 'An Old Soldier', it drew attention to the fact that Cardigan had 'some time since grossly and wantonly insulted an officer at the mess-table', and when called to account had 'pleaded his privilege as a commanding officer'. A second insult had led to 'charges' being 'sent in against his lordship for "conduct arbitrary, unjust, and offensive to the feelings of a gentleman"', but they had been ignored.

> Lord Cardigan [it continued] has now insulted the senior captain
> of the regiment – *a private insult*; and, when called upon for redress,
> has again claimed the privileges as commanding officer, and placed
> Captain ———— in arrest for resenting such insult. Many a gallant
> officer has waived the privilege which nothing but wealth and an
> earldom obtained for Lord Cardigan.

The letter ended with a call for an inquiry, and the hope 'that it may no longer be imagined that a commanding officer may outrage every gentlemanly feeling of those under his command with impunity'.[1]

Given that only details of the second Reynolds affair had by this time reached the press, and the letter was signed 'An Old Soldier', Cardigan immediately suspected Harvey Tuckett, who was still in contact with some of his officers. He received confirmation in a matter of days when he was 'informed upon good authority that the Editor of the *Morning Chronicle* had stated that Mr Tuckett was the author'. At last his hands were free. Tuckett was no longer a serving officer, and to fight a duel with him would not be contrary to the Articles of War. That it contravened the civil law of the land either did not occur to him or was considered of no import.

Tuckett was working as an agent for the East India Company at this time, and on 11 September Captain John Douglas arrived at his office in the Poultry to demand 'satisfaction' for Lord Cardigan. Admitting to being the author of the letter, Tuckett asked for time to go into the country to consult his friend, Captain Henry Wainright. The following day Wainright met Douglas and requested in writing the reason for the duel. At 2.30 p.m., Douglas handed him a note from Cardigan stating that 'many parts' of Tuckett's letter 'contained matters entirely false, and the whole of it was slanderous, insulting and calumnious'. The duel was fixed for 5 o'clock that afternoon on Wimbledon Common.[2]

Shortly before the appointed hour, a post-chaise containing Tuckett and Wainright arrived in the northern corner of the Common. Soon after, a second post-chaise drew up a short distance away, out of which climbed Cardigan, Douglas and Sir James Anderson, Cardigan's surgeon. With Anderson hanging back, the parties advanced towards each other. The seconds, both carrying a case of duelling pistols, met on a piece of open ground where they knelt to charge the guns. Then, standing back to back with a gun in each hand, they marked out six paces before beckoning the principals forward. Handing the weapons over, they moved a little way to the side.

Cardigan now faced Tuckett, his body side-on, his pistol pointing towards the ground. At the command, both raised their arms and fired. Neither shot struck home and Cardigan threw his pistol away before walking up to Douglas to rearm. Tuckett did likewise. A second signal was given and, almost simultaneously, both fired. Again Cardigan was unscathed, but Tuckett had been hit, the ball shattering the upper part of his right hip-bone before exiting close to his spine. Seeing him stagger, Anderson rushed forward.

At that moment, Thomas Dann and his son arrived on the scene. Proprietor of a mill a couple of hundred yards away, Dann had been appointed as the parish constable to intervene on just such an occasion. He had seen the carriages arrive and, but for a brief delay while he went indoors to collect his staff of office, might have prevented the damaging second shot. Ignoring the stricken but still standing Tuckett, he strode up to Cardigan, put a hand on his shoulder and announced that 'for a breach of the peace' he must consider himself in his custody, 'in the name of Her Majesty, Her Sovereign Lady, the Queen'. Then he relieved the astonished earl of his smoking pistol, turned to the others and declared that they, too, were under arrest. Anderson now intervened, requesting that the wounded gentleman be taken back to Dann's house where he could be treated. Dann agreed, pausing only to take possession of the other pistols and their cases.

After a brief time at the mill, Anderson asked if Tuckett could be allowed home and Dann acquiesced on the condition that he left his card. Anderson went with him, as did Wainright after writing his name and address on the back of Tuckett's card. Dann would later claim that he never gave Wainright permission to leave. Cardigan and Douglas were then escorted by Dann to the station-house of the Metropolitan Police at Wandsworth, where Inspector John Busain was on duty when a knock sounded at the door. Opening it, he noticed two gentlemen and bowed before asking them their business.

'I am a prisoner, I believe,' said Cardigan.

'Indeed, sir,' replied Busain, 'on what account?'

Walking past Busain into the station-house, Cardigan said: 'I have been fighting a duel, and I have hit my man. But not seriously, I believe, merely a graze across the back.' Pointing over his shoulder, he continued: 'This gentleman also is a prisoner; my second, Captain Douglas.'

Cardigan then took out one of his cards and handed it to Busain. The name was instantly recognisable as that of the notorious commanding officer of the 11th Hussars, who had recently arrested one of his own officers. Assuming that this man might have been his opponent, Busain asked: 'Not with Captain Reynolds, I hope?'

'Oh no, by no means,' Cardigan said disdainfully. 'Do you suppose that I would fight with one of my own officers?'

Dann then entered and handed over the two cases of pistols, one of which bore a silver crest which Cardigan identified as his own. It only remained for Busain to enter the charge in the ledger, before granting Cardigan and Douglas bail on condition that both appeared before magistrates the following Monday, 14 September.[3]

The hearing took place at Wandsworth Magistrates' Court, Church Row. Depositions were read by Dann, Busain and Anderson, the latter adding that he had visited Tuckett the day before and that his wound 'was looking well' and he was 'free from fever'; he considered him 'not dangerously wounded'. After a short consultation, the chairman of the magistrates announced that, as the case was 'one of a very serious nature, they could not be contented with ordinary recognizances': bail was set at £1,000 for Cardigan and £500 for Douglas.[4]

That evening the Queen discussed the duel over dinner at Windsor Castle. 'Talking to Ld Melbourne who sat next to me,' she wrote in her journal, 'of Cardigan's having had a duel with Lieut. Tuckett who had offended him by a letter in the papers. Cardigan shot him in the body, though he did not kill him. Talked of what Cardigan had done previously, & Ld. Hill having restored him very unwillingly. Consequently Ld. H. was sure to be in a great fuss about this.'

Details appeared in Wednesday's edition of *The Times*, and on the same day Cardigan's woes continued when *The Globe* printed the first full account of the 'Black Bottle Affair'. Reproducing the correspondence in its entirety, the article spilled over into the following day's edition. Beside himself with rage at the partiality of the report, Cardigan took it out on the nearest available target. It was probably no coincidence that the subject of his ire was Lieutenant William Forrest, the officer who had exchanged commissions with Tuckett, a close friend of the Captains Reynolds, and a man whom Cardigan was reputed to have said was too 'Indian' for promotion.[5]

In the afternoon of 17 September, Forrest locked his room in the cavalry barracks and rode into Brighton to relieve Lieutenant Cunningham on the Pavilion Guard. Normally, officers on such duty would give up their rooms in the barracks, as a temporary room was provided at the infantry barracks in nearby Church Street. But Forrest had only been posted there for a week and did not think it was necessary. At 5 p.m., he was hailed in the street by Lord Cardigan passing in his phaeton. 'What do you mean, sir, by locking your door and taking away your key?' Cardigan asked.

Forrest replied that he had certainly done so.

'Do you suppose, sir, that you can hold two rooms?'

'The room which I have locked is my own room, the one I will be occupying for the next week is a guard-room and it will be a great inconvenience to me having no room in barracks to dress in for mess and to retire to after mess,' explained Forrest.

'Oh! You mean to come the letter of the law with me, sir, do you,' said Cardigan threateningly. 'I can tell you this, sir, that were I to do so with you, I could find more faults than I do, which are now a great many. What were you doing in the mess-room this morning after the Stable Trumpet had sounded?'

Forrest replied that as he had neither stable nor servant at the Pavilion, he was obliged to bring his horse back to barracks himself, and that he had gone into the mess-room to get some breakfast.

'Do you suppose, sir, that it is necessary for an officer to eat after Field Exercise?'

Disdaining to answer the question, Forrest again explained the inconvenience he would have to face if he had to give up his room.

'Well, sir, I as commanding officer of this regiment order you to give up the key of your room and that instantly.'

Forrest saluted and withdrew.

About an hour later, Cardigan arrived at the Pavilion Stables accompanied by Adjutant Knowles. Lieutenant Jenkinson needed to use his room, he told Forrest, so what did he mean by locking his door? Forrest repeated what he had said earlier, adding that he did not forfeit his room in barracks whilst on duty at the Pavilion.

Cardigan exploded. 'This is some plan of yours, sir, and I would tell you that military lawyers do not get on in the service. I could understand you feeling inconvenienced if you had been accustomed to live in two or three suites of apartments at St James's. But, really, for a cavalry officer to require two rooms is ridiculous.'

Forrest replied that he had many things in his room that he needed; if he had been asked for the loan of his room he would have made no objection to allowing Lieutenant Jenkinson or any other officer into it.

'What . . .' stammered Cardigan, hardly able to speak because he was so angry, 'I . . . sir, as commanding officer, ask you for the loan of your room! Why, if I choose I can keep you down here for a month and you have no business to go into the barrack yard at all except for your breakfast and dinner. I again order you to give up the key to your room to Lieutenant Jenkinson before night, do you understand the order?'

'Yes,' Forrest replied.

But that did not mean that he intended to comply with it – which he did not – and when Cardigan learnt of this the following day he put him under arrest and, once again, a report was despatched to the Horse Guards. On 20 September, Lord Hill's reply reached Brighton; it strongly censured Forrest's conduct and ordered him to give up the key 'for the good of the service'. Forrest had no option but to comply, but later that day he sent a personal account of the episode to Hill, blaming Cardigan's 'offensive and irritating manner and language' for his unwillingness to surrender the key. As all correspondence with the Commander-in-Chief had to be forwarded by Cardigan, this was guaranteed to worsen relations between them.[6]

Although still officially supportive, the Horse Guards was rapidly losing patience with Cardigan. He was too quick to temper and could not be absolved of all responsibility for his repeated clashes with junior officers. On 29 September, Lord Fitzroy Somerset wrote to Colonel Richard Egerton, Lord Hill's private secretary, informing him that Adjutant-General Macdonald was 'sadly vexed and annoyed' about the duel, while he, Somerset, considered it 'an injudicious *complication*'. As far as the Forrest incident was concerned, both officers were to blame. 'Cardigan mismanaged this matter to my idea grossly,' he wrote, 'but it was too much of Lieutenant Forrest to complain of insulting language when he disobeyed an order before Lord Cardigan spoke to him at all.'

He added, gloomily: 'The hell hounds of the press are let loose upon Cardigan and the Horse Guards.'[7]

A nasty shock was in store for Lord Cardigan when he and Captain Douglas returned to London on Saturday, 19 September, to attend a second hearing at the Wandsworth Magistrates' Court, in connection with the duel with Harvey Tuckett. Since it was assumed that the charge would be for a breach of the peace, an excited buzz spread through the packed courtroom when the clerk announced that Cardigan was to be charged with 'shooting at Captain Harvey Tuckett with a pistol, with intent to murder him or do him some bodily harm'. Douglas was to be charged for aiding and abetting.

Asked by the chairman under what statute the offence would come, the clerk replied: '"1st Victoria, Cap. 85, Section 2", under which, amongst other offences, it was enacted that "Whosover shall stab, cut, or wound any person, or shall by any means whatsoever cause to any person any bodily injury, dangerous to life in such aforementioned case, with intent to commit murder, shall be deemed guilty of felony, and on conviction suffer death".' The public gasped, but Cardigan never altered his fixed expression.

After the witness depositions had once again been read out, the chairman announced that as one of the accused was 'a peer of the realm, it was rather a singular and peculiar case, and one with which they scarcely knew how to deal'. They had applied to the proper authorities for an opinion, and would not pass judgement until it had arrived. Therefore the accused would be released on the same bail to reappear nine days later. Cardigan pointed out that, on order of Lord Hill, he 'had very important business to attend to' (the court-martial of Richard Reynolds) which 'would occupy at least a week or ten days'. He was told curtly by Captain Page, the most hostile of the three magistrates, to 'organise his business' round his court appearance.

Earlier, during the hearing, Page had taken it upon himself to examine Cardigan's duelling pistols. A rumour had begun to circulate in the press that they had rifled barrels, thereby giving Cardigan an unfair advantage over Tuckett. But when Page put his finger into the muzzle, he could feel only smooth metal. 'You see they are not rifled,' said Cardigan.

'Yes, I perceive they are not,' Page replied.

According to Robert Baldick, author of *A History of Duelling*, rifling 'flouted the duelling code' and 'was strictly forbidden, but unscrupulous duellists circumvented the ban by using pistols which were rifled at the breech end but not at the muzzle'. Inspected by an amateur, such weapons would escape detection. Page was well aware of this, and to be certain he asked Inspector Busain to send one of each pair to Mr Parker, a well-known Holborn gunsmith. With Parker away, the examination was carried out by his deputy, John Field. Once in possession of the results, Busain wrote to Page: 'Capt. Tuckett's are of the commonest and plainest kind of duelling pistols. His Lordship's on the contrary, are of the best kind, with stop locks, hair triggers and French rifle barrels, rifled from the breech to about an inch from the muzzle, and will hit with unerring precision when fired by a steady hand.'[8]

On Monday, 28 September, Cardigan and Douglas made their third appearance before the Wandsworth magistrates. The Reynolds' court-martial had already begun, but Cardigan had managed to obtain an adjournment for the day. The charge, the clerk confirmed, was still 'shooting with a pistol at Captain Harvey Tuckett, with intent to murder or do him some bodily harm'. Dann was the first to be re-examined, followed by Sir James Anderson. The latter told the court that Tuckett's wound 'continues to heal rapidly', that 'his general health was good' and that he had given him 'permission to go down into the drawing-room'. He would be well enough to appear before the court in about two weeks.

Captain Wainright was then called, but Dann was unable to identify him as one of those present at the duel. Anderson, on the other hand, could confirm that he 'was one of the acting parties in the affair'. Finally

Mr Nottidge, the chairman, announced that although the case had been 'of a very painful nature', the Bench was 'of opinion a felony had been committed, and therefore that they should not do their duty to the country were they not to send the parties accused to trial'. All three were bound over to appear at the Old Bailey on 19 October. Cardigan's bail was set at £2,000; the other two at £1,000.

One other episode of note occurred during the hearing when Captain Page reopened the controversy over the pistols by reading out the letter from Field confirming that Cardigan's pair had both hair triggers and rifled barrels. Mr Nottidge and his fellow magistrate, Mr Wilson, insisted that this information was irrelevant to the charge, but Cardigan still leapt to his own defence. Denying both claims, he once again offered the pistols to the Bench for inspection, remarking that he had bought them from Mr Manton 'as common duelling pistols, and knew nothing more about them'. If there was any doubt, he said, why not call the maker 'who would say they were like every other brace of pistols which he sold'. 'Nobody,' Cardigan insisted, 'would think of fighting a duel with hair triggers.'[9]

On 1 October, Field responded to Cardigan's denial in a letter to the *Morning Chronicle*. The pistol belonging to Cardigan was made by John Manton, had 'a "French" or "fine scratch" rifle barrel, a detented, or what is more commonly known as a hair trigger and a bolted lock'. Tuckett's pistol was made by Samuel Nock, 'had a smooth inside, not rifled, and without hair triggers or bolt lock', and was of the 'usual duelling kind' though 'of the best manufacture'.

A couple of days later, the makers of Cardigan's pistols, Manton & Hudson of Dover Street, made a counter-claim in the same newspaper. Worried that the recent statement reporting the barrels as rifled 'may lead the public to suspect they were of peculiar make, and not the ordinary and usual kind of duelling pistols, and consequently, create an unfavourable impression against his lordship', they wished to certify that the pistols supplied to Lord Cardigan 'are in every aspect similar to other duelling pistols of their manufacture for the last half century'. Furthermore, they had been made 'previous to his lordship going to India, and no particular directions were given respecting them when ordered'.

This was, of course, far from being a flat denial of the claim that the guns possessed rifled barrels and hair triggers. The latter innovation, which enabled a duellist to get in his shot before his opponent, and with less disturbance of aim, had actually been developed by Manton, and by this time may well have been standard issue on their pistols. Rifled barrels, on the other hand, were considered to contravene the duellists' code of honour. Therefore, the most favourable interpretation that can be put on the whole business is that Cardigan asked Manton & Hudson to produce the *best* duelling pistols available without being specific, and that he was genuinely unaware that his guns possessed either innovation. It is, of course, possible that Cardigan knew about the rifling all along, and had deliberately sought to gain an advantage against anyone foolish enough to provoke him to a duel, but this scenario flies in the face of his undoubted preoccupation with 'honour'.[10]

Shortly before 11 a.m. in the morning of Friday, 25 September 1840, the court-martial of Captain Richard Reynolds opened in a hospital ward of the Brighton cavalry barracks.

Ranged behind a long table at the head of the room were the 15 members of the court: Major-General Sir Hercules Packenham, the president, eight colonels, two majors and four captains from various cavalry, infantry, artillery and guards regiments, 'all arrayed in the most gorgeous uniforms'.

Lord Cardigan and Sergeant Wrangham, the barrister he had engaged to prevent a repeat of the Wathen fiasco, were at a small table to their right. Opposite them sat Reynolds and his counsel, Sergeant Watson; he, too, was taking no chances. Though deprived of his sword, Reynolds still cut a dashing figure; while his countenance, reported *The Sun*, 'exhibits the deep bronzed colour of one who has been for many a year exposed to the burning rays of an Indian sun, still his figure and free buoyant action prove him to be one still possessed of all the vigour of youth. His hair and mustachios are jet black; and these, with the dark flashing eyes of one who has encountered many a peril (but so different from that to which he is now exposed), exhibit him to be what he is – a brave and gallant "Indian officer".'

Every extra available inch of space in the improvised courtroom was taken up by the press and public.

The charge – read by Major Pipon, the deputy judge-advocate – was for conduct 'unbecoming an officer and a gentleman, prejudicial to the interests of this service, subversive of good order and military discipline'. Reynolds had sent Lord Cardigan – in 'direct violation and disobedience' of an order that all future letters should be 'strictly official' – a 'most disrespectful, insubordinate, offensive, and insulting letter, imputing to him conduct calculated to excite him to depart from his duty as Commanding Officer'.

'Extremely agitated', according to *The Sun*, Cardigan opened for the prosecution by appealing to the court not to be swayed by the 'torrent of misrepresentation directed against him by the press, and against which, however gross, he was deprived of all defence by that positive order of the Service which prohibited any officer on full pay from communicating with the press' (though such a prohibition had not prevented him from doing just that in the past).

It was with 'no animosity, but with feelings distressing to himself, and only in obedience to the strictest dictates of duty', that he called the court's attention to the offence of which Captain Reynolds was accused. He then rapidly narrated the sequence of events, but became so 'very much excited' during the reading of Reynolds' second letter that he 'actually began to weep', uttering the last words 'in tones tremulous with feeling' before throwing the document on the table.

Next, Cardigan appeared as a witness, and in cross-examination Reynolds asked the court if he could put questions 'respecting the treatment to which' he 'was subjected at Brighton and Canterbury'. After clearing the room and taking advice from the deputy judge-advocate, the court decided that 'in putting his questions he must confine himself strictly to the charge under their consideration'. Technically the court was right: previous provocation is no justification for an offence; it is merely a mitigation as to sentence and should only be introduced after the verdict.

Stripped of this line of cross-examination, Reynolds had little option but to put the crucial question: 'Did you say to the young lady, in the conversation you have mentioned, "As long as they live they shall not enter my house"?'

'Certainly not,' came the predictable reply, albeit qualified by the words, 'to the best of my recollection.'

The rest of the day was taken up with the examination and cross-examination of the remaining prosecution witnesses, Captain Jones and Lieutenant Knowles, but – unlike in the Wathen trial – neither could be coaxed to say anything that was of benefit to Reynolds. By 4 p.m., the case for the prosecution was complete and the court adjourned until the following Tuesday, thereby enabling Cardigan to make his third appearance before the Wandsworth magistrates on the previous day.

In the event, the court only reconvened for a short time on Tuesday the 29th because Reynolds requested a further adjournment of two days to complete his defence. But it sat long enough for the president to chastise those newspapers which had ignored the ban on publicising the proceedings until the end of the trial. They were, he said, in contempt of court and he would be reporting the matter to the Judge-Advocate-General. While some newspapers heeded the warning, others like the *Brighton Guardian* continued their reporting regardless.

When Captain Reynolds arrived to begin his defence on 1 October, all classes of people were gathered round the doors of the barrack hospital 'to catch a glimpse' of the defendant 'whose manly bearing and bold open countenance it is difficult to see without being prepossessed in his favour', reported the *Brighton Herald*. Those who could not gain entry crowded at the windows.

Reynolds told the court that he had prepared 'a very large body of evidence . . . to prove that Lord Cardigan's conduct' towards him 'had been very irritating and offensive', but that it had already been ruled inadmissible. Now he would like to set out the reasons why he thought this ruling was wrong. In the first place, if he could show that the 'second letter was written under irritating conduct on the part of Lord Cardigan', the 'degree of irritation' would 'materially' affect his offence, if indeed he was guilty of one. And it followed 'that provoking and offensive conduct on this occasion' was to be 'measured' by Cardigan's 'conduct on other and former occasions'. This was also evidence that affected his 'guilt or innocence of the charge itself'.

Reynolds then turned to the alleged incident at the party. 'Lord Cardigan had a perfect right to choose his visitors; but neither as a man, nor a Commanding Officer, was he justified in saying that I should never enter his doors again; for that necessarily implies that I had been guilty of some improper, dishonourable, or immoral conduct . . . I owed it to myself, my family, and to my station, that such report should be speedily contradicted.'

His case could be summarised in a few words: 'I, the senior Captain of the regiment, respectfully solicit a denial from Lord Cardigan of a report affecting my character. He now says the report was untrue – he could, but would not deny it. In effect, he said I *can*; but I will *not* do an act of the commonest justice to an Officer of unimpeachable character under my command.'

Reynolds admitted that in his second letter there were 'strong and what, under other circumstances, might be considered offensive expressions'. But 'whether insolent or aggressive under the particular circumstances must be judged by the aggravating conduct of Lord Cardigan'.

He would call past and present officers from the regiment to prove that he had always been 'attentive' to duty and 'respectful' to his superiors, and that what Lord Cardigan called 'conduct unbecoming the character of an officer and a gentleman . . . proceeded not from an insolent or insubordinate spirit, but from the goading and oppressive conduct of Lord Cardigan'.

'Up to this time,' Reynolds concluded, 'whatever annoyance I suffered at the hands of Lord Cardigan I had borne from a sense of duty; but when his oppressive conduct was pushed to the extreme, my patience was exhausted, my feelings overcome. And I hope by your verdict of "*Not Guilty*" you will prove to Lord Cardigan that wealth and rank do not license him – although the Commanding Officer of a regiment – to trample with impunity upon honourable men who devote their lives to the service of their country.'

There was hardly a dry eye in the room, and the packed audience expressed their sympathy for Reynolds by prolonged applause and cheering. General Packenham had to threaten to clear the court before it was quiet enough for the proceedings to continue. For the remainder of the day, and the whole of the next, Reynolds called a procession of officers in his defence. Lieutenant Cunningham and Captain John Reynolds merely confirmed the sequence of events. The purpose of examining Major Morse Cooper, an officer who had been promoted to an unattached majority the previous January, was to illustrate Cardigan's tendency to insult officers; but as soon as Reynolds' questions moved in this direction, the court judged them to be inadmissible, as it had warned that it would.

The main pillar of his defence undermined, Reynolds now had to rely on his character witnesses: Major Rotten, Captains Forrest and Reynolds, and Surgeon Sandham who were still with the regiment; and Majors Morse Cooper and Brown, Captain Roebuck and Lieutenant Peterson who were not. All confirmed that Reynolds was a zealous and efficient officer, incapable of an act of insubordination. But Morse Cooper qualified this last assertion with the words, 'Not without some extraordinary provocation'. Brown, too, considered Reynolds 'utterly incapable of forgetting the respect due to a commanding officer, unless under provocation which no man of honourable feelings can endure'. Similar, if less extreme, sentiments were expressed in writing by six other officers, including Major-General Sir John Brown, and Colonels Childers and Brutton, the two previous commanding officers of the 11th.[11]

After Cardigan had made his closing speech on Monday, 5 October, the proceedings came to an end and the court retired to consider its verdict.

This would not be announced until it had been confirmed by the Queen, but many onlookers felt that Reynolds deserved to be acquitted. A letter to the *Morning Chronicle*, signed 'An Officer' and sent from Brighton on 9 October, complained that the trial had been an 'ordeal' for Reynolds to which no other officer had 'hitherto been subjected'. Only four out of the 15 officers of the court had been of the same rank as the accused, whereas 'one half' was the 'usuage of the service'. In addition, the president and the deputy judge-advocate had suppressed 'all evidence in favour of the prisoner which might risk the exposure of Lord Cardigan's revolting language and manner'.[12]

On Monday, 19 October, Cardigan, Tuckett and both seconds – Captains John Douglas and Henry Wainright – appeared in front of a grand jury at the Old Bailey. Five days earlier Tuckett, looking 'wan and delicate, as though he had undergone much suffering', had been indicted by the Wandsworth magistrates on the same charge as Cardigan – 'feloniously shooting, with intent to murder' – and bailed for £2,000.

The whole day was taken up with the giving of evidence, and on Tuesday the jury announced that it had found true bills against Cardigan, for 'firing a pistol . . . at Captain Harvey Garnett Phipps Tuckett, with intent to murder him, or do him some grievous bodily harm', and Douglas, as an accessory. The significance of stating Tuckett's full name in the charge would not become apparent until the actual trial.

But for some inexplicable reason the jury found no true bill against Tuckett and his second, Captain Wainright, and they were free to go. This was strange because, in law, they were every bit as guilty of a crime as Cardigan and Douglas. It is probable that, as members of the public, the jury had been influenced by the amount of adverse press coverage directed against the so-called 'Homicidal Earl'. He was, however, a peer of the realm and, on Wednesday the 21st, Mr Justice Bosanquet accepted the application by his counsel, Mr Adolphus, that the 'proper course would be to remove the case . . . to the House of Lords'. The trial would take place on 16 February 1841, and Douglas would have to wait for its result before he too was tried.[13]

Lord Cardigan was at the Old Bailey when the verdict of the court-martial was read out to Captain Reynolds in his Brighton hotel room on 20

October by Colonel Cochrane, Assistant Adjutant-General, accompanied by Major Jenkins and Adjutant Knowles.

> The Court, having duly weighed, and most maturely considered, the whole of the Evidence adduced on the part of the Prosecution, together with that advanced by the Accused in support of his Defence, is of opinion, that, he, Captain Richard Anthony Reynolds, of the 11th (Prince Albert's own) Hussars, is *Guilty* of the Charge exhibited against him, which being in breach of 'The Articles of War,' The Court does in virtue thereof Sentence him . . . to be *Cashiered*.

In addition, the General Order noted that two witnesses had stated that they considered Reynolds to be incapable of insubordination unless provoked, thus 'apparently sanctioning the idea that there might be circumstances of private irritation which would justify a Soldier breaking from the established order of Military Discipline'. This was a 'doctrine so totally subversive of the fundamental principles by which all Armies are governed' that the court felt called upon 'to stamp it with marked Reprobation'.[14]

Both the finding and the sentence of the court had been approved and confirmed by Her Majesty, stated the General Order. Indeed they had, and with a lot more feeling than might have been imagined. On 12 October, Queen Victoria had noted in her journal that Reynolds was 'to be cashiered, & I think rightly, for Ld. Cardigan has behaved quite well, in the business, & discipline must be maintained'. Her entry four days later described Reynolds' conduct as 'outrageous', but also recorded a lunchtime conversation about 'this ever unfortunate business of Cardigan's' with Lord Melbourne, who was of the 'opinion that Reynolds must be cashiered, but thinks something must be done with the Regt'.[15]

The Duke of Wellington was in agreement, stating in a memorandum sent to Lord Hill on 14 October that the court-martial had 'no alternative' but to cashier 'an officer who provokes another to send a challenge', and that a 'perusal of Captain Richard Reynolds' letter of the 28th August can leave no doubt that it was intended as a provocation to Lord Cardigan to take steps which would have terminated in a duel'. To avoid a repeat, Cardigan should be advised 'to interfere as little as possible in personal matters, to conduct them through the official channels of the Regimental staff'. Consequently, he will have time 'to consider every Act and every

Expression' and he 'will have Witnesses for the whole of his conduct and it will not be so easy for Parties to act against him'. In the covering letter, Wellington suggested sending 'a general officer to the 11th Hussars to communicate to the officers your feelings and opinions on the state of the Regiment in consequence of their disputes'.[16]

Following this advice, Lord Hill drafted a memorandum of his own and sent Adjutant-General Macdonald to read it to Cardigan and his officers behind locked doors on 23 October. The day before, Reynolds had left Brighton for London. The memorandum noted that the 'proceedings of the late general court-martial', and the 'various disputes amongst' the officers, 'complaints and instances of disobedience, insubordination, and disrespect towards the commanding officer recorded therein, as well as in the correspondence with the Adjutant-General', made it obvious that the 11th Hussars 'is not in a state in which a regiment ought to be'.

Hill then warned that the 'Mutiny Act, and the rules, articles, and regulations for the government of the British army, require that the officers thereof should conduct themselves as ought gentlemen, men of truth, honour, and morality'. If they did just that, he was certain that there would be 'no more complaints – that all that has passed will be buried in oblivion, and that henceforward the officers of the 11th Hussars will serve together with cordiality'.

But if an officer *did* have 'serious reason to complain of his commanding officer', and the necessary proof, 'it should be stated to his lordship in the manner clearly pointed out in the regulations of the service, and his lordship will immediately order those steps to be taken to enable him to form a judgement on the course which his duty may require that he should take'. However, Hill hoped that 'the officers will not be too ready to draw conclusions from, or impute motives to, looks or casual expressions in conversation'.

Up to this point, with three-quarters of the memorandum read, Cardigan was more than satisfied that Horse Guards had seen things his way. But as Macdonald read on, there was an implicit censure for Cardigan too. 'The commanding officer of the 11th Hussars,' stated the memorandum, 'should feel that he has an arduous duty to perform.' Particularly as he had a 'corps of officers either recently returned from service in a tropical climate, in which the habits and customs of the service must differ from those in European service, or who have been but a short time in the army'. Furthermore, he 'must recollect that it is expected from him not only to exercise the military command over this regiment, but to give an example of moderation, temper, and discretion, blended with the zealous activity and ability for which he is noted'.

But Lord Hill was wise enough to sweeten the pill and ended by assuring Brudenell of 'his anxious desire to support the fair exercise of his authority, and his determination to discountenance, check, and, even when necessary, to bring to trial every act of wilful disobedience, insubordination, and disrespect manifested towards him'.[17]

All sides of the press were dissatisfied with this attempt to pour oil on to troubled waters. Staunch Tory publications like the *Morning Post* and the *Naval and Military Gazette* felt that Hill had been wrong to criticise Cardigan; the *Morning Chronicle* and *The Globe* supported Captain Reynolds and were angry that Cardigan had escaped a more severe censure. More worrying for Cardigan was the fact that non-partisan newspapers were quick to condemn him. On 26 October, *The Times* noted that when Cardigan 'found that he was to come off scot-free a second time in his life, be whitewashed from his offences – offences which would have cashiered any officer in the service not protected and sheltered by overwhelming influence – he was delighted beyond measure'.

Two days later, *The Times* provided its own interpretation of the memorandum: 'Let him, therefore (so advises Lord Hill, with a silence more emphatic than words), now retire at once, while he can do so with honour. All that I can do (his Lordship would say) is to give him this last opportunity. Let him take the only step which can restore unananimity to Prince Albert's Hussars . . . I request, I command, the officers to spare me the necessity of going further than this, to spare Lord Cardigan the mortification of doing, under compulsion, what is more expedient that he should do of his own accord.'

On 31 October, the *United Service Gazette* described Adjutant-General Macdonald's speech to the officers of the 11th Hussars as a 'rose-water reproof', adding that 'to maintain arrogant, overbearing, intemperate, and imbecile conduct of the Cardigan kind, is to render authority odious, and make disobedience of orders seem meritorious and praiseworthy'.[18]

The public were not slow to take up the lead given by most of the press. Across the land meetings were held to demand the dismissal of Lord Cardigan, and a subscription was set up to reimburse Captain Reynolds for the loss of his commission. While some had a genuine sympathy for Reynolds, seen as the victim of an aristocratic tyrant, others were more

interested in political gain. Melbourne's fragile Whig/Radical government was daily in danger of being defeated in Parliament, and any publicity
that concerned the misbehaviour of a notorious Tory was welcome.

But as donations from all over the country began to flow in to the
offices of the *Morning Chronicle* and *The Globe* newspapers, Reynolds
realised that his cause was being manipulated by the Radicals for their own
political ends. The point they seemed to have missed was that he was as
blue a Tory as Cardigan, rode with the Fitzwilliam Hunt, and was horrified at the idea of becoming the symbol of a Radical crusade. From his
gracious home, Paxton Hall in Huntingdonshire, he wrote to the editor of
The Globe on 30 October to request an end to the subscriptions.

'I cannot,' admitted Reynolds, 'I dare not, as an officer, brought up in
her Majesty's service, lay my hand on my heart and say that I have not
grievously offended the laws established for the government of the army.'

> My loss has indeed been a bitter one [he continued] but it is not of
> a nature to be alleviated by pecuniary compensation; and it would
> certainly be augmented by any proceeding which might be con-
> strued into an admission on my part that the members of the hon.
> Court meant anything but rigid and necessary justice. I have paid
> too close an attention to my duties as an officer not to know that
> military subordination *must* be enforced; and although I cannot
> subscribe to the sweeping doctrine that *no degree* of provocation can
> ever justify a subordinate in breaking from the strict line of respect-
> ful submission, I feel that I am much too deeply and too personally
> interested on this occasion to consider myself a fair witness as to the
> nature and degree of mercy . . . which might have been extended
> to me . . . I hope and trust that my assertion will be received as sin-
> cere, when I state it as my most anxious desire that no subscription
> of any kind be entered into on my account. But I am, if possible,
> even more anxious that no attempt should be made to influence
> the Crown on my behalf . . . [If] her gracious Majesty may see in
> her always faithful servant only the rashness, the transient rashness
> of a temper too finely sharpened in her service to bear with
> patience what he considered a reflection on her honour, she may
> yet deem his hand worthy to bear again the sword which he has so
> long carried in defence of his Queen and country.[19]

Such a noble letter did much for Reynolds' cause. In time, the Queen did indeed forgive him, and in April 1842 he was gazetted a captain in the 9th Lancers. But his supporters among the press felt betrayed. The *Sun* described him as 'the now subservient and obedient craven of the Horse Guards', while the *Examiner* noted: 'His disposition to kiss the rod does not remove the public quarrel with the rod.'[20]

But what did the ordinary hussar think about his commanding officer in general and the 'Richard Reynolds Affair' in particular? George Loy Smith, no admirer of Cardigan's, was then a corporal in Reynolds' C Troop. 'I have often,' wrote Loy Smith, 'on parade, witnessed Lord Cardigan's overbearing manner to Captain Reynolds, which he did not submit to quietly, often replying in a manner that I was surprised that his Lordship did not then and there place him under arrest. Captain R.A. Reynolds was tried by a general court-martial . . . and was cashiered. The troop was not at all sorry at losing him.'[21]

Soon after, 'A Soldier of the 11th Hussars' – angered by the cruel treatment that Cardigan was receiving in the press – wrote to the *Naval and Military Gazette* 'to state what the soldiers under his command think of him'.

> That he is an impartial, indulgent, and considerate officer is confessed by all – one of the best Colonels in the British Army; ever alive to the interests and *eclat* of his regiment, he has not been sparing of his wealth, rest, or personal exertions, since he commenced the reorganisation of the 11th Hussars; and it was owing to the exaction of a little work, such as he did a great deal of himself, that first occasioned dissatisfaction amongst some of his officers, who were little accustomed to the active duties of their profession.

Those officers who had left were a 'good riddance, and the regiment would not be anything worse if the remainder of the cabal followed them'. The 'necessary attentions which a young regiment required from all ranks *quite disturbed them*, and put them in a fit of temper to talk of his Lordship, his former corps, their own *hard* duty, and the easy idle years they had spent before'. Consequently, 'the bottle of one, and the marked disrespect of the other, were purposefully presented and persisted in to annoy or get up a case to effect the designs of the clique who were formed against their Colonel.'

But Cardigan 'has disappointed them, and the men rejoice at it'. For 'he is deservedly respected, a *good* man, whom not a soldier under him but would follow into action with confidence, nor hesitate a moment to shield from danger by his own body in the battle-field'.[22]

The proof of this final remark would be shown 14 years later at Balaclava.

Together, these two soldiers provide the clue to Cardigan's perennial quarrels with his officers. His standards of smartness, discipline and efficiency were that much higher than many of his regimental officers were used to; when they could not, or would not, meet them, they were berated and the more headstrong responded in a manner calculated to provoke their commanding officer. Thus developed an anti-Cardigan faction, much as it had done in the 15th Hussars. From the publicity surrounding his removal from that regiment, many of them had probably prejudged him as a tyrant even before he arrived.

Cardigan's quick temper and overbearing manner have traditionally been blamed for the disharmony within the 11th Hussars. What has not been acknowledged is that some of his officers were not prepared to put up with his rigorous regime and so used his outbursts as an excuse to challenge his rightful authority; possibly with the intention of causing his dismissal. Two soldiers do not tell the whole story, but they at least confirm that it was the officers leaving the regiment, rather than Cardigan, who were unpopular with the ordinary hussars.

The public, however, believed what they read in the press and, after the announcement that Reynolds was to be cashiered, Cardigan was well on his way to becoming the most unpopular man in the kingdom. Soon after the verdict of the court-martial had been announced, he was booed at Brighton railway station on his way to London. A few days later his appearance in a box at Brighton's Theatre Royal provoked a 'storm of hisses, which lasted at least half an hour'. To enable the performance to begin, he was forced to withdraw, at which point 'three cheers were called for for Captain Reynolds, and responded to most lustily'.

In late December, the same thing happened at the Drury Lane Theatre in London when a crowd gathered beneath his box, shaking their fists and shouting, 'Black Bottle!' and 'Turn him out!' Again, seemingly unperturbed, Cardigan remained sitting while the clamour grew; but eventually he had had enough and 'advancing very deliberately to the front of the box, put on his great coat, and making a bow, retired amid one universal shout of disapprobation'.

The following month, shortly before his trial for shooting Tuckett, he was back at the Drury Lane Theatre to attend a promenade concert in the company of some friends, two of whom were ladies.

> At the end of the first act [wrote an eye-witness to *The Times*] a few young gentlemen, actuated . . . to a considerable extent by the desire of 'a bit of fun,' and two or three members of the respectable Hebrew community, gathered into a corner of the stage, and began hissing. It soon spread; and in about ten minutes there was a complete uproar; every eye in that vast circle fixed upon one spot; necks craning, bodies twisting round pillars, vernicular [sic] all to gaze upon, or to cast insult at, one small party. Now, Sir, in that house there must have been at least 700 or 800 men; the individual on whom the attack was directed was one . . . From 9 o'clock until 11 there was one continued uproar. Not a note of music could be heard.

But the correspondent, at least, was sympathetic towards Cardigan, noting that 'the playhouse is not a court of justice, nor the audience a fit jury', and that a 'more violent' and 'less creditable scene' he had 'never witnessed'. He was 'proud' to record that by the end of the performance 'a very considerable party had manifested itself against this spirit of outrage'. All the while, Cardigan's demeanour 'was perfectly correct and dignified – respectful towards the audience, but firm and determined not to be bullied from a place where he had as good a right to be as all those clamourers.'[23]

Learning of the incident from Lord Melbourne, the Queen was horrified that people had 'behaved so brutally' to Cardigan by 'hissing, yelling, & calling out to him'. 'Really too bad,' she concluded her journal entry.[24]

The public's perception of Cardigan was shaped by the publicity that surrounded his repeated 'turn-ups' with regimental officers; it was either unaware of, or ignored, the generous, sympathetic side to his nature. There was no better example of this than when Major Jenkins, Cardigan's second-in-command, suffered an apoplectic seizure on 28 October 1840. Aged 52, he had been in the regiment since 1806 and had seen action in the Peninsula, at Waterloo and at Bhurtpore. Cardigan both liked and admired him, and on hearing of his illness rushed to his bedside. While his eldest son, William (a young clergyman at Oxford) was sent for, Cardigan sat up with the delirious Jenkins for two whole nights.

On Saturday, 31 October, Jenkins died and the following Wednesday was buried with full military honours in St Peter's churchyard, Brighton. Between the barracks and the church, the 11th Hussars marched in twos with arms reversed, followed by the coffin carried by troopers, the pall by officers, and Jenkins' black horse with his riding boots round its neck. Next came the remaining officers, also in twos, with Cardigan and Adjutant Knowles last. Bringing up the rear was a black mourning coach with William Jenkins and the commanding officers of three other regiments, and a private carriage containing the major's doctors. A large crowd lined the route and, appreciating the solemnity of the occasion, managed to maintain a respectful silence despite Cardigan's presence.

The public might have changed their feelings towards Cardigan if they had been made aware of his generosity towards Jenkins' family. Having lost, by his father's death, the considerable value of a major's commission, William Jenkins had little money and so Cardigan paid for the cost of the funeral, bought the major's horse for him, and 'begged his acceptance of a sum of money for his immediate use, pending the settlement of the Major's affairs'. On parting, Cardigan told him: 'Pay me again when you are a bishop, but not before.'

Cardigan also paid £400 to get elected as a governor of Christ's Hospital so that he could give his nomination to Jenkins' younger son. 'It is a great pity that such hard-hearted tyranny as this is not more general,' remarked the *Naval and Military Gazette*.[25]

Years later, in a book fiercely critical of Cardigan's conduct in the Crimea, George Ryan conceded that the pre-war public perception of him had been one-sided:

> Unpopular with civilians, where best known his lordship was a great favourite. While the outcry against him was at its full height, with the private soldiers in his regiment his character stood high to a degree, notwithstanding his having been obliged to guide a few unruly hussars with a vigorous hand. Not only was he ever ready to minister to the pressing necessities of the married men, but many officers were in the moment of difficulty succoured by his lordship. The Earl of Cardigan's career has been daubed dark as night. His good deeds have had no public sitting, or their fair light would have materially toned dawn the harshness of the picture.

His purse was open to the claims of civic charities, but he had an abhorrence of having his contributions paraded in lists of sub-scriptions.[26]

Needless to say, Cardigan's open-handedness extended to his favourite pastime: hunting. When Lord Chesterfield resigned the mastership of the Pytchley before the start of the 1840 season, Cardigan bid for Squire Osbaldeston's old hounds with the intention of taking over the country himself. But the local gentry, fearing Cardigan's overbearing manners would bring a repetition of the unpopular Chesterfield regime, preferred 'Gentleman' Tom Smith of the Craven Hunt. Despite the rebuffal, Cardigan – 'the one bright exception' – was still willing to subscribe £1,000 to keep the hunt solvent.

Far from resenting Smith, Cardigan quickly came to respect his qualities as a master, and 'so delighted' was he at the end of one excellent run that he 'fairly embraced' Smith for being the 'means of causing him so much pleasure'. In another of the season's fine early runs, Cardigan 'had the best of everyone'.[27]

With Lord Hill's memorandum still fresh in his memory and his trial looming large, Cardigan might have been expected to tread warily for a few months. But that was not his way and, on Sunday, 8 December, he was involved in another 'turn-up'. As the regiment was leaving church, Dr Sandham, the junior surgeon of more than 35 years' service, was delayed while adjusting the fastening to his cap and, to catch up, he used the side entrance of the churchyard. Back at the barracks, he was confronted by the adjutant: 'It is his lordship's order that you fall in with the troops.'

'I don't understand you,' replied the doctor.

'It is his lordship's order,' repeated the adjutant before taking his leave.

After the troops had been dismissed, Sandham went to seek an explanation from Cardigan. 'My lord,' he said, 'I have been ordered to fall in with the troops.'

'Those are my orders, sir,' said Cardigan.

'But I don't understand them, my lord.'

'They are my orders, sir,' Cardigan repeated. After a pause, he then asked: 'Did you not come out at the small gate?'

'I did.'

'Then I order you in future, sir, to come out of the large gate.'

Sandham withdrew to his room, where some junior officers visited him to inquire what the trouble had been. 'I came out of the small gate instead of the large one,' Sandham explained.

Before long he was again summoned before Cardigan, who told him: 'Your conduct was highly improper and reprehensible in having made such a statement to the young officers who have just left you.'

Sandham replied that he had made no complaint but had simply described his fault.

'Be quiet, sir!' barked Cardigan. 'I shall not listen to any reply!'

'My lord, I have not failed to use my best endeavours to please your lordship, but I now find that it is impossible to do so,' said Sandham.

'Well sir, you had better state that fact in writing. And now, sir, *leave the room!*'

Taking his commanding officer at his word, Sandham wrote immediately to Lord Hill; before forwarding the letter, Cardigan enclosed his own version of events.

On 17 December, Hill replied, expressing his 'regret that if your lordship thought it your duty to notice this apparent irregularity, a fault of an unimportant character of which Mr Sandham was wholly unconscious, you did not at the same time take the necessary steps to enquire into the circumstances which gave rise to it . . . Had this obvious course of action been adopted . . . the valuable time of Lord Hill would not again be occupied by regimental controversies of this painful nature between your lordship and an officer of the 11th Hussars.'

In addition, Cardigan was instructed to read the admonition in Sandham's presence.[28]

Also in December, the 'Black Bottle Affair' once again reared its ugly head. Now without the support of his cousin, Richard, and fearing that Cardigan would make his life increasingly difficult, John Reynolds had applied for leave to join the Senior Department of the Royal Military College, Sandhurst – the predecessor to the Staff College. Predictably, Cardigan refused, causing Reynolds to apply to the Horse Guards for permission to sell his commission.

Fearing more adverse publicity, Lord Fitzroy Somerset invited Reynolds' uncle, Captain Basil Hall, to the Horse Guards to discuss the matter. Hall told him that Reynolds had had enough of Cardigan's 'overbearing and tyrannical conduct', and that he did not feel that the value of his commission was secure 'for even one day whilst under the Earl's command'. Then Reynolds himself was summoned to London, and on Boxing Day Somerset reported the gist of the meeting to Lord Hill. Reynolds would not withdraw his resignation 'unless you [Hill] allow him to go to the College and in arranging this for him we must take care not to give life to the supposition that you have any motive in wishing him to continue in the service'.

But of course he did have a motive, and that was to prevent more criticism of Lord Cardigan. Through Macdonald, Hill wrote to Cardigan, asking his reasons for refusing Reynolds leave to attend the Senior Department. The answer was obviously not satisfactory because – according to a report in the *Alligator* – at a further meeting between Somerset and Reynolds in early January, Reynolds agreed to withdraw his resignation but only on the following terms:

> A recantation of the censure given by General Sleigh . . .; six months' leave of absence . . .; two years at the senior department of the Military College, and a distinct and express understanding that Captain John Reynolds should never again be required to serve for a single day under the Earl of Cardigan.[29]

While it is unlikely that the first condition was ever granted, the rest seem to have been and Reynolds never returned to the 11th Hussars. His card was marked nonetheless; after leaving the Senior Department he spent long periods on half-pay, and it was not until 1859 that he was appointed to a staff post as deputy adjutant-general in Jamaica. Six years later, by then a major on half-pay, he again came face to face with Lord Cardigan at a regimental dinner. Spontaneously, the former protagonists clasped hands as officers past and present looked on amazed. Still hand in hand when dinner was announced, they walked in together and sat down side by side. In the year of Cardigan's death, and seven years before his own, Reynolds became a major-general.

9

'Plague-spot of
the Army'

In early January 1841, Lord Cardigan was summoned to Windsor Castle for an audience with Prince Albert. According to a report in the *Morning Chronicle*, they discussed the possibility of Cardigan being replaced at the head of his regiment by young Prince George of Cambridge, the Queen's cousin. A more likely scenario is that Albert talked about the possibility of having to give up the colonelship of the 11th Hussars if Cardigan was found guilty at his forthcoming trial.[1]

But not all was doom and gloom. The charge Cardigan was due to face on 16 February could have been worse. When Wellington fought Lord Winchelsea, even to take part in a duel was to commit a crime punishable by death. In July 1837, however, the law against duelling had been modified and it was now only a capital offence 'if a bodily injury dangerous to life' was inflicted. Tuckett had been wounded, but his speedy recovery and Sir James Anderson's testimony on 14 September that he had not been 'dangerously wounded' had resulted in the lesser charge of 'intent to murder, maim and cause grievous bodily harm'. The maximum sentence was transportation to the Colonies for life.

Furthermore, even if found guilty there was the possibility that he could plead 'Benefit of Clergy', a statute dating from Edward VI's reign that made peers immune from the penalty of felony. Lords Mohun, Warwick and Byron had all killed men in duels, and all had successfully pleaded the privilege after being found guilty of manslaughter by their fellow peers. The statute was meant to have been abolished by an act of

1824, but the wording was said to have been too defective to carry the intention of the legislature into effect. On 31 January, Lord Melbourne told the Queen that he thought the privilege was still in existence. 'Talked of the Cardigan business,' Victoria noted in her journal, '& he, as a Peer, having the benefit of Clergy, so that even if he were pronounced guilty, Ld M. understands, he could not be punished.' Confirmation that a loophole in the law existed was given in June 1841, after the trial, when the original statute was repealed, making all peers convicted of a felony 'liable to the same punishment as any other of Her Majesty's subjects'.[2]

Cardigan could also take comfort from the fact that, as recently as June 1838, the young Lord Castlereagh (son of the famous statesman who had committed suicide in 1822) had been wounded in a duel on Wormwood Scrubs with a French nobleman, but neither had been prosecuted.

Two months later, on the other hand, a fatal duel on Wimbledon Common had resulted in death sentences; but this was hardly a typical 'affair of honour'. A Mr Mirfin, son of a thriving linen-draper, had quarrelled over a bet of £100 with Francis Elliot, the son of an officer but also the nephew of a Taunton innkeeper. Neither came from the type of aristocratic or gentry background usually associated with duels.

Mirfin was given due warning when Elliot's first shot went through his hat; but he insisted on a second and was killed. The jury at the inquest returned a verdict of 'wilful murder' against Eliott as the principal. His second, Edward Broughton, Mirfin's second, Henry Webber, John Young (a friend of Mirfin's), and two other persons unknown, were named as principals in the second degree. But Elliot and Broughton skipped bail, and only Webber and Young could be found to be tried in September 1838. Both received the death sentence, later commuted to 12 months on the treadmill at the infamous Guildford House of Correction.[3]

The Times, for one, was anxious that Cardigan should share the same fate:

> Let his head be cropped, let him be put on an oatmeal diet, let him labour on the treadmill. Let not the occasion be given for anyone to say that the same which was visited as a felony on the associates of the linen-draper Mirfin is excused as an act worthy of a man of honour in the Earl of Cardigan.[4]

That Cardigan took the possibility of conviction seriously is shown by his decision to transfer his property to Viscount Curzon, the eldest son of his

157

favourite sister, the late Countess Howe. This was to avoid the confiscation of his estates by the Crown which was mandatory when a peer was found guilty of a felony. The cost of this deed of gift, 'arising from fines upon copyholds, and the enormous stamp duties', was said to have been 'upwards of £10,000'. The same fee would be necessary to transfer it back.

But he still had one very influential supporter – the Queen. On 28 January she discussed the forthcoming trial with Lord Melbourne, who described it as 'so awkward'. Indeed it was, but only one verdict would satisfy the Queen. 'My hoping he would get off easily,' she wrote.[5]

The last peer to be tried in the House of Lords was the Duchess of Kingston for bigamy in 1776. Seven years earlier she had obtained a divorce *a mensa et toro* in the Ecclesiastical Court from her first husband, the Earl of Bristol. But ignoring the restriction against remarriage in her husband's lifetime, she had immediately wed the Duke of Kingston, who died four years later. Found guilty, her second marriage was declared null and void and she was threatened with branding if she reoffended.

Sixty-five years later, Lord Cardigan was facing an infinitely more serious penalty. By 10 o'clock in the morning of the trial – Tuesday, 16 February 1841 – the approaches to the Houses of Parliament were thronged with people keen to observe the spectacle and anxious for a glimpse of the defendant. As well as a strong police presence, a battalion of the Scots Guards had been deployed to keep order. Richard Mayne, the Commissioner of Police, feared an attack on Cardigan, but his offer of personal protection had been turned down.

Carriage after splendid carriage, complete with liveried attendants, rolled down Parliament Street before disgorging nobles at the entrance to the House of Lords. The Queen and Prince Albert had decided not to attend, but her uncle, the Duke of Cambridge, was there, as were her Ladies-in-Waiting in the royal carriages.

With just half an hour to go, the queue of coaches was directed to one side to enable a single gorgeous carriage to reach the entrance of the House unimpeded. Arriving at the gallop, its door emblazoned with an instantly recognisable coat of arms, it contained the splendidly attired 7th Earl of Cardigan.

The Painted Chamber, where the peers had met since the fire of 1834, was a breathtaking sight, newly festooned in crimson cloth and thronged with nobles in their elaborate ceremonial robes and cocked hats. Yet, of the 300 or so peers eligible to sit in judgement, fewer than half were present, among them Cardigan's brother-in-law, the Earl of Lucan, Lady Cardigan's elderly lover, Lord Colville of Culross, and two of his contemporaries at Christ Church, Lord Godolphin and the Earl of Wilton. His cousin, the Marquis of Ailesbury, had stayed away, as had his other brother-in-law Earl Howe.

Members of the House of Commons were allowed standing room below the bar of the House, while the galleries, newly extended to allow room for up to 340 spectators, were packed with foreign ambassadors and peeresses, including Elizabeth, the notorious Countess of Cardigan, who at 43 was still strikingly handsome.

It only remained for the Lord High Steward, the presiding judge, to make his appearance and the trial could begin. Normally, this office was undertaken by the Lord Chancellor, but he was ill and Lord Denman, the Lord Chief Justice, had taken his place. On the stroke of 11 o'clock, Denman entered the chamber, preceded by the Serjeant with the Mace, Black Rod carrying the Lord High Steward's white staff of office, and Garter with the Sceptre.

After prayers and a roll-call of peers, the royal commission was read and Denman took his seat in the chair of state on the step below the empty throne. Then the Deputy Clerk of the Crown in the Queen's Bench read the three counts of the indictment: firing with a loaded pistol at Harvey Garnett Phipps Tuckett with intent to murder him; to maim and disable him; and to do him some grievous bodily harm.

Proclamation was then made for the Yeoman Usher to bring Lord Cardigan from the ante-chamber to the bar of the House. There he bowed three times, once to the Lord High Steward and once to the peers on either side, before being conducted to a stool within the bar next to his counsel, Sir William Follett. The indictment was read by Lord Denman and the Deputy Clerk asked Cardigan how he pleaded.

'Not guilty, my lords,' Cardigan replied.

'How will your lordship be tried?' asked the clerk.

'By my peers.'

'God send your lordship a good deliverance.'[6]

Presenting the case for the prosecution was Sir John Campbell, the Attorney-General. A formidable Scots lawyer who later became Lord

Chief Justice and ultimately Lord Chancellor, he also wrote the celebrated tome, *Lives of the Lord Chancellors.* Tall, with a high forehead and hawk nose, he gave the impression of a bird of prey about to swoop on to its unsuspecting victim.

But Cardigan was far from unprepared. To defend him he had engaged the brilliant Sir William Follett, a former Solicitor-General in the brief Peel ministry of 1834–5. Also tall, his features were softer and his manner less aggressive than Campbell's. But his superior intellect made him a more effective lawyer and, if he had not been afflicted by a disease that was to cause gradual paralysis leading to death within four years, he would probably have been made Lord Chancellor. In addition to this cerebral advantage, he had the incentive of revenge. For in 1836, in the notorious Norton divorce action, he had represented the husband while Campbell had appeared for the co-respondent, Lord Melbourne. Campbell had won.

As prosecutor, Campbell spoke first. Convinced that his case was water-tight, he could afford to be generous. 'I am rejoiced to think,' he told the House, 'that the charge against the noble prisoner at the bar does not imply any degree of moral turpitude, and that if he should be found guilty the conviction will reflect no discredit upon the illustrious order to which he belongs.'

Then Campbell gave a long, 'masterly exposition' of the law relating to duelling and the facts of the case. He followed this with a list of his witnesses, adding that neither Douglas, Tuckett nor Wainright was among them. Douglas had been 'jointly indicted with the Earl of Cardigan' and would soon face a trial of his own. The grand jury had 'thrown out' a bill of indictment against the other two, he said, but they were 'still liable to be tried, and it would not be decorous' for them 'to give evidence which might afterwards be turned against themselves'.

Campbell continued with another concession to the defendant: 'My lords, I at once acquit the Earl of Cardigan of anything unfair in the conduct of this duel. Something has been said respecting his lordship's pistols having rifle barrels, and those of Captain Tuckett not having rifle barrels. My lords, however that may have been, I have the most firm conviction that nothing but what was fair and honourable was intended, and that the Earl of Cardigan most probably imagined, when he carried these pistols to the field with him, that one of them would be directed against his own person . . . Whether his lordship gave or received the invitation, I am willing to believe that his only object was to preserve his reputation, and to maintain his station in society as an officer and a gentleman.'

To redress the balance, he added: 'But although moralists of high name have excused or even defended the practice of duelling, your lordships must consider what it is by the law of England. My lords . . . there can be no doubt that parties who meet deliberately to fight a duel, if death ensues, are guilty of the crime of murder.'[7]

But the damage had been done. Campbell had, in effect, acquitted Cardigan of the moral responsibility for his 'crime', and this was hardly likely to aid the prosecution when many of the peers present had fought in 'affairs of honour' themselves.

The first witness to be called was the miller Thomas Dann. Examined by Mr Waddington, Campbell's deputy, he began to recount the sequence of events from the arrival of the duellists on Wimbledon Common. But it soon became clear from Follett's constant interruptions that the case for the prosecution had a fundamental flaw:

> Waddington: You tell us that you saw the pistols fired a second time; did you observe whether either of the shots took effect?
>
> Dann: I thought Captain Tuckett was wounded – or at least the other gentleman: I did not know who it was.
>
> Q: You thought that the gentleman that you afterwards ascertained to be Captain Tuckett was wounded?
>
> A: Yes.
>
> Q: Did you see what the gentleman did with his pistol after the second shots were fired?
>
> A: No.
>
> Waddington: You did not see whether he held it in his hand, or what he did with it?
>
> Q: Which are you alluding to?
>
> A: I am speaking of Captain Tuckett.
>
> Follett: He says he did not know who he was.[8]

Follett's intuitive intellect had enabled him to identify Cardigan's only hope of escaping conviction: the prosecution failing to prove the identity of the wounded man. Normally, this would be achieved by calling the victim as a witness; but, as Campbell had explained in his opening address, Tuckett would not be appearing because he was still liable to be tried. Instead, Campbell was relying on the card that Tuckett had given to Dann, as well as evidence from other witnesses, to prove his identity.

Waddington: The wounded gentleman gave you a card of his
   address?
Dann: I have a card of his, but whether he gave it me or another
   gentleman I am not sure.
Q: Have you got it here?
A: I have.
Q: Produce it.
Follett: We cannot have that card in evidence unless it came from
   Lord Cardigan; it cannot be made evidence against him unless
   that be shown.[9]

Then followed a convoluted legal argument, with Waddington demanding
to be allowed to read the card in evidence, and Follett insisting that it was
inadmissible on the grounds that Cardigan had been unaware of the transaction and that the identity of its donor was uncertain. This was Follett's
master stroke. He knew that Denman would eventually rule against him,
but he wanted Campbell to think that his hopes rested on the inadmissi-
bility of the card. In fact they did not, because the inscription on the card –
Captain Harvey Tuckett, 13 Hamilton Place, New Road – was not the
identical name to that on the indictment: Harvey Garnett Phipps Tuckett.
When, in response to Follett's objection, Campbell agreed to postpone
presenting the card as evidence until later in the trial, everything was
going to plan.

After Dann's son and wife had backed up his evidence, Cardigan's physician, Sir James Anderson, was called. Before he began his testimony, Lord
Denman warned him that he was 'not bound to answer any question
which may tend to incriminate' him, and he took this advice literally. 'Are
you acquainted with Captain Tuckett?' asked Campbell.

'I must decline answering that,' Anderson responded, and so on to subsequent questions until it was obvious that he could be of no assistance to
the prosecution.

Inspector Busain was next. He testified that during the conversation in
the police station Cardigan had actually confessed to his crime:

Campbell: You asked what his business was. What did his lordship
   say to that?
Busain: He said he was a prisoner, he believed.
Q: Just give us the language his lordship used?
A: 'I am a prisoner, I believe.' 'Indeed, sir,' said I; 'on what

account?' . . . His lordship said, 'I have been fighting a duel, and
I have hit my man; but not seriously, I believe; slightly; merely
a graze across the back.'[10]

Next, in an attempt to provide proof of Tuckett's identity, Campbell called
Mr Walthew, a chemist of 29 the Poultry. In response to Waddington's
questions, Walthew confirmed that a Captain Tuckett had been running a
business from rooms in his house for the past 15 months, and that he lived
at 13 Hamilton Place, New Road. But when he was then asked if he knew
Tuckett's christian names, Follett objected on the grounds that no evidence
had yet been provided to connect that gentleman with the crime.
Waddington persisted, however, claiming that the prosecution simply
wanted to know 'the name of that individual who rents rooms of the witness at the Poultry'. At this, Follett relented, but he need not have worried.

'The only names I know him by are Harvey Tuckett,' replied Walthew.
There was still no evidence to prove that a man called Harvey Garnett
Phipps Tuckett had been wounded by Cardigan in a duel.[11]

Seemingly unaware of this glaring omission, the prosecution called their
final witness, Edward Codd, an Army agent. Questioned by Campbell,
Codd said that for the past three or four years he had been giving Captain
Tuckett his half-pay. Unlike Walthew, he knew him by all four of his
christian names but he had only paid him at his own residence, 15 Fludyer
Street. He had once seen him at the Minerva Life Insurance Office, but
never in the Poultry.[12]

With his case almost over, Campbell requested permission to read the
card that Tuckett had given to Dann; this, he assumed, would prove
Tuckett's identity. By now, however, some of the peers betrayed the fact
that they were aware of the fatal flaw in the prosecution's case. 'Is this your
case, Mr Attorney?' asked Lord Brougham, a former Lord Chancellor,
incredulously.

'I should first wish to know whether that card is to be received or
rejected?' replied Campbell, not realising that it would not make any difference.

But Follett was perfectly aware of this, and after asking to look at the
card he withdrew his objection to it being read. On one side, it was
announced, the words 'Captain Harvey Tuckett, 13, Hamilton Place, New
Road' were engraved, on the other 'Captain H. Wainright' was handwritten.

'Is that your case, Mr Attorney-General?' asked Follett anxiously.

'This, my lords, is the case on the part of the prosecution,' came the fateful reply.[13]

It was now late afternoon. Follett had no witnesses and no evidence in defence of Lord Cardigan, but he did not need any. 'This being the case on the part of the prosecution,' he announced, 'I shall venture to submit to your lordships that no case has been made out which calls upon the prisoner at the bar for an answer; and I think your lordships will see at once that my learned friends have failed in proving an essential part of their case.'

Every count in the indictment, he said, contained the name 'Harvey Garnett Phipps Tuckett'. It was the prosecutor's duty 'to prove the christian and surname of the person against whom the offence is alleged to have been committed, and that if he fails in proving either . . . he fails in the proof of his case'. Yet there was 'no evidence whatever to prove that the person at whom the noble earl is charged to have shot upon the 12th of September was Mr Harvey Garnett Phipps Tuckett':

> Now, your lordships will observe [Follett continued], that the evidence is this: they have called a person of the name of Codd, who is stated to be an army agent, and who receives the half-pay of a Captain Tuckett, who was formerly an officer in the 11th Dragoons, and who states that the Mr Tuckett for whom he received half-pay is named Harvey Garnett Phipps Tuckett. Is there any thing at all before your lordships to identify that Mr Tuckett with the person who is said to have been at Wimbledon Common on the 12th of September? There is nothing whatever. Mr Codd does not know where that Mr Tuckett lives; he never saw him at any place but at his own office in Fludyer Street, and once at an insurance office . . . Then, my lords, what is the other evidence on this point? A witness is called who comes from the Poultry, and who states that a Captain Tuckett occupies rooms in his house, where he carries on the business of an Indian and colonial agent, and he states that his name is Harvey Tuckett, but that he does not know where he lives. There is, therefore, no evidence to connect the Captain Tuckett spoken of by Mr Codd as bearing those christian names with the Captain Tuckett spoken of by the other witnesses . . . and, therefore, I submit that my learned friend has entirely failed in one essential part of the proof in this prosecution.[14]

Campbell's desperate response had all the hallmarks of a drowning man. 'Now, my lords, how does the case stand?' he asked. 'My learned friend withdrew all objection to the reading of the card. Well, then, the gentleman who was wounded, at whom the Earl of Cardigan shot on the 12th of September, was a Captain Tuckett. It was Captain Harvey Tuckett. We have got so far as to one of his names. Now, my lords, how does it stand with regard to the rest? Am I obliged to call the clerk of the parish where he was baptized, in order to prove his baptismal register? Am I obliged to call his father or his mother, or his godfathers and godmothers, to prove the name that was given to him at the baptismal font? I apprehend that such evidence is wholly unnecessary, and that if from the facts that are proved any reasonable man would draw the inference that we wish to be drawn, there is abundant evidence to be submitted to a jury, and to be submitted to your lordships.'

After Campbell had waded through that evidence, Follett calmly demolished his main points:

> It is not that we object that the clerk of the parish or the parents should be called; but what we object is this, that they have called a person of the name of Codd, who has proved that he knows a Captain Tuckett who bears these christian names, but he gave no evidence . . . to connect that Captain Tuckett with the gentleman who was upon Wimbledon Common on the 12th of September . . .
>
> My learned friend said that he obtains from the card one of the christian names '*Harvey* Tuckett'. Is that to be proof that the person named in this indictment 'Harvey Garnett Phipps Tuckett' is the same person? I ask whether any one of the judges would leave that question to a jury. There might be two persons of the name of 'Harvey Tuckett' . . . The question is this, – not what your lordships know out of this house, nor what your lordships may surmise or conjecture, – but, sitting as judges in a criminal case, looking at the evidence alone, is there any evidence before your lordships to prove that the gentleman who was upon Wimbledon Common bears the christian name and surname of 'Harvey Garnett Phipps Tuckett'?[15]

Before giving his opinion, Lord Denman gave instructions for the galleries to be cleared of spectators and for the Yeoman Usher to take Lord

Cardigan into the ante-chamber. The Archbishop of Canterbury then requested that he and his fellow peers-spiritual be allowed to withdraw before judgement was given, and this was granted. At last, Denman spoke. After summarising the inadequacy of the evidence, he explained how simply the prosecution could have proved Tuckett's identity:

> No fact is easier of proof in its own nature, and numerous witnesses are always at hand to establish it with respect to any person conversant with society. In the present case the simplest means were accessible. If those who conduct the prosecution had obtained your lordships' order for the appearance at your bar of Captain Tuckett, and if the witnesses of the duel had deposed to his being the man who left the field after receiving Lord Cardigan's shot, Mr Codd might have been asked whether that was the gentleman whom he knew by the four names set forth in the indictment. His answer in the affirmative would have been too conclusive on the point to admit of the present objection being taken.

But, for reasons of their own, they had failed to do this and he had no hesitation in asserting that in an ordinary court of law 'the jury would at once return a verdict of acquittal'. Consequently, he gave it as his own opinion that 'the Earl of Cardigan is entitled to be declared Not Guilty'.[16]

To hear the verdict the spectators were re-admitted, but not Lord Cardigan. Denman then stood up and, reading from a list, addressed the junior baron. 'John, Lord Keane, how says your lordship; is James Thomas, Earl of Cardigan, guilty of the felony whereof he stands indicted, or not guilty?'

Keane, a general famous for his recent exploits in Afghanistan, rose bareheaded, put his hand on his heart and replied: 'Not guilty, upon my honour.'

One by one the 120 assembled barons, viscounts, earls, marquesses and dukes gave the same reply. Only the Duke of Cleveland qualified his response by saying: 'Not guilty *legally*, upon my honour.'

It only remained to inform the accused. His heart thumping, Cardigan was brought back to the bar and told by Lord Denman that he had been pronounced 'not guilty by an unanimous sentence'. Mightily relieved, he bowed and withdrew. Denman then broke the white staff of office in two and what was arguably the most dramatic trial of the century came to a close.[17]

★

The Queen heard the welcome news that 'Lord Cardigan had been acquitted on the ground that Captain Tuckett could not be identified, his Christian name not being known', from the Duchess of Sutherland. The government, too, was relieved, with Lord Melbourne telling the Queen after dinner 'that it was just as well the trial ended as it did, & that Lord Brougham, Lord Lyndhurst . . . & all the judges agreed completely in the ground of acquittal'.[18]

Less enthusiastic was the audience of the Drury Lane Theatre when Cardigan and his wife were spotted in a box before the start of a promenade concert on the evening of 17 February. An exercise in public defiance of almost staggering proportions, it infuriated a rowdy minority of the audience who responded with 'a storm of yells and hisses which lasted nearly half an hour'. Noting that Cardigan sat through the tirade seemingly 'unmoved', while his countess appeared amused, one eyewitness made clear his own sympathies in a letter to the *Morning Post*: 'For myself, though considering the unpopularity of Lord Cardigan by no means undeserved, I confess to you that I witnessed the attack of last night with a feeling of shame for the cowardice and barbarity displayed by some scores of my countrymen.'[19]

Richard Reynolds was at his Huntingdonshire home when he received news of the verdict. A couple of days later he wrote to his friend, Lieutenant Henry Moysey, who was in the process of sending in his papers:

> You are quite right to retire from the regiment. Treadmill is better than serving under Cardigan and I am no means sure that he will be much better of the lesson he has had, for this trial will give him confidence, as the vain blockhead no doubt will suppose that the peers acquitted him because they approved of his conduct. The boast of having *hit his man* and his explanation to the policeman of his ideas on regimental etiquette I consider good and not likely to tell much in his favour, but he is really such an out and out bad one that I have given up troubling myself about him, so long as I am not under him and Captain Jones. I do not envy those who are . . . Nobody ever supposed that the fellow had not pluck enough to knock his head against a wall, but a man who will insult another who has not the power to resent is, in my opinion, as despicable a fellow as ever lives. But enough of the subject, I am sick of it.[20]

On the whole, the press reaction to Cardigan's acquittal was predictable.

The *Morning Post* and the *Naval and Military Gazette* were delighted; *The Globe* and the *Morning Chronicle* outraged, with the latter describing the trial as a ' solemn farce'. But it was the response of the non-partisan *Times* that best mirrored the view of the man in the street. 'The extraordinary termination of the proceedings of the highest court of criminal judicature in Lord Cardigan's case reflects deep disgrace upon the present state of English law,' howled its editorial of 17 February, 'and suggests very grave doubts as to the manner in which the officers who represented the Crown on this occasion have discharged their duties.'

Was it possible, the editorial asked, that the peers had conspired to shield 'one of their order from the consequences of his actions, at the expense of decency, truth, and justice?' 'No', it answered, but a questionable legal technicality had enabled Cardigan to escape in a 'pageant' that had cost the public £3–4,000. 'What earthly difference could it make in a moral or social, or ought it to make in a legal point of view, whether that British subject was rightly or wrongly described in the indictment . . . so long as it was distinctly proved by sufficient evidence that the law had been broken . . .?'

The following day, a second *Times* editorial continued the theme that there must have been either incompetence or complicity displayed by the law officers involved. 'Altogether, we deeply lament the whole of this affair,' it said, 'because it will be difficult to persuade the people (as indeed it is difficult to believe) that due diligence has been used to procure a conviction.' It was also lamentable 'because it must inevitably give a great encouragement to the practice of duelling', 'must as certainly discourage magistrates from exerting themselves to suppress duels', and 'because an opinion, most dangerous to the aristocracy, prevails, that in England there is one law for the rich and another for the poor'.[21]

It was, indeed, inexplicable that a future Lord Chancellor had failed to prove the identity of the victim, one of the fundamental requirements of a successful conviction. As Lord Denman pointed out during the trial, this could easily have been achieved by insisting on Tuckett's presence so that witnesses would have been able to confirm that he was the man in question. He need not even have spoken, so removing the possibility that he might incriminate himself. Instead, Campbell relied on a calling card with an incomplete name, and a witness who had never visited Tuckett at home and who was unable to connect the half-pay captain he knew with the man who had been shot on Wimbledon Common.

Over-confidence may have been the cause, but Campbell was surely too careful a lawyer for that, and the more likely explanation is that it was deliberate. After all, the establishment – including the Queen, the government, the House of Lords and the vast majority of the House of Commons – were in favour of an acquittal. Cardigan, they believed, had been provoked into breaking the law in a manner which many of them had emulated without punishment. And if he had been found guilty, the political consequences of a successful appeal against punishment on the grounds of 'Benefit of Clergy' were incalculable. The government admitted this by hastily removing any doubt as to the repeal of this anachronistic privilege soon after. But if there was a conspiracy, Cardigan was not privy to it. If he had been, he would hardly have gone to the massive expense of paying £20,000 to have his property transferred to his nephew prior to his trial, and then back again after his acquittal.

But *The Times* was wrong in its assumption that Cardigan's acquittal would give encouragement to the practice of duelling. Instead, this hammered another nail in its coffin by turning public opinion even more firmly against the practice. For this was a time of rapid social, economic and even political change, with a rising middle class challenging the outdated mores of a seemingly corrupt ruling élite. Duelling was one of the first anachronisms to be done away with.

The final straw came in July 1843 when Lieutenant Colonel David Fawcett of the 55th Regiment was mortally wounded by his brother-in-law, Lieutenant Alexander Munroe of the Royal Horse Guards. An Anti-Duelling Association was then set up, and within a year the Articles of War had been amended to make it an offence punishable by cashiering for any officer to send or accept a challenge, or, if aware of a duel, not to take active measures to prevent it. The result was dramatic. Duels became extremely rare – one exception was in 1845, when one of Cardigan's officers had to flee to France after killing a naval lieutenant – and by 1850 had all but ceased to occur.[22]

Undaunted by the largely adverse reaction of the press, Cardigan celebrated his deliverance at a dinner given by his royal friend, Lord Adolphus Fitzclarence, at St James's Palace on 18 February. Among the distinguished guests were the Duke of Cambridge, his son Prince George and Lord Fitzroy Somerset.

However the Radicals, in particular, were not prepared to let the events of the previous year be forgotten; on Friday, 5 March, during a debate on Army Estimates, Joseph Hume attacked both Lord Hill and the government for failing to censure 'the conduct of the commanding officer of the 11th Dragoons – conduct such as no man holding the character of a gentleman could possibly tolerate or permit'. Henceforward, he said, no man could join the 11th Hussars 'without having "slave" branded on his forehead'. Furthermore, the fact that Captain Richard Reynolds – 'an officer of twenty-six years standing, who had received the sanction and praise of every individual officer under whose command he had served' – had been dismissed for an offence with 'many extenuating circumstances', led him to conclude that the 'rank of the offenders caused some difference in the punishment meted out to them'.

Thomas Macaulay, the celebrated historian and then Secretary-at-War, replied by admitting that the topic of Lord Cardigan was one of 'violent irri-tation' and that the government had acted in the 'face of the whole press' and 'the general cry of the whole country'. But it had done this because Cardigan's unpopularity was in no way warranted. 'Could Lord Cardigan go to a theatre that he was not insulted?' he asked. 'Could he take his place in a railway train without having a hiss raised against him? Was there ever a case in which a man was more violently and intemperately assailed?'

In any case, Cardigan was a Tory and a Whig government had nothing to gain by shielding him. The truth, he said, was that they could not have dis-missed Cardigan 'without a court-martial', for it would be 'in the highest degree prejudicial to the army to establish a precedent for the dismissal of an officer for imputed faults of manner and temper'. 'I say nothing of Lord Cardigan,' concluded Macaulay, 'I don't pretend to say he is faultless, but I insist that the principles on which the Government acted are sound ones.'

But Lord Howick, Secretary-at-War when Cardigan was restored in 1836, was far from satisfied. He wanted Richard Reynolds to be reinstated, and said that it had been a great error not to order an inquiry into Cardigan's conduct. Many in the House agreed, and a vote was passed to schedule a debate for the following Friday.

By then, however, the mood had changed. Wellington had let it be known that the Army was not to be dictated to by the House on matters of discipline, and the majority of members had swung behind him. During the debate, only Radicals like O'Connell and Hume continued to press for an inquiry and it ended without a division.[23]

Despite the public clamour, Lord Cardigan remained high in his sovereign's estimation, and in early April 1841 the 11th Hussars were ordered to leave

Brighton to take up the Queen's Duty at Hounslow, with detachments at Hampton Court, Kensington and Sandhurst.

The night before departure, Private William Rogers went absent and returned to barracks drunk in the early hours of the morning. As punishment, he was ordered to march to Hounslow on foot, leading his horse. He refused. Cardigan regarded drunkenness as only marginally less serious than disobedience and, coming as both offences did on the eve of the regiment assuming the honour of guarding the Queen, was triply determined to make an example of the perpetrator. A district court-martial was convened at Hounslow on 8 April and the 26-year-old Rogers was sentenced to the maximum 100 lashes. Confirmation of the sentence arrived from the Horse Guards on the morning of 11 April, and Cardigan ordered the flogging to be carried out forthwith.

The problem lay in the fact that 11 April was Easter Sunday, and it was not the custom of the Army to administer corporal punishment on the Sabbath. There were examples of this unwritten rule not being adhered to, but usually during active service or when a regiment was on the march. Cardigan compounded his error by defying convention at a time when his stock with the public could not have been lower.

The flogging took place in the riding-school, where just half an hour earlier the Easter service had ended. With the regiment formed into a hollow square, Rogers was led into the centre to hear the adjutant read out the proceedings of the court-martial, including the charge, finding and sentence. The prisoner then stripped down to his overalls and boots and was fastened by the wrists and ankles to a large iron triangle. At a signal two burly farriers, also stripped to the waist, began to administer the lashes.

By the fifteenth blow, the white flesh of Rogers' back had turned a livid purple in an oblique line from shoulder to waist. After 25, the blood had begun to flow freely. Seeing this, a private in the ranks fainted and was left where he fell. As the hundredth and final lash fell with a dull thud, Rogers was slumped against the triangle, his back a gory mess. Cut down, he was covered with a cloak and taken to the hospital to have salt rubbed into wounds that would leave permanent scars. He had endured his punishment 'without emotion', recalled the watching Corporal Loy Smith.[24]

Three days later a horrified *Morning Chronicle* broke the story of the flogging – describing it as 'a violent outrage offered to the religion of the country', but incorrectly stating that it had taken place immediately after divine service – and this was soon repeated by the other dailies. Only the *Morning Post* attempted to excuse Cardigan by pointing out that Lord Hill had ordered the punishment and that the commanding officer must have conceived 'that it was his duty not to allow a parade to pass without it being carried into execution'.

The same paper also stated that 'far from [Cardigan] being an advocate for corporal punishment, no case has occurred in his regiment since the end of 1839'. Another man had been found guilty of drunkenness on the march from Brighton to Hounslow, and sentenced by a regimental court-martial to receive 100 lashes, but Cardigan had remitted the whole sentence because of his previous good conduct, and it was well known 'that his Lordship is considered by the soldiers of the 11th Hussars as a most kind and indulgent commanding officer'. Furthermore, there were 'abundant precedents, both in the army and navy, of corporal punishment having been inflicted on Sundays'.[25]

Lord Hill immediately ordered Adjutant-General Macdonald to investigate. In response to Macdonald's letter, Cardigan confirmed that the flogging had taken place but maintained that he could not understand what all the fuss was about. At a loss how to react, Hill consulted Wellington; he was told that while Cardigan was guilty of considerable impropriety, he had not broken the Articles of War and was therefore only liable to be reprimanded. With Wellington's help, therefore, Hill drafted a General Order censuring Cardigan.

Meanwhile, in the House of Commons on 20 April, Joseph Hume asked the government to comment on Cardigan's behaviour. Macaulay's reply was greeted with loud cheers: The 'immediate infliction of punishment on a Sunday after divine service was clearly contrary to the religious feelings and habits of the people of this country,' he admitted, 'and could not be reconciled either with good taste or good feeling.' However, 'whatever imputations might be cast on Lord Cardigan', a 'disposition to inflict corporal punishment' was not one of them. This was the first flogging 'in the regiment for two years'. Even so, he told the House, 'such further notice' of the event 'would be taken, as to render it impossible that a recurrence should take place'.[26]

Macaulay was referring to the General Order that was duly issued on 22 April:

> It is well known that it is not the practice of this country to carry the penal sentences of the law into execution on the Lord's Day; neither is it the practice of the army, whether abroad or at home.

[Lord Hill] is therefore surprised that an officer in the situation of Lieutenant-Colonel commanding a regiment should have carried such a sentence into execution on Sunday.

[Lord Hill] desires that it may be clearly understood that the sentences of military courts are not to be carried into execution on the Lord's Day, excepting in cases of evident necessity, the nature of which it cannot be requisite for him to define.[27]

To the press, this was too little, too late. *The Times* demanded nothing less than Cardigan's head:

We doubt if in the whole series of 1800 years which have elapsed since the great Event which the church commemorates at Easter, anything parallel to this act has before occurred; and, under all the circumstances, we can hardly speak of it as less than diabolical. Precedents there have been for the infliction of corporal punishments in the British Army on Sundays, under circumstances of peculiar emergency. But for their infliction on *Easter* Sunday, we trust . . . that no precedent has ever been known; and we can imagine no exigency, short of mutiny itself, by which it could possibly be justified . . .

What, then, is to be done with this inveterate offender, this plague-spot of the British Army, who seems to exist for the single purpose of setting public opinion at defiance, and bringing discredit upon the unwise clemency which restored him, after one well-merited disgrace, to employments for which he is by temper and character thoroughly disqualified . . . [We] trust some independent member of the House of Commons will take an early opportunity of cutting the Gordian knot, and move an address to the Crown for the removal of the Earl of Cardigan from the Lieutenant-Colonelcy of the 11th Hussars.[28]

Such hysterical ranting, however, was more a reaction to a career of indiscretions than to the flogging incident itself. After all, while Cardigan had displayed a massive lack of judgement and sensitivity, he had not contravened Army regulations. Furthermore, it is probably safe to assume that had Cardigan been the commanding officer who ordered the flogging of a soldier at Dover barracks on Good Friday, the event would not have passed without censure.

As it was, the press had whipped the public into a frenzy over the Sabbath flogging, and on 24 April the Cabinet met to devise a solution. Later, Lord Melbourne sent a record of the day's events to the Queen at Buckingham Palace:

> We have had under our consideration at the Cabinet the unfortunate subject of the conduct of Lord Cardigan. The public feeling is almost certain that a Motion will be made in the House of Commons for an Address praying your Majesty to remove him from the command of his regiment. Such a Motion, if made, there is very little chance of resisting with success, and nothing is more to be apprehended and deprecated than such an interference of the House of Commons with the interior discipline and government of the Army. It was also felt that the general order issued by the Horse Guards was not sufficient to meet the case, and in those circumstances it was thought proper that Lord Melbourne should see Lord Hill, and should express to him the opinion of the Cabinet, that it was necessary that he should advise your Majesty to take measures as should have the effect of removing Lord Cardigan from the command of the 11th Hussars. The repeated acts of imprudence of which Lord Cardigan has been guilty, and the repeated censures which he has drawn down upon himself, form a ground amply sufficient for such a proceeding, and indeed seem imperiously to demand it.
>
> Lord Melbourne has seen Lord Hill and made to him this consideration. Lord Hill is deeply chagrined and annoyed, but will consider the matter and confer again with Lord Melbourne upon it to-morrow.[29]

The point Melbourne was trying to make was that it was better to remove Cardigan before the House of Commons made it impossible *not* to do so, and thereby created a dangerous precedent. At least then they could maintain the fiction that the lower chamber had not interfered with the internal government of the Army. But he reckoned without the Horse Guards' determination not to be dictated to by politicians *per se*. Hill's annoyance had been not so much with Cardigan as with the Cabinet for presenting him with such an unpalatable ultimatum. His inevitable reaction had been to buy time to re-consult Wellington.

The Queen, too, appreciated the danger ahead and urged caution. 'I wrote to Ld M,' she recorded, 'that this was a serious question, as affecting the discipline of the Army, in general, & that I hoped the matter would not be hurried, but duly weighed, before anything was finally determined upon.'[30]

Next morning, Melbourne returned to the Horse Guards for Hill's response to the demand for Cardigan's head. He was told that the Duke of Wellington had vetoed any further action:

> The opinion of the Duke [Melbourne wrote to the Queen] is that the Punishment on Sunday was a great impropriety and indiscretion upon the part of Lord Cardigan, but not a Military offence, nor a breach of the Mutiny Act or of the Articles of War; that it called for the censure of the Commander-in-Chief, which censure was pronounced by the General Order upon which the Duke was consulted before it was issued, and that according to the usage of the Service no further step can be taken by the Military Authorities. This opinion Lord Melbourne will submit to-day to the Cabinet Ministers.[31]

Later that afternoon, Melbourne again wrote to the Queen, telling her 'that the Cabinet had decided that nothing should or could be done respecting Cardigan, besides the General Order'. It had bowed to Wellington's opinion, but over dinner that evening Melbourne told the Queen that he still feared repercussions in the House of Commons. 'Could Cardigan not be persuaded to resign,' asked the Queen. He would 'rather be shot dead on a Parade', replied Melbourne. His next remark to the Queen indicated that he, for one, did not consider the flogging incident to be as serious as had been made out: 'I don't think so much of this last act of Cardigan's, it was a piece of misadventure, but with the present feeling in the country, & then the act having been committed over Easter Sunday, makes it very difficult.'

But Melbourne had taken seriously Victoria's suggestion that Cardigan should be asked to resign, and the following day he sounded him out. Cardigan's answer, Melbourne told the Queen, was that he did not want to 'unless perhaps the Prince were to speak to him'. Hoping to forestall this possibility, Cardigan sent 'a very proper' letter to Lord Fitzroy Somerset at Horse Guards 'expressing his regret for having punished this man on a Sunday, in doing which, he had *only* thought he was carrying out his duty, but now felt it had been *want of judgment*'. This must have had the desired effect, because Prince Albert was never called to ask Cardigan to resign.

Melbourne was certainly impressed, reporting the gist of the letter to the Queen on 29 April, and adding that as he had once been guilty of a similar piece of 'misadventure' he had told the Cabinet he sympathised with Cardigan.[32]

But on 6 May, Melbourne's initial fears were realised when an M.P. by the name of Muntz gave warning that he intended to introduce a motion asking the Queen 'to institute an inquiry into the conduct' of Lord Cardigan during his command of the 11th Hussars, 'with the view of ascertaining how far such conduct has rendered him unfit to remain in Her Majesty's service'. However, the time delay had allowed the anti-Cardigan atmosphere to dissipate, causing Melbourne to tell the Queen that the motion 'will not have many votes'.[33]

The debate took place during the evening of 13 May. Proposing the motion, Muntz told the House that the flogging on the Sabbath was 'but the last of a series of misdeeds on the part of the noble earl which made it impossible to believe that there was not something more culpable than neglect on his part'. The fact was that Cardigan had 'a total want of command over his own temper' which 'rendered him totally unfit to command others'. To illustrate this, Muntz said that in Cardigan's first two years in command, when the regiment was 350 strong, he had held 105 courts-martial, put men on defaulters more than 700 times, and placed 90 men in Canterbury jail. Yet during 20 years in India, when the regiment was 700 strong, the number of punishments was fewer.

Macaulay replied for the government, pointing out that the discipline of the Army was the responsibility of the Queen and 'ought not to be submitted to large popular assemblies of men, who were too apt to be influenced by party and factious impulse'. Whatever his faults, Cardigan was 'one of the most unfortunate men of the present time' and M.P.s 'should beware how they hastened to take advantage of the unpopularity of an individual, to introduce a precedent which, if once established, would lead to the most fatal effects to the whole of our military system'. In any case, he said, Lord Hill and the Duke of Wellington had decided that Cardigan had not committed a military offence and could only be reprimanded by a General Order which had already been issued.

Lord George Lennox spoke next, defending Cardigan's record of punishment by pointing out that 'the discipline of regiments returning from foreign stations was . . . more lax than that of regiments which had passed the same period at home'. Cardigan was 'an abused man' and 'had he not been the Earl of Cardigan, the press would never have raised the cry it did'.

A Mr Stanley then alluded to Richard Reynolds by saying that it was unfair that certain long-serving officers, 'placed under the command of an officer whose temper seemed to be incorrigible, should be driven to acts which deprived this country of their service'. Consequently, he would vote for the motion.

Sir Hussey Vivian, Master-General of the Ordnance, rose and said that the Sunday flogging had arisen from an 'error in judgement' and that 'Lord Cardigan had authorised him to express to the House his deep regret. He was followed by more speakers, but the number was roughly two to one in opposition to the motion. When the House eventually divided, this proportion was maintained: 58 for the motion, 135 against – the latter number including Sir Robert Peel, William Gladstone, and the 36-year-old Benjamin Disraeli who had first entered Parliament in 1837.[34]

The cost of Cardigan's singleminded determination that his regiment would be the smartest and most efficient in the British Army had been the string of controversies which had made him one of the most unpopular men in the land. Yet he was still in command, and seemed to be close to achieving his ambition.

On 3 and 5 May, the 11th Hussars was again inspected by General Sleigh who expressed his entire 'approbation of its appearance in the field, and the quickness and steadiness with which the manoeuvres were performed'. He was also 'much pleased with the inspection of the regiment in barracks'. On 9 June, Prince Albert reviewed the 11th Hussars and spoke of 'his high approbation of the appearance and movement of the regiment'.

Throughout the summer the regiment provided escorts for the Queen on journeys to Nuneham in Oxfordshire, Woburn Abbey in Bedfordshire, and Woolwich to launch HMS *Trafalqar*. Both from the Queen and Lord Hill, Cardigan received fulsome praise. After the visit to Woburn, the seat of the Duke of Bedford, Lord Hill recorded his 'great satisfaction at the judicious arrangements made by Lieutenant Colonel Earl of Cardigan for carrying his instructions into effect; and also at the precision and regularity with which they had been acted upon by the officers, non-commissioned officers, and private men'.[35]

Such approbation was far from routine, given that the young royal couple had already been the target of two assassination attempts in the space of a year. In June 1840, they were driving up Constitution Hill in an open phaeton when Edward Oxford, 17, a waiter in a 'low inn', fired at them with two pistols from a distance of just six feet. Both shots missed, Oxford was seized by onlookers and later judged guilty but insane. Almost a year later, another failed attempt was made by a man called John Francis when the Queen and Prince Albert were out near Buckingham Palace in an open carriage. This time the gunman got away, but instead of confining themselves indoors they showed remarkable courage by going out the very next day. Again Francis struck, this time from just five paces, but he missed and was arrested. Initially condemned to death, the sentence was commuted to life imprisonment.

Victoria and Albert had been lucky – within two years Peel's private secretary, Edmund Drummond, would be killed by an assassin targeting the Prime Minister. Henceforth the purpose of their military escorts was far from simply ceremonial, and Hill's praise of Cardigan reflected this extra responsibility.

However, when Cardigan tried to join the most prestigious military club in Britain – the United Service Club – the efficiency of his regiment counted little when set against his record of bad relations with fellow officers.

Founded as the Military Club at the Thatched House Tavern in St James's Street in May 1815, to provide a meeting-place for senior officers not on foreign service, it became the United Service Club in January 1816 when it amalgamated with the Navy Club. Absent then in Brussels, the Duke of Wellington was not among the 80 founding officers but accepted an offer of membership on 13 June, just five days before the battle of Waterloo. Originally based in Charles Street, in 1828 the Club moved to its Beau Nash-designed residence on the former site of Carlton House, which was demolished after George IV had moved into Buckingham Palace.

It did not help Cardigan's application that so-called 'Indian' officers – both those who had served with the Queen's regiments in India, and those in the service of the East India Company – made up a sizeable number of Club members. Many of them were unwilling to forgive certain insulting remarks attributed to him and, when the election took place on 6 July 1841, he was blackballed 28 times. 'The number of ostracisms recorded against his lordship may, therefore, be taken as a tolerable example of the estimation in which he is held by the unbiassed members of the club,' gloated the *United Service Gazette*.

Seven years later he tried again, and this time was blackballed by 18 members. 'Courage, my Lord, courage! "Once more unto the breech!"' scoffed the same paper, suggesting that after another twelve years and two more attempts the excluding balls 'may disappear altogether!'[36]

But Cardigan had his pride, and in December 1848 it was announced that he had founded the Military and County Club in St Martin's Lane. 'A home for the blackballed,' sneered the *United Service Gazette*. When that Club folded, Cardigan started another, the St James's Military Club, but this too was quickly crippled by huge debts. On 1 November 1852, at a meeting of creditors who were owed a total of £10,000, the following resolution was reached:

> That Lord Cardigan be applied to, through the solicitor attending this meeting, to ascertain from his Lordship whether he had arranged with his co-committee men for the *immediate discharge* of the now long outstanding debts . . ., and if not, whether such would be done before the 12th; if not, then a second meeting stands appointed for that date, for the purpose of determining on suing his Lordship for the debts, the creditors looking chiefly to him for their discharge.

In the event, the Club was wound up and its total debts of almost £20,000 were paid off by members' contributions of £60 each, although some had to be taken to court before they paid.[37]

There was more disappointment in store when Cardigan tried to take advantage of the long-awaited change in administration. In late May 1841, the Melbourne government had been defeated by one vote on a motion of no confidence, and at the subsequent General Election the Conservatives gained a majority of more than 70 seats. When Parliament reopened on 27 August they promptly defeated the government on an amendment to the Address, and three days later Sir Robert Peel kissed hands and became Prime Minister.

Cardigan did not waste any time in renewing his request to be made the next Lord-Lieutenant of Northamptonshire, particularly as the health of Lord Westmorland, the incumbent, was rapidly failing. On 24 September he wrote to Peel from Deene Park, noting that he was 'very anxious to obtain the high post' in his 'own County' and hoping that his trial in the

House of Lords would not be seen as 'any disqualification for the appointment'. He reminded Peel that he had been 'a steady and consistent
supporter of every Tory government under *all circumstances*' during the 16
years he had spent in the Commons, and that he was 'the first to establish
Toryism in the Northern part of Northamptonshire after the passing of the
Reform Bill'.

Five days later, Peel sent a curt reply. Only *when* a vacancy had occurred,
would he 'consider with the Secretary of State for the Home Department'
the advice to be given to the Queen regarding 'the nomination to an
appointment involving so high a trust and responsibility'.

Lord Westmorland duly died on 15 December and Cardigan hurried to
London to press his claim. During an interview with Peel, he again
emphasised how much he had given to the Conservative party and what it
owed him in return. Back at Deene, he wrote once more on 23 December
to remind Peel that he had been forced to vacate his original seat 'in consequence of my determination to support you and the Duke of
Wellington's administration upon the Catholic Question', and that 'at no
considerable pecuniary sacrifice' he had then obtained Fowey 'for the sole
purpose of supporting the Government then in power'. Furthermore, he
added, the lord-lieutenancy was 'the only appointment' he had ever asked
for either for himself or any one of his family during the 23 years that he
had been 'the undeviating supporter of yourself & Colleagues in
Parliament'.[38]

But unbeknown to him, Peel and his Home Secretary, Sir James
Graham, were already in the process of persuading the Marquess of Exeter,
Lord-Lieutenant of Rutlandshire, to accept the vacancy – Exeter's reluctance being based on the fact that he was unwilling to leave his existing
post. On Christmas Day, Graham wrote to Peel, suggesting that Exeter be
allowed to assume both posts 'on an understanding that he shall resign
[Rutlandshire], when you require it, and when support given to your
administration by young Gil. Heathcote or by Ld. Gainsborough might
justify the appointment of one or other of them'.

Clearly, there was nothing unusual about a request for a position as the
reward for political support; Cardigan was simply disqualified on account
of his notoriety. The irony of Graham's suggestion is that Cardigan's old
adversary, Sir Gilbert Heathcote, stood to gain from his disappointment.

Eventually, Lord Exeter agreed temporarily to assume both lord-lieu-
tenancies and, on 6 January 1842, Peel wrote to Cardigan to give him the
bad news: Exeter's name had been submitted for Her Majesty's approval.

Again Cardigan hurried to London, hoping to change Peel's mind. Anxious to avoid an unseemly confrontation, Peel arranged for him to see Graham, who hinted at the reason for his disappointment by telling him that he, Graham, disapproved of his 'conduct in matters which have appeared before the Public in the course of the last two or three years'.

Writing to Peel from Portman Square on 9 January, Cardigan rejected Graham's criticism by saying that his conduct had been 'on *each separate occasion as it occurred, in detail* (with one exception) approved of by my military superiors'. It was a fair point to make, although in truth there had been two exceptions – Sandham and the Sunday flogging – not one.

'I cannot,' he continued, 'but feel deep regret & disappointment that the concern and persecution of the Public Press, which has invariably pronounced me in the wrong when my military superiors, and all judicial tribunals, had decided in my favour, should have prevented the honour being conferred upon me to which I may safely say it is *generally* considered I have the strongest pretensions.' He was particularly bitter, he said, because 'in the selection of Lord Exeter, a person already loaded with honour and favours by Her Majesty, and for many years holding the situation of Lord Lieutenant in an adjoining county, has been brought into Northamptonshire in which county he *does not reside*, contrary to his Lordship's wishes, as by himself openly declared . . .; thereby inflicting upon me (to say the least of it) a *marked slight*, and, as it were, affixing a stigma upon me in my own County'.

The following day, Peel sent his final response. There were 'several competitors' for such a post, he wrote, and no unsuccessful candidate could 'be entitled to consider his non-appointment on a vacancy as a mark of slight or disrespect'. While Lord Exeter had not put himself forward, 'other Peers connected with Northamptonshire' had, and each had been disappointed. 'I think you will find,' wrote Peel, 'that Burleigh is within the County of Northampton.'[39]

Cardigan may have forfeited any potential patronage from Peel's government, but his stock still remained high at Buckingham Palace. Prince Albert Edward, the heir to the throne, had been born in early November 1841, and seven weeks later the 11th Hussars escorted the King of Prussia from New Cross to Staines on his way to Windsor Castle for the christening.

On 28 January 1842, the regiment was reviewed with the Royal Horse

Guards at Windsor by the Queen, accompanied by the King of Prussia, Prince Albert, the Duke of Wellington and others. The Queen's 'approbation' was communicated to the men in regimental orders. When the King of Prussia took his leave a week later, Cardigan's regiment was chosen to escort him to Woolwich, where he embarked for Ostend.[40]

It was at about this time that John Anstruther Thomson, the celebrated horseman, had a curious encounter with Lord Cardigan. Then a cornet in the 13th Light Dragoons – recently returned from India and billeted near Hampton Court – his squadron commander was none other than Major Augustus Wathen, formerly of the 15th Hussars.

One evening, the officers of the 13th Light Dragoons received an invitation to dine with the 11th Hussars in their unofficial regimental mess, the Mitre Hotel at Hampton Court. Wathen, not surprisingly, made his excuses, but Thomson and a number of others went. After a sumptuous dinner, a group of them retired to one officer's room where they sat on the floor and 'chaffed'. Among them was Lieutenant John Cunningham, a favourite of Cardigan's who had testified against Richard Reynolds at his court-martial. Cunningham kept a pack of stag-hounds at a nearby public house, but the ground was frosty and considered too hard to hunt. Then the weather turned:

> About three in the morning [wrote Thomson] it began to rain, and so we all wanted to hunt, but there was a watering parade ordered for the morning, so it was settled we should send a deputation to Cardigan to ask leave.
>
> Johnny Vivian and I were selected. We knocked at his door and a gruff voice said 'Come in.' He was sitting on the side of his bed, with a shawl dressing-gown on and his hair all dishevelled and standing on end. He had not slept a wink we had made such a row. We stated our request, and he said 'Certainly, certainly,' so we thanked him and retired. In the morning he put his head cautiously outside the door and said, 'Have all those d——d fellows gone?'[41]

Contrary to public perception, Cardigan could be remarkably indulgent towards his officers, particularly when hunting was involved. And if the quarry was the fairer sex, then so much the better. A much-repeated anecdote of the time involved one of his captains requesting a short leave which Cardigan refused, citing an inspection as the reason. But despite his chief's growing anger, the captain pressed his request, saying: 'The fact is, sir, I must have leave; I have arranged to elope with Mrs———.'

Cardigan's ire instantly dissipated. 'My *dear* fellow, why didn't you say so before? Of course you may have your leave. A most hussar-like action!'[42]

But even Cardigan's favourites faced dire consequences if they emulated his financial extravagance too closely, and Lieutenant Cunningham was a prime example. Commissioned as a cornet in January 1839, he soon became – according to the *United Service Gazette* – the 'peculiar pet and *protégé* of his Colonel', visiting Deene to shoot and hunt. Yet with an annual income of £464 – £164 pay and £300 allowance from his father – he was spending ten times as much.

In 1841, Cunningham's father paid off £4,000 of his debts, but they continued to mount. His stag-hounds cost £800, two racehorses £160. He owed £660 to six different tailors, £435 to his jeweller, £359 for hosiery, £131 for a watch and a lady's dressing-case, £202 for cigars and £118 for the hire of a four-in-hand. In addition, he had taken out a number of discounted loans which eventually cost twice their nominal value.

By the summer of 1842, with debts of more than £17,000, his creditors were closing in and he was forced to sell his commission for £1,800. His father agreed to pay all *bona fide* debts, but insisted on him applying to the Insolvent Debtors' Court to free himself from engagements made with extortionate moneylenders.

The *United Service* Gazette was in no doubt who was to blame: '[Cardigan] is a man of large fortune himself, and corresponding habits of expenditure, and accordingly considers the neophyte as little better than a snob who cannot emulate to a certain extent the example of his commanding officer.' An example of this extravagance was the regiment's crimson overalls – 'pseudo-Austrian brick-dust-tinted unmentionables' that 'cost their wearers some twice or thrice the money they would pay for similar articles of attire of legitimate colours'.

While there was some truth in this, the same paper admitted that many parents of young officers 'belonging to what are commonly called "crack regiments"' were continually complaining 'of the ruin entailed upon them by the habits of profligate extravagance'. If Cardigan deserves censure for Cunningham's ruin, it is because he failed to arrest his downward slide rather than that he encouraged such profligacy in the first place. 'We believe,' noted the *United Service Gazette*, 'we are correct in affirming that Lord Cardigan was fully aware of the circumstances of Mr Cunningham; of his means and those of his family; while there can have been no sort of mistake as to the rate at which he was running to ruin.'[43]

Criminal Conversation

In early March 1842, Cardigan again wrote to Peel. A vacancy had
appeared in the Order of the Garter – the highest rank of British knighthood, founded by Edward III in 1347 – and by recommending him Peel
could make up for his earlier oversight. 'I beg to remind you,' Cardigan
added, 'that I rank high amongst the Earls, there being but few senior to
me, that the knighthood of the Garter has already been held in my family –
viz. by George Earl of Cardigan – and that all his successors in my family
down to myself have held places about the person of George the 3rd.'[1]

Peel's response was non-committal. It was his duty, he wrote, to carefully weigh the 'many competitors with very high qualifications' and 'to do
justice to the best of my power, bearing in mind the considerations which
have generally influenced the selection of knights of the Garter'. Privately
he was exasperated with Cardigan's gall. On 20 March, he sent a short-list
of seven to the Queen, adding that 'those Peers who may severally be considered from their rank and station candidates to this high distinction,
have behaved very well in respect to it', and that 'excepting in the cases of
the Duke of Buckingham and recently of Lord Cardigan' he had never
received 'a direct application on the subject of the Garter'.[2]

All seven on the short-list – two dukes and five marquesses – were
senior in rank to Cardigan, but two of them could be said to have led
equally controversial lives. Like Cardigan, the Marquess of Londonderry
commanded a cavalry regiment and had a history of pestering Horse
Guards with his problems. Soon after replacing the retiring Lord Hill as

Commander-in-Chief in August 1842, the Duke of Wellington received yet another complaint from Londonderry. Slamming the papers on his desk, he exclaimed: 'By——, these two lords, my Lord Cardigan and my Lord Londonderry, would require a Commander-in-Chief for themselves; there is no end to their complaints and remonstrances.'

The Marquess of Hertford, on the other hand, was notorious for his licentious living, and was said to have regularly hosted orgies at St Dunstan's, his mansion in Regent's Park, at which 'the prettiest members of the *corps de ballet*' served his guests 'wearing less than what is now considered good form to appear in Salome'.[3]

In the event, neither Londonderry nor Hertford was chosen. But Peel's preference and the man who was appointed, the Duke of Cleveland, was just as unpalatable to Cardigan because it was he who had qualified Cardigan's acquittal in the House of Lords.

This disappointment, however, was insignificant in comparison with the mark of royal disfavour that was about to befall Lord Cardigan. Peel had long been worried about the adverse affect of Prince Albert's association with a regiment as controversial as the 11th Hussars. In mid-April 1842, an opportunity arose to do something about it when the colonelship of the Scots Fusilier Guards became vacant. Peel immediately offered it to the prince, pointing out that the regiment was senior to the 11th Hussars, had been raised as a bodyguard for the monarch, and was therefore a more suitable colonelship for a royal consort to hold.

At first Albert 'had some doubts', the Queen noted in her journal, 'but the fact of the Duke of Wellington having given up the Blues for the Grenadier Guards, make him feel he could not do less'. On 20 April at Wimbledon Common, the Queen reviewed the 11th Hussars for the final time with her husband as Colonel-in-Chief:

> The Regt. looked very handsome [she noted in her journal], & the Review was a very pretty sight. I never saw anything handier than the maneuvring. The day was beautiful. Ld. Cardigan rode a very fine horse & looks very well in uniform & on horseback. At the conclusion of the Review, Albert rode by at the head of his Regt., mounted on his little white Arab, & saluted me as he passed, just as the officers did. He also appeared at the head of the Regt. when the last general Salute was given.

That evening the Queen wrote to Peel, enclosing Prince Albert's acceptance of the colonelship of the Scots Fusilier Guards. Both 'the Prince and the Queen feel much regret at the Prince's leaving the 11th, which is, if possible, enhanced by seeing the Regiment out to-day, which is in beautiful order'. She added:

> The Queen fears, indeed knows, that Lord Cardigan will be deeply mortified at the Prince's leaving the Regiment, and that it will have the effect of appearing like another slight to him; therefore, the Queen much wishes that at same fit opportunity a mark of favour should be bestowed upon him . . .

The following evening, Lord Cardigan was invited to dinner at Buckingham Palace so that Prince Albert could break the bad news. According to the Queen, he took it 'quite quietly, saying he had expected it'. The one consolation was that the 11th Hussars would continue to be known as 'Prince Albert's Own' and their patron would 'still be able to wear the beautiful uniform'.[4]

Despite his brave face, the Queen was right to suspect that Cardigan was deeply upset by Albert's desertion. His humiliation was compounded by the announcement on 18 April that the findings of Richard Reynolds' court-martial had been annulled, and he had been gazetted a captain in the 9th Lancers. Cardigan suspected Peel's involvement, but the initiative seems to have come from the Horse Guards with Wellington's backing. On 29 March, Lord Fitzroy Somerset had written to Colonel Egerton, Hill's private secretary, that 'the Government [is] quite with us in this Reynolds affair' and that Wellington had approved a 'draft letter' for the Queen concerning Reynolds' vindication and reappointment.[5]

Now Cardigan was doubly anxious to attain a symbol of royal favour, and on the afternoon of 27 April he arrived at Buckingham Palace in full-dress uniform for an audience with the Queen. She recorded the interview in her journal:

> He said he came in order to ask me to authorise his being made one of my ADCs [aides-de-camp] on the following grounds. 1st, because he had been Lieut. Col. of Albert's Regt. for 3 years; 2nd, (which I think is of no weight) because I had no Hussar ADC, & lastly, because in the last Brevet several officers, junior to him, had been promoted. His anxiety about it, at the present moment arose, he said, from Capt. Reynolds being restored which I said was

very unfortunate (& I think was *very wrong*), but had been an old promise. *That* Ld Cardigan remarked did not lessen the fact of its being prejudicial to him as it had the appearance before the whole world of his having treated Reynolds harshly – whereas he had it in writing that the Horse Guards approved his conduct. I told Ld Cardigan that he must know I was fettered, & could not do as I liked. However, I *would* bear in mind, what he had said, though I could make no promise at the present moment. I then expressed Albert's & my regret, at A's leaving the Regt., which seemed to gratify Ld C, & I should have liked to be able to promise him, what he wanted, but that would have been imprudent.[6]

The Queen's caution was based on the fact that in mid-April she had already sounded out Lord Hill as to this very possibility, and his reply had been unenthusiastic. Mentioning Reynolds' court-martial, Hill had noted that 'in the course of the proceedings upon it, it did appear that in the exercise of the command of the 11th Hussars, the Earl of Cardigan, tho' distinguished for zeal and anxiety for the service, had not always displayed the soundest judgment nor merited the unreserved expression of Your Majesty's approbation'. He had also pointed out that not a year had passed since he had been forced to censure Cardigan for flogging a soldier on a Sunday, 'an act of indiscretion which excited a strong feeling in the country' and which almost caused Hill to recommend he be removed from his command.[7]

Yet the Queen was only partially discouraged because in July she sent her personal adviser, Baron Stockmar, to gauge Peel's reaction to such an appointment. Stockmar reported that Peel 'had made it a rule with the Commander-in-Chief never to interfere with their appointments for political purposes of his own, but in return, never to share the responsibility attached to the qualifications for the appointments made'. Reading between the lines, Stockmar was sure that Peel 'neither could nor would raise an objection to the execution of Your Majesty's good intentions for Lord Cardigan, yet he could read on his face, that he is inclined to consider it as a very objectionable one'.[8]

Under the circumstances, with neither the Prime Minister nor the Commander-in-Chief in favour, the Queen felt unable to appoint Cardigan. Once again, and not for the last time, Peel had stood in his way despite the Queen's appeal for Cardigan to be shown a 'mark of favour'. In both September 1842 and February 1845, when new vacancies appeared in the Order of the Garter, Cardigan wrote to Peel asking to be recommended, and on each occasion he was not even short-listed.

At the end of April 1842, shortly after the replacement of Prince Albert by General Sir Arthur Clifton as colonel of the regiment, the 11th Hussars was relieved of the Queen's Duty by Cardigan's original corps, the 8th Hussars, and moved to York with detachments at Burnley, Sheffield, Barnsley and Colne. This was a response to a resurgence of Chartist activity, particularly in the north.

The movement had begun three years earlier, in May 1838, when the London Radical William Lovett had drafted the People's Charter – a demand for sweeping parliamentary reform as the only solution to the social injustices of the new industrial order. Born out of the economic depression of 1837–8, when high unemployment and the effects of the Poor Law Amendment Act of 1834 were causing suffering throughout the country, the People's Charter appealed to all shades of the working class. Its six demands – universal manhood suffrage, equal electoral districts, vote by secret ballot, annually elected parliaments, payment of parliament members, and abolition of the property qualification for membership – seem tame by today's standards (with only annual parliaments not yet law), but to the ruling classes of 1838, just six years after the passing of the Great Reform Act, they were seen as nothing short of revolution.

Threats by the more extreme leaders like Irishman Feargus O'Connor to resort to 'ulterior measures' if their demands were ignored only hardened the government's stance. When a massive petition in support of the People's Charter was presented to Parliament in July 1839, it was rejected out of hand. There followed in November an armed uprising of extremists at Newport, but this was swiftly crushed and its leaders transported to Australia. Even the moderate leaders who had eschewed violence were arrested and given short prison terms.

By early 1842, with the moderates once again in control and an efficient national organisation in place, the Chartist movement began gathering signatures for a second national petition, and it was to guard against any consequent public disorder that the 11th Hussars were sent north. Cardigan, however, remained in London for the summer Season, content to let his second-in-command, Brevet-Colonel Rotton, take charge of policing operations in York.

The massive Chartist petition, containing an estimated three million signatures – many of them fakes – was finally presented to Parliament in August. Again it was rejected, and again there were disturbances, particularly in Lancashire, Yorkshire and Derbyshire. With detachments in all three counties, the 11th Hussars was in the thick of it. Perhaps the most serious riot took place in Halifax when a troop under the command of Captain William Forrest, a company from the 61st Regiment and a force of special constables were caught between two mobs entering the town from different directions. The *Halifax Guardian* reported:

> The whole of North Parade was densely crowded, and many of the bludgeon men made their way into the bye streets. The mob not appearing willing to disperse, but becoming rather more furious in their behaviour, Captain Forrest was ordered to clear the streets. The scene was now becoming rather serious, but owing to the admirable courage and coolness of the Hussars, the mob dispersed at that place, without we believe a single wound being inflicted.[9]

Forrest, Cardigan's particular *bête noire* since the departure of the two Captains Reynolds, also distinguished himself in the eyes of the Establishment at Elland in Yorkshire. There, after his troop had been stoned and three men unhorsed, he managed to disperse the violent crowd and rescue the badly beaten troopers by ordering his men to charge while firing their carbines in the air.

Absent from the regiment for much of the year in London and Northamptonshire, Cardigan missed all the excitement, but this did not prevent him from exercising a long-distance authority that soon caused more controversy. The first officer to provoke his ire was Captain John Reynolds, by now at the Senior Department of the Royal Military College. Reynolds had insisted on taking with him a batman from the 11th, but the man drank and was becoming a menace. Reynolds applied for a replacement, but Cardigan would not hear of it. More angry letters were exchanged and eventually Cardigan sent all the papers to the new Commander-in-Chief, the Duke of Wellington. Exasperated by the pettiness of the disagreement, Wellington advised Cardigan to let the matter drop 'for my sake, as I really have not leisure time to consider all the nice details of these trifles'.[10]

This was followed by an equally trivial disagreement between Cardigan and Captain Forrest. At the end of October 1842, Forrest applied for leave; his health had been poor for some time and he needed a rest to recover. Back came a letter from Cornet Hanson, recently promoted from regimental sergeant-major to adjutant, telling him that Major-General Sir Thomas Arbuthnot, the district commander, had granted him leave of absence for a week, but that he was to remain on duty until relieved by Lieutenant Harrison.

Forrest wrote back, demanding to know under whose authority he had been detained, and was told that Lord Cardigan had set the conditions. He then protested to Cardigan in person and was informed that his leave had been cancelled 'until further orders'.[11]

This time Forrest's brother-in-law, Major Carmichael Smyth of the 93rd Highlanders, notified Wellington of the dispute. Normally, an officer would have been chastised for interfering in another regiment's business, but Carmichael Smyth's brother, Sir James of the Engineers, had drawn up the plans for Waterloo and the Duke had a soft spot for the whole family. After making inquiries, Wellington wrote firmly to Cardigan. It was, he said, his 'earnest suggestion that you carry out the provisions of the General Regulations and orders of the Army in a spirit of Conciliation and Indulgence, and, above all, exercise your command in such a manner as shall prevent your being involved in fresh disputes on trivial regimental matters'.[12]

For a time Cardigan seemed to be heeding this advice; but in the spring of 1843, he and his regiment were despatched to Ireland. Since the formation of Peel's Conservative ministry in 1841, Daniel O'Connell, the great Irish patriot, had been actively campaigning for the repeal of the 1801 Act of Union which had joined England and Ireland as a single state. Even without this political threat the country was highly unstable, with the majority of its 8 million inhabitants relying on the notoriously unpredictable potato crop. So three infantry regiments that were due to return to England were ordered to stay, and they were joined by one other, the 60th Rifles, and two cavalry regiments, the 11th and 15th Hussars.

Now back with the regiment on a full-time basis, Cardigan found it impossible to avoid still more 'turn-ups' with his officers. In late August, at a field day in Phoenix Park, he ordered the arrest of one of his subalterns for unsoldierly conduct. The officer was only released after being chastised by Lieutenant-General Sir Edward Blakeney, the Commander-in-Chief in Ireland. A couple of days later, during another field day, Cardigan ordered the brigade to dismount. Thinking that the exercise was over, Lieutenant

Harrison told his groom to return his horse to the stables, but then Cardigan ordered the brigade to remount and the forlorn figure of Harrison was left standing. Explaining his mistake, he added that he had already sent a message for his horse to be returned.

'Go for him yourself, sir!' shouted Cardigan.

Later, at an interview with Cardigan, Harrison objected to his treatment in front of the regiment and said that if it was repeated he would not obey such an order. Predictably, he was put under arrest and only released on the intervention of General Blakeney.

In early October, the orderly officer Lieutenant Weguelin was arrested on Cardigan's orders after arriving ten minutes late for morning stables. This time Major-General Wyndham, commanding the Dublin Garrison, had to insist on his release. Soon after, another officer complained to Wyndham of Cardigan's language in the drill field. Eventually, Wellington came to hear of this catalogue of ill-feeling, and he immediately issued a final warning to the officers of the regiment in the form of a memorandum:

> The constant disagreement between Lord Cardigan and the offi-
> cers serving under him having been brought to the notice of the
> Commander-in-Chief the Duke of Wellington, he proposes,
> should these dissensions continue, to put a stop to them by dis-
> persing all the officers through various regiments in the service . . .
> In future should any officer of the Regiment address any com-
> plaint or remonstrance to Lord Cardigan, such letter, together
> with a copy of the proposed reply from the Lieutenant-Colonel is
> to be submitted to the General Officer who should be so unfor-
> tunate as to have the Regiment under his command.[13]

Clearly, Cardigan took this more as a warning to his officers than to himself, because his own high-handed behaviour altered little. In the winter of 1843, Captain Forrest was finally granted leave to take his heavily pregnant wife back to friends in England for the period of her confinement. The baby was born but Mrs Forrest became ill and, on the advice of the doctor, Forrest applied for an extension of leave. This was turned down by Cardigan, but Forrest stayed anyway. Once again the papers were sent in to Wellington, and this time Lord Cardigan received the brunt of opprobrium:

> It became necessary for Captain Forrest to apply for an extension,
> and the Duke considers that Captain Forrest had a perfect right to

do so until after his wife's confinement and until after such time as her medical advisers and her friends should cease to wish for his presence . . . The Duke must observe that in the whole of his experience he had never known the time of the staff of the Army to be taken up in so useless a manner as in the present instance, that if any other Regiment in Her Majesty's Service gave such trouble and could not be commanded without such voluminous correspondence and such futile details an additional staff would be necessary for conducting the affairs of that Regiment. The details of the foolish quarrels of the officers of the 11th among themselves had gone to such an extent that if they continued the Duke might think it necessary to submit to Her Majesty some plan to relieve the Department from an intolerable annoyance.[14]

Wellington's threat must have had some effect on both Cardigan and his officers, because for a time there were no more incidents. Such tranquillity may have been aided by the exchange of Cardigan's arch foe, Captain William Forrest, to the 4th Dragoon Guards in March 1844. They would not come into professional contact again until the Crimean War.

But Cardigan was never far from public derision. In the autumn of 1843, O'Connell planned an enormous demonstration at Clontarf to demand the repeal of the Act of Union. The Lord-Lieutenant of Ireland promptly issued a proclamation prohibiting it, and a military force was earmarked to back this up. According to a letter in the *Freeman's Journal* of 21 October – from an officer who cited an informant 'high in command' – Cardigan was called to London and told by the Secretary-at-War that he would command the combined force of cavalry, infantry and artillery with the task of arresting O'Connell. Hearing this, Cardigan was said to have replied: 'Leave him to *me*, I'll *nab* him at the onset; my life on it.'

The correspondent, 'Captain Outall', was not amused: 'Cardigan to lay hands on O'Connell!!! Irishmen, hear you that! If I were near, and saw Lord Cardigan approach O'Connell, I would risk my life to – make SOMEBODY the richer of an earl's coronet.'[15]

In the event, O'Connell drew back from inciting civil war and ordered his followers not to attend the meeting. Cardigan and his troops marched to Clontarf to make sure of this and George Loy Smith, recently promoted to sergeant in Captain Douglas's troop, recorded a curious encounter:

On arriving at Clontarf, where the meeting was to be held, there was not a person to be seen. After a time we dismounted on the sands and fed our horses, remaining there till evening. On our march back, by the roadside sat an old woman. Just as Lord Cardigan was passing her, she sprang up and shouted, 'Arrah bad luck to ye's. We'll have the repeal in spite of your red arses. Three cheers for Daniel O'Connell!' Lord Cardigan and all within hearing had a good laugh at the old woman.[16]

Peel ordered O'Connell's arrest, nonetheless, and it was a detachment of the 11th Hussars that escorted him to Kilmainham Gaol. 'We were frequently confined to barracks during his trial and held in readiness to turn out at a moment's notice,' wrote Loy Smith. O'Connell was convicted by a jury, but released on appeal when the law lords voted three to two in his favour.

Cardigan's chief motive for offering to nab O'Connell, according to a lady who knew the Earl well, was in the hope that it might 'help him in the quashing of the Lady William Paget affair'. Born Frances de Rottenburg (and known as Fanny), the beautiful but penniless daughter of a general, she had married the second son of the 1st Marquess of Anglesey in 1827. Then aged 24, and already a post-captain in the Royal Navy, Lord William Paget appeared set for a glittering future. But 'from this turning point in his career,' wrote the 7th Marquess of Anglesey, author of *One-Leg*, the biography of the 1st Marquess, 'he launched himself, ably seconded by his wife, along the road to ruin, which was to lead him to a debtors prison and eventually to permanent exclusion from Britain.'

Within two years the couple had accumulated debts of £20,000, and Lord William was threatening to give up his seat in Parliament – M.P.s being immune from arrest for debt – as a means of forcing his father to bail him out. Anglesey was outraged, but conceded that 'he has me in his clutches'. Given a full list of his son's debts, he wrote: 'I am shocked, disgusted, shamed, at all I *hear*! What a catalogue of meanness – of shuffling shifts – of prodigality – of selfishness.'

Nevertheless, to save his son from prison he raised a loan on his estates to pay off the most pressing debts. Out of respect for Anglesey, a former Lord-Lieutenant of Ireland who had supported Catholic emancipation, Lord William's Irish creditors offered to accept ten shillings in the pound; but Anglesey insisted that they should be paid in full. He also increased

Lord William's allowance and arranged for him to be given command of a frigate due to sail for the West Indies.

But, like Cardigan, controversy dogged Lord William and, on his return in January 1831, he requested and was granted his own court-martial. The ship's boy had failed 'to lock the tank after going for water', a serious offence, and Lord William had ordered his flogging. Recently flogged for another offence, he had thrown himself overboard rather than submit to the 'cat' a second time. Two courts of inquiry in Nova Scotia had honourably acquitted Lord William, as did the court-martial in Portsmouth, but no sooner did he step ashore from the flagship after his trial than he was arrested for debts incurred before his departure. This time his older brother, Lord Uxbridge, secured his release at a cost of £500.

Soon back at sea he was out of trouble, but in 1833 he resigned his command and went to live abroad, first in France, then Brussels. For a while he served in Spain as a mercenary in the British Auxiliary Legion, raised to defend the Queen Regent in the civil war against the Carlists. All the time his expenditure far outweighed his income. In 1836 he returned to Britain, was arrested for debt and again his father paid what was necessary, but this time under strict conditions that Lord William took his family and lived in France.

Towards the end of 1839, he was once more in England, ostensibly to find employment in the Navy but in fact to get more money out of his father. In February 1840, at a family council, Anglesey stated that since 1830 he had had to raise almost £27,000 – three times his son's patrimony – to pay Lord William's debts, and that it was only out of consideration for him that William's name was retained on the Navy List. Even so, Anglesey agreed to raise his income by £100 to £780, to pay off his debts in France and to try to obtain employment for him. He then kissed his son's hand and told him he forgave him 'in the hope that you will yet prove worthy of my affection and regard'.

Lord William and his wife then returned to France, but were back again before the end of the year. Ignoring his father's demands that he leave the country, Lord William got himself elected M.P. for the borough of Andover in the General Election of 1841, making him immune from arrest and necessitating his residence in England. But his debts continued to rise, so that by 1843 the whole of his allowance was under stoppages and he was living exclusively on his naval half-pay of £3 15s a week.[17]

For many years Lord William had been friendly with Lord Cardigan, so he was well aware of the latter's reputation as a womaniser, and the fact that he had been forced to pay damages to Lady Cardigan's first husband for adultery. It is, therefore, highly probable that he saw the mutual attraction between his wife and the notorious hussar as an opportunity to obtain temporary relief from his straitened circumstances. Cardigan was a regular visitor during the three months in 1842 when the Pagets took a house in Queen Street, Mayfair, and it may well have been during this period that Lord William first suspected that Cardigan was having an affair with his wife. The following year he made plans to obtain proof that would stand up in court.

In early August 1843, Lord William again took the house in Queen Street, this time for just a week, and bade his wife join him from Portsmouth where she had been living alone for the previous six months. She arrived on Friday, 4 August and, at her husband's suggestion, sent a note to Lord Cardigan – in residence at 36 Portman Square – inviting him to pay a call the following day. The ostensible reason was to ask Cardigan if he could obtain a situation for a friend of Lord William's. Unbeknown to Fanny, however, her husband had engaged a shady character by the name of Frederick Winter to observe what took place. The house had two adjoining drawing-rooms, with folding doors between them, and Winter – with the assistance of Lord William's valet, John Thomas – was hidden under a sofa in the rear of the two.

Shortly after midday, Cardigan called and was taken into the front drawing-room. Lord William then departed, leaving his wife alone with Cardigan. On this occasion, according to Winter, the folding doors between the two rooms were closed and, though he heard whispering and kissing, he could not be certain that Cardigan and Lady William had actually made love. After an hour, Cardigan left and Winter, sweating profusely, was helped out from under the sofa. That evening, after receiving Winter's report, Lord William and his wife joined Cardigan at the opera in his private box, and later husband and wife slept together in the same bed.

The following day, Fanny sent another note to Cardigan asking him to come at 6 p.m. This time Lord William left before Cardigan arrived, telling his wife that he was taking their eldest son to Woolwich; in fact he was waiting in a cab in nearby Berkeley Square to hear the outcome of the interview. When Cardigan appeared in full-dress uniform 15 minutes early, Fanny had not returned from her airing in Lady Fremantle's carriage and Winter had yet to carry out Lord William's instructions to hide under the sofa in the front drawing-room. So Winter fled downstairs while Lord William's valet told Cardigan that Lady William would be back soon and took him into the front drawing-room to wait. Asked by Cardigan about Lord William's whereabouts, Thomas said that he was out of town in Woolwich.

It was now impossible for Winter to secrete himself in the front drawing-room so, while Thomas created a diversion by raising the blinds, he used a door off the hall to return to his previous hiding-place beneath the sofa in the adjoining room. At this point, according to Winter, the folding doors were closed.

While Thomas was drawing up one of the blinds, Cardigan said, 'Never mind, they will do very well.'

But realising that his movement with the blinds would mask Winter's clumsy efforts to conceal himself, Thomas replied, 'I had better pull them up.' In the event he only partially opened one before going next door to check on Winter.

At 6 p.m. Fanny returned and went to greet Cardigan in the drawing-room. According to Winter, she then went into the back drawing-room to shut the window and the blind, before doing the same with the single open blind in the adjoining room. In the course of doing this she left at least one of the folding doors open, and Winter overheard the subsequent conversation.

'Are you come again?' asked Fanny.

'Yes,' said Cardigan. 'How do you do? Where is Lord William?'

'He is gone to Woolwich with Billy.'

Fanny then asked if he had enjoyed the opera, and he replied 'very well' but not as much as if he had been 'able to have a little closer conversation' with her.

Winter later testified as to what then took place:

> There was then a whispering, but I could not distinctly hear what passed. I could hear kissing distinctly. In a moment all was quite quiet, and I could hear nothing but breathing. The breathing was hard, like that of persons distressed for breath after running. There was a cracking of boots and a creaking of the sofa. I drew myself from under the sofa along the floor, in order to make the less noise, and put my head round the corner of the door. (The witness here describes circumstances which, if true, could leave no doubt that a criminal connexion had taken place between the parties.) After I had satisfied myself, I crept back to my place as quickly as I could. I then heard his lordship as if in the act of getting up from

the sofa, and then walking about, as if he was adjusting his dress. Lady William then came into the back drawing-room and pulled up the blind. She then went into the front drawing-room and pulled up the blinds there. They then appeared to sit down.

Fanny now used the opportunity to ask Cardigan if he could arrange a situation for a respectable man in the Post Office on £120 a year. Cardigan said he could not, on the grounds that he was 'not in very good favour with the current Administration'. Fanny then suggested that he might be able to do it with the assistance of a certain nobleman, but again Cardigan demurred.

'Oh, you ought to do so,' persisted Fanny, 'it is for me and it will make Lord William in a good humour.'

Winter now heard more whispering, followed by sounds that left him in no doubt that they were making love a second time. After this, and in reply to Cardigan's query, Fanny said that she was due to dine with the Duke and Duchess of Richmond. Still apparently unsated, Cardigan asked her if she 'would not stay away under the plea of a headache, or meet him somewhere?'

'Don't you know Lord William better than that?' she replied. 'If he should call and not find me there, he'll go stark staring mad, and go to all the policemen in town.'

She then whispered to Cardigan, and from his answer Winter assumed she had asked if he was fond of her. 'Oh, indeed I am,' said Cardigan, 'I never loved anyone as I do you. Is not Lord William very kind to you?'

'Oh no,' came the reply, 'he is very unkind. He calls me all the damnded bitches he can think of.'

'Does he?' said Cardigan. 'It is very wrong of him.'

Kissing Fanny a final time, he took his leave. By then, Winter had been under the sofa for almost one and a half hours.[18]

(There is no truth, of course, in Harry Flashman's assertion that he was 'locked in the frenzied embrace' of Fanny when Cardigan arrived, and was forced to 'dive trouserless beneath the sofa' where he found Winter 'already *in situ*'. Nor in the claim that he then 'had to lie beside the brute while Cardigan and Fanny galloped the night away two feet above our heads'. For, as we have seen, Fanny arrived after Cardigan; there was barely room for one under the sofa, let alone two; Winter was not beneath the sofa on which the couple were making love; and they definitely did not gallop 'the night away'.)[19]

No sooner had Fanny retired upstairs to change for dinner than Winter left the house to report to Lord William in Berkeley Square. Hearing the news, he rushed home and blacked his wife's eye. The following day he instructed his solicitor to begin proceedings against Cardigan for criminal conversation with the aim of obtaining £15,000 in damages.

According to the *Freeman's Journal* of 8 September, Lord William soon had second thoughts and offered to drop the case if Cardigan agreed to give him 'satisfaction' either 'in England or on the Continent'. Cardigan is said to have responded by rejecting the accusation as 'a foul conspiracy' and pointing out that, since the Tuckett duel, he was no longer 'a free agent' in affairs of honour. Well aware of this, Lord William was able to take the moral high ground in the certain knowledge that Cardigan was not in a position to give him 'satisfaction' – even abroad. The offer was little more than a publicity stunt. Lord William was never going to throw away the opportunity of being awarded a fortune in damages for the sake of his honour.

Needless to say the press had a field day with the scandal, although for once the consensus of opinion was that Cardigan was more sinned against than sinner. On 24 September the *Age* attacked Lord William, arguing that he had been prostituting his wife to Cardigan in order to claim a substantial sum in damages. Cardigan was urged to seek a prosecution for conspiracy. When Lord William then sued the newspaper for criminal libel, it responded by accusing him of being a beater of women.

In October, in the same letter to the *Freeman's Journal* that denounced Cardigan for offering to nab O'Connell, 'Captain Outall' quoted a lady's view that the two events were linked:

> A lady who was present when this communication was made to me, and a lady long acquainted with Lord Cardigan, exclaimed – 'Well, and it may be that Cardigan supposed the *nabbing* of O'Connell would certainly also help him in the quashing of the Lady William Paget affair, etc, etc; but, upon my honour,' added the lady, 'I acquit Cardigan of THAT, for I do not believe there exists a woman who would risk herself and her reputation with such a downright forbidding looking man; – he has something fiendish about him, and is the perfect personification of what the Germans call a 'Gemeine kerl'. Why look at his head, his hair, his colour, his walk. Oh! he is a most mean-looking fellow!' So thought *that* lady, and I know so think some dozen of others.[20]

In preparation for the case – due to be heard in December – Lord William's solicitor, Mr Bebb, tried to persuade Lord Anglesey to appear as a witness, and also to give permission for William junior – his ward since 1838 – to testify as to the affection that existed between his parents. Anglesey's reply was unequivocal:

> I really do not believe it would be possible for Lord William's counsel to extract from my testimony any fact that could be deemed favorable to his case and I have no doubt that the counsel for the Defendant might upon cross-examination elicit facts that might materially damage Lord William's case.
>
> In regard to their son, William Paget, I think it would be highly indecorous . . . that a *son* – a youth of 13 years, should be brought into court with a view of criminating his mother, and I must believe that such a step would produce feelings in the court that would be entirely sinister to Ld. William's interests. Under these circumstances I must deprecate the idea of calling into court William Paget or myself: and in addition I have to say that I am by no means in a state to undertake the journey.[21]

On 22 December 1843, the case was due to be heard before Lord Chief Justice Tindal and a special jury at the Court of Common Pleas in the Guildhall. The case opened at 9 a.m., but within minutes the packed court was told that the record had been withdrawn. 'The announcement came like a thunderclap on all present,' said *The Times*, 'and seemed to excite greater astonishment among the counsel engaged in the cause . . . than among the remainder of the audience.'

Apparently Frederick Winter, the chief witness, had disappeared. Earlier he had walked with Lord William and Mr Bebb as far as Middle Row, Holborn, where they had caught a cab, but he had not been seen since. It later transpired that the previous evening Bebb had refused to pay him two sovereigns for testifying. Winter had been led to believe that there would be some reward in it for him, and when he was disabused of this notion he decided not to appear.

Lord William suspected that Cardigan was involved and immediately wrote accusing him of buying his witness. Copies were sent to a number of newspapers, though *The Times* refused to publish more than a small extract because of its 'violent language'. Even the *Age* would only print the following expurgated version:

MY LORD, – My Solicitor, Mr Bebb, has this instant made known to me that my principal witness, Winter, who was with him until a few minutes of the opening of the Court at Guildhall, had suddenly disappeared.

My Lord, I charge you with the *wicked and infamous crime* of having bought him, and sent him 'out of the way'.

Having done so, you may go forth to the world and declare your innocence, and legally speaking you are so; but you are not in my opinion, one jot the less of a scoundrel for having debauched my wife, nor of a liar and a coward for having acted the part you have done.[22]

As before, Lord William knew that Cardigan could not challenge him to a duel and that his only redress was through the courts. At the resultant hearing, on 30 January 1844, in the Court of Common Pleas, Cardigan's counsel secured a retraction of the slander. Lord William now knew that Cardigan had had nothing to do with Winter's disappearance, because the latter had since resurfaced and was now willing to testify, presumably for a fee.[23]

Meanwhile, Lord William was busy trying to enlist support for his cause – but without much success. He wrote to both the Duke of Wellington and Lord Haddington, First Lord of the Admiralty, sending copies of his correspondence with Cardigan and demanding a full inquiry. Both replied that it was a civil matter and beyond their jurisdictions. Lord William also wrote to his father, imploring him not to believe the rumours that he had set up the whole affair: 'I am an INJURED MAN & GOD IS MY WITNESS; as far as Lady Wm. is concerned, *a most innocent one* . . . I will give up . . . all my old associates, every one of them. FORGIVE THIS ONCE!! and shame and disgrace befall me if I disappoint you. Only don't make me afraid of you, the only thing on earth I fear! . . . *Try me!*'

Anglesey's anguished response is testimony to the strength of blood-ties:

Although I think your whole conduct perfectly atrocious, and as regards myself and knowing as you do my nervous sufferings, absolutely inhuman, yet I do not abandon you. I feel that I ought to have discarded you long ago without a single shilling nevertheless I have continued your allowance after having repeatedly paid your debts and I have taken charge of your 3 sons. All this I shall continue to do, but . . . at present I am most unhappy to say that it is wholly out of my power to throw a shield over you; and I feel perfectly assured that your presence in my house would close my doors against every friend & relative which I have.[24]

All would be settled at the trial and, on 27 February 1844, it reconvened before Lord Chief Justice Tindal and a special jury in the Court of Common Pleas. 'The courtroom was crowded throughout the day to suffocation,' reported *The Times*. 'Every seat was occupied, and the passages were so densely thronged that it was almost impossible, even for the privileged few, to obtain either ingress or egress.'

This was hardly surprising given the allegation and the cast of characters that included the two most notorious noblemen of the time, a vanishing 'private detective', an adulteress called Fanny and a valet by the name of John Thomas. It was far better than theatre; it was real life.

Sir Thomas Wilde, a former Attorney-General, opened the case for the plaintiff, describing the sequence of events in a manner intended to dispel the suspicion of a conspiracy:

> For many years the plaintiff and the defendant had been on terms of the closest friendship, but upon late occasions, from some intimations which had been given to the plaintiff, he entertained a suspicion that an improper intimacy existed between Lord Cardigan and Lady William Paget. In August last Lady William Paget came to town, and in consequence of the suspicion which he felt on the subject, the plaintiff took steps to watch the conduct of his wife and Lord Cardigan. He procured a person who, being placed in a certain situation, would be capable of seeing what passed between these parties.

On Saturday, 4 August, Cardigan had 'called on Lady William Paget, they had some conversation together of a familiar nature, he kissed her, and they sat down on the sofa together. Nothing, however, occurred on that day which was sufficiently well ascertained to warrant any legal steps on the part of the plaintiff, but on the Sunday, the next day, Lord Cardigan arranged to come again':

> Lord William Paget told his wife on that day that he was going to take his son to Woolwich, and while the plaintiff and his son were out together, Lord Cardigan called upon Lady William Paget, and,

after some kissing and toying together, they placed themselves upon the sofa, and, according to the testimony of the witness, a distinct criminal connexion took place between them. This occurred a second time before they separated. Upon being informed by Winter of what had taken place Lord William Paget was considerably excited, and going home challenged his wife with the fact; and even went so far, under the influence of his feelings at the time, as to use considerable violence.

Wilde concluded his address by assuring the jury that he would show 'that their union had been upon the whole a happy one prior to the occurrence in August last', and he would prove 'that the plaintiff had evinced much warmth of affection towards his wife, although he was occasionally subject to sallies of temper'.

After two witnesses had briefly testified to the validity of the marriage, Winter was called and examined by Wilde. He related in detail the two visits made by Cardigan to the house in Queen Street, assuring the court that on Sunday, 6 August, he had been left 'in no doubt that a criminal connexion had taken place'.

Representing Cardigan once again was the brilliant Sir William Follett, Solicitor-General since the formation of Peel's government in 1841. It was during his lengthy cross-examination that Winter's credibility as a witness began to unravel. Winter said that he had met Lord William in 1842 while acting as a clerk for a Mr Samuel Hamer, but would not comment on an alleged 'disgraceful and swindling transaction' in which Lord William and Hamer had been engaged. He had not himself 'been engaged in any swindling transaction', he told the court. When Follett accused him of being forced to leave Hamer's service because he had been embezzling funds, he replied lamely: 'He never charged me with embezzlement, that I heard of, till about six weeks ago.'

Referring to a subsequent employer, Follett asked him: 'Did you not receive money from Mr Bartlett which you afterwards applied to your own purposes?'

'I cannot answer that question,' Winter replied.

It got worse as, with little prompting, he told the court that he had been receiving £1 a week from Mr Bebb, Lord William's lawyer, but that these payments had 'ceased before the day appointed for the trial in December last'. After some more discourse, Follett asked him if he expected to be paid for giving evidence.

'I expect that Lord William Paget will not turn round on me, after my coming here, I may say, at the hazard of my life,' he rejoined.

With the cross-examination over, Sir Thomas Wilde re-examined Winter by asking him about his absence from the original trial. The response did not do Lord William's case any favours:

> I had seen Mr Bebb the evening before, and he asked me whether I would go to the court the next morning, and I said I would. I then asked him if he could oblige me with a couple of sovereigns. He refused, with great indignation, turned on his heel, and walked away. I then resolved that I would not come, as I had not been served with any subpoena.

The implication was obvious. If Winter had refused to testify in December because he had been denied payment, it was only natural for the jury to assume that he had been promised adequate recompense in the meantime – particularly as he had admitted as much during cross-examination. Furthermore, his inability to refute Follett's charges of embezzlement while in the employ of Hamer and others had put the honesty of his remaining testimony in serious doubt.

John Thomas, Lord William's valet and the next witness, only made matters worse. He testified that on Friday, 4 August, he had delivered a letter from Lady William to Lord Cardigan, and that the following day 'my master made a communication to me about some person coming'. In the course of his narrative he also admitted that Lord William had been present in the house when Cardigan had arrived on Saturday, although not when he returned the following day. Again the visit was in response to a letter from Lady William. That night, Lord William had slept in his own room, though previously he 'had been in the habit of sleeping with Lady William'.

Thomas concluded with a feeble attempt to bolster his master's credentials as a family man. While he 'seemed to be attached to his children', Lady William 'did not seem so fond of them'. And, generally speaking, Lord William 'seemed kind and attentive' to his wife and 'used to stay at home in the evenings, and seemed attached to home'.

But Follett's cross-examination of Thomas gave the lie to this and more besides. Thomas admitted that for at least six months prior to the alleged adultery, Lord William had resided alone at the White Bear, a tavern in Piccadilly, where he had spent his time smoking and drinking in the company of certain low friends and had, at least on one occasion, brought back a woman 'to sleep with him'. Turning to the events of the previous August, Thomas said that Lord William had been present when Lady William had given him the first note requesting Cardigan to come to the house in Queen Street – which had only been taken for a week – 'in order that he might get a place for a friend of Lord William's'. Furthermore, on Saturday evening, after Winter had reported Lady William kissing Cardigan, Lord William and his wife accepted the latter's hospitality at the theatre and that night slept together.

Re-examined by Wilde, Thomas said that on Saturday night Lord William 'had not wanted to sleep with one of whom he had suspicions, and thereupon I told him that he ought to do so, in case she suspected, especially as he had agreed to make another trial by Mr Winter next day'.

Finally, the Duke of Richmond, Lady William's brother-in-law, was called to the stand. 'I have seen Lord William sometimes show great atten- tion to his wife, and on other occasions he has appeared to me not so attentive as he ought to be,' he answered ambivalently. 'He always appeared to have a great affection for his children.' Under cross-examination he went further, admitting that Lord William's absence from his wife 'has been so frequent, and of such duration, that I cannot say that he has shown to her the regard which, as her husband, he ought'.

And so ended the case for the plaintiff. Follett then stood and proposed that the defendant, Lord Cardigan, had no case to answer.

'If he rose with the feelings of deepest anxiety,' he told the court, 'it was not the question of a verdict in favour of Lord William Paget that excited these feelings, but that an amiable lady had been made the victim of an atrocious attempt to extort money from the defendant.'

He then reviewed Lord William's lifestyle. 'He, possessing a wife ami- able and accomplished, was found spending his time at the White Bear, and at Dubourg's in the Haymarket. Was he the companion of the other members of his family? No, but of persons whose names were known and associated with the want of honour and character . . . His wife was all that time away from London.'

As *The Times* reported the following day, Follet's rhetoric was only warming up:

> He repeated, that the whole was an atrocious plan concocted from the beginning, and that there was no one step of it to which Lord William Paget was not a party. The proof showed that he was privy

to the appointments made with Lord Cardigan in order to get him into the house. Why had he not obtained one of his own servants instead of Winter to watch under the sofa? If a husband could so far forget what was due to himself and his family, when he suspected that an improper intercourse was going on, as to place some one in the room in which it took place – to seat himself in a cab in the street while this was going on, and then to come back and bring an action, was that such a person as a jury could trust with their confidence? He might have placed one of his servants there . . . But what had he done? He sought in London for a person reckless of consequences – a person who was admitted to be in abject distress – whom he knew to have been dismissed from Mr Bartlett's employment for making false entries, and whom he himself charged with embezzling a bill of exchange of which he was the acceptor . . .

Follett pressed on, and the logic of his arguments was virtually unanswerable:

The jury had been told that Lady William Paget had sent a letter to Cardigan and he (the Solicitor-General) now asked them whether the impression of his learned friend's opening was not that she had sent the letter unknown to Lord William Paget? That impression he had been able to set right by making it manifest that the letter was sent by both Lord and Lady Paget jointly . . . Either [they] were scheming together to get money out of Lord Cardigan, or he was doing so reckless of the consequence to others . . . Lord William was in the house when Lord Cardigan called [on Saturday]. The case for the plaintiff endeavoured to establish that Lord William Paget had sent for his wife and that it was his hand which led her to the room, and left her with a person whom he supposed to be an adulterer . . . He (the Solicitor-General) did not think that he contemplated that such would be done, but that he got Lord Cardigan into that room, and that he put the witness Winter there, not for the purpose of seeing what took place, but to state that such an act was committed, which, if he really believed to have been committed, no language could describe the infamy of the act . . . Here was a man under the sofa – Lord Paget in the house, and in the course of examination it was elicited that the doors were not fastened. Any of the servants, the landlady or landlord of the house, Lord William himself, or any of the children, might have gone into the room.

The case was now all but won, but Follett had one last potent point to make:

> Did the jury suppose that a man with affection in his heart could for any purpose take the woman he loved into a room, and leave her with a party whom he believed to have come for the purpose of committing adultery? Such might be possible, but it was not human nature. It was incredible, and therefore he was driven to the conclusion that Lord William Paget expected nothing of the kind, that he cared not for his wife, that he cared not for the infamy which would he brought upon the mother of his children, if he could obtain the object for which he was seeking, viz. to extort money from a wealthy nobleman unpopular with the public.

Without even bothering to retire, the jury found for Lord Cardigan. 'It was received throughout the court with an applause which the criers found it difficult to subdue,' reported *The Times*.[25]

Whether Cardigan actually was innocent of the charge of adultery with Fanny Paget is doubtful. Effectively separated from his wife by this time, he had had a number of affairs and his chivalrous nature meant that he was particularly susceptible to damsels in distress – a category into which any woman married to Lord William would fall (it would not have occurred to Cardigan that to succour a woman by sleeping with her could hardly be described as chivalrous). Furthermore, it was well known within the Paget family that Fanny was no angel either. Therefore, she might easily have had an affair with Cardigan. Certainly, Winter's detailed recollection of their conversation on Sunday, 5 August, has a curious ring of truth.

The irony of the whole business is that, given his own unpopularity, Cardigan was unlikely to have been acquitted if the action had been brought by any man other than Lord William, possibly the only aristocrat in England more notorious than Cardigan himself. Then again, no other aristocrat would have used such disreputable methods to secure his 'proof'. Needless to say, Lord William failed to mend his ways and three years later, no longer an M.P., was forced to flee the country to avoid arrest for using his father's name to sell government offices. Far from disowning him, Lord Anglesey increased his allowance by £200 a year in 1848. He spent the rest of his life abroad, and died at the age of 70 in 1873.

One great lady with whom Lord Cardigan undoubtedly had a lengthy affair was the beautiful Marchioness of Ailesbury. Born Maria Tollemache, the first cousin once removed of Lady Cardigan and the grand-daughter of the Countess of Dysart, she had married the Marquess of Ailesbury in 1833 when he was a 60-year-old widower and she just 20 years of age. If the Duke of Wellington had been less tardy, she might have become a duchess. Also a recently widowed sexagenarian, he rode up to her father's house to ask for her hand, only to be told that her betrothal to the marquess had just been announced. The Duke remounted and galloped off, muttering, 'Too late, too late.'[26]

With a fine figure and a remarkably handsome face framed by golden ringlets, the young marchioness was a much-sought-after guest in Victorian society. As lady of Tottenham House, the Ailesbury seat in Wiltshire that had been redesigned in the 1820s by the architect Thomas Cundy at a reputed cost of £250,000, she lived in great state, never engaging a manservant under six feet tall and lining her hall with liveried servants whenever guests arrived. She was also highly eccentric, given to wiping her mouth on the tablecloth and appearing in unconventional garb.

Although her husband lived on until 1856, his frail constitution was unable to keep up with Maria's notorious libido. It was inevitable that she would look elsewhere for satisfaction, and she found it with, among others, the Earls of Cardigan and Wilton. Cardigan's main advantage was the family connection. As the wife of his cousin and a close relation of Lady Cardigan, Maria was a frequent unescorted guest at Deene and Portman Square. On the other hand, Wilton – a handsome man whose many love affairs earned him the sobriquet 'The Wicked Earl' – was unmarried, equally rich and a possible future husband.

The rivalry came to a head in the 1850s during Cowes' Week, which followed on from the close of the London Season in August. Cardigan was aboard his luxury steam yacht *Dryad*, while Wilton, Commodore of the Royal Yacht Squadron, preferred the canvas of his schooner *Xarifa*, a former slave-trader. Adeline de Horsey, later Cardigan's second wife, takes up the story:

The Ailesburys visited us at Cowes for several seasons, and then, as they liked the place, they took a house every summer. Although Lady A. was considered a beauty she was excessively thin, and her scragginess was the source of a joke some years later. She was devoted to Lord Wilton, but one day she went on board Lord Cardigan's yacht, which was lying off Calshot, and stayed the night before returning to Cowes. Lord Wilton, who was furious about it, made quite an unnecessary scene with Cardigan, and some kind friend said that after all it was only a case of two dogs fighting over a bone![27]

Childless, and with little in common beyond their self-possessed natures, Cardigan and his wife had long since ceased sexual relations. Their pretence at matrimony ended in 1846 when Lady Cardigan's intrigue with the 8th Lord Colville led to a definite separation. The son of a man who had fought at Culloden, Colville had joined the Navy in 1780 and had risen to the rank of full admiral. Aged 78 (with just over three years to live), he still felt honour bound to offer Cardigan satisfaction (perhaps in the knowledge that it could not be accepted). Cardigan's reply was a deliberate echo of the answer he had been given by Lady Cardigan's first husband, 22 years earlier. In taking her off his hands, Colville was performing 'the greatest service one man may render another'.[28]

For some years both had sought solace in others and Cardigan, with his wealth, handsome figure and roguish reputation, was desired by many. One such was Mrs Browne, well-known in society. According to Cardigan's second wife, this lovesick lady was so smitten that she took to sending him 'quantities of *billets doux* begging for an interview'. Lady Cardigan, however, 'accidentally got hold of one of these letters' and decided to take revenge by arranging for Cardigan's agent, Mr Baldwin, to impersonate her husband.

> The unsuspecting lady received a note purporting to come from Cardigan, saying he would visit her on a certain evening. He further stipulated that as he was so well known he did not wish to see any of Mrs Browne's servants, and that she must receive him in the dark! Any one but an infatuated woman would have queried the genuineness of the letter, but Mrs Browne did not, and when Mr Baldwin arrived, he was duly received in darkness as black as Erebus. He and Mrs Browne were mutually well pleased with the

The Allied Generals with the officers of their respective staffs before Sebastopol. A portrait by Thomas Barker. Lord Raglan is in the centre, wearing a dark tunic with two rows of buttons and a cocked hat crowned with feathers. General Canrobert, the French commander, is on his immediate right, riding the Grey. Omar Pasha, the Turkish general, is to his left, grey-bearded and wearing a red fez. Lord Lucan, wearing a grey overcoat and peaked cap, his arms crossed, is to the right of Canrobert. Lord Cardigan, in the uniform of the 11th Hussars, is immediately behind him. *(Bridgeman Art Library)*

Harvey Tuckett, a former lieutenant in the 11th Light Dragoons who preferred to exchange on to half-pay rather than serve under Lord Cardigan's command. In 1840 he was wounded in a duel with Cardigan. Tried by his peers for intent to murder, Cardigan was acquitted on a technicality. *(Courtesy of Robin Baird-Smith)*

'Farewell to the Light Brigade'. A member of the 11th Hussars, destined for the Crimea, says goodbye to his wife. A portrait by Robert Collinson. *(Bridgeman Art Library)*

Elizabeth, Countess of Cardigan,
the 7th Earl's first wife.
(Courtesy of Edmund Brudenell)

Maria, Marchioness of Ailesbury,
the 7th Earl of Cardigan's mistress.
A portrait by Sir William Beechey.
(Courtesy of Edmund Brudenell)

James Thomas Brudenell, 7th Earl of Cardigan, wearing his various orders and decorations. Among them is the Crimean medal with clasps for the various battles (the troops likened them to decanter labels and christened them 'Port', 'Sherry' and 'Claret'). A painting by R. Buckner. *(Courtesy of Edmund Brudenell)*

Ronald, Lord Cardigan's chestnut charger, in the Crimea. *(Courtesy of Edmund Brudenell)*

The siege of Sebastopol from the new 32-pounder battery manned by the Royal Navy, October 1854. *(Bridgeman Art Library)*

The Charge of the Heavy Brigade at the Battle of Balaclava, 25 October 1854. An engraving after a painting by William Simpson. (*Bridgeman Art Library*)

Lord Cardigan describing the Charge of the Light Brigade to Prince Albert and the Royal children at Windsor on 18 January, 1855. A painting by James Sant. Queen Victoria was present on this occasion, but is said to have insisted on her image being removed from the original picture after discovering some unpleasant detail about Cardigan's private life. *(Courtesy of Edmund Brudenell)*

'Relief of the Light Brigade.' A painting by Richard Caton Woodville. The survivors of the second line of 11th Hussars reach the Russians' guns. *(Bridgeman Art Library)*

The Charge of the Light Brigade, seen from the Russian positions on the Fedioukine Hills. An engraving after a painting by William Simpson. *(Bridgeman Art Library)*

Lord Cardigan's engagement with two Cossacks behind the Russian battery, 25 October 1854. A painting by George Henry Laporte. *(Courtesy of Edmund Brudenell)*

The Charge of the Light Brigade at the Battle of Balaclava, 25 October 1854. Lord Cardigan is leading the first line of 17th Lancers (foreground) and 13th Light Dragoons. (*Bridgeman Art Library*)

Lord Cardigan in general's uniform. A painting by R. Buckner. *(Bridgeman Art Library)*

Adeline, Countess of Cardigan, the 7th Earl's second wife, with her hair dyed blonde and wearing her peeress's robes. A painting by R. Buckner. Note Lord Cardigan's sword and uniform, and A. de Prades' painting of him at the 'charge', in the background. *(Courtesy of Edmund Brudenell)*

result of their meeting, and under cover of darkness of the small hours of a winter's morning they said good-bye. It was not long afterwards that Mrs Browne found out that she had entertained an agent unawares, and no doubt she hated Lady Cardigan for the unkind deception of which she had been the victim.[29]

(Once again, there is no truth in Flashman's claim that he, rather than Baldwin, had stood in for Cardigan during that night of abandoned passion!)[30]

Until his remarriage in 1858, Cardigan was, in the words of his second wife, 'a grass widower, consoled by many fair friends, and bills no doubt being as numerous then as they are now, certain ladies were always ready to stop at Deene without their husbands'.[31]

11

The Sick Man of Europe

In September 1844, the 11th Hussars left Dublin for Dundalk, with the raw recruits and heavy baggage travelling by train on the newly opened line to Drogheda. Soon after their arrival Lance-Corporal Davidson, on duty at the canteen, was arrested for neglect of duty after failing to prevent a defaulter gaining entry. As punishment, Major Inigo Jones, acting C.O. in Cardigan's absence, ordered him to be reduced to the ranks and given seven days' dry room and kit drill. An hour later Davidson loaded his carbine and shot himself. 'He was a promising young soldier,' wrote Sergeant Loy Smith, 'and much respected by his comrades.'[1]

Ironically, the punishment might not have been so severe, and Davidson might not have felt driven to committing suicide, if Cardigan had been present. A disciplinarian he may have been, but he was generally seen as fair. According to Loy Smith, this was particularly true of his dealings with the ordinary soldier:

> Although Cardigan was considered one of the strictest and most severe officers in the army, still he always saw for himself and did not at once take the evidence of others, but enquired into matters – particularly if he suspected that any injustice was being practised on the non-commissioned officers or men by those in authority over them. This, in a great measure, reconciled the men to the strict régime to which they were subject. His Lordship had a wonderful gift for remembering men's names.[2]

But once back with the regiment, Cardigan quickly showed the other side of his nature:

> The only place available for field days was on the sands when the tide was out [wrote Loy Smith]. On one occasion, the tide hemmed us in so that the water was up to the horses' girths; the consequence was the crimson overalls were much discoloured by the salt water. The same evening, Lord Cardigan ordered that the whole regiment was to be put under stoppages for new overalls. This caused great discontent among the men, many that had two good pairs objected to it. Those men that did not object received a new pair at the expense of his Lordship.[3]

After seven months at Dundalk, the regiment marched to Newbridge for summer training. Having then spent June to October in Dublin for the drill season, it returned to Newbridge and was still there, in February 1846, when Captain Charles Colville, nephew and heir of Admiral Lord Colville, became the latest officer to attempt to avoid service under Cardigan. The reason was that his elderly uncle's affair with Cardigan's wife was making his position in the regiment untenable.

Admiral Colville's wife was the sister of the 1st Earl of Ellenborough, Governor-General of India between 1842 and 1844, and during this period Captain Colville had been absent from the regiment serving on Ellenborough's staff. Now he enlisted his former patron, serving in Peel's government as First Lord of the Admiralty, to ask the Horse Guards to approve an exchange. On 18 February 1846, Wellington replied to Ellenborough's solicitation: No, he would not agree to the exchange with Captain Jenkinson of the 8th Hussars because he was aware that the latter officer wished to sell out of the Army and would not stay long in his new regiment. In addition, if Colville was allowed to exchange this would not be fair on the senior lieutenant of the 8th Hussars, who 'has been above six years in the army, and is entitled to be promoted by purchase'.

'I much prefer to endeavour to obtain leave of absence for Captain Colville,' Wellington wrote, 'though that is very unpleasant for me, as I must communicate upon the subject with Lord Cardigan.' He concluded: 'The real truth of this whole affair is the desire to avoid getting under the command of Lord Cardigan, which desire I have no objection to gratify, but I desire to do so without injury to a meritorious officer serving abroad.'[4]

A month later, after almost exactly three years in Ireland, the regiment returned to England and was stationed at Coventry, with detachments at Northampton and Weedon. Its return coincided with the second consecutive year that the potato crop had been blighted in Ireland and parts of England. What made this failure so catastrophic for Ireland was the fact that half its 8 million inhabitants ate only potatoes because they could not afford bread.

Even England, with an eighth of its 16 million population relying on the crop, suffered from the great scarcity and high price of potatoes and, according to Loy Smith, 'the issue of them to the troops had to be discontinued and extra bread provided in lieu'. With Cardigan away, as he was for much of the time the regiment was based at Coventry, Major Jones, 'fearing that scurvey might break out for lack of vegetables, ordered parties from each troop under a corporal to go daily into the country lanes and gather nettles'. This earned them the nickname 'donkey robbers' from the townsfolk.[5]

One far-reaching consequence of the famine in Ireland was that it accelerated Peel's plan to abolish the Corn Laws. In 1828, a sliding scale had been introduced so that the duty on imported corn rose as the domestic price fell. Peel had reduced this duty at the lower end of the scale in 1842, and by 1845 had been completely won over to Cobden and Bright's argument that free trade would hold the brightest future for all classes in Britain. The Irish famine was simply the moral excuse to put this philosophy into practice sooner rather than later.

For, as the great historian Robert Blake wrote, the 'mass of the Irish peasantry lived so far below the bread level that the relatively slight fall in the price, which might be expected to follow, could not have made bread a substitute for potatoes'. Even Peel's distribution of American maize – 'Peel's brimstone' – at a penny for 1 lb and the paid relief work could not prevent a million Irish deaths, many from disease, and the forced emigration of millions more.[6]

In late November 1845, Lord John Russell, the leader of the opposition Whigs, announced that he had been won over to repeal because, as with parliamentary reform, he wanted to avoid 'a struggle deeply injurious to an aristocracy which (this quarrel once removed) is strong in property, . . . strong in opinion, strong in ancient associations, and the memory of immortal services'. Ten days later Peel concurred, saying that he was willing to bring in a Bill 'involving the ultimate repeal' of the duties.[7]

In the face of protectionist opposition, particularly within his own party, Peel doubted whether he could carry 'ultimate repeal' unless he had the solid backing of his Cabinet. When two of its members, Lord Stanley and the Duke of Buccleuch, could not be talked round, he resigned on 5 December. Russell, too, was doubtful whether he could pass such reform without his ablest supporters, and was forced to reject the opportunity to form a government when Lord Grey refused to serve in a ministry in which Palmerston was Foreign Secretary. Within 15 days, Peel was again Prime Minister.

With a reshuffled Cabinet – Gladstone replacing Stanley as Secretary for War and Colonies, among other changes – Peel used the reconvening of Parliament on 22 January 1846 to announce his Corn Importation Bill. This catered not for immediate abolition, but the gradual reduction of import duties over a three-year period. The Tories received their leader's words in silence, but were soon electrified when Disraeli got to his feet to reply. In a masterful speech, he portrayed Peel, in Robert Blake's words, 'as a slightly pompous, priggish mediocrity who was betraying the party by which he had risen'. He closed with a rousing plea:

> Let men stand by the principle by which they rise, right or wrong. I make no exception. If they be wrong, they must retire to that shade of life with which our present rulers have so often threatened us . . . Do not then because you see a great personage giving up his opinions – do not cheer him on, do not give so ready a reward to political tergiversation. Above all maintain the line of demarcation between the parties, for it is only by maintaining the independence of party that you can maintain the integrity of public men, and the power and influence of Parliament itself.[8]

He sat down to Tory cheers that lasted several minutes. Battle had been joined and Disraeli, hitherto anonymous, had launched himself on the path to greatness. When the House voted to take the Bill into committee stage on 27 February, the motion was passed by 339 votes to 242. But only 112 Tories had voted for repeal – many simply out of personal loyalty – while the rest were Whigs, Irish and Radicals. At four in the morning of 16 May, a similar proportion supported the Bill and it passed a third reading by 98 votes. Only the House of Lords now stood between it and law.

Cardigan, like most landed Tories, had long supported the Corn Laws, believing them essential for the well-being of agriculture and the 'landed' interest in general. Peel's *volte face* over the issue of repeal gave him a chance to vent his anger on a Prime Minister who had consistently thwarted his applications for honours. On 26 May 1846, he gave one of his most eloquent speeches in Parliament in favour of the Duke of Richmond's amendment to delay a second reading of the Bill by six months.

For 25 years he had been a legislator, he told the House, and if his vote had not always been 'consistent', he had always given 'faithful support to the measures of Her Majesty's Government'. Catholic emancipation in 1829 was an example of his inconsistency, but that was because of his 'high opinion' and 'profound respect' for the Duke of Wellington who was then Prime Minister. 'But how,' he asked rhetorically, 'could he possibly have imagined that the carrying of that measure into law would be but the prelude to concede every other important measure, so that the end would be that the Government would in truth have no fixed or definite political opinion of its own; but that its whole career would consist in borrowing the principles or carrying out the measures of others?'

He then turned to the government's justification for repealing the Corn Laws. 'It was unfortunately true that, to a certain extent, distress did exist during the winter months in the sister kingdom [Ireland], and though he believed that these statements had been much exaggerated, yet, be that as it might, His Majesty's Government had taken a prudent course in applying temporary relief to the distress of that country.'

While the attempt, in his previous point, to belittle the famine in Ireland did him no credit, his next was more valid: 'Was there any man living who consciously believed that a temporary calamity was a sufficient ground for Her Majesty's Government calling upon them to repeal the protection existing upon the agricultural interests?'

Having laid the ground, he launched into a personal attack on Peel: 'The right honourable Baronet had encouraged by his conduct and his speeches the cry which had been raised at the last general election, when the representatives of the people offered themselves . . . on the cry of protection to agriculture as opposed to the cry of cheap bread . . . What was the success of that appeal to the country? Was it not most triumphant? Was there not an enormous, preponderating majority returned to the House of Commons in favour of protection?'

Since then, he continued, M.P.s had voted for protection to agriculture, 'by large majorities, no less than four or five different times'. Now they were expected 'to reverse all their former votes'. While he could not pretend to have 'finer feelings than other people' – 'nay, likely less' – he could not 'refrain from saying that he thought they had been placed in an unfortunate predicament – either to disunite themselves from their party, which, were it not for the conduct of their leaders they would be sincerely attached to, or to reverse their former votes and decisions, and place themselves in a position which, in his humble judgement, would be derogatory to their position as legislators, or even as gentlemen'.

And if they did reverse their former decisions, 'what would be the opinion of the respectable middle classes . . . the yeomanry . . . the farmers . . . – a respectable race, who loved honesty and plain dealing, and hated duplicity and sudden change?' His suggestion was to let the country decide in a General Election – 'yield up to the demand of a great body of people, but not to a vacillating and inconsistent Minister'.

He had long supported the government, he concluded, 'but thinking the measure proposed would bring confusion and ruin on the country, he must give it his decided opposition'.[9]

Cardigan's sterling effort was to no avail, however, because two days later, after a particularly stormy debate, the second reading of the Bill was passed by 211 votes to 164. Parties and family alike were divided by the issue. Staunch Tories like the Earls of Winchilsea and Wilton were in opposition, while Cabinet ministers including Wellington, Buccleuch and Aberdeen were in favour. Even Cardigan's brothers-in-law were torn, with the normally conservative Earl Howe voting for and the Earl of Lucan against. Within a month the Bill had become law.

The short-term effect of the repeal on agriculture in general, and the price of domestic corn in particular, was minimal. For two decades after 1850, agriculture thrived and the price of corn remained steady, albeit at a time of rising world prices. It was not until 1870, when the fall in the cost of transport on sea and land enabled American corn to compete with the British harvest, that prices began to tumble and agriculture suffered.

But the ruling classes could not anticipate this in 1846, and it is difficult to overstate the bitter divisions that were produced by Peel's 'betrayal'. The Duke of Newcastle, for example, disowned his Peelite son, Lord Lincoln, used his influence to ensure Lincoln's defeat in the election for Nottinghamshire, and was reconciled only on his deathbed. The rank-and-file Tories preferred a more dramatic manifestation of their anger. On 25 June, the day the Speaker announced that the House of Lords had passed the third reading of the Corn Importation Bill, the House of Commons debated the second reading of the Coercion Bill, a measure to combat the agrarian outrages in Ireland provoked by the famine. Normally, the Tory majority would have happily passed such a Bill to restore law and order, but many were out for revenge and, with Disraeli and Lord George

Bentinck taking the lead, more than 70 voted against the government, while a further 80 members abstained. Added to most of the Whigs, Radicals and Irish, they were enough to defeat the bill by 73 votes. 'A blackguard combination,' remarked Wellington.[10]

Four days later, Peel resigned and the Queen sent for Lord John Russell. The Tory party had been shattered and over the next 40 years only one Conservative government – Disraeli's between 1874 and 1880 – would enjoy a clear majority in the House of Commons. The rest were short-lived administrations relying on their opponents' dissensions. Cardigan, of course, was not to know this and at White's, in October, he bet Lord Adolphus Fitzclarence £100 that Lord Stanley, the leader of the Tory protectionists, would become Prime Minister before Peel. He won by default when Peel was thrown from his horse and killed in the summer of 1850 – divine justice, some said, for his betrayal. Within two years, Stanley, by then the Earl of Derby, was asked to form a government.[11]

As the 1840s wore on, Cardigan spent less and less time with his regiment, leaving the day-to-day running to Major Jones. Now over 50 years old, and periodically afflicted by an irritating bladder complaint and chronic bronchitis, he entered a period of semi-retirement: spending more and more time in London, socialising and attending Parliament. Even without a hostess, the scale of his entertainment was lavish, particularly at Deene where his house parties included notables such as the Duke of Cambridge, the Prince of Mecklenburg and Lord Adolphus Fitzclarence.

And of course there was his hunting, which he approached in the same fearless manner as when he was a boy of 16. According to Nethercote, author of *The Pytchley Hunt* and a man who rode with Cardigan, 'there were few harder men across country', and, 'at a time when the Quorn and Pytchley were well furnished with "bruisers", it was no easy matter for the best of them to get in front of the gallant Earl'. It was about this time, during Charles Payne's immensely successful term as Master of the Pytchley, that Cardigan was said to have had a number of run-ins with his tenants. One incident occurred after Payne had run a fox to ground near Deene and was in the process of digging it out. Up rode Cardigan and ordered him to cease and draw for another fox.

'But, my lord,' said Payne, 'your tenants are complaining that he takes their lambs.'

'Tenants complaining!' responded Cardigan incredulously. 'The land is mine; the woods are mine, and the tenants are mine; and my tenants are not in the habit of complaining about anything.'

Dick Christian, the famous steeplechase jockey, recalled a similar incident when the covers near Deene were drawn blank by the hunt and Cardigan blamed his tenants, threatening to turn them out and raise the rent. 'They were very put out,' wrote Christian, 'and lays their heads together that night in the inn back parlour, and decides to lay a drag next time over the Stonton Brooke, where it was too wide to jump; and one was to ride each side of his mightyship and a big heavy man called Stopps behind, to jump on him when the other two got him down. But I never heard as anything come of it.'

Clearly, such tenants would have been the last to respond when their master, in danger of drowning in a brook after a fall, was heard to exclaim: 'Is there no one to help and save the 7th and last Earl of Cardigan.'[12]

On the whole, however, Cardigan got on remarkably well with his tenants. Undoubtedly he was brusque, as he was with his troops, but he could also be extremely generous, as when he made regular gifts of food to the poor, gave the neediest 2s 6d a week, and clothed the children who attended the local school he maintained. Lady Augusta Fane, a first cousin of the second Lady Cardigan, recalled that he 'considered education to be of the first importance' and, as 'village schools were few and far between, he had the children conveyed to and fro in his own wagons'. Even 30 years after his death, wrote Lady Augusta, the 7th Earl 'was still spoken of by the villagers with love and respect as though he were alive'.[13]

In June 1848, after two quiet years at Coventry, the 11th Hussars returned to Hounslow for Queen's Duty. With his love of ceremonial, Cardigan now spent more time with his men than had recently been the case and was in command when, soon after its arrival, the regiment was reviewed on Hounslow Heath by the Queen, Prince Albert and the Duke of Wellington. George Loy Smith, now a troop sergeant-major, recalled:

> The ground being very soft and slippery, several of the horses fell, which much annoyed Lord Cardigan, so that he threatened to send us all to everlasting riding school. A few minutes after this threat, his and Trooper Connor's horse fell together. His Lordship's foot, being in the stirrup iron under the horse, was severely injured so that we did not see him again for several months. As he lay on

the ground, all smothered in mud, one of the men in the ranks exclaimed in a loud tone, 'Behold the Lord is down,' which caused a tittering amongst the men. I have no doubt the officers joined in it, for they were under the law as well as ourselves.[14]

One officer who undoubtedly did so was Captain the Honourable Gerard Noël, M.P. for Rutlandshire and the son of the Earl of Gainsborough. According to an article in *John Bull*, Cardigan had twice ordered his arrest before the regiment left Coventry: once for being late for stables when he was orderly officer, and once for not returning to duty during the Easter recess of Parliament. On both occasions he was released on the authority of the district commander, Major-General Brotherton, but soon after the second arrest there was a third incident. Noticing Noël slightly out of position during a field day, Cardigan called out: 'Captain Noël, go to your troop, sir!'

'I am with my troop, sir,' came the defiant reply, in the full knowledge that Cardigan allowed no answering back on parade.

'You are not, sir,' Cardigan rejoined, 'none of your London manners here!'

Noël fell silent, but after the parade was over he gained a private interview and asked Cardigan why he had been insulted in the presence of his troop. 'Get out of my room, sir!' was the angry response.

Immediately, Noël drafted a letter of complaint to Wellington, but the reply was disappointing since the Commander-in-Chief ordered him to apologise to Cardigan for his three errors. Adjutant-General Macdonald was sent to supervise the apology, only to find a recalcitrant Noël. A challenge seemed likely, and it required Wellington's personal intervention before peace prevailed. Inevitably, the press blamed Cardigan for the feud, yet it seemed to follow a familiar pattern. Over-reaction by Cardigan, certainly, but with a certain amount of provocation from his subordinate. In any case, the Horse Guards had once again come down on Cardigan's side despite the fact that Wellington could hardly stand the sight of him.[15]

If Cardigan was often given the benefit of the doubt, it was because he was seen to have produced a remarkably fine regiment. After a review of the 11th Hussars on Wimbledon Common in July 1849, Prince Albert congratulated Cardigan on the appearance of his men and the 'precision and celerity with which the field movements were executed'. Wellington also praised the regiment, and added in a letter his 'approbation at the admirable system of discipline established in the corps, which was brought to his notice by the Inspecting General's confidential report'.[16]

But it was precisely this preoccupation with discipline and efficiency, even when away from the regiment, that caused a number of disagreements between Cardigan and his second-in command, Major Inigo Jones. In March 1850, unhappy with Cardigan's habit of interfering with the running of the regiment when absent, Jones gave his C.O. a piece of his mind in the orderly room and was arrested for his trouble. Wisely, he apologised to Cardigan before higher authority could become involved and was released. But that September, after the 11th Hussars had been moved to Norwich and Ipswich, a similar incident occurred; this time General Brotherton, the Inspector-General of Cavalry, had to travel to Norwich to induce Jones to apologise.

Horse Guards, however, was not under any illusions as to Cardigan's share of the responsibility. On 30 September, Wellington wrote him a stern letter, advising him that manners between gentlemen must be 'gentle, without asperity or appearance of violent temper'. If he did not drop his haughty tone, the Duke warned, he would be ordered to remain permanently at his own headquarters. Such hard words were necessary, the Duke explained, so that the public might not be deprived of Cardigan's 'military qualities'.

The following day Cardigan received a private letter from Major-General George Brown, a Peninsula veteran who had recently replaced Macdonald as Adjutant-General. One of the sternest disciplinarians in the Army, even he was alarmed by Cardigan's methods of command. 'I trust I may not be considered intrusive,' Brown wrote, 'if I venture to offer Your Lordship a word of advice, and to point out to you how much more agreeable it would be to yourself, if you would manage to live on friendly terms with your second-in-command.'

Admitting he had been strict when in command of a regiment, Brown added: 'I never had a quarrel with any of my officers in my life, and during the 19 years that I commanded a Regiment, I cannot remember that I had an officer in arrest.'

His explanation for this was that while he 'required close attention to all essential points of duty', he made it understood that he was 'actuated by no other motive than for the interests of the Public Service' and that he was always ready to grant his officers 'any indulgence they might reasonably require'. Therefore, as the easiest means of appeasing Jones, he suggested offering 'to procure him any reasonable term of leave that he may require'.

A week later, on 8 November 1850, Cardigan replied from his head-quarters, saying he had acted on Brown's advice and offered his second-in-command leave of absence. Jones only wanted a week, although Cardigan had said he could have longer, and the following day Jones had thanked him. Turning to Brown's comments regarding his time in command of a regiment, Cardigan distinguished between their respective positions: 'Your officers did not dare oppose you. Mine, at least the [clique of which] I class Major Jones the Chief and Leader, always hope to be assisted by the Press and the Public & by repeated appeals . . . at last to [bring] down the displeasure of the Commander in Chief upon me their Commanding Officer.'

Cardigan had a point, but in reality it was a circular argument. From his time with the 15th Hussars, he had rubbed certain officers up the wrong way and they had reacted in a manner bound to provoke him. They felt that they were not being treated with the respect due to gentlemen, while he justified his overbearing manner on the grounds of discipline. How else could he achieve an efficient regiment? he would have asked. What he failed to understand was the point that Brown had hinted at in his original letter – without the goodwill and cooperation of his officers the 11th Hussars would never be a truly effective unit. His ambiguous parting comment to Brown hardly inspired confidence that he was about to mend his old ways: 'I shall not spare my exertions to keep matters as quiet as possible for the future.'[17]

By spending less time with his regiment, Cardigan was able to devote more energy to his duty as a legislator. With the passing of the years he undoubtedly became wiser and, despite the public perception of him as a blustering fool, his words were listened to with a certain amount of respect by his fellow peers. In the summer of 1850, he made one of his more compelling speeches when he denounced Lord Palmerston's record as Foreign Secretary.

Born Henry Temple in 1784, the son of an Irish viscount not eligible to sit in the House of Lords, Palmerston had, like Cardigan, been educated at Harrow before becoming a Cabinet minister at the age of 23. Since 1807 there had been only three administrations – Wellington's of 1828–30, and Peel's of 1834–5 and 1841–6 – in which he had taken no part. In all, he had served a total of 14 years as Foreign Secretary.

While never restricting his policy to a 'system', he did adhere to certain principles, notably that constitutional states were the natural allies of Britain. Inevitably this caused him to support nations struggling for independence, which in turn brought accusations of 'meddling' from the foreign ministers of absolutist states such as Tsarist Russia and Imperial Austria. So it was that in 1831, much to Cardigan's anger, he had supported the nascent state of Belgium; and 17 years later, during the year of revolutions, had encouraged liberals throughout Italy to rebel against their autocratic rulers: both Austria in the north, and the Kingdom of Naples in the south.

In 1850 Palmerston managed to alienate both Russia and republican France by his high-handed action towards Greece. Don Pacifico, a Portuguese moneylender with British citizenship courtesy of his birth in Gibraltar, demanded compensation after his house in Athens had been sacked. Palmerston took his exaggerated claims as genuine and, seeing the issue as the last straw after years of Greek hostility and dishonesty towards Britain, advised the Greek government to pay all outstanding debts to British subjects. When it failed to do so, he ordered the Royal Navy to blockade Greek ports without consulting either France or Russia, co-guarantors with Britain of Greek independence.

As if this was not bad enough, he then agreed a settlement to the crisis with France without notifying the British minister at Athens who, meanwhile, had authorised warships to bombard the Greek coast. The French were outraged and, when Palmerston failed to censure the minister's conduct, withdrew their ambassador from London.

His enemies now had a perfect opportunity to attack his methods of conducting foreign policy and, on 17 June, Lord Stanley proposed a motion of censure designed to bring down the Whig government. While recognising the 'duty of the Government to secure to Her Majesty's subjects residing in foreign States the full protection of the laws of those States', Stanley condemned the fact that 'various claims against the Greek Government, doubtful in point of justice or exaggerated in amount', had been 'enforced by coercive measures directed against the commerce and people of Greece, and calculated to endanger the continuance of friendly relations with other Powers'.

One of the first peers to speak in support of the motion, Cardigan made it clear that he, for one, did 'not think that either the claims or complaints we had against [Greece] were of sufficient magnitude and importance to justify the risk' that the government had incurred 'of bringing on a general war in Europe'. The recall of the French ambassador, he reminded the House, was 'the usual prelude to a declaration of war', while a recent communication from Count Nesselrode, the Russian foreign minister, made it clear 'that we have, with the most extraordinary ingenuity, succeeded in arraying against us, if not in open hostilities, yet with the most hostile feel-ings, two of the most powerful nations of Europe, directly opposed to each other in all their national and political institutions, those of one being founded upon republican and democratic principles, those of the other upon arbitrary and despotic government'.

Palmerston's foreign policy he considered 'one of the most extraordinary anomalies'. By pandering to the 'dictates' of Richard Cobden, the 'very influential and talented leader' of the 'Manchester School of reformers', the government had cut expenditure on the Army and Navy to the extent that it no longer had a force sufficient to defend its own shores. At the same time, it was 'unceasingly quarrelling with every other nation in Europe'.

Was it 'either wise or prudent', he asked, to encourage the Sicilians 'in open revolt' against the Kingdom of Naples, one of Britain's 'oldest allies' and a country 'to which they as lawfully belonged as nine-tenths of the pos-sessions of this country, in different parts of the world, belong to the dominion of this country?' Was it 'requisite for the honour and permanent interests of the country that we should have given every encouragement to the Sardinians in their hostile and aggressive proceedings against Austria?' Was it wise 'to send a British fleet in a hostile and menacing manner to the confines of Russia, and afterwards even to have permitted that fleet to anchor within the precincts of the Dardanelles, in direct breach of existing treaties?'

Would it not have been wiser, he asked, to have sent the fleet, return-ing from its 'unlawful anchorage', direct to Malta rather than allowing it 'to deviate from its course, for the purpose of making a violent and hostile attack upon a small and insignificant kingdom, on account of claims which it is evident, up to that time, had not been very clearly defined?'

Surely, redress for those claims should have been sought with the coop-eration of France and Russia, 'our co-guarantees for the integrity of the Greek nation'. Given that Britain 'would ill brook, indeed would not tol-erate, the slightest advice or interference from any foreign Power without internal concerns,' Cardigan concluded, 'it is much to be regretted that we do not refrain from interfering with the internal affairs of other nations'.[18]

Such noble sentiments were appreciated by many of the peers present, both Tory and Peelite, and when it came to a vote the motion of censure against the government was carried by 169 votes to 132. But real power lay in the House of Commons, and the government would not step down until it had been defeated there.

The inevitable motion of censure was duly introduced on 25 June but, despite the condemnation of every leading statesman bar his Cabinet colleagues, Palmerston triumphantly vindicated himself with a masterful speech setting out the principles of British foreign policy since the death of Canning. Its stirring finale, which could not fail to appeal to any man who held himself a patriot, did much to secure a government majority of 46: 'As the Roman, in days of old, held himself free from indignity, when he could say "*Civis Romanus sum*", so also a British subject, in whatever land he may be, shall feel confident that the watchful eye and the strong arm of England will protect him against injustice and wrong.'[19]

In May 1852, after a year at Nottingham, Cardigan and the 11th Hussars were despatched to Ireland and stationed at Newbridge. The move was a response to a chain of events which had begun the previous December when Louis Napoleon, Bonaparte's nephew, carried out a successful *coup d'état* against the Second French Republic.

In February 1852 – to calm renewed fears of a French invasion – Lord John Russell proposed the forming of a local militia. Palmerston, recently sacked for his premature approval of the *coup*, sought revenge by demanding a national militia: The protectionist Conservatives supported Palmerston, and in a vote on 20 February the Whig government was defeated. Lord Derby formed a minority Conservative administration and the customary General Election was set for late July. With feelings in Ireland running high against landowners – who, as a consequence of the famine, had evicted almost 37,000 families over the previous three years – the government decided to send the 11th Hussars and other regiments to help keep the peace during the voting.

Towards the end of June, with the elections still a month away, the regiment moved from Newbridge to Dublin and Cardigan returned to London on leave, taking the opportunity to speak in a House of Lords debate on two Bills to regulate the new militia. It was also during this period of absence from the regiment that he again fell out with his second-in-command. Hearing that Major Jones had committed the cardinal sin of allowing the regiment to wear forage caps during a parade in Phoenix Park, he sent strict instructions for the indiscretion not to be repeated. He also informed Adjutant-General Brown at the Horse Guards, who in turn wrote to Lieutenant-General Sir Edmund Blakeney, Commander-in-Chief in Ireland, demanding an explanation. Eventually the complaint found its way to Major-General William Cochrane, the commander of the Dublin garrison and the senior officer at the parade.

On 9 July 1852, Cochrane sent a spirited reply to Brown's inquiry. General Blakeney had 'always permitted the Cavalry, except on review occasions, to appear in the Park in forage caps', he wrote, and 'was justified in doing so by the fourth paragraph, page 97, of the Dress Regulations'.

'This "Horse Guards pet",' he continued, referring to Cardigan, 'ought not to receive any encouragement to interfere with the . . . command and dress of his regiment when absent from it.'

Cochrane then said that he had been informed that Brown had given Cardigan leave of absence 'but no *official* intimation to that effect has been received here'. His wish was that Brown 'would keep him altogether in England'.

Realising that he had been a little too candid, Cochrane was relieved when Brown sent a cordial reply on 20 July. Two days later he wrote back, expressing his delight 'at seeing your handwriting again for I began to fear that you had taken offence at some nonsense which I wrote to you ten days ago about Cardigan'.[20]

Meanwhile Cardigan, back with his regiment, had given Jones a severe dressing-down. Not only had he allowed the regiment to be, in Cardigan's opinion, improperly dressed on parade; he had also failed to supply his commanding officer with regular reports during his absence. The upshot was that Cochrane sent a report of the disagreement, favouring Jones, to the Horse Guards and, on the strength of this, Brown wrote back warning Cardigan not to interfere with the running of his regiment when absent.

In August Wellington received the inevitable appeal from Cardigan against Brown's thinly disguised censure. Now 83 (and with less than a month to live), the Duke could have been forgiven for ignoring Cardigan's pleas on a subject that had been taking up his time unnecessarily since 1842. Instead, at a morning discussion with Brown at Apsley House on 25 August, Wellington dictated a response that conceded certain points to Cardigan.

While the Duke was 'prepared to maintain inviolable the direct responsibility to his immediate superiors of the Majors or other officers left in the actual command of a regiment during the temporary absence of its Lieutenant-Colonel,' wrote Brown, 'he is willing so far to modify the interpretation of my letter [of 27 July] . . . as not to deprive Lord Cardigan of those reports from his Majors which may be considered necessary to give him such a knowledge of what takes place in his absence, as an officer in his position, zealously anxious for the welfare of his corps, could reasonably require.

'In making this communication, however (which his Grace trusts will be the last on the subject which has already fruitlessly occupied much of his time & attention),' Brown continued, 'I am directed specially to refer to that portion of the standing orders of the Army in which "unanimity & good understanding" are pointed out as intimately "*connected to the character & discipline of a regiment*".'

As Wellington was perusing the draft of this letter, Brown asked him 'whether in receiving Reports from his Regiment during his absence on leave or otherwise, Lord Cardigan would be justified in issuing orders to his Regiment?' Wellington replied, 'Certainly not.' That day he left Apsley House for Walmer Castle in Kent – his official residence as Warden of the Cinque Ports – never to return. He died of a stroke on 14 September, hounded to the last by Cardigan's petty squabbles.[21]

'The death of the Duke of Wellington has deprived the Country of her greatest man, the Crown of its most valuable servant and adviser, the Army of its main strength and support,' wrote Prince Albert at Balmoral on 17 September.

That same day a grief-stricken Queen Victoria wrote to her uncle, King Leopold of the Belgians, of Britain's 'irreparable' loss. She had had her differences with Wellington, particularly at the outset of her reign, but was now in no doubt as to his worth:

> He was the GREATEST man this country ever produced, and the most *devoted* and *loyal* subject, and the staunchest supporter the Crown ever had . . . To think that all this is gone; that this great and immortal man belongs now to History and no longer to the present, is a truth we cannot realise. We shall soon stand sadly alone . . .

Wellington's successor as Commander-in-Chief was Lord Hardinge (formerly Sir Henry Hardinge, one of the generals who had supported Cardigan's reinstatement in 1836). He was replaced as Master-General of the Ordnance by Lord Fitzroy Somerset, who was raised to the peerage as Lord Raglan. Although Cardigan could not have known it then, Wellington's death was to prove extremely timely in terms of his career. It raised to the head of the Army a man who admired the zeal with which he had brought his regiment to a high state of efficiency, and who sympathised with the way the press had persecuted him. It removed a man all too aware that disharmony between officers could prove fatal on the battlefield.

Had he been alive at the outset of the Crimean War, it is highly unlikely that Wellington would have agreed to Cardigan's appointment as commander of the Light Brigade of cavalry.

The protectionist Conservatives increased their numbers in the summer General Election of 1852 but, without the support of the Peelites, remained in a minority. Nevertheless, Derby's government limped on until December when Disraeli, Chancellor of the Exchequer, presented his first budget. Faced with a majority in the House in favour of free trade (a stance even he was moving towards), he decided on a budget of 'compensation instead of protection'.

'Disraeli's problem,' wrote Blake, 'was to satisfy the "interests" that deemed themselves to have been damaged by free trade, and at the same time to avoid reuniting against him the whole of the opposition in the House of Commons.' These 'interests' were the landed, the sugar and the shipping lobbies, and he included three measures specifically for their benefit: a reduction of the malt tax; the privilege of refining colonial sugar in bond; and the reduction or abolition of certain minor shipping dues.

To pay for this, he made the error of doubling the highly unpopular House Tax while at the same time halving the exemption limit to houses of £10 rateable value. He also tampered with the Income Tax, reducing the levy of 7d on 'precarious' or earned income by a quarter; but also lowering the exemption limit from £150 to £100 and to £50 for earned and unearned incomes respectively.

On 3 December, in a speech spanning five hours, Disraeli presented his controversial financial package. A week later an acrimonious four-day debate began in which almost every point of the budget was attacked. 'Disraeli's enemies had little difficulty in showing that the boons which he had conferred with one hand upon the middle-class householder in the form of earned income relief were neatly removed with his other when he imposed the house tax and lowered the income-tax exemption limit,' wrote Blake.

Finally, as the debate came to a close in the early hours of 17 December, the chamber of the House lit by flickering gaslight and a violent thunderstorm raging outside, Gladstone rose and, displaying the full extent of his extraordinary mastery of financial detail, dismantled Disraeli's budget piece by piece. When the division was taken at 4 a.m., the whole of the opposition voted against it and the government was defeated by 305 votes to 286.[23]

Barring a second General Election, the only alternative to a Conservative government was a coalition, and this depended on the Peelites joining forces with the Whigs, Radicals and Irish. They agreed to do so for a price. Of the 13 Cabinet posts, six went to Peelites, with Lord Aberdeen as Prime Minister and Gladstone as Chancellor of the Exchequer. Whigs filled a further six places, including Russell and Palmerston as Foreign and Home Secretaries respectively. The lone Radical Cabinet minister was Sir William Molesworth, the M.P. who had tried to prevent Cardigan's reappointment in 1836; he became First Commissioner for Works.

Even as Aberdeen was forming his administration, discussions were taking place in St Petersburg, capital of the Russian Empire, that were destined to plunge Europe into the first continental war for almost 40 years. They centred on the so-called 'Eastern Question': the future of the ramshackle and corrupt Ottoman Empire.

At its height in the early seventeenth century, the empire had included not only modern Turkey but the whole of the Balkan peninsula, the central Hungarian plain, the Ukraine, the shores of the Black Sea, the Arab lands of the Middle East and most of the African shore of the Mediterranean. In the eighteenth century, Austria 'liberated' Hungary and the Russians advanced south round both sides of the Black Sea, reaching the Danube delta in the west and the mountains of the Caucasus in the east. Successive Sultans also relinquished control of outlying provinces in the Balkans and North Africa; Serbia and Egypt were to all intents and purposes autonomous, while Greece was given independence in 1829.

Yet the Ottoman Empire still contained more than 13 million orthodox Christians who looked to Russia as their protector. To enforce their rights Nicholas I, the Russian Tsar, had fought a victorious war against the Turks in 1828–9, receiving generous concessions in the subsequent Treaty of Adrianople. By 1841 the British and Russians had engineered a Straits Convention closing the Dardanelles and the Bosphorus to all foreign warships so long as Turkey was at peace. This allowed Russia freedom of movement in the Black Sea and Britain peace of mind that its quickest route to India, via the isthmus of Suez, would not be at the mercy of the Russian fleet.

So it was that Tsar Nicholas arrived secretly in London in June 1844 to discuss the 'Eastern Question' with Peel and his Foreign Secretary, Lord Aberdeen. 'Turkey is a dying man,' Nicholas told them, but it was vitally important to prevent its early collapse because of the danger that a single foreign power, particularly France, might then dominate the strategic capital of Constantinople. The following month, Aberdeen and the Russian Foreign Secretary, Count Nesselrode, signed a memorandum affirming the desire of both powers to preserve the Ottoman Empire as long as possible; if it was in danger of collapsing, they would discuss 'the establishment of a new order of things to replace that which exists today'. The agreement was so secret that it was not even discussed in Cabinet and was kept not in the Foreign Office, but in Aberdeen's private papers.[24]

What upset this delicate balance was the election of Louis Napoleon – nephew of the emperor who had invaded Russia in 1812 – to the presidency of the Second French Republic in 1848. Two years later, to whip up clerical support at home, he began to sponsor Roman Catholic rights to the Palestinian Holy Places of the Ottoman Empire, the most important of which were the Holy Sepulchre in Jerusalem and the Church of the Nativity in Bethlehem. Russian fears about Louis Napoleon's hidden agenda were increased after his successful *coup* of December 1851, elevating him to virtual dictator. (A year later the Second Empire was proclaimed and he became Napoleon III.)

In February 1852, Sultan Abdul Medjid made certain concessions to the French over the issue of access to the 'Holy Places'. Impressed by French military might – in the form of the steam-powered warship *Charlemagne* which, in breach of the Straits Convention, carried the French ambassador through the Dardanelles in the summer of 1852 – the Sultan turned increasingly towards France as his primary ally. In December he succumbed to French pressure and ordered Orthodox monks to hand over to their Latin counterparts the keys to the church in Bethlehem and its Holy Grotto, believed to have been the birthplace of Christ. As Aberdeen was forming his coalition government, Latin monks were placing a silver star engraved with the arms of France in the Holy Grotto.

Tsar Nicholas was furious and, encouraged by reports of clan warfare along Turkey's north-west frontier, suggested to Count Nesselrode that the time had come to draw up partition plans for the Ottoman Empire. Nesselrode warned him that such talk would alienate Britain, but Nicholas was not to be deflected. On 11 January, in a despatch to the Foreign Office, the British Ambassador, Sir Hamilton Seymour, gave an account of an informal conversation he had had with the Tsar two days earlier. Nicholas had spoken of 'the close alliance which ought always to exist between us, saying that if England and he . . . were on good terms . . . what anyone else thought mattered little'.

As Nicholas was taking his leave, Seymour had asked him for some assurances as to Turkey and he replied: 'We have a sick man on our hands, a man who is seriously ill; it will be . . . a great misfortune if he escapes us one of these days, especially before all the necessary arrangements are made.'

Over the next three months, Nicholas had a number of other conversations with Seymour on the subject of Turkey. Each time he returned to the same theme: the Ottoman Empire was dying and it was important to come to an agreement over its dismemberment. Serbia, Bulgaria and the Danubian Principalities should become independent states under Russian protection, Nicholas suggested, while in return Britain could have Egypt and Crete. While not overtly hostile to these suggestions, Aberdeen's government could not sanction any action which would precipitate Turkey's collapse, particularly as Nicholas had hinted that it might lead to Russia 'temporarily' occupying Constantinople.

Believing that he had reassured Britain, Nicholas now turned to deal with France. Towards the end of February he sent the 66-year-old Prince Menschikoff, Chief of Naval Staff, to Constantinople to secure a convention recognising Russia's right to protect Turkey's Orthodox Christians. If France opposed these terms, the Sultan was to be offered a secret defensive alliance. On 5 May, Menschikoff was given guarantees about the 'Holy Places', but this was no longer enough and he repeated his original demand. For the Sultan to have agreed would have meant effectively ceding sovereignty over his Danubian provinces to Russia. He refused, and on 21 May Menschikoff left the Ottoman capital.

A majority in Aberdeen's Cabinet were in favour of action to dissuade the Russians from war, and on 5 June Admiral Dundas was ordered to sail the fleet from Malta to the anchorage of Besika Bay, ten miles south of the entrance to the Dardanelles. France promised naval support. 'We are drifting towards war,' Aberdeen told Lord Clarendon, Foreign Secretary since Russell's resignation in February (Russell continued in the Cabinet as Minister without Portfolio).[26]

He was right. On 3 July, Russian troops entered the Danubian principality of Moldavia, but the British Cabinet was too divided to agree on decisive action. It was left to Austria, with much of her trade passing through the lower Danube, to convene a conference in Vienna attended by British, French and Russian envoys, but no representative from Turkey. The outcome, the 'Vienna Note' of 1 August, sought to guarantee joint Franco-Russian supervision of the Sultan's Christian subjects.

The British Ambassador at Constantinople, Lord Stratford de Redcliffe, told the Sultan that his government was anxious for him to sign the Note. But the Sultan knew that, unofficially, Lord Stratford felt it would be unwise to give in to the Russians, and he was convinced that neither the British nor the French would allow Russia to take Constantinople. Also, public feeling in his capital was running high and within days anti-Russian riots would break out. Therefore he suggested an amendment, giving Turkey a say in the protection of the Christian religion within its borders.

Russia refused, and within a few weeks a Berlin newspaper was quoting Nesselrode as saying that he interpreted the Vienna Note as allowing Russia a right to interfere in the interest of all Orthodox subjects of Turkey. These comments finally dispelled the belief in the British Cabinet that Tsar Nicholas sought a reasonable settlement to the 'Eastern Question'. On 23 September, Clarendon ordered Stratford to summon Dundas's naval squadron to Constantinople. Anxious to seek a diplomatic settlement, Stratford delayed, but Russia refused to withdraw from Moldavia and Wallachia and on 4 October Turkey declared war.

Still Aberdeen held back from direct involvement, but all this changed on 30 November when a Russian naval squadron destroyed a light flotilla of Turkish ships in the small harbour of Sinope on the Anatolian coast. Three thousand Turks died, either in the fires or in the sea. It was said that after the battle, the Russians had cleared the wounded off the Turkish ships with grapeshot.

When news of the 'massacre' reached the British press on 12 December, the public were outraged. Where before there had been lukewarm enthusiasm for war, with the majority of newspapers urging a settlement, now the reverse was true. 'The English people are resolved,' declared *The Times*, 'that Russia shall not dictate conditions to Europe, or convert the Black Sea, with all the various interests encompassing its shores, into a Russian lake.'

A week later the formerly anti-war *Morning Chronicle* stated: 'To stop the unprofitable contest by striking down the aggressor with a blow is as plain a duty towards humanity as it was to send succour to Sinope.'

'War with Russia at this time was the principal topic of conversation, at Mess, at stables – in fact everywhere when we met and had an opportunity of discussing the subject,' wrote Troop Sergeant-Major Loy Smith as the 11th Hussars spent Christmas 1853 quartered in the Portobello barracks in Dublin. Cardigan, of course, was on leave enjoying the comforts of Deene.[27]

Responding to the Sinope 'atrocity', the British and French governments made war all but inevitable by sending their respective naval squadrons into the Black Sea to prevent the Russian fleet from making another sortie from its Crimean base at Sebastopol. On 9 February the Duke of Newcastle, Secretary for War and the Colonies, issued orders for 10,000 troops to be transported by steamship to Malta, from where they could quickly be deployed in the defence of Constantinople. Five days later the 1st Battalion, Coldstream Guards, left its Trafalgar Square barracks and, with the regimental band playing 'The Girl I Left Behind Me' and cheering crowds lining the route, marched towards Waterloo Station, en route to Chichester and ultimately to troopships at Portsmouth and Southampton.

The first ships sailed on 23 February. Four days later Clarendon sent an ultimatum to the Russians to evacuate the Danubian principalities by April or face war. The French did likewise. Early the following morning the Scots Fusilier Guards, with the regimental band at its head, marched out of the Wellington barracks in Birdcage Walk in slow time and made its way through cheering crowds lining the Mall to the forecourt of Buckingham Palace. Waiting to see the Guards off were the Queen, Prince Albert and several of the royal children including the 12-year-old Prince of Wales:

> They passed through the courtyard here at seven o'clock this morning [the Queen wrote to her uncle Leopold]. We stood on the balcony to see them – the morning fine, the sun rising over the towers of old Westminster Abbey – and an immense crowd collected to see these fine men, and cheering them immensely as they with difficulty marched along. They formed line, presented arms, and then cheered us *very heartily*, and went on cheering. It was a *touching and beautiful* sight; many sorrowing friends were there, and one saw the shake of many a hand. My best wishes and prayers will be with them all . . .[28]

With their band playing 'O Where, and O Where is my Highland Laddie Gone?', the Guards left Buckingham Palace and marched in extended column towards Waterloo Station and trains for Portsmouth.

Meanwhile, Cardigan had been avidly following newspaper reports of the drift to war, anxious that he would not miss any opportunity to serve. There was every chance that the 11th Hussars, still in Dublin, would be joining the expeditionary force, but Cardigan was not content with the prospect of commanding a single regiment in battle. After all, at a number of field days in Phoenix Park during the summer of 1853, the 11th Hussars had been brigaded with the rest of the mounted Dublin garrison – including the 1st and 2nd Dragoon Guards, the 16th Lancers and a troop of Royal Horse Artillery – and each time Cardigan had been in command. So when Lord Raglan (the former Lord Fitzroy Somerset) was named as Commander-in-Chief of the British expeditionary force in February, Cardigan immediately wrote to Lord Hardinge offering his services.

For a time there was silence. Then finally, on 23 March, four days before Britain officially declared war, he received notification from the Horse Guards that he would command the Light Brigade of Cavalry which included his own regiment. Present when the news arrived was Lieutenant-Colonel Edward Hodge, commander of the 4th Dragoon Guards, a regiment also due to join the expeditionary force. 'Went to Lord Cardigan to find out all I could,' Hodge noted in his diary. 'He was very civil. He received his order of Brigadier-General when I was with him. I learnt much that was worth knowing.'[29]

The official announcement that Cardigan would command a brigade was made on April Fool's Day . . . but it was no joke. Nor was the appointment of the Earl of Lucan, Cardigan's hated brother-in-law, to command the Cavalry Division – made up of the Light and Heavy Brigades. Three years younger than Cardigan, the then Lord Bingham had entered the Army as a 16-year-old ensign in the 6th Regiment of Foot in 1816. Within ten years – by a series of exchanges, switches to half-pay and purchases (the last of which was reputed to have been for £25,000) – he had risen to the rank of Lieutenant-Colonel in command of the 17th Lancers.

Like Cardigan, Bingham was obsessed with making his regiment the finest in the service and would stop at nothing to achieve this. 'Officers and men began to groan,' wrote Cecil Woodham-Smith, his biographer, 'Drills, parades, inspections came upon them in an unending procession, followed by reprimands, punishments, floggings.' What distinguished him even from Cardigan is that he did not have a lighter, hedonistic side to his nature that enabled him to unwind. Rising at dawn, he worked unceasingly, ate and drank sparingly, and had little interest in social pursuits.

Anxious to see action, Bingham managed to get himself seconded to the staff of Prince Woronzoff during Russia's victorious war against the Turks in 1828. There he won many admirers, although at times his zeal and gallantry were bordering on the irresponsible. 'Lord Bingham never let slip an opportunity to be in the fighting, even more than I could wish,' wrote

Woronzoff that September. When Tsar Nicholas I was told of the young Irishman's feats, he conferred on him the Order of St Anne, Second Class.[30]

Returning to Britain in early 1829, Bingham was the most eligible of eligible bachelors: dark and handsome, heir to an earldom with estates in Ireland and England, and a war hero to boot. In June he married Lady Anne Brudenell, Cardigan's youngest sister – 'worldly and not over-wise' according to Queen Adelaide – and after a lengthy honeymoon resumed command of the 17th Lancers. But in May 1837 he exchanged on to half-pay to enable him to put in order the vast neglected family estates in Ireland. His wife detested Castlebar, the cold and forbidding mansion in County Mayo, preferring instead the comfortable drawing-rooms of London. Her husband was a tyrant, she claimed, expecting her to live on a shoestring; despite the birth of two sons and a daughter, they had permanently separated by 1854. Cardigan was said to have been infuriated by the alleged maltreatment of his sister, and would undoubtedly have challenged Lucan to a duel if that had still been a possibility.

Needless to say, Cardigan was far from happy to learn that he would be serving under his despised brother-in-law and, given that all of London knew of their feud, it is difficult to explain their respective appointments, particularly as Lucan had been on half-pay since 1837. In his book *The Great War with Russia*, William Russell wrote:

> Lord Lucan was a hard man to get on with. But the moment the Government of the day made the monstrous choice of his brother-in-law, Lord Cardigan, as the Brigadier of the Light Brigade of the Cavalry Division, knowing well the relations between the two officers and the nature of the two men, they became responsible for the disaster; they were guilty of treason to the Army – neither more nor less.[31]

Soon after publication of his book, Russell received a letter from an 'officer and politician', for whose 'opinion' he had 'respect', claiming that when Lord Hardinge, the Commander-in-Chief, 'made the appointments it was not thought there would be war'. What he meant was that it was not thought likely that British troops would actually be involved in fighting. Yet, as Russell rightly points out, even if that had been the assumption it still does not explain why Cardigan and Lucan 'were allowed to retain their commands, not only when it was plain that they were likely to be engaged on active service against the enemy, but after positive proof had been forced on the attention of the Commander-in-Chief, when actually in the presence of the enemy, and immediately after the battle, that the feeling between the . . . Lucan . . . and . . . Cardigan was such that friendly co-operation between them was impossible.'[32]

The method of appointment for generals of divisions and brigades was for Hardinge, the Commander-in-Chief, to consult Raglan, the expedition commander. The names would then be submitted to the Duke of Newcastle for the government's approval, and finally sent to the Queen for her sanction. Aware of this, many historians have assumed that Raglan was partly responsible for the injudicious appointments. In fact, according to John Sweetman, Raglan's most recent biographer – who refers to a conversation between the Honourable Somerset Calthorpe, Raglan's nephew and aide-de-camp, and Martineau, Newcastle's biographer – Raglan was 'not consulted about the appointments of either Lucan or Cardigan'. When he was informed, he 'protested strongly to Hardinge about placing in such close professional proximity two such irreconcilable men whose antipathy for each other was well-known'. Hardinge overruled his objections.

Sweetman also quotes from a letter from Hardinge to Newcastle of 13 March 1854, in which the Commander-in-Chief 'apologized . . . for recommending the appointments of Lord Lucan and Brigadier-Generals Torrens and Goldie to the Queen without reference to him'. Newcastle decided not to exercise his veto, therefore Hardinge must shoulder the majority of the blame. It could be argued that Raglan, as the commander on the ground, should have relieved either Cardigan or Lucan once they began to disagree on active service. Yet Hardinge had overruled him once, and he may have assumed that he had to put up with what he had been given.[33]

The Army, of course, was well aware of the breach between the two brothers-in-law, and Colonel Hodge voiced the fears of many in the cavalry when he wrote on 5 April 1854: 'Lord Lucan commands the whole. He is brother-in-law to Lord Cardigan, and they do not speak. How this will answer on service I know not.'[34]

12

Off to War

No less controversial than the appointment of the two brothers-in-law, Cardigan and Lucan, was the choice of Lord Raglan as Commander-in-Chief of the expeditionary force. Almost the whole of his career had involved staff work rather than the command of troops, although he had had the benefit of learning at first hand from Britain's finest soldier.

During the Peninsular and Waterloo campaigns he had been Wellington's Military Secretary, his right hand, and it had cost him his own when his right elbow was smashed by a musket ball during Napoleon's final defeat. The arm had to be amputated between shoulder and elbow and, despite the lack of anaesthetic, he is said to have endured the crude operation in silence. Only when his severed limb was tossed aside by the surgeon did he pipe up: 'Hey, bring my arm back. There's a ring my wife gave me on the finger.'[1]

After Waterloo, Raglan continued as the Duke's secretary, accompanying him on a number of diplomatic missions before being sent to Spain on one of his own in 1823. Four years later, when Wellington became Commander-in-Chief for the first time, the then Lord Fitzroy Somerset was appointed Military Secretary to the Horse Guards and remained in this post until 1852. Yet in almost 50 years of service he had never commanded a formation larger than a battalion, even in peacetime, and now, aged 65, was expected to head an army.

The truth is that Raglan, a fluent French speaker, was chosen more for his ability to ensure cordial relations with the French and Turkish commanders, Marshal St Arnaud and Omar Pasha, than for his skill as a

battlefield tactician. Lord Hardinge emphasised these diplomatic qualifications in a letter to Newcastle on 8 February 1854, recommending Raglan's
appointment:

> [The] officer the best qualified to be sent with a British force to
> the East would be Lord Raglan . . . He possesses great professional
> experience acquired under the Duke, and he has for this service
> personal qualifications most desirable in a chief who has to co-
> operate with a French force. His temper and manners are
> conciliatory, and he would command the respect of Foreigners and
> the confidence of our own force.

Newcastle, however, was sceptical, citing Raglan's lack of 'experience of
the personnel of the army' and want of recent active service. In the event
he was overruled by the Queen and the Cabinet, and Raglan was officially
appointed on 21 February. Renowned for the charm, tact and efficiency
with which he carried out his duties, a diplomatic role was well suited to
him. But he was used to acting on orders, not giving them, and this fatal
flaw in a commander would be exposed to the full before his death the following year.[2]

If Raglan had his deficiencies, then so too did many of his subordinates;
men over whose appointments he had only a limited say. Of his six divisional generals, only two had experience of commanding a formation
bigger than a battalion in action against trained troops, and only one, the
35-year-old Duke of Cambridge, was under 60. The Duke had never
been to war and owed his appointment to the fact that he was the Queen's
cousin.

The pick of the bunch was probably Sir George de Lacy Evans, the 67-
year-old commander of the 2nd Division, who had fought in the
Peninsula, India and America, and who had been knighted for commanding the British Legion in Spain during the Carlist Wars of the 1830s.
Since then he had spent much time in Parliament, first as M.P. for Rye,
then Westminster, espousing radical views unusual in a soldier.

Yet it was typical of the class bias of the British officer corps that Sir
Colin Campbell, 61, the most outstanding soldier available to Raglan,
was still only a brigadier-general in command of the Highland Brigade.
The son of a Glaswegian carpenter by the name of Macliver, he had been
given the name of his uncle, Colonel John Campbell, owing to a mistake
by the Duke of York when he was commissioned. But lacking money and

social influence, his promotion had been slow. Nevertheless he had displayed remarkable military talent in a number of foreign campaigns, including the War of 1812 against the United States, the Opium War of 1842 and the Second Sikh War of 1848–9 when he was knighted for his services.

In many other respects, Raglan's position was an unenviable one. His expeditionary force of 25,000 men was a hotch-potch of semi-independent departments that well reflected the administrative chaos of the early Victorian Army. While the infantry and cavalry were under his immediate authority, the artillery and engineers owed their theoretical (and often practical) allegiance to his former fiefdom, the Ordnance Department in London. In addition, he had no direct control over the supply of his army which was the responsibility of the Commissariat Department, a civilian organisation under the auspices of the Treasury. The Medical Department, too, was largely independent and woefully under-equipped.

Even the regiments and battalions under Raglan's command had a history of independence. As commanding officers had often paid well over the regulation price for their rank, they tended to view their regiments as their own personal property and resented interference from the Horse Guards. In particular, they opposed suggestions that their regiments should join in large-scale manoeuvres, with the result that few of them had experience of operations on even a brigade scale. Instead, in line with the belief that battles should be fought in close formation, their regiments spent hours perfecting repetitive drill movements at the expense of battlefield tactics.

Soon after taking over at the Board of Ordnance, Lord Raglan had tried to rectify this by establishing a training camp at Chobham for 8,000 men. But the field days which took place were a fiasco, with units getting jumbled and moving in the wrong direction. 'This Army is a shambles,' noted Captain Biddulph of the Royal Artillery.[3]

One area of the expeditionary force over which Raglan did have decisive influence was his staff – but even this was indicative of a flaw in the system. Good staff work is usually the key to any army's success, but in Britain an independent staff college did not then exist. Instead, the Senior Department of the Royal Military College was the only place where an officer could gain theoretical experience of staff work. Yet few 'smart' officers aspired to such training, and only 15 of the 221 staff officers assigned to the expeditionary force had studied at the Senior Department. As ever, 'influence' rather than ability was the key to gaining such an appointment.

All four of Raglan's aides-de-camp were relatives: two nephews and two great-nephews. A fifth who joined later was a relation by marriage.

On 21 March, Lieutenant-General Sir George Brown, formerly Adjutant-General and now commanding the Light Division, left London on board the hired steamer *Golden Fleece*. Accompanied by a battalion of riflemen, two companies of sappers and William H. Russell of *The Times*, his task was to prepare the forward British base at Boulahar on the Gallipoli peninsula.

Arriving on 6 April, he discovered Generals Bosquet and Canrobert with 2,000 French troops already in residence. Over the next few days, sappers from both nations traced out the camp lines and a number of infantry regiments arrived from Malta. But it soon became apparent that the French were far better prepared. On 4 May, *The Times* published a letter from an officer in the 50th Regiment: 'Our encampment is very wretched, and hardly anything except the men's rations to be got to eat . . . The French have everything – horses, provisions, good tents and every kind of protection against contingencies.'[4]

Not only was there no cover at Boulahar, but water was scarce and sanitation non-existent. Furthermore, it was poorly placed in a strategic sense, a long way from Constantinople and particularly the battle-front in northern Bulgaria. For all these reasons it was decided to establish a forward base closer to the Turkish capital; after some indecision the British Ambassador, Lord Stratford, managed to obtain Turkish permission for the British to use the empty military barracks at Scutari, opposite Constantinople on the Asian shore of the Bosphorus.

On 28 April, Lord Raglan arrived and set up his headquarters in a small hut between a line of cypress trees and a beach 'which somewhat resembled that of Folkstone at high water'. Marshal St Arnaud, the French commander, preferred a villa at Yenikov, 12 miles distant on the European side of the Bosphorus. Until recently the French Minister of War, St Arnaud, 55, had earned his military reputation by suppressing a serious native revolt in Algeria. Earlier, in the late 1820s, he had learnt to speak English while living for two years among the prostitutes and pimps of Drury Lane, teaching fencing and dancing to earn a crust. Yet he had long suffered from intestinal pains, and before long they would sap his enthusiasm for war.

★

The force of cavalry earmarked for service in the East consisted of ten regiments of roughly 300 sabres each. They were equally divided between Cardigan's Light Brigade and the Heavy Brigade of the Honourable Sir James Scarlett, 55, the younger son of Lord Abinger and, until recently, Lieutenant-Colonel of the 5th Dragoon Guards. With his white whiskers, florid face, unorthodox dress and easygoing manner, Scarlett was immensely popular with men and officers alike and could not have been more of a contrast to Cardigan and their immediate superior Lucan. Never before in action, he would prove his worth in the Crimea.

Scarlett's heavy cavalry was made up of five regiments of dragoons and dragoon guards, including the renowned Royals, Inniskillings and Scots Greys. With bigger recruits, heavier horses and weightier weapons than light cavalry, their role was as a shock force to break up enemy formations of infantry or cavalry. All but the Scots Greys wore brass helmets to protect them from sword cuts during a mêlée. Cardigan's five regiments of light cavalry, on the other hand – made up of light dragoons, hussars and lancers – were designed for mobility and wore fur caps or shakos. In theory, their tasks would be escort and outpost duty, skirmishing and reconnaissance.

The uniforms worn by the cavalry could not have been less suited to such work, with their fantastic head-dresses and elaborate slung jackets, and all in bright colours of red, blue and gold that announced their presence from some distance. None, however, were as distinctive as the uniforms of the 11th Hussars. 'The splendour of these magnificent light horsemen, the shortness of their jackets, the tightness of their cherry-coloured pants make them as utterly unfit for war service as the garb of the female hussars in the ballet of Gustavus, which they so nearly resemble,' read a letter to *The Times* of 22 April.

Intending himself to wear the uniform of his former corps on active service, Cardigan took offence and wrote back: 'It would be scarcely necessary for me to state, except to show the falsehood and ignorance of this anonymous writer, that in the 11th Hussars the men's Jackets are longer and Overalls looser than in almost any other Cavalry regiment in the Service.'[5]

The men of the 11th Hussars were far too busy preparing for war to worry about such flippant comments, however. Ordered to take out two service squadrons of two troops each, totalling 310 men and 280 horses, and to leave two troops behind to form a recruiting depot, they were forced to break up the regimental band to make up the numbers. Other regiments had to borrow both men and horses from units staying behind. Once up to full strength, the 11th had frequent field days in Phoenix Park under Lord Cardigan during April while they waited for the order to embark. Their swords were sharpened under the supervision of men from the Tower of London, while the officers' mess plate and the regiment's heavy luggage were deposited in the Bank of Ireland.

To preserve the horses from the adverse effect of a long sea voyage, the original plan had been to march the cavalry across France before embarking them at Marseilles for the onward journey. In the event, comfort was sacrificed for time. One of the first cavalry regiments to depart was the 8th Hussars from Plymouth on 25 April. Accompanying part of the regiment on the sailing ship *Shooting Star* was Fanny Duberly, the vivacious young wife of Captain Henry Duberly, the 8th's Paymaster.

Recognising the tradition of women following troops to war, the Horse Guards had allowed room for 16 per regiment (Loy Smith would later pronounce this 'a mistake as women on campaign, unless they could be employed in the hospitals, become a useless encumbrance'). But this number did not include officers' wives – who were thought unsuited to the rigours of campaigning – and only those with 'influence', like Mrs Duberly, managed to obtain special dispensation.[6]

Three days into the voyage, she was beginning to regret her daring. 'The breeze,' she noted in her journal, 'which had been gradually freshening during yesterday, increased last night. I, sick and almost helpless in my cabin, was told the disastrous news that both the mizzen-top and the main-top gallant were carried away; that fragments of the wreck – masts, ropes, and spars – strewed the deck: one poor fellow was lying seriously injured, having broken his leg, and crushed the bone.'

Once through the Bay of Biscay, the weather improved but the horses still suffered. 'A fourth horse died last night,' wrote Fanny Duberly on 4 May. 'They tell me he went absolutely mad, and raved himself to death. The hold where our horses are stowed, although considered large and airy, appears to me horrible beyond words. The slings begin to gall the horses under the shoulder and breastbone; and the heat and bad atmosphere must be felt to be understood.'

Finally, on 22 May, after almost a month at sea, the *Shooting Star* reached Scutari. Fanny Duberly soon realised that the external looks of the barracks could be deceptive. 'They appear from the outside to be a very fine building, close to the sea, and with a very handsome facade,' she wrote. 'But the inside – the dilapidation! the dirt! the rats! the fleas!'

Her opinion of the town generally was, if anything, even lower: 'Turkish dogs, lazy and dirty, were lying about in all directions; while horribly filthy beggars were hovering everywhere, interspersed with Turkish soldiers and Greeks. The little harbour is filled with cabbages, and refuse of every description, – a dead dog floating out, and a dead horse drifting close to the shore, on whose swollen and corrupted flanks three dogs were alternately fighting and tearing off the horrible flesh . . .'[7]

The 11th Hussars left Dublin in five small sailing vessels in early May, and also took more than a month to reach Constantinople. Thanks to Troop Sergeant-Major Loy Smith, the long voyage passed without mishap for the 43 men and 39 horses of F Troop on board the 700-ton *Asia*:

> I had brought some sticks and baskets for the men to practise attack and defence, and for amusement. When they were tired of this, dancing and singing songs were resorted to, so that the evenings were spent pleasantly. Everyone on board seeming happy – Captain Cook leaving all the arrangements to me. The men's conduct was so good that I do not recall having to report one of them.
>
> The trumpeter sounded 'Stables' three times a day, and every man attended to his horse as far as possible the same as at barracks. Several barrels of vinegar were shipped for the purpose of refreshing the horses, by sponging their heads well over with it, particularly their nostrils. Slings were provided too for the horses to rest on. These I soon began to suspect must be made on a wrong principle for, if a horse slipped, they rather tended to throw him down than support him, and there was more difficulty to get a horse up . . . than if he had fallen without one. So convinced was I . . . that I discontinued their use. The consequence was that every horse was disembarked . . . in splendid condition: this I believe did not happen with any other sailing vessel that went out . . . The other four vessels that took out the 11th lost 11.[8]

One of the luckier regiments was the 5th Dragoon Guards, which left Cork on 28 May in one ship, the 3,500-ton steamship *Himalaya*, and arrived at the Bosphorus 16 days later. Lieutenant Richard Temple Godman, the adjutant, noted that the only hardships were trying to keep the horses calm in rough weather and the excessive vibration of the ship which made it difficult to write letters![9]

Most regiments lost a few horses during the voyage, but only the 6th Inniskilling Dragoons suffered human casualties. Its headquarters was aboard the *Europa*, a small sailing ship which caught fire 200 miles out from Plymouth and had to be abandoned. The dead included the commanding officer, Lieutenant-Colonel Willoughby Moore, the veterinary surgeon, 16 other men and two women. All the horses, equipment and baggage were also lost.

At Malta, the regimental sergeant-major and 11 other survivors were transferred to the sailing ship *Deva*, carrying Lieutenant-Colonel Hodge and the headquarters of the 4th Dragoon Guards. Hodge soon discovered that the tragedy was the fault of the sailors, and that had they 'behaved properly every man would have been saved'. On 24 June, he wrote in his diary: 'I have been questioning the Sergeant Major of the 6th. The *Europa* caught fire at 10 p.m. on 31 May, 123 miles west of the Scilly Isles. The two mates and three able seamen at once deserted the ship in a boat. The rest of the crew took to their boats. The soldiers behaved well.'[10]

Like most other senior officers, Lord Cardigan chose to avoid the long sea voyage by taking a short cut through France. Accompanied by Lieutenant Maxse, his aide-de-camp, he left London for the French capital on 8 May. Two days later, he gave a sumptuous dinner party at the Café de Paris, and on the 11th was received by Napoleon III and the Empress Eugénie at the Tuileries.

Continuing his journey south, he left Marseilles in a steamer and, after a couple of days sightseeing in Athens, reached Scutari on the 24th. He immediately went to pay his respects to Lord Lucan, who had arrived before him, and two days later they dined together. But the veneer of cordiality would not last.

That same day, Raglan issued orders for two regiments of the Light Brigade – the 8th Hussars and 17th Lancers – to proceed by sea up to the Black Sea port of Varna. The Russians had crossed the Danube to invest the Bulgarian river fortress of Silistria, and Raglan was responding to the Turks' request for assistance. At a conference with Omar Pasha, the Turkish commander, he and St Arnaud had agreed to move all their troops up to the vicinity of Varna from where they could combat the Russian threat.

Hearing of the move, Cardigan immediately applied to Raglan for permission to accompany his regiments, which would have the dual benefit of placing him close to the action and far from Lucan's control. But by not sending his request via Lucan, his immediate superior, Cardigan was in breach of standard practice, having taken unfair advantage of Raglan's generous concession that he could write directly to him in a private capacity. Choosing to ignore the fact that the content of Cardigan's letter was in fact official, Raglan agreed to his request and then notified Lucan so that he could make the necessary arrangements. Already irritated at having been bypassed, Lucan was incensed to discover that Cardigan had issued his own orders for embarkation; cancelling these, he substituted his own.

But despite the fact that twice Cardigan had acted without his knowledge, Lucan did not protest to Raglan. Instead, on 2 June, he sent Cardigan a private reproof: 'It is obvious that the service cannot be carried on as it should be,' Lucan wrote, 'and as I hope in my division it will be, if a subordinate officer is allowed to pass over his immediate and responsible superior and communicate direct with the General Commanding in Chief.' While he considered 'the error deserving and requiring notice', he was writing in an unofficial capacity as he wished 'this, like all other communications between us, to be of the most friendly nature'. Cardigan did not reply.[11]

To some extent, Cardigan may be excused for wishing to be apart from a commander who was prone to interfering in every aspect of his division's day-to-day life. While at Scutari, a stream of petty orders flowed from Lucan's headquarters, encompassing everything from the amount of facial hair ('Below the mouth there is to be no hair whatever, and the whisker is not be worn more forward on the chin than the corner of the mouth') to the wearing of gold sword knots ('The officers . . . are to wear their regulation sword knots and no others'). As the days wore on he would pass sentence on, among other duties, the picketing of horses, the care of baggage animals, the packing of valises, the carriage of ammunition, reports, tents, boots, trumpet-calls, watch-setting, marching and drill.[12]

Fanny Duberly almost became a victim of his officious nature when she was forbidden to accompany her husband and his regiment to Varna. But she was a determined woman and made plans to bribe the crew of the *Shooting Star* to stow her away; if that failed she would 'purchase a pony, and ride 130 miles (up to Varna) through a strange and barbarous country'. As it turned out, neither recourse was necessary as Raglan, asked by Lucan to adjudicate, had 'stated that he had no intention of interfering' with Mrs Duberly. When the 8th Hussars left Scutari on 31 May, she went with them.[13]

Raglan had more important things to worry about. On 30 May,

Colonel Alexander Gordon – a Guards officer in the 1st Division – outlined the main problem in a letter to his father, the Prime Minister Lord
Aberdeen:

> We are ready to go up to Varna, but the commissariat is not . . .
> They have no horses or mules for the transport of tents, provisions
> or baggage – and instead of setting to work to get them they are
> engaged in objecting to everything proposed and thwarting Lord
> Raglan in everything. Until you send out an order that Lord R. is
> to command the army and not Commissary General Fidler we
> shall not get into ready working order.[14]

Three days later, Raglan was faced with another headache when St Arnaud
informed him that he had decided against sending up all his troops to help
the Turks relieve Silistria. Now only a small force under General Canrobert
would proceed to Varna. Instead, he proposed that the main Anglo-French
force should defend Constantinople by holding the Balkan passes. But
Raglan had already sent part of the Light Brigade, and more regiments –
both infantry and cavalry – were almost ready to depart. He continued
with arrangements and was vindicated when, on 9 June, he was told that
St Arnaud had reverted back to the original plan.

Meanwhile, Cardigan had arrived at the small Bulgarian port of Varna
on 4 June. Mrs Duberly, approaching it from the sea three days earlier,
thought it 'a small but clean-looking town'. But as with Scutari, looks
could be deceptive. On closer inspection the buildings were ramshackle,
although recently whitewashed, and the streets were narrow, pot-holed and
each angled towards an evil-smelling central drain.[15]

With Varna and its immediate hinterland incapable of sustaining the
50,000 Allied troops that were about to descend upon it, Lieutenant-
General Brown, the senior British officer present, scouted inland for
alternative sites. The one chosen for the light cavalry was the small town
of Devna, 16 miles due west of Varna. On 7 June, Cardigan was ordered
by Brown to take command there; his task, Brown told him, was to make
contact with cavalry outposts of the main Turkish army, based at the
fortress of Shumla about 40 miles further inland, and patrol with them for
any signs of Russian penetration south of the Danube.[16]

The 8th Hussars had already set up camp on the outskirts of Devna on
5 June, joined soon after by the 17th Lancers. Mrs Duberly recorded her
impressions of the exhausting march:

Was awoke by reveillée at half-past two; rose, packed our bedding and tent, got a stale egg and a mouthful of brandy, and was in my saddle by half-past five.

I shall never forget that march! It occupied nearly eight hours. The heat intense, the fatigue overwhelming; but the country – anything more beautiful I never saw! – vast plains, verdant hills, covered with shrubs and flowers; a noble lake; and a road, which was merely a cart track, winding through a luxuriant woodland country, across plains and through deep bosquets of brushwood.

In a subsequent journal entry, Mrs Duberly described the camp as 'most picturesque, in the midst of a large and fertile plain, near a sparkling river, and carpetted with brilliant flowers'. The nearby town, however, was a different matter. Lieutenant Temple Godman, who arrived with the 5th Dragoon Guards on 25 June, thought it a 'wretched place – any village you saw in Connemara is much better – hardly anyone to be seen, not even a chicken'.[17]

Lord Cardigan reached the new camp on 7 June and the following day, in line with Brown's instructions, despatched Captain Tomkinson and ten men of the 8th Hussars on a three-day patrol towards the north. Although the summer nights were cold, Cardigan forbade them to take their cloaks to wrap around themselves because he considered such a practice to be 'effeminate'.

Established in a house on the outskirts of the town, built over a stream and shaded by a tree, Cardigan began to suffer from a relapse of bronchitis but still found enough strength to give 'everyone as much trouble as he possibly can', wrote Lieutenant Seager of the 8th Hussars. 'No end of reports, returns and official letters, even more than at home.'[18]

Assuming his command was a detached one, Cardigan ignored Lucan (still at Scutari) and forwarded all official reports to the senior officer at Varna – General Brown. Lucan, needless to say, was furious at what he saw as a fresh attempt to usurp his authority. Left twiddling his thumbs while his division was sent up to Varna, he accused Raglan of favouritism. 'The whole of the horse artillery, and the whole of the cavalry present, full half of what is expected, and composed of troops of the two brigades, are to be in the field with the headquarters of the army under a brigadier (Lord Cardigan), whilst I am to be left behind without troops, and for all I can see without duties,' he wrote to Raglan on 11 September.

When appointed to the Cavalry Division, it had 'occurred to very

245

many, that the great difficulty would be to command Lord Cardigan'. He had not shared that view, Lucan wrote, confident that he 'should receive from Lord Raglan that support which a divisional commander may fairly expect to receive from the Commander of an Army'. Yet he could not hope to receive 'submission' from Cardigan 'if his lordship is allowed to continue in the opinion he is well known to entertain, that the position of a brigadier is one of independence towards his divisional superior'.

At the same time, Lucan sent Cardigan an official reprimand, ordering him to forward all returns and reports to his divisional general as was customary in the service.

Raglan was the first to respond, despatching Lord de Ros, his Quartermaster-General, to placate Lucan. Eccentric in his habits and dress, with a penchant for sunbathing, de Ros lacked the experience and constitution needed for his high staff appointment which combined the duties of a modern chief of staff and quartermaster. But, like Raglan, he was good with people and soon managed to soothe Lucan's ruffled feathers by telling him that Cardigan had been ordered to keep him fully informed; furthermore, far from trying to sideline him, Raglan wanted him up at Varna.

Cardigan's reaction to being chastised by his hated brother-in-law was predictably defiant. 'I consider that being sent forward in advance of the Army,' he wrote to Lucan on 15 June, 'and not being very far distant at the present moment from the enemy, that my command may be considered as a separate and detached command, and that I am not bound to anybody except the general officer in command of the forces in the country in which the brigade under my command is serving.' He concluded the letter by saying that, independently, he 'was submitting an appeal to . . . Raglan upon the subject for his decision'.

Regarding it as grossly insubordinate, Lucan forwarded the letter to Raglan with suitably caustic comments. But in place of the decisive action he expected Raglan to take against Cardigan, he received more flimsy assurances. On 20 June, the day Raglan left for Varna, General Estcourt, the Adjutant-General, replied privately on behalf of the Commander-in-Chief. 'I am directed to say that the misapprehensions which Lord Cardigan has entertained on the nature of his command have already been rectified by private communication from me, written by Lord Raglan's desire,' wrote Estcourt. 'Lord Cardigan, I am sure, will quite understand now, that you may call for what returns you think necessary to inform yourself of the condition of the cavalry belonging to your division, and that you may and ought to visit detached parties, and look to their efficiency in every respect for which you are responsible to Lord Raglan.'

For Lucan, such a response was far from satisfactory and simply added to his conviction that Raglan had neither the inclination nor the strength of character to chastise Cardigan properly. On 22 June, he wrote back to Estcourt, pointing out that not only had Cardigan written him 'a very insubordinate letter' but he had also 'appealed to the Commander of the Forces *direct*' and not through his commanding officer, 'as is required by the regulations of the Army'.

Estcourt replied that, in Raglan's eyes, the matter was now settled. However, Raglan did accept that there should be 'no departure from the regular and usual channel of communication' and that this point would be emphasised in a letter to Cardigan. But 'it will be a *private* communication,' Estcourt wrote, 'as indeed all the correspondence on this occasion has been.'[19]

If Raglan was too easy on Cardigan at this juncture, thereby storing up trouble for the future, part of the responsibility must lie with Lord Hardinge. It was he who had ignored Raglan's warnings about the respective appointments of the brothers-in-law, leaving Raglan no option but to try to keep the peace when the inevitable disagreement took place.

In any case, Raglan had more pressing concerns. On 19 June, the Russians detonated an 8,000-lb mine under the outer walls of the main bastion at Silistria, and the resultant explosion could be heard in Raglan's headquarters at Varna, more than 60 miles away. Assumed to be the prelude to an attack, the Allies waited anxiously for news. But an hour before the main assault was due to take place, Prince Gorchakov, the Russian commander, was ordered to raise the siege.

This was done in response to increasing pressure from the Austrian Empire. On 2 June, fearing Russian control of the lower Danube, Austria had called on Russia to evacuate the Principalities or risk war. To show she meant business, troops had been massing on her Transylvanian border. Now faced with the Turkish, British and French armies in front, Austria on their right flank, and the Black Sea controlled by the Allied fleets on their left, the Russians had little option but to withdraw. 'How sad and painful for me, dear Gorchakov,' wrote Tsar Nicholas, 'that I had to agree to the insistent arguments . . . as to the danger threatening the army, from the faithlessness of Austria, whom we had saved [by helping to suppress the revolt in Hungary in 1848].'[20]

The good news arrived in the form of a letter from Omar Pasha marked 'urgent' as Raglan was having dinner at his headquarters with Sir George

Brown, the Duke of Cambridge and 15 other guests on the evening of 24 June. Fearing it heralded the fall of Silistria, Raglan was 'agreeably surprized' to learn that the siege had been raised and the Russians were recrossing the Danube.

But the message also posed the possibility that a large portion of the Russian force had, instead of recrossing the Danube, marched down the right bank in the direction of the Dobruja marshes – the area of land between Silistria and the sea. To find out one way or the other, Raglan immediately dictated a brief order and despatched Lord Burghersh, one of his aides-de-camp, to deliver it to Cardigan. He was to 'proceed in person early tomorrow . . . with two squadrons' to Karasou 'to ascertain the movements of the enemy'.

Not long after, a second aide, Lord Poulett Somerset, was sent off with a more detailed order from Raglan drafted by General Brown. At Bagodish Cardigan was to team up with a detachment of Turkish cavalry and continue on to Karasou. Once there, he would 'patrol with small parties to the left towards the Danube' until he either fell in with enemy posts or ascertained the direction of their march. He was to carry three days' forage and provisions, and a party from the commissariat would follow with supplies for another four days.[21]

Choosing a squadron from the 8th Hussars and another from the 13th Light Dragoons, Cardigan had them roused at 4 a.m. the following morning. But a delay ensued while forage was gathered and rations for three days were cooked, and the 200-strong column with Cardigan at its head did not leave the cavalry camp until 10.30 p.m. Each horse was carrying a man in full marching order, 3 lbs of salt beef or pork, 3 lbs of hard biscuit, a 3-pint keg of water, 36 lbs of barley or oats, 20 lbs of hay, two blankets and extra ammunition. The total burden was in excess of 25 stone.

Cardigan was later roundly condemned for what came to be known as the 'sore-back reconnaissance', but his critics included few who were actually present. One officer who was, Captain Soame Jenyns of the 13th Light Dragoons, later described it in a letter to a friend as 'a most interesting patrol, but precious hard work'. He continued:

> We started to Bagadish and on next day north, but had to return from want of water. The whole country is deserted, not a soul to be seen, and the villages burned down and battered – such a desolate scene. We had only salt beef and biscuits and what we had on. No tents, of course, which in this hot weather on plains is no joke.[22]

In fact, there was a tent – Cardigan's – 'about six feet square, just large enough to cover a spring sofa bed'.

Through the heat of the day, weighed down by their absurd loads, the horses trudged onwards. Cardigan, understandably, was anxious to complete his first mission on active service, but the real imperative behind the succession of long marches was the lack of water. 'No fountains were to be found at any intermediate places,' wrote Cardigan.[23]

By 30 June, the column had passed through Karasou and reached the edge of the Dobruja marshes. From there Cardigan sent Lieutenant Maxse, his aide-de-camp, to report to Raglan that he had 'found no part of the Russian Army in the neighbourhood' and that his only information was that it had 'retreated' north by 'Babadagh in the direction of Tula' at the mouth of the Danube delta.'[24]

That same day, Cardigan received new instructions from Raglan to advance towards Bassora on the Danube, not far from Trajan's Wall. 'There is hardly a tree between Bagadish and Bassora, and very little water,' Jenyns noted. 'We went by long marches to Bassora, where we first saw an enemy in the shape of Cossacks on the other bank of the Danube looking at us. We bivouacked close to the bank under the old camp of the Russians, which was a curious sight.'[25]

On 2 July, word from 'an indirect source' reached Raglan that Cardigan had arrived at Bassora and found no Russians on his side of the river. 'You have thus fulfilled your mission and are now I conclude on your return,' wrote Raglan the following day, adding:

> I am very much obliged to you for the pains you have taken to carry out my instructions. By so doing you have ascertained for me that the Russians have withdrawn from the end of the Dobruja and that the country between this and Trajan's Wall is not only clear of the Enemy, but is wholly deserted by the inhabitants. These are important facts . . . and I hope that the fatigue that you and your squadrons have undergone in obtaining the information will not prove injurious to your health and that of the officers and men under your orders.[26]

If Cardigan had terminated the patrol at this juncture, as Raglan expected him to do, he could have returned to Devna none the worse for wear and comfortable in the knowledge of a job well done. That he did not was probably because he was enjoying himself and was keen to explore further. Without informing Raglan, he set off along the Danube in the direction of Silistria where the main body of the Russian army had last been seen. Over the next few days, according to Colonel Hodge at Varna, two parties of cavalry were sent 'to look for him' as 'it was thought he was lost'.[27]

Five miles from the town, wrote Jenyns, they 'saw the whole camp of the Russians on the other side in such a jolly country, all grass and a lovely view'. Observing them in turn, the Russian general, Lüders, decided not to take the responsibility of firing the first shots in the war against the Allies. Instead, he sent over a captured Turkish officer under a flag of truce to discover their identity: French or British. Having put the Russians right, the column continued on towards the town.

'We stayed all day at Silistria,' wrote Jenyns, 'and it was such a rum sight, the town riddled with shot and shell, and up at Arab Tabia [the main bastion] just as it was when they left. The Russian battery being within thirty feet of the Turkish one, the Turks must have fought like demons.'[28]

From Silistria the increasingly weary expedition continued on to Shumla, Omar Pasha's headquarters, and finally arrived back at Devna on 11 July after 17 days in the saddle. They had travelled, according to Cardigan, over 'a perfectly wild desert, for a distance of 300 miles' – 120 of them 'without ever seeing a human being'. Cardigan had 'borne it well', eaten 'almost the same food as the men', and only changed his clothes once – which was once more than the men. But the relentless pace had exacted a high price. Fanny Duberly wrote:

> The reconnaissance, under Lord Cardigan, came in this morning at eight, having marched all night. They have . . . seen the Russian force, lived for five days on water and salt pork; have shot five horses, which dropped from exhaustion on the road, brought back an araba [wagon] full of disabled men, and seventy-five horses, which will be, as Mr. Grey says, unfit for work for many months, and some of them will never work again. I was riding out in the evening when the stragglers came in; and a piteous sight it was – men on foot, driving and goading on their wretched, wretched horses, three or four of which could hardly stir. There seems to have been much unnecessary suffering, a cruel parade of death, more pain inflicted than good derived; but I suppose these sad sights are merely the casualties of war, and we must bear them with what courage and fortitude we may.[29]

Many others at the cavalry camp were shocked by the poor condition of the returning column. 'They had started in robust health,' wrote Private Albert Mitchell of the 13th Light Dragoons, 'but returned mere shadows of their former selves.' Lieutenant Temple Godman of the 5th Dragoon Guards described both horses and men as 'terribly knocked up'.[30]

Not surprisingly, given Cardigan's reputation, the details had become grossly distorted by the time they reached Varna. 'A precious business it appears to have been and will cost 50 horses to say nothing of the 150 with sore backs,' wrote Major William Forrest, formerly of the 11th Hussars, now second-in-command of the 4th Dragoon Guards. Lord George Paget, brother of Lord William and commander of the 4th Light Dragoons, wrote to his wife that Cardigan 'has brought back only 80 horses out of 200'.[31]

Another man at Varna who was particularly unimpressed with Cardigan's handling of the reconnaissance was Captain Louis Nolan, aide-de-camp to the Quartermaster-General. Born in Milan in 1818, the son of the British vice-consul – a distinguished Irish infantry officer – and his beautiful Italian wife, Nolan had a reputation for brilliant horsemanship even before the age of 14. Brought to the attention of the ruling Austrian Grand Duke, his first commission was in the 10th Imperial Hussars and by the age of 21 he was already its senior lieutenant. But he was keen to serve in the British cavalry, and was delighted when his father bought him a cornetcy in Cardigan's former regiment, the 15th Hussars.

In 1839, he accompanied his regiment to India and within five years had been appointed regimental riding-master, proving himself a superb swordsman and steeplechaser. During the Second Sikh War he served as aide-de-camp to the Commander-in-Chief, Madras, and by the end of the decade had perfected a system for breaking in and training remounts which formed the subject of a successful book. In 1851 he returned to Britain and the following year, during a continental tour, he studied the cavalry systems of the major European powers, including Russia. The result was a second, highly acclaimed book: *Cavalry: Its History and Tactics* (1853).

Now 35, an accomplished linguist, musician and amateur jockey, exceedingly handsome with dark curly hair, Nolan was probably the most brilliant young cavalry officer in the British Army. He was also insufferably arrogant and, in the words of William Russell of *The Times*, 'impetuous, vehement, restless'. Such a man had little respect for aristocratic cavalry commanders who, in his eyes, owed their appointments to influence rather than ability. Meeting him at Varna, Russell was 'astonished at the angry way in which he spoke of Lord Lucan and Lord Cardigan, especially of the former, though, after "the sore back reconnaissance" to the Danube he was full of invective against the latter'.[32]

George Ryan, on the other hand – author of a post-war pamphlet fiercely critical of Cardigan's wartime conduct – was positively restrained when writing of the Dobruja patrol: Cardigan had 'discharged a very difficult duty in making a *reconnaissance* which lasted some days, to the perfect satisfaction of the Commander of the forces'. 'This duty lost us many horses,' he added.[33]

Back home, the public was hungry for news of derring-do and even Cardigan's former enemies in the press were willing to eat humble pie. 'Their intrepidity and sense of duty carried them close to the Russian lines, even within view of the enemy, and it was a miracle they got free,' wrote an admiring *United Service Gazette*. 'We have henceforth every confidence in Lord Cardigan.' Horse Guards clearly agreed, because on 20 June they had promoted him to major-general.[34]

Captain Jenyns, who shared the privations of the patrol and who, therefore, had most reason to criticise his chief, described him in a letter home as 'a capital fellow to be under at this work'.[35]

Perhaps the last word should go to Lord Burghersh, Raglan's aide, who accompanied the patrol for 15 of its 17 days. 'I do not consider that either the men or horses were unnecessarily harassed,' he later wrote to Cardigan. 'The marches were some days very long, but this was not your fault, as we could only halt where there was water, which was anything but plentiful in that country.'[36]

Even Raglan chose not to censure Cardigan for his unauthorised absence of more than a week. Instead, he simply inquired after his health and was relieved when Cardigan replied on 21 July that he was 'none the worst' after his 'slight service'. His aide-de-camp, Maxse, had 'been very ill', but Cardigan was convinced 'he will get right for he has my cot "plush"'. He concluded on an upbeat note: 'As there are rumours of war . . . about the Crimea, I hope if only a part of the Cavalry go there the proper position of the Light Brigade "*to the Front*" will be favourably considered by your Lordship.'[37]

For once the rumours were accurate. Ever since Sinope, the more bellicose of Aberdeen's ministers had seen Sebastopol, the Crimean base of the Russian Black Sea fleet, as the prime military objective. As early as March,

Sir James Graham, the First Lord of the Admiralty, had told Lord Clarendon that he had his heart set on the 'capture and destruction of Sebastopol'. He added: '[The] Eye tooth of the Bear must be drawn.'[38]

News of the Russian withdrawal from Bulgaria meant that Constantinople was safe and troops were available for such an operation. On 27 June, Sir Charles Wood, President of the Board of Control, wrote to Sir George Grey, Secretary of State for the Colonies since the division of Newcastle's ministry two weeks earlier: 'Now comes the Sebastopol question and that turns on whether the French can go forward.'[39]

Alexander Kinglake, the distinguished author of *The Invasion of the Crimea*, claimed that the final decision to attack Sebastopol was taken at the famous post-prandial Cabinet meeting of 28 June at Pembroke Lodge, Lord John Russell's Richmond home, where the balmy summer air and the lateness of the hour caused a number of ministers to doze off. In fact, the doves – particularly Gladstone and Aberdeen himself – had already been won over, and the meeting was simply to approve the wording of Newcastle's despatch. In its final form it stated that a 'safe and honourable' peace could only be arrived at after the capture of Sebastopol. The timing was in Raglan's hands, but he should be aware 'that delay would be dangerous' because the retreating Russian troops could be 'poured into the Crimea'.[40]

Too important to be sent by telegraph, the despatch did not reach Raglan until 16 July. Lacking intelligence about the terrain and troops in the Crimea, Raglan's first instinct was caution. The following day he expressed his doubts to Sir George Brown, his senior divisional commander, who sympathised but warned him that any hesitation might lead to his recall. This decided Raglan, and on 18 July he called a Council of War with the French. Again, a number of misgivings were expressed by both sides, but it was finally agreed to bow to the political will and prepare for an invasion. Generals Brown and Canrobert were ordered to make a reconnaissance of the Crimean coast north of Sebastopol, to decide on the most suitable landing site. They left by the steamship HMS *Fury* on the 21st.

By now, Cardigan's command at Devna had expanded to include a regiment of Turkish cavalry, the 11th Hussars, 13th Light Dragoons, 17th Lancers, 8th Hussars and a troop of Royal Horse Artillery. Also occupying part of the valley floor was Brown's Light Division and two regiments of the Heavy Brigade under Brigadier-General Scarlett. Lucan was still at Varna with Scarlett's remaining regiments, much to the delight of those at Devna and the disgust of those left behind. Lieutenant Temple Godman, one of the former, wrote on 17 July:

> Our Brigadier is come, which we are glad of. One half of our brigade is here; they leave the rest at Varna, so as to keep Lord Lucan there, for he and Lord Cardigan would be sure to fight if together, so we suffer for their folly. Lord Lucan inspected us the other day and taking the command of the regiment clubbed it completely; he is a regular muff. General [Sir Joseph] Thackwell [formerly of the 15th Hussars] would, I expect, have been better. There seem to be a good many muffs among the chiefs.[41]

Major Forrest, one of those still at Varna, wrote on the same day: 'Lord Lucan is here and a rum one he seems to be, I hear his staff all wish themselves off it, he is so uncertain and difficult to get on with. Report says something disagreeable happened between him and Scarlett, the latter has gone to Devna and told me he found he was nobody here, Lord Lucan had all reports made direct to himself.'[42]

Hodge, Forrest's colonel, noted: 'He is of violent temper and an unreasonable man to deal with.' Five days later, after a brigade field day, he added: 'Lord Lucan commanded, and gave such words of command as were never invented. We could not understand him.'[43]

Meanwhile, back at Devna, Cardigan's preoccupation with drill was making him equally unpopular. 'The Major-General amused us by giving us regulation Phoenix Park Field Days,' wrote Captain Cresswell of the 11th Hussars, 'such a bore he is, comes round stables just as if he was Colonel instead of Major-General.' To Captain Shakespear of the Royal Horse Artillery, he was 'the most impracticable and most inefficient cavalry officer in the service . . . We are greatly disgusted with him.'[44]

The troops, however, soon had a genuine reason to grumble. 'The cholera is amongst us!' wrote a horrified Fanny Duberly on 23 July. 'It is not in *our* camp, but it is in that of the Light Division, and sixteen men have died of it this day in the Rifles.'[45]

Such epidemics were common during prolonged periods of hot weather – thousands had died in Paris during the summer of 1848 – and the disease found a welcome breeding ground in the tightly packed and poorly sanitised camps of the Allied armies. The French were the first and worst affected, particularly after three of their divisions moved into the notoriously unhealthy marsh region of the Dobruja, although the disease soon spread to the British. By the time the Allies embarked for the Crimea in early September, they had lost more than 10,000 men – a sixth of their total strength – to cholera, fever and dysentery.

At first, the Light Brigade was unaffected, and to keep it that way Raglan ordered Cardigan to move his camp about 30 miles further west to Jenibazar, a small village just 11 miles from Shumla. He was to take with him the troop of horse artillery, but not Scarlett and his two regiments which were to move just five miles west to Kotlubei. After a two-day march, the first light cavalry units reached Jenibazar on 28 July and set up camp about a mile from the village. The only shade was provided by a clump of large trees near a natural fountain, and it was here that Cardigan sited his two marquees – one for dining and working, one for sleeping. All remaining shade was occupied by his staff and servants.

As if this did not cause resentment enough, Cardigan placed a sentry on the fountain, day and night, to prevent the troops from filling their water bottles or watering their horses. 'Instead of being able to get water at about a hundred yards,' wrote Private Mitchell, 'we had to go upwards of a mile, and climb a steep hill on our return loaded.' This was particularly annoying because at night the stone troughs in front of the fountain 'overflowed and a large quantity of water ran away to waste'.[46]

Mitchell's regiment, the 13th Light Dragoons, soon had another reason to feel aggrieved. Having set up its tents on the right of the camp, the position reserved for the senior regiment, Cardigan ordered it to change places with the 8th Hussars. Even then he was not satisfied. 'Our tents when changed were not quite in line, though I confess it was barely perceptible; but at evening we had to strike and move all our tents about a foot and a half further back,' wrote Fanny Duberly.[47]

The following day, an artilleryman died of cholera and a major outbreak at Jenibazar seemed inevitable. 'Several men died, as well as a soldier's wife,' wrote Mitchell. 'At first we had regular funeral parties, with trumpets sounding in front of the procession, but as it soon became an every-day occurrence, and the number of men in hospital increased daily, the "Dead March" was ordered to be discontinued; for to say the least of it, it was a most doleful noise, and must have had a depressing effect on the sick.'[48]

In fact, there were remarkably few deaths due to cholera in the Light Brigade. According to Troop Sergeant-Major Loy Smith, the 11th Hussars only lost three men during the whole of August. As late as 12 August, Cardigan wrote to Raglan that 'there is no appearance of cholera amongst us' although the sick list was 'very large' and there had been 'several deaths from fever and diorrhoea [sic]'. A week later, Cardigan reported 'another case of cholera', but added that the 'camp is in a healthy place with plenty of water'.[49]

Cholera was, however, ravaging the rest of the Army, including the two regiments of heavy cavalry near Kotlubei. The 5th Dragoon Guards was so badly hit – with three officers and 35 men dead, and its colonel ill – that it was sent back to Varna for temporary attachment to its sister regiment, the 4th.

To try to stem the flow of casualties, Raglan took the advice of his medical men – that alcohol helped to stave off illness – and ordered his troops to be issued with half a gill of rum per day. The net result was much drunkenness. An offence which Cardigan could not forgive, he dealt with it in his usual summary fashion. 'There were few days passed without a parade being ordered before breakfast for someone to be flogged,' wrote Mitchell. 'In some cases three or four in the morning.'[50]

But Cardigan could also be touchingly solicitous of the welfare of his men who, due to the extreme heat – often more than 90 degrees in the shade – had become listless, with little appetite. When a bizarre General Order in early August increased the daily ration of meat – mainly beef – from 1 lb to 1½ lbs, Cardigan's response was to inform Raglan that 'the men cannot & will not eat so much meat' as 'they found 1 lb too much even'. Instead, they were 'generally anxious to get more rice' and 'would be satisfied with a couple of ounces of it per diem'.

It seems that the commissariat was unable to satisfy this request, although Cardigan's subsequent demand for the occasional issue of mutton, for variety, was complied with. According to Mitchell, however, seasoning was the missing ingredient: 'If we could have had a little pepper and salt, we should have got on nicely.'

In the interests of 'comfort', Cardigan also asked for – and received – permission for officers and men to 'be allowed to wear their beards & whiskers as they like out in this climate' in line with the General Order, as he did not think 'it would tend to want of cleanliness'. This request was, of course, in direct contradiction to Lord Lucan's divisional order at Scutari, which had ignored the directive from Horse Guards by forbidding the men to wear beards.[51]

Cardigan did not always seem so concerned about the welfare of his horses, however. Determined that his brigade would be prepared for any eventuality, he insisted upon regular early-morning field days during most of August. Skirmishing drill, outpost drill, charging in line and by squadrons, and rallying after a dispersal were all practised incessantly. 'The poor horses felt the effects of it, for instead of them looking better, they looked worse, if possible,' wrote Mitchell.

'Cardigan kills horses with pace,' lamented Captain Shakespear of the Royal Horse Artillery. 'We wish we were with Scarlett and his Heavy Cavalry.'

Loy Smith, on the other hand, omits any mention of overwork in his diary, stating instead that the horses of the 11th Hussars 'were in first-rate condition'.[52]

Perhaps mindful of Cardigan's reputation as a hard taskmaster, Raglan gave him some kindly phrased advice in a letter of 20 August: 'I hope the men are not exposed more than is absolutely necessary to the influence of the sun. If they take good care of their horses & give them plenty of food, I do not wish you to require more of them. This is a very debilatory climate & trying to the English constitution.'

Eight days later, Cardigan sent the following inexplicable reply: 'The Brigade has had *very little* drill under me.'[53]

Why he felt the need to lie is unclear, particularly as such drill was necessary given the paucity of brigade training in peacetime. As things turned out, this monotonous work in Bulgaria probably prevented the disaster of the charge at Balaclava from becoming a total catastrophe.

Despite the rumours, Cardigan spent much of August in the dark as to the eventual destination of the Light Brigade, telling Fanny Duberly on 30 July that they would probably spend the winter quartered in Adrianople. Two days earlier, Generals Brown and Canrobert had returned from their reconnaissance, having chosen the mouth of the River Katcha, seven miles north of Sebastopol, as the site for the invasion.

But the expedition was then further delayed while Raglan obtained more intelligence, supplies were arranged and flat-bottomed caiques were collected from the Bosphorus to enable the artillery to be landed. Consequently, it was not until Lieutenant Maxse returned from sick-leave in Varna on 23 August that the Light Brigade's imminent embarkation for the Crimea was finally confirmed. 'We are reanimated!' wrote Fanny Duberly. 'The sickness decreases; cooler weather is coming on; things look more cheerily now. . . .'

Next day, Cardigan was inspecting evening stables with Colonel Doherty of the 13th Light Dragoons when he noticed a staff officer cantering across the plain from Varna. 'Hullo!' he exclaimed. 'A cocked hat, by Jove!'

Spotting Cardigan's unmistakable figure in the peacock uniform of the 11th Hussars, the staff officer rode up and handed him a despatch from Raglan. Having read it, Cardigan looked up and said: 'Hurrah! Doherty, we are for the Crimea! We march tomorrow morning for Varna, for immediate embarkation.'

The camp was suddenly full of frantic activity as trumpets sounded 'Orders' and orderly sergeants appeared so as to take down instructions. 'Everyone was in the highest spirits, for we had been at this place long enough,' wrote Mitchell. Not so in the 8th Hussars' lines where, according to Fanny Duberly, a reaction had set in and the 'order was heard silently; not a single cheer: we have waited in inaction too long'.[54]

Two days later, during a halt in the march back to Varna, a number of cavalrymen were revisiting the village of Devna when they came across a man they knew as Johnny – a Bulgarian canteen worker who had earlier been run out of the cavalry camp for selling bad spirits – sitting on top of an araba cart packed with provisions. After a violent argument over the sale of one of his goods, an angry mob of more than 30 soldiers formed and surrounded his cart.

'Just at this time,' wrote Private Mitchell, 'who should come galloping up but Lord Cardigan with the brigade-major, and two or three other officers. He asked what all the row was about, and before Johnny could get a word in, one of the 8th Hussars stepped forward, and, saluting his lordship, said: "I beg pardon, my lord, this is the man who was turned out of camp for selling bad spirits, and now he has been cheating one of our men, and because he told him of it, he tried to run him through with a sword."'

Uttering an oath, Cardigan said: 'Give it him; give the fellow a good thrashing.'

He then rode off, at which point the terrified Bulgarian fled into the nearest house and the troopers satisfied themselves by looting his araba; Mitchell making off with 'a dried tongue, a jar of anchovies, and a loaf of tolerably white bread'.[55]

Fanny Duberly and the last of the Light Brigade reached Varna on 29 August to discover that most of the infantry had already been embarked. By now rather taken with this bold and attractive young woman, Cardigan went to ask Lord Raglan's permission for her to accompany her husband to the Crimea. Fanny recalled: 'Lord Cardigan was at the trouble of bringing me Lord Raglan's answer himself. It was a decided negative. "But,"

258

added Lord Cardigan (touched perhaps by my sudden burst of tears, for I was so worn and weak!), "should you think proper to disregard the prohibition, I will not offer any opposition to your doing so."[56]

Cardigan was, of course, well aware that Lucan was violently opposed to officers' wives accompanying them on active service, and he was not about to miss an opportunity to irritate his superior. Also, his sense of independence had been enhanced by recent orders from Raglan that he and Scarlett were in charge of organising the embarkation of their brigades which would proceed to the Crimea while Lucan remained, for the time being, at Varna. Major William Forrest, for one, would have approved of the arrangement because, while he had no great respect for Cardigan, he had even less for Lucan:

> We have not much confidence in our Cavalry General [he wrote to his brother on 27 August], and only hope he will allow the several Brigadiers to move their own Brigades. I much fear he will not do so and I think he will stick to the heavies for he and Cardigan would be sure to row directly – Lord Lucan and Scarlett are not upon the best of terms and the general feeling is that he has behaved ill to Scarlett. Lord Lucan is no doubt a clever sharp fellow but he has been so long on the shelf that he has no idea of moving cavalry . . . I write this in order that if any mishap should occur to the Cavalry you may be able to form a correct idea how it happened. Do not say anything about Lord Lucan unless we come to grief.[57]

Lord George Paget of the 4th Light Dragoons felt differently. 'I get on very well with our chief (Lord Lucan); I only hope to remain under his immediate command,' he wrote on 14 August, adding: 'What jolly slaves we soldiers are – praying for one master instead of another!' Perhaps understandably, he did not look forward to serving under Cardigan, a man who was alleged to have cuckolded his (albeit disreputable) half-brother, Lord William.[58]

But Lucan was determined not to be left out in the cold for a second time. All his pent-up frustration was released in a strongly worded letter to Raglan on 29 August:

> . . . I find myself left, as on former occasions, without instructions regarding myself, the commander of the division, except, as I read

them, not to accompany the Light Cavalry Brigade and not to interfere with their embarkation . . . I cannot conceal from myself, what has not been concealed from the Army – that during the four months I have been under your Lordship's command, I have been separated, as much as it was possible to do, from my division . . . and I have been left to discharge duties more properly befitting an inferior officer; whilst to Lord Cardigan has been intrusted, from the day of his arrival, the command of nearly the whole of the cavalry . . .

It is a subject of remark that I do not command the division; it is said it is not left to me, to prevent any collision between Lord Cardigan and myself. Now, as I happen never to have come into collision, or had a disagreement with a single officer during the very many years I served in the Army . . . no apprehension of the sort should be entertained of me, but of Lord Cardigan, whom it might be supposed was not to be controlled by any superior authority. It is surely unfair, on that account, to make his lordship independent of his immediate commanding officer . . .[59]

As Lord de Ros was convalescing in Constantinople, suffering from a variety of nervous and physical complaints that would soon necessitate his replacement as Quartermaster-General by Brigadier-General Richard Airey, Raglan went in person to placate Lucan. Accepting the cavalry commander's argument that Wellington had allowed his generals to accompany any part of their divisions they saw fit, he gave him permission to sail with part of the Light Brigade in the steamship *Simla*. He also said that he would, in no uncertain terms, order Cardigan to report directly to his immediate superior, who was to be gazetted a lieutenant-general to underline his authority. All in all, it was a triumph for Lucan and a slap in the face for his brother-in-law.

'From this date my position in the cavalry was totally changed,' wrote Cardigan in hindsight and with, one suspects, a certain amount of exaggeration. 'All pleasure ceased in the command which remained to me, and I had nothing to guide me but a sense of duty to the service.'[60]

13

Crimea

By the evening of 6 September 1854, more than 64,000 French, British and Turkish troops had been crammed into a vast array of vessels. Lord Cardigan and his staff were on the steamship *Himalaya* with the 17th Lancers and 8th Hussars. Also aboard was Fanny Duberly who, with Cardigan's encouragement, had disguised herself in plain dress and arrived at the quayside in the back of a baggage-cart.

'Lord Lucan, who was there, scanned every woman, to find traces of a lady,' she recalled, 'but he searched in vain, and I, choking with laughter, hurried past his horse into the boat. Here the crew received me very hospitably, gave me some water, and a compliment on the clearness of my cheeks, which "did not look as though I had done much hard work in the sun" . . .'[1]

In order to make room for the huge number of troops, many essentials had to be left behind, including tents, medical equipment, ambulances, baggage animals and cavalry officers' spare horses. Conditions were so overcrowded on the steamship *Jason* that the 'numbers of our sick kept on increasing,' wrote Private Albert Mitchell, 'and in a few days we had to consign three poor fellows to watery graves'. Cholera was still claiming lives and the bay was already filled with the ghastly sight of bloated corpses bobbing in the water, their makeshift weights having proved inadequate.

On 7 September, as the vast invasion armada got under way, Mitchell marvelled at its size: '. . . six hundred sail of all kinds: English, French and Turkish, including men-of-war of all sizes, from the huge three-decker to the tiny gun-boat; steam transports of the heaviest tonnage, sailing ships of all sizes laden with troops, horses, munitions of war, and stores of all kinds that could be got together.'[2]

The following day, after keeping a rendezvous with French warships at the mouth of the Danube, the combined fleets paused. It was now decided that the initial choice of landing site was too close to Sebastopol and, to settle the issue, Raglan decided to see for himself aboard his steam-driven flagship, *Caradoc*. He was accompanied by a party of Allied generals and admirals, and escorted by three warships. Arriving off the Crimean coast on the morning of the 10th, they eventually decided on Calamita Bay, a low-lying section of coast which, at 45 miles north of Sebastopol, would enable the armies to be landed before any counter-attack could take place.

Meanwhile, as the fleet waited impatiently at anchor, the brothers-in-law continued their bickering. First Lucan chastised Cardigan for authorising a court-martial without his sanction, then he sent him a memorandum reminding him to submit embarkation returns to his superior immediately after landing. Cardigan's angry response was to ask for his 'exact position' in the expedition to be clarified. After all, he said, Raglan had assured him that the Earl of Lucan 'did not in any way intend to interfere or deprive me of the command of the Light Cavalry'. With no immediate reply, Cardigan sent a second letter saying that it was 'impossible for him to carry out his duties with any satisfaction until his position in the expedition was defined. This time Lucan replied via one of his staff:

> To circulate a memorandum that disembarkation returns would be required immediately on landing, a memorandum which has been circulated to all senior officers, is not an irregularity, still less respectful or any encroachment on your authority and Lord Lucan much regrets that you should entertain what his Lordship considers a great misconception. In reference to the rest of your letter, the Lieutenant-General instructs me to add, that whilst he knows his own authority he equally respects yours; and that your position as a Major-General commanding a brigade . . ., will not, so far as depends on him, differ from that held by the other brigadiers, of whom there are so many in the six divisions of this Army.[3]

Before Cardigan could think of a suitable response, Raglan returned from his reconnaissance on 11 September and the whole fleet got under way.

The following morning it gained its first glimpse of the Crimean coast. 'Twelve days accomplishing 300 miles!' wrote an exasperated Fanny Duberly. 'The delay puzzles me as much as it grieves and disgusts. Lord Cardigan, too, is growing very impatient of it . . .'[4]

On the 13th, the fleet sailed north past the entrance to Sebastopol harbour and that evening anchored off Calamita Bay, a 'low, flat strip of sand' that reminded Private Mitchell of Romney Marsh. The following morning was fine and the landings began in an almost carnival mood, with bands playing and flags flying. 'For nearly a mile, flat-bottomed boats filled with armed men – our Light Division being first – were being towed by the sailors rowing in other boats,' wrote Sergeant-Major Loy Smith. 'We saw them leap cheerily on to the beach. Grave thoughts now passed through my mind: how many of these fine fellows will never again leave that shore!'[5]

By afternoon, however, the weather had deteriorated and the disembarkation of the cavalry was postponed. This was just as well, because those who had gone ashore were without tents and had to endure a night of torrential rain without cover.

There was still a heavy surf on the 15th, but the landings continued regardless. Each cavalryman took ashore three days' rations and corn, a spare shirt, pair of socks and towel rolled in his blanket and strapped on the back of the saddle. He left behind his valise, pelisse, spare overalls and shoes, and did not see them again for almost three months.

'The beach is a vast and crowded camp,' wrote Fanny Duberly, 'covered with men, horses, fires, tents, general officers, staff officers, boats landing men and horses, which latter are flung overboard, and swum ashore. Eleven were drowned to-day. I am glad to say we lost none. Lord Cardigan begins to be eager for the fray, and will be doing something or other directly he has landed, I fancy.'[6]

She was not far wrong, for Cardigan landed with his staff towards evening and spent the first night on the beach with his men, their horses picketed nearby. After a makeshift breakfast the following morning, he paraded the advance guard in a hollow square and told them that he had been ordered to take out a patrol of three squadrons, a battalion of the Rifle Brigade and two guns of the Royal Horse Artillery to try to intercept two regiments of Russian dragoons which were believed to be advancing towards the landing area.

I am determined to cut them off if possible [he said]. I have every reason to believe – in fact, I am certain – that whatever service you are ordered on, you will do it with credit and honour to your name as British Dragoons. I wish to give you a little advice and caution. It is this: In case we fall in with them and charge them, ride close, and let the centre be a little in advance of the flanks, and when you get within a hundred yards of them ride with the utmost impetuosity. But mind whatever you do after you have passed through their ranks, don't go too far, but turn about as quick as possible, and rally together and charge back again, that is if they have not bolted by that time.[7]

In fine weather, the patrol moved inland, crossing salt lakes and passing through villages thronged with inhabitants anxious to greet the invaders. Some offered water-melons and black bread, others knelt making the sign of the cross to show they were Christians – clearly a ruse, given that the majority were Tartar Muslims. But no Russian cavalry was sighted and the greatest hazard proved to be the heat and the lack of fresh water, with the result that many of the infantrymen had to be carried back in arabas.

For the next two days, as supplies were landed and baggage-carts requisitioned from the surrounding countryside, the light cavalry undertook a number of smaller patrols, one of which led to a minor skirmish with Cossacks and Russian cavalry but no casualties. This was more than could be said for an undignified incident that took place in the cavalry camp on the night of 18 September when a jumpy sentry fired at a noise in the dark, sparking off a volley of undisciplined firing from the other vedettes. Before long, the whole camp was in uproar. Sergeant-Major Loy Smith recalled:

> About midnight, we were awakened by musketry fire, the bullets whizzing over us. Thinking the Cossacks were attacking us, the brigade was soon mounted and in line, ready. Lord Lucan and Lord Cardigan were in front. On enquiry, it turned out to be a false alarm .˙. . One unfortunate circumstance occurred through this alarm. Lieutenant Annersley, seeing Lieutenant Dunn's servant who was running to bridle up his master's horse, and taking him for a Russian from the fact of his wearing a long grey coat – he being a private servant, the only one with the regiment – fired and shot him through the thigh.[8]

According to private Mitchell, there would have been more casualties but for the bravery of the Brigade-Major, Colonel Mayow, who rode round the vedettes ordering them to cease fire.

At 9 a.m. the following morning – 19 September – the Allied armies at last began their advance on Sebastopol. The French, 28,000 strong, were on the extreme right nearest to the coast, with 7,000 Turks immediately behind them; further inland, astride a narrow post road, was the British army of 25,000, marching in two double columns with pipes and drums playing and colours flying. As the heavy cavalry had yet to arrive and the French had no horsemen, the Light brigade was given the task of protecting the line of march. Cardigan, needless to say, was in the van with Raglan, the 11th Hussars, 13th Light Dragoons and a troop of horse artillery; Lucan was covering the exposed left flank with the 8th Hussars and 17th Lancers; Lord George Paget and the 4th Light Dragoons brought up the rear.

The gay atmosphere did not last long. With the men weakened by illness, Raglan had given them permission to march without knapsacks, carrying just their rifles and their possessions in blankets. But given the extreme heat and the lack of water, even this light load proved too heavy and many collapsed by the roadside as the bands fell silent and their comrades trudged wearily on. 'I never saw such a scene in the last five miles of it,' wrote Paget. 'An occasional shako and mess-tin lying on the ground first bore evidence that the troops in our front had begun to get fatigued . . . A little further a man, and anon another, were found lying down . . . This went on gradually increasing until ere a mile or two was passed the stragglers were lying thick on the ground, and it is no exaggeration to say that the last two miles resembled a battle-field! Men and accoutrements of all sorts lying in such numbers . . .'[9]

Reaching the River Bulganek in the early afternoon, Raglan could see Cossack outriders on rising ground the other side. There was no mistaking these much-feared irregular troops, with their bulky coats, sheepskin caps and laced leggings, carrying huge 15-foot lances and riding shaggy ponies. Cardigan was ordered forward to investigate. Pausing just long enough to allow his men to fill their water-barrels and water their horses in the knee-deep river, he led the cavalry up the hill in two columns with skirmishers out in front and the Cossacks retiring before them.

'On gaining the crest,' wrote Sergeant-Major Loy Smith, 'we came in sight of the main body of Cossacks, spread out in skirmishing order in a beautiful valley about a mile across and two miles in length.' At this moment, to Cardigan's fury, Lucan arrived and took command.

As the Light Brigade advanced along the valley, the Cossacks retired before them until they had reached the top of some steeper rising ground. Here they made a stand, and opened fire when the skirmishers of the 13th Light Dragoons had come within a hundred yards. 'They hit none of us;' wrote Private Mitchell, 'a few of theirs got hit, which proved that bad as our carbines were, theirs were still worse.'

This skirmishing had continued for about half an hour when suddenly the crest behind the Cossacks 'lit up with the glitter of swords and lances'. Identifying them as regular cavalry, Cardigan leapt at the chance to engage them with the order, 'Draw Swords – skirmishers In – Trot.'[10]

Meanwhile, Raglan had reached the crest of the first rise and could see what Cardigan and Lucan could not: that behind the mass of Russian cavalry was a large force of infantry (3,200 men of the Tarutinsky regiment). Realising the danger to the four advancing squadrons of cavalry, he brought up two divisions of infantry and two more regiments of cavalry, and sent Airey, his Quartermaster-General, to order Lucan to withdraw. His arrival put a stop to an argument between Lucan and Cardigan over troop dispositions. 'We then retreated by alternate squadrons in one line,' recalled Cardigan, 'which was performed with great steadiness.'

As they did so, wrote William Russell of *The Times*, an eyewitness, the Cossacks advanced 'jeering and cheering', and then 'a heavy block of cavalry came over the hillside' with a battery of Russian cannon which quickly halted, unlimbered and opened fire. Its targets were the alternate squadrons of 11th Hussars and 13th Light Dragoons, waiting motionless as their comrades retired. 'Several shells burst close to us, and some fell in the ranks,' recalled Private Mitchell, 'one struck a troop horse a few files on my left . . . in the side, and bursting inside the horse, cleaned him out as though a butcher had done it. His rider and the next man were both wounded and taken to the rear . . .'

According to Cornet Palmer of the 11th, Private Williamson 'rode out of the ranks, his leg shot off and hanging by his overall. Coming up to me he said, quite calmly, "I am hit, may I fall out?"'[11]

Meanwhile, two troops of Royal Horse Artillery had arrived and opened fire – as had some field artillery – with such accuracy that the Russians were forced to retire too. After dark the cavalry rejoined the main body of the army, bivouacked on the banks of the Bulganek. In addition to five men wounded (one mortally) and five horses killed, it had also suffered the humiliation of being forced to retreat in the face of the enemy. 'Serve them bloody right, silly peacock bastards,' commented a private of the 41st Foot.

Unaware of the reason for their withdrawal, many light cavalrymen blamed Lucan. Cardigan knew the truth, but felt foiled nonetheless. 'I don't know how it is, but whatever I propose is always frustrated,' he is said to have muttered on receipt of the order to retire.

Shortly after the engagement, as his men were resting on the grass, Cardigan took out his frustrations on some officers of the 11th who, against regulations, had removed their busbies and were wearing forage caps. He is said to have called them 'a damned set of old women', at which point Colonel John Douglas – Cardigan's second at the Tuckett duel and now commander of the 11th – defended his officers 'and there were quite high words on the subject for a while'. Later, in his tent, Cardigan apologised to Douglas for his 'use of some nasty expressions'.[12] That evening Raglan conferred with St Arnaud. Naval reports had confirmed that the main body of the Russian army was entrenched on the heights above the Alma river, just five miles away. It was agreed, therefore, that supported by naval gunfire the French would carry the poorly defended 350-foot cliff by the sea, while the British would attack the right of the Russian position.

Next morning the Allied armies continued their advance over a three-mile front in the same order of battle as before, with the marching in columns of divisions, artillery in between, and the Light Brigade protecting the left flank and rear. Once again, Cardigan was at the front with the 11th Hussars and 13th Light Dragoons.

Before midday, they crested a rise and were met, in Sergeant-Major Loy Smith's words, 'with one of the most magnificent sights that ever man beheld . . . We were now in full view of the Russian Army that crowned the opposite heights of Alma, their lance points, swords and bayonets glistening in the sun – it was a lovely day. Between us ran the River Alma . . . two or three small villages . . . and a gently sloping plain about a mile across'.[13]

Minutes earlier, Raglan and St Arnaud had met on a rise between the British and French armies and made their final plans. In addition to the advance up the cliffs, the French would also assault Telegraph Hill, the heavily defended feature in the centre of the Russian line. The British, meanwhile, would make a frontal attack on the even more formidable Kourgane Hill, 450-foot high and protected by two powerful redoubts. As the British had the toughest nut to crack, St Arnaud agreed to attack first.

The armies moved forward until the British were within a mile of the river. There, in gently sloping land dotted with vineyards, they deployed from column into lines and lay down to wait. Unfortunately, they were within range of the Russian cannon on Kourgane Hill. By 3 p.m., the French were making good progress up the cliffs, but Telegraph Hill still held out and they were desperate for assistance. But with his troops suffering unacceptable casualties from shellfire and round shot, Raglan could delay no longer and launched the 10,000 men of his leading divisions. Within an hour, Kourgane Hill had been taken and the Russians were in full retreat thanks to the heroic efforts of the Guards and Highlanders of Cambridge's 1st Division, although Brown's Light Division had done well and suffered appalling casualties.

It was now that Lord Lucan, on his own authority, ordered Cardigan and four of his regiments to advance. 'We ascended the hill at a gallop in column of troops,' wrote Private Mitchell. 'Many poor fellows we passed who begged for assistance, but we could not stay to render any, and after getting some distance farther up we saw to what a fearful extent the enemy had suffered. His dead were lying by scores, and we could also see that our own poor fellows had suffered terribly. There were Guardsmen, Highlanders and Light Division men in great numbers killed and wounded. We pushed on in haste, expecting to be called into play on the top of the heights.'

At this moment, Raglan and his staff rode across the front and up went a tremendous cheer as the Highlanders threw their bonnets into the air. Mitchell and his comrades joined in, but were soon silenced by their troop commander: 'What are you shouting for? We have done nothing to shout for yet!'[14]

There seemed to be the perfect opportunity to put this right with the enemy in headlong retreat just over the brow of the next hill. However, Adjutant-General Estcourt now arrived with orders that the Light Brigade was not to pursue because Raglan was certain that the Russians would make a stand. Instead, Lucan was to take two regiments and escort some field guns ahead of the army to the left, while Cardigan did the same on the right. 'Mind now,' Estcourt concluded, 'the cavalry are not to attack.'[15]

But on this occasion Lucan was not so easily deflected and, leaving a few troops to protect the guns, he led the 8th Hussars and the 17th Lancers forward to the left while Cardigan took the 11th Hussars and 13th Light Dragoons to the right.

> The road we took, being the only one available, was down the hill to our right front [wrote Loy Smith of the 11th]. This brought us directly in front of our own infantry. They cheered us on as we passed up the opposite hill. Where the infantry columns were when they were overtaken by the fire of our artillery, the ground was literally covered with dead and wounded. On arriving at the brow of the opposite hill, before us was a vast plain. In the distance could be seen the Russian Army in full retreat, with many stragglers. We now sent out pursuers to make prisoners of all that could be overtaken. A number were brought back – most of them wounded.

Lieutenant Wombwell of the 17th Lancers recalled 'the enemy running as hard as they could go, throwing away their knapsacks, arms and even their coats to assist them in their flight'. Even so, a 'good many' were captured after 'they dropped on their knees and begged for mercy'.[16]

Seeing that Lucan had disobeyed his first order, Raglan sent a second, and when that produced no result he sent a categoric third – the cavalry was to break off its pursuit. At last a fuming Lucan obeyed. 'I was near Lord Lucan when the recall order was delivered to him and witnessed his vexation at having to give up the pursuit,' recalled James Blunt, his civilian interpreter.

Immediately on his return, Lucan sent a thinly veiled message of protest to the Commander-in-Chief: 'Lord Lucan trusts that Lord Raglan has that confidence in him, as commanding the cavalry, that he would allow him to act on his own responsibility, as occasion should offer and render advisable, for otherwise opportunities of acting will frequently be lost to the cavalry.' There was no reply.[17]

So why did Raglan rein in the cavalry with his foe in disarray? He provided the answer himself two days later in response to Lord George Paget's inquiry as to 'whether the cavalry might not have been of more use': 'his object all day had been to – what he called "shut them up" (those were his words, the enemy's cavalry being so superior in numbers.'

He certainly had a point. Throughout the battle the Light Brigade – fewer than 1,000 in number – had been faced by a body of Russian cavalry roughly three times its size. As the light cavalry was taking prisoners, Lieutenant Wombwell of the 17th could see in the distance 'an immense force of cavalry . . . advancing'. Loy Smith, too, recalls prisoners escaping because Russian cavalry were moving forward.[18]

Furthermore, Raglan had twice asked the French on Telegraph Hill to take the Russians retreating from Kourgane in the flank, but there had been no response. St Arnaud later excused himself by saying that his soldiers had to retrieve their knapsacks from the other side of the river; the sick and wounded needed medical attention; and his gunners were short of ammunition. Therefore, any pursuit would have to have been by the British alone, in failing light, with a superior force of Russian cavalry in the way. Under the circumstances, Raglan was probably right to be cautious with his only cavalry brigade.

Unfortunately, Captain Nolan did not see it this way and that evening he vented his frustration in William Russell's tent. To think, he raged, that 'there were one thousand British Cavalry looking on at a beaten enemy retreating – guns, standards, colours, and all, with a wretched horde of Cossacks and cowards who had never struck a blow ready to turn tail at the first trumpet – within a ten minutes' gallop of them – is enough to drive one mad! It is too disgraceful, too infamous. They ought all of them to be———!'

Later in the campaign, Nolan was heard to remark to Major McMahon, Lucan's Assistant Quartermaster-General, that had he commanded the Light Brigade at Alma 'he would have pursued the Russians to the very gates of Sebastopol'.[19]

The irony is that both Lucan and Cardigan were in sympathy with these sentiments. Lucan, unaware of Raglan's reasons, blamed the Commander-in-Chief; Cardigan did too, but was more incensed with Lucan for again assuming direct command of his brigade in the field.

As Cardigan and his men were coming down from the Heights after dark, they met their commissary officer with his waggons and some bullocks. 'That's right, Mr Crookshank, I am glad you have come up,' said Cardigan. 'What have you got with you?'

'I have got plenty of everything, my lord,' Crookshank replied. 'Beef, biscuit, coffee, sugar, and rum.'

'Well, I hope you will let my men have some as soon as possible, for they have had nothing to-day,' said Cardigan pointedly.

That night, the Light Brigade bivouacked in the middle of the battlefield, wrapped in their cloaks and blankets, each man lying near his horse so as to be ready to mount at a moment's notice. Private Mitchell was on night patrol with 20 men and did not turn in until the early hours. By that time most were asleep, and he could hear all around him 'the groans of the wounded and dying; some calling for the love of God for a drop of water. Others were praying most devoutly, well knowing this to be their last night.'[20]

As well as 60 French, 362 British and 1,801 Russians killed, 6,000 troops of all nationalities had been wounded. The British had landed 'without any kind of hospital transport, litters or carts or anything', and many of the wounded were forced to spend the night on the battlefield.

One man who could not sleep through 'the horrors of that night' was William Russell. Tortured by the cries of fallen soldiers, he and a small group went out with flasks of water. 'We were out for hours among the wounded on the hill-side,' he wrote, 'but all we could do was but the measure of our great helplessness . . .'[21]

For two more days the armies remained at the Alma. Raglan was keen to press on but St Arnaud, weakened by an illness that would soon prove fatal, urged caution. He was convinced that the Russians would vigorously contest the two intervening rivers – the Katcha and the Belbec – and was aware that the Allies did not yet have siege artillery to bombard the defences of the Severnaya, the fort guarding the north of Sebastopol harbour. Instead, he suggested a gradual advance so that the outer defences could be probed while reinforcements, including the heavy cavalry, arrived from Varna and Constantinople.

While the dead were being buried and the sick and wounded carried aboard ship, Cardigan found time to pen a long letter of complaint to Raglan about Lucan's treatment of him, describing it as 'a grinding and humiliating system of discipline on the part of one general officer to another'. He had been promised that Lucan would not interfere with his command of the Light Brigade and yet he had done so, both at the Bulganek and at Alma. Furthermore, Lucan insisted on seeing all orders that Cardigan received from Raglan, and wrote him orders and memoranda as if he were a junior officer. Raglan had to intervene, pressed Cardigan.

As procedure demanded, the complaint had to go through Lucan and on 22 September he forwarded it with a covering letter, pointing out that he had 'neglected nothing to show courtesy and attention to Lord Cardigan' since his appointment. 'To avoid any personal difference,' he continued, 'I have studiously communicated on all matters of duty with him either by written memoranda or divisional orders; and on no one occasion have I ever allowed to drop from me one sentence of reproof, reserving my opinion when I could not approve, and only expressing it when it was likely to be agreeable to him . . .'

It was more than a week before Raglan could find the time to reply with reference to this latest petty squabble, and he left both in no doubt as to whom he held responsible:

> I have perused this correspondence with the deepest regret, and I am bound to express my conviction that the Earl of Cardigan would have done better if he had abstained from making the representation which he has thought fit to submit for my decision. I consider him wrong in every one of the instances cited. The General of Division may interfere little or much with the duties of a General of Brigade as he may think proper or see fit. The Earl of Lucan and the Earl of Cardigan are nearly connected. They are both gentlemen of high honour and elevated position in the country, independently of their military rank. They must permit me, as the Commander of the Forces, and I may say the friend of both, earnestly to recommend them to communicate frankly with each other, and to come to such an understanding as that there should be no suspicion of the contempt of authority on the one side, and no apprehension of undue interference on the other.[22]

After starting the letter so forcefully, Raglan had let his equable temper get the better of him. William Russell, for one, was under no illusion as to the effect such a request would have:

> He recommends two men, each as proud as Lucifer, the one impetuous, dominant, as hard as steel; the other proud, narrow, jealous, and self-willed, to communicate 'frankly' with each other! There was ample evidence already that neither of these officers would follow his Lordship's advice. Fretful, discontented, each probably not disinclined to 'let the other into a hole', they were allowed, like two jibbing horses, to pull against each other until the coach was upset.

In Russell's opinion, Cardigan should have been relieved of his command the moment the 'Adjutant-General had to explain to him the nature of his

duties to his superior' in Bulgaria. With the benefit of hindsight, he may
have been right, although it should be remembered that few of Lucan's
subordinates appreciated serving under him during the campaign. On the
other hand, if Cardigan had been the superior no doubt he would have
been just as irksome in behaviour towards Lucan as he claimed the latter
had been towards him. This leads back, therefore, to the original appointments and the fact that Raglan's objections were overruled. From that
point on, he seems to have disregarded the possibility of sacking either of
them – hardly surprising given his quietly spoken, unassertive nature and
the fact that he knew both men socially – preferring instead to cajole them
not to quarrel.[23]

On 23 September, the slow march towards Sebastopol resumed, and Lucan
was ordered to take most of the cavalry and a troop of horse artillery south
of the River Katcha to occupy the village of Duvankoi on the Belbec. A
disgruntled Cardigan went too. Watched by Cossacks all the way, they
approached the village, hemmed in between the river and high cliffs,
through a narrow defile. It was a natural trap, but Lucan had his orders.
Only when night fell would he consider his duty done and retire closer to
the main armies, by this time camped on the north bank of the Katcha.

The following morning, Lord George Paget recorded a conversation
with his brigade commander: 'Cardigan has just ridden in from the cavalry
(three miles off) and describes a dreadful night they had of it, having got
into a narrow pass, in which he says one battalion might have annihilated
them, but then he added, "Mind, Lord Lucan was in command," which
accounts, in his mind, for it, and perhaps for his colouring of it.'[24]

That day, the cavalry was sent on a reconnaissance south of the River
Belbec down the main road leading to Sebastopol, and this time Cardigan
was in command. As they were moving down a stretch of the road between
two hills, with marshy ground on either side, Captain Walker – one of
Lucan's aides-de-camp who was riding on high ground above them – called
out that there was a masked battery on the opposite hill. 'Lord Cardigan
immediately gave the order, "Threes about. Gallop,"' recalled Sergeant-
Major Loy Smith of the 11th. 'So back we went much quicker than we
went down, expecting every moment to be assailed with shot and shell.'[25]

Returning to the main army, now near the River Belbec, Cardigan
reported an 'impracticable' marsh and a causeway dominated by enemy
cannon and supported by infantry and cavalry. This information, along

with French fears about the strength of the defences in their path and the belief that the north side of the harbour had no safe anchorage from which they could be resupplied in poor weather, led to the decision to skirt round Sebastopol so that it could be attacked from the south. The small port of Balaclava would enable supplies and fresh troops to be landed.

That night, long after most of the men were asleep, Loy Smith was lying on the ground in front of a 'splendid fire' with the orderly room clerk and his troop sergeant when out of the darkness came two figures. 'After looking at us for a few moments,' he wrote, 'they seated themselves on the ground close to the fire and entered into conversation. One was no less a personage than the Earl of Cardigan, the other Colonel Douglas. Unfortunately I had nothing to offer them, or I certainly should have done so for I looked on them as guests, although they had come without invitation.'

Such condescension (in the true sense of the word) by Cardigan towards his men was not unusual and explains why he was so popular. Private Mitchell of the 13th recalled a similar encounter the following night when he and some colleagues, frying beefsteak and onions, 'were honoured by a visit from Lord Cardigan' who 'conversed with us as freely as though we were his equals'. Mitchell always regretted not having offered Cardigan some meat, 'for he must have been as hungry as ourselves. But the difference in our respective ranks was so great that I felt afraid to do so.'

The ordinary soldier had always respected Cardigan. According to Private Pennington of the 11th Hussars, he was known to his men as 'Jim the Bear', and 'they with a somewhat extravagant opinion of his gifts as a cavalry officer regarded him as the Murat of the British Army'. Pennington was at a loss, however, to explain by 'what standard of judgment they arrived at such a measure of his capacity . . . for he never gave any evidence of those attributes of prescience or inspiration which at an important crisis mark a great military leader'.[26]

The famous 'flank march' began the following morning in a south-easterly direction through forest towards the Sebastopol–Bakchisarai road near Mackenzie's Farm. The cavalry (less the 4th Light Dragoons but plus the Scots Greys, who had landed at Katcha) were to lead the way, supported by a battalion of rifles and a battery of horse artillery.

They set off down a track through the thick brushwood at 8.30 a.m., closely followed by Raglan and his staff, and after a while came to a fork. Lucan's guide, an officer from General Airey's staff, did not have it marked on his map so he chose the right fork because, although the smaller of the two, it seemed to be heading in the correct compass direction. This was a mistake. The cavalry were now heading towards, not away from, Sebastopol.

'After some time I happened to look to my right rear, when to my surprise through an opening in the trees I had a full view of Sebastopol,' wrote Sergeant-Major Loy Smith. 'I called out involuntarily, "Sebastopol." All within hearing halted and for a few moments sat gazing at the beautiful town with its church spire and white buildings reflected in the sun.'

'Fortunately,' recalled Cardigan, 'Captain Maude of the horse artillery had ventured to disobey the order he had received of going down the same road. Feeling that the [other] road . . . was the proper one he took the responsibility upon himself by saying that he would give as a plea the impracticability of getting the guns through the wood that way.'[27]

Raglan and his staff, meanwhile, had followed the cavalry but realised their error when Sebastopol appeared in the distance to their right. By cutting through the woods they rejoined the right track and soon met the horse artillery. Onward they rode until a clearing loomed in the distance, and Airey was sent ahead to reconnoitre. Suddenly he raised his arm in warning. They had stumbled on the rearguard of the Russian army near Mackenzie's Farm as it withdrew from Sebastopol.

'Instantly the words "Get Lord Raglan out of the way" were said by everyone – and away he went with his Staff of course,' recalled Captain Shakespear of the Royal Horse Artillery. 'Maude [his commander] and I instantly saw that . . . nothing could save us but a dashing action . . . He accordingly took 4 guns to the right road: I took two howitzers to the left. We unlimbered and fired shells at the shortest range. Captain Walker had been sent back to hasten up the cavalry.'

Not bothering to wait for the cavalry, Shakespear's troop then 'wheeled to the left and came into action, the enemy flying before us. We limbered up and pursued as hard as our guns would go for 10 minutes. Suddenly the road turned to the right . . . and to our astonishment a regt. of infantry was formed across the road, front ranks kneeling within 30 yards of us. They fired a volley, but were so bewildered *nothing* touched us . . . They then bolted into the bush.'[28]

By now, Captain Walker had found and deployed some of the missing cavalry. When Lucan appeared soon after, leading the rest, Raglan called out: 'Lord Lucan, you are late!'

Quickly into action, Cardigan and his men pursued the Russians three miles down the road to Bakchaserai, until they came to the top of a hill which overlooked a large plain. 'Down this hill the Russians had fled,' wrote Private Mitchell, 'and our Horse Artillery having now come up, they sent a few shots after them. The 17th Lancers followed them some distance, but were recalled.'[29]

Raglan had issued the order because, as at Alma, he feared the cavalry would pursue too far and get itself into difficulties. An added incentive was the fact that his headquarters was then defended only by some horse artillery and the Scots Greys. Later, still smarting from his close shave, he confronted Cardigan.

'What could have induced you to take the wrong road?' asked Raglan.

'My lord,' Cardigan replied, 'I was a junior officer, the order was not mine. I had only to obey.'[30]

The troops, both officers and men alike, had then been given permission to pillage the captured wagon-train. 'In a few moments,' wrote Lieutenant the Honourable Somerset Calthorpe, one of Raglan's aides, 'the ground was strewed with every sort of thing – handsome Hussar uniforms, rich fur cloaks, every kind of undergarment, male and female. Several wigs I saw being offered for sale, amidst the laughter of the men. French books and novels of an improper kind were not infrequently met with in the baggage of the Russian officers . . . A gold Hussar pelisse would sell for about 30s or £2.'

Sergeant-Major Loy Smith managed to secure for himself 'an officer's undress jacket and shabrack [sic] embroidered with gold lace, a dress shirt, towel, a large bag of Turkish tobacco and some scores of cigarettes . . . giving one each first to the officers, then to the non-commissioned officers and men of my troop'. But Private Mitchell was too late, as other troops had 'helped themselves to everything worth having, so there was nothing left for us'.[31]

By evening, the cavalry had reached the banks of the River Tchernaya, south-east of Sebastopol. Cardigan spent the night in a small summer-house; Raglan in a post-house beside the Traktir Bridge. The rest of the Allied armies were strung out between the Tchernaya and the Belbec: the French and Turks on the heights east of Sebastopol, the British infantry lower down in the Tchernaya plain.

To Raglan's relief, however, no attack came and the British were able to continue their march the following day, taking the port of Balaclava in the afternoon after its defence force of 70 militiamen had put up only token resistance.

★

To troops approaching from the north, the harbour of Balaclava had the appearance of a lake, being almost completely landlocked and surrounded by high hills obscuring its narrow exit. A mile long and half a mile broad, the anchorage was deep enough for even the largest men-of-war. On the south-eastern side was the small picturesque town, its green-tiled villas festooned with roses, clematis, honeysuckle and vines. Many of the 1,500 inhabitants had fled, leaving their possessions to be pillaged by the callous British troops.

'Several of the houses were well and even elegantly furnished,' wrote Private Mitchell, 'having sofas, chimney glasses, pianos, etc. Many of these articles were ruthlessly destroyed, drawers and boxes ransacked, female attire held up and made the subject of ribald jest and laughter, for by this time some liquor had been found . . .'[32]

Up a steep gorge to the north of the town lay a large plain, almost four miles long and three wide, divided into two equal valleys by an east-west range of hillocks known as the Causeway Heights. The Woronzoff Road, the main route into Sebastopol, ran along part of the Heights before dropping down into the North Valley and then rising sharply again up the Sapouné Ridge and on to the Chersonese Plateau. It was from this large upland, which could also be reached from the South Valley by a rough track known as the Col, that the Allies intended to attack the great port.

With the Fedioukine Hills above it and a series of mountain gorges and deep ravines to the east, the North Valley was almost completely enclosed. It was through a gap in the Fedioukine Hills that the British army had entered the North Valley before crossing over the Causeway Heights into the southern part of the plain, where it spent the night of the 26th. Well cultivated, the South Valley was dotted with cottages surrounded by vineyards and orchards full of ripe grapes, melons and other fruit. It also contained two villages: Kadikoi, on rising ground immediately above Balaclava, and Kamara, towards its eastern end. Villagers from both were friendly, offering the British bread and salt.

On 27 September, the day the French and Turks arrived in the South Valley, Raglan met General Canrobert – the dying St Arnaud's successor as Commander-in-Chief – on a detached feature to the south-east of the Causeway Heights and known thereafter as 'Canrobert's Hill'. A short, dapper man with a high forehead and a heavily waxed moustache, Canrobert agreed to Raglan's suggestion that the British would retain Balaclava and place their infantry on the right of the Allied line on the Chersonese Plateau facing Sebastopol; the French would occupy the left and would be resupplied from two wide bays, Kamiesch and Kazatch, 10 miles west of Balaclava.

What Canrobert would not agree to, however, was an immediate assault on the city. French tactics were dominated by the perceived importance of artillery preparation, and Canrobert was not willing to attack until the Russian forts had been reduced by continuous bombardment. Raglan has often been criticised for not ordering an immediate *coup de main*, but he could hardly have done so without his main ally, and in any case his chief engineer, General Burgoyne, was in agreement with Canrobert. But not even the bombardment could begin until the heavy siege guns had arrived and been dragged into position, and this gave the Russians a crucial breathing space in which to strengthen their defences.

With its right flank 'in the air', the British army was vulnerable to attack from the Russian troops which had evacuated Sebastopol and were now gathered to the east. To guard this open flank, the cavalry were camped near to the village of Kadikoi in the South Valley, from which point they could carry out regular patrols and picket duty. At first, with two regiments of the Light Brigade – the 4th and the 11th – attached to infantry divisions on the plateau, they were short on numbers, and the arrival of the remaining four regiments of Scarlett's Heavy Brigade over the next ten days was particularly welcome. Unfortunately, these regiments had lost more than 220 horses during an exceptionally stormy crossing from Varna.

Cardigan, needless to say, was on worse terms than ever with his brother-in-law. On 29 September, a day after receiving Raglan's rebuff to his earlier complaint, he and Lucan had a 'turn-up' because the latter would not allow the regiments in the valley to have forage until those on the plateau had been provided for. 'Good man!' applauded Lord George Paget, whose regiment was to receive priority.[33]

Matters hardly improved when, on 4 October, Lucan issued a memorandum explaining the Light Brigade's 'chief duties', which were primarily 'to ensure the safety of the Army from all surprises'. It was not, on the other hand, its duty 'needlessly, without authority, to engage the enemy' and 'on no account should any party attack or pursue, unless specially instructed to do so.'[34]

The following day, Cardigan succumbed to the debilitating effects of diarrhoea and was ordered aboard the *Southern Star* in Balaclava harbour by the cavalry division's medical officer. 'Lord Cardigan is always in front I hear,' wrote an unsuspecting Colonel Hodge of the 4th Dragoon Guards, also ill aboard a transport.[35]

Cardigan was absent, therefore, when the cavalry was involved in two controversial episodes on consecutive days. First, on the 6th, an outlying picket of 4th Dragoon Guards, commanded by Cornet Edward Fisher, was surprised by a regiment of Polish lancers, and three men 'who could hardly get their horses to canter' were 'run into and speared in the most merciless manner'. Fisher tried vainly to assist them, and only escaped himself by shooting one assailant with his pistol.

Next day, a large force of Russian cavalry advanced over the hill near Kamara into the South Valley, driving the outlying picket before them. The entire Cavalry Division was called out but as the Russians manoeuvred to and fro, inviting attack, Lucan stayed his hand. Eventually the enemy withdrew, and many of those present were furious at this latest humiliation. The 'finest opportunity for thrashing the Russian cavalry, was *thrown* away', wrote Captain Shakespear of the Horse Artillery.

At dinner that evening, the cavalry camp was alive with criticism. Fanny Duberly, who had landed at Balaclava on the 4th, noted: 'By judicious generalship, they say, the whole force might have been taken, or severely punished; but a hesitation at the wrong moment allowed them all to retire out of range, after having killed two or three of our men, while they escaped unhurt.'

Cardigan no doubt joined in the general condemnation and, as a result of this incident, Lucan acquired the sobriquet 'Lord Look-on'. This was particularly hard on a man who knew from bitter experience that his chief, Raglan, was determined not to fritter away his cavalry on senseless charges against an enemy of uncertain strength. Events at Alma and during the flank march had shown that Raglan did not trust his judgement, and he did not intend to give him another opportunity to chastise him. Instead, he gave the opportunity to his officers. But not all of them blamed him. Lord George Paget was on the Chersonese Plateau when the actual event took place, but later spoke to all 'those whose opinions are worth anything' and came to the conclusion 'that a more unjust accusation never was made'.[36]

On 12 October, with Cardigan feeling a little better, Raglan decided the wise thing would be to give him command of the two cavalry regiments on the Chersonese Plateau. 'There are Lucan and Cardigan again hard at it, because they can't agree, and it is found desirable to separate them,' wrote a disappointed Lord George Paget. 'Cardigan must needs be ordered up here to command the 4th and the 11th, both of which are usefully placed, with their respective divisional generals, and all this must be upset to part these two spoilt children.'[37]

In a letter home that day, Major William Forrest of the 4th Dragoon Guards was even more scathing about the cavalry commanders: 'We have no faith in the generalship of my Lord Lucan, we all agree that two greater muffs than Lucan and Cardigan could not be. We call Lucan the cautious ass and Cardigan the dangerous ass. Between the two they got us into two or three very awkward positions at Alma and also in the previous day and then began to dispute who commanded the brigade.'[38]

Next day Cardigan, 'looking ill', pitched his tent on the plateau. 'The Earl is very gracious to me,' Lord George noted with surprise, 'but I always "My Lord" him, though he has returned to "George Paget".'[39]

Cardigan's jaunty mood may have been due to the fact that he was expecting good news. That evening, as he was sitting in his tent on a bullock trunk, dining off soup from a jug, boiled salt pork and Varna brandy mixed with rum, an impeccably dressed civilian entered: it was his great friend Hubert De Burgh, the husband of Lady Cardigan's sister, who had brought out his luxury steam yacht, the *Dryad*, from England. Together they returned to the yacht for champagne and a meal cooked by the French chef. Two days later, citing a recurrence of his diarrhoea, Cardigan was given permission by Raglan to sleep aboard his yacht while still retaining command of the Light Brigade.

Fanny Duberly, noticing on the 14th that two yachts (Cardigan's and a Mr Carew's) had entered the harbour, commented: 'What a satire is the appearance of these fairy ships amidst all the rough work of war! They seem as out of place as a London belle would be; and yet there is something very touching in their pretty gracefulness.'[40]

Needless to say, Cardigan's fellow officers were not terribly impressed – forced as they were to suffer the privations of camp life and army rations – and he was soon given the derisive nickname of the 'Noble Yachtsman'. Those invited to share his hospitality felt differently: 'Paid Lord Cardigan a visit on board his yacht,' wrote Colonel Hodge. 'This is the way to make war. I hope he will take compassion on me sometimes.'[41]

Having received information from Tartar spies that a Russian army was marching towards the Tchernaya, Raglan decided to bolster the defence of Balaclava, his vulnerable supply depot, by ordering the construction of six redoubts on Canrobert's Hill and along the Causeway Heights. They were to be armed with British naval 12-pounders and garrisoned by Turkish militiamen. More naval guns were sited on the high ground immediately above Balaclava and manned by 1,200 Royal Marines, while the 93rd Highlanders (less four companies at Balaclava), a battalion of Turks and a battery of six field guns were given the task of defending Kadikoi. Placed in overall command of these troops on 14 October was Raglan's most experienced soldier, Sir Colin Campbell.

Also on that day, Raglan strengthened Lucan's hand by instructing Cardigan and the two regiments on the plateau to rejoin their comrades on the plain below. Cardigan duly issued the necessary orders but was mystified when Lord George Paget and his 4th Light Dragoons failed to keep the rendezvous. The reason was that Sir George De Lacy Evans, commanding the division to which the 4th had been attached, had asked Paget to wait while he appealed to Airey against the decision. By the time a compromise had been agreed – one officer and 20 men would be left behind to assist De Lacy Evans – Paget was more than an hour late. As he and his men trotted over to join the 11th Hussars on parade at the appointed place, he reasoned that upon the result of the forthcoming confrontation would depend his future under Cardigan, and he ground his teeth 'in the determination that no amount of provocation should tempt me to commit myself'. As expected, he found Cardigan 'in a very angry state'.

Calling the commanders of the two regiments aside, and with a preparatory twist of his moustache, Cardigan said icily: 'Pray, Lord George Paget, I wish to be informed why my brigade order has not been obeyed, and why I have been kept waiting for you for the last hour?'

'If your lordship will give me the opportunity of explaining the reason, I think I can satisfy you,' Paget quietly replied.

'Proceed, my lord.'

Paget then explained the events as they had happened and was pleasantly surprised when Cardigan, after another twist of his moustache, said: 'Quite satisfactory, my lord, be pleased to join your regiment.'

'Now talk of general actions and great victories!' Paget wrote later. 'I pride myself on this one, I assure you.'

It was made all the sweeter when both Colonel Douglas and Hubert De Burgh – 'who had only just arrived on the yacht, and whose London hat and well-shaven chin looked odd but pleasant' – congratulated him on his 'success'. They then 'rode down in harmony together' to the cavalry camp, now sited in orchards to the south of the Causeway Heights.[42]

Three days later, at about 6.30 a.m., the bombardment of Sebastopol finally began when 126 Allied guns opened up on the main Russian redoubts. The original plan had been for the Allied navies to begin firing simultaneously from the sea, but the admirals decided at the last minute that they had too little ammunition for a day-long barrage, and it only got under way in the afternoon. Long before then – at around 10.30 a.m. – two lucky hits on the French ammunition magazines had brought their firing to a halt. Later in the day, British shells did manage to blow up a Russian magazine and reduce their main redoubt, the Great Redan, to rubble, but Canrobert refused to attack and the British could not go in alone.

Leaving Lord George Paget in command, Cardigan had ridden over to the siege lines with De Burgh to observe the bombardment. They were joined by a young Royal Engineer officer and William Russell, who recorded the conversation:

> 'Ah,' said Lord Cardigan, 'I see! Those fellows below are our men and they are firing at the Russians. Those fellows who are firing towards us are the Russians. Why don't we drive them away?' The officer explained there were certain difficulties in the suggested operation, but the gallant General was by no means satisfied, and insisted on his views with an air of haughty conviction. At last, putting up his glasses and turning to remount his horse, he exclaimed, 'I have never in my life seen a siege conducted on such principles, Squire.' The Squire assented: he had never seen such a siege either; and they rode back to Balaclava.[43]

Still weak and sleeping aboard his yacht every night, Cardigan often reached the Light Brigade long after it had completed its tedious morning stand-to when, with the Heavy Brigade, it remained mounted for an hour either side of daybreak. On 18 October, in response to Russian cavalry activity, the whole division was turned out from 9 a.m. to 8.30 p.m. Cardigan did not arrive until 11 a.m. and only stayed a couple of hours having been, De Burgh told Paget, 'very unwell all night'. 'I believe really he is ill,' wrote Paget, 'and that this will be the end of him.'

Next morning, as Cardigan had not arrived, Colonel Mayow, the Brigade-Major, asked Paget if he would form up the brigade for the daily divisional parade. Paget duly gave the necessary directions, but five minutes later Cardigan appeared, saying: 'Lord George Paget, why were you to assume that I was not coming on parade?'

When Paget explained that it was in response to a request from Colonel

Mayow, Cardigan 'flew off . . . very irate' at his Brigade-Major.

Paget's conclusion was particularly perceptive: Cardigan 'is easily managed, with calmness and firmness, and when one is in the right – which it is not difficult to be with him'.[44]

If only Cardigan's other subordinates had shown the same perspicacity, how different his career might have been.

Warned of large-scale Russian troop movements in the direction of Tchorgoun, a village on the Tchernaya behind the Fedioukine Hills, Raglan decided to see for himself. Accompanied by his staff, he rode to the edge of the Sapouné Ridge in the morning of 18 October. But after an hour straining his eyes through field-glasses, he decided there was no immediate threat and returned to watch the bombardment.

He was wrong. On that day, near Tchorgoun, General Liprandi, the commander of the Russian 12th Division, completed the assembly of more than 20,000 infantry, 3,400 cavalry and 2,300 artillerymen with 78 guns. His task: to capture Kadikoi and cut off the British supply base of Balaclava. Two days later, and again on the 22nd, he probed forward with cavalry and each time withdrew with valuable intelligence. A full-scale attack was planned for the 25th.

As luck would have it, Rustem Pasha, the commander of the Turkish troops on the Causeway Heights, received word from one of his Tartar spies on the 24th that 'the enemy had concentrated behind the Tchorgoun heights 28,000 [men] . . . preparatory to an early attack on Balaclava'. The spy was then interrogated by Campbell and Lucan. Considering the news to be of the first importance, Campbell at once wrote a report which was conveyed to Raglan by Lucan's son and aide-de-camp, Lord Bingham. Unfortunately, the Commander-in-Chief had little faith in the reliability of spies; a similar report had resulted in an infantry division being marched down from the Chersonese Plateau on the 20th, and back again the following day when it proved a false alarm. This time he simply acknowledged the message with the words 'Very well' and a request that 'anything new was to be reported to him'.[45]

His inaction was particularly unfortunate given that – according to James Blunt, Lucan's interpreter – the chain of redoubts on the Causeway Heights was incomplete and hopelessly inadequate:

These works, six in number, were of a very superficial type, and were hastily constructed by Turkish troops under the personal direction of English Engineers. I went into most of them shortly after they were made, and among other defects I observed that their ditches and parapets were so low, that a horse could easily have leaped over some of them. Only 3 . . . were armed: the redoubt (No. 1) on Canrobert Hill, by far the highest of the range, with three guns, and the two succeeding ones (No. 2 and 3) with two guns each, all ships' iron twelve pounders. The three works with No. 4 were garrisoned by about 1,400 Turkish Rediffs [militia] from Asia Minor and Tunis, most of whom, I was informed by their Officers, had never been under fire before, or seen any active service. Some 600 . . . garrisoned No. 1 redoubt, and the remainder were distributed in about equal numbers in Nos. 2, 3 and 4 . . . Nos. 5 and 6 were not armed or manned nor were the works of No. 6 completed.[46]

That evening, riding back to headquarters after having visited the cavalry camp, William Russell fell in with Captain Nolan who lent him his cloak to keep out the chill. 'Mind you send it back to me tomorrow; I shall not want it tonight,' said Nolan.

They then discussed the rumours of an imminent Russian attack, with Nolan prophesying that the cavalry would be greatly handicapped by its commanders. 'We are in a bad way I can tell you,' he concluded ominously.

At dinner, Russell mentioned this conversation, but his listeners had little sympathy with Nolan's opinions. 'He is an inveterate croaker and I wish he was away in Jericho with his cavalry,' growled Captain Burke, General Burgoyne's aide-de-camp. 'What do we want with cavalry here?'[47]

14

'Charge!'

An hour before daybreak on 25 October, as Cardigan slept aboard his yacht and the Cavalry Division stood mounted on parade, Lucan and two staff officers rode out of camp in the direction of Canrobert's Hill. They were joined by Lord George Paget.

As the small knot of riders approached to within 300 yards of the most easterly of the six redoubts, it was just light enough for them to see two flags flying.

'Holloa,' said Lord William Paulet, the Assistant Adjutant-General. 'What does that mean?'

'Why, *that* surely is the signal that the enemy is approaching,' replied Major McMahon, the Assistant Quartermaster-General.

Hardly had the words left his mouth when a cannon from the redoubt opened up, to be met by counter-fire from a Russian battery. Paget galloped back to the camp.[1]

It was now about 6 o'clock.

An hour earlier, General Liprandi had crossed the Tchernaya with 25 battalions of infantry, 35 squadrons of cavalry and 78 guns – 25,000 men in all. With three battalions in possession of the village of Kamara, another five now moved forward to attack No. 1 Redoubt on Canrobert's Hill. A further three had orders to take No. 2 Redoubt while four battalions, a field battery and three squadrons of Cossacks were advancing from the Traktir Bridge to assault No. 3. All these columns were supported by a huge force of Russian cavalry.

Before long, Lucan was joined by Sir Colin Campbell who concurred with the opinion that the attack was serious. Lucan, therefore, sent one of his aides to warn Raglan and another to bring forward the Heavy Brigade and the horse artillery. The Light Brigade – still under Paget, as Cardigan had not yet appeared – was to follow in reserve.

Rushing ahead, Captain Maude's troop of horse artillery halted on the ridge between No. 2 and No. 3 Redoubts and began firing on the Russian skirmishers and artillery in the plain below. But what, asked one of their officers later, 'could 6-pounders do against 18-pounders at 1800 yds? However, Maude stuck to it, and fell severely wounded in the first twenty minutes.' His position had received a direct hit, killing one man, wounding many more and putting one of his six guns out of action.[2]

Even the Light Brigade, halted beneath the hill of No. 2 Redoubt, was suffering casualties. Roundshot – like 'huge cricket-balls' – were coming over the hill, and one caught a man in the front rank of the 4th Light Dragoons and spun him round. 'I can well remember the slosh that sounded, as it went through the centre of his belly,' wrote Lord George Paget.[3]

It was not long before the horse artillery ran out of ammunition – their wagons having been sent to supply the siege guns before Sebastopol – and Captain Shakespear, now in command, ordered them to retire below the ridge. Cardigan, having at last arrived from his yacht, noticed this and called out: 'Where are you going with your guns, Captain Shakespear? Who ordered you to retire?'

'We are going for more ammunition, my lord,' Shakespear replied, adding: 'Our guns are of no use over a thousand yards, and the enemy's guns are a mile away.'[4]

Finally, after a stout defence of an hour and a half, and having lost a quarter of their strength, the heavily outnumbered and outgunned defenders of No. 1 Redoubt broke and began to run down the hill in the direction of Balaclava. 'They appeared to fight bravely against overwhelming odds,' wrote Sergeant-Major Loy Smith of the 11th, 'for, as the last of them came over the parapet, I noticed that the Russians were close at their heels and, as they retreated down the hillside, many of them turned around and fired.'[5]

At the last moment, the Royal Artillerymen had spiked the redoubt's three guns, but the Russians soon dragged up more and began to concentrate their fire on the neighbouring redoubt. 'A short, a very short struggle on the hill,' wrote Lord George Paget, 'and down came the "Buono

Johnnys", helter skelter down the almost perpendicular descent, as if the Devil were at their heels.'[6]

On Campbell's advice, Lucan now began to withdraw the cavalry west to a line between No. 4 and No. 5 Redoubts. This would give Campbell's artillery at Kadikoi a clear field of fire and enable the cavalry 'to take in flank any Russian forces marching against Balaclava'.[7]

Looking down from his vantage point on the Sapouné Ridge, from where the 'field of Balaclava was as plainly seen . . . as the stage and those upon it are seen from the box of a theatre', William Russell noted 'a panorama of exceeding beauty . . . – a picture of green valley and plains, framed with mountain ridges on all sides – with the sun-like waters of the harbour on our right flashing in the sun, and down below us the wheeling squadrons of our cavalry seeming very much as though they were "showing off" for our inspection'.

He could distinctly see the 'Heavy Cavalry, further away on the right of the Light Brigade, making a very gallant appearance – the sunshine playing on scarlet and blue uniforms, brass helmets, flashing swords – though the Scots Greys were conspicuous by their horses and bearskins'. They were 'plainly retiring before an actual enemy'.[8]

Raglan and his staff reached the edge of the Sapouné Ridge at about 7.30 a.m., just in time to witness the fall of Canrobert's Hill. Immediately, the Commander-in-Chief despatched two divisions down to the plain: Cambridge's 1st was in reserve and was directed down the Col and into the South Valley; Cathcart's 4th was in the siege lines two miles from the ridge, and was ordered to follow the Woronzoff Road down into the North Valley. Neither would arrive before 10.30 a.m. At the same time, the French ordered two infantry brigades and a cavalry brigade down the Col to a position under the lee of the ridge at the western end of the South Valley.

Raglan was also anxious to preserve his cavalry until the infantry arrived, and he sent a galloper to Lucan with what came to be known as the First Order: 'Cavalry to take ground to the left of the second line of redoubts occupied by the Turks.' In other words, beyond No. 6 Redoubt, as it and No. 5 were known as the 'second line'. As a result, the cavalry was withdrawn further to the west than Lucan had originally intended, through its own camp and into vineyards beneath the unfinished No. 6 Redoubt.

Meanwhile, not wishing to share the fate of their comrades, the defenders of No. 3 and No. 4 Redoubts decided to flee even before they were attacked. 'We were much annoyed at seeing the Turks come flying down past us crying, and calling upon "Allah",' wrote Private Mitchell of the 13th Light Dragoons. 'However great their haste, they were very careful of their kettles and pans, for they rattled and clattered as they ran past us.'

But unlike their compatriots on Canrobert's Hill, who escaped without molestation, the Turks from the remaining redoubts were harried by Cossacks. William Russell likened the pursuit to the bursting of 'a dark cloud' which had been 'lowering' on the Heights. 'We could hear the yells of the fugitives, and had to witness the work of lance, sword, and pistol on the unfortunates,' he wrote.

'Some of them, unarmed, raised their hands imploringly,' noted Sergeant-Major Loy Smith, 'but it was only to have them severed from their bodies. This we had to witness close in front of our squadrons, feeling the while that had a dozen or two of us been sent out numbers of these poor fellows might have been saved.'

Fanny Duberly was supervising the striking of her husband's tent in the cavalry camp when she noticed that the crest of the nearest hill was 'covered with running Turks, pursued by mounted Cossacks, who were all making straight for where I stood'. Without ceremony, her husband threw her on to her horse and together they rode 'a little to the left, to get clear of the shots, which now began to fly towards us'.[9]

On the Cossacks rode, galloping actually into the cavalry camp where they wounded a number of spare horses that had been left tied up in the lines. Cardigan now gave the order, 'Draw Swords', but the despatch of a troop of the 13th Light Dragoons was enough to encourage the Cossacks to retreat back over the Heights. Observing this, Raglan sent Lucan a second order (rarely acknowledged by historians) 'to take some cavalry forward and protect the camp from being destroyed'. According to Sergeant-Major Loy Smith, the aide carrying the order also had one for Campbell at Kadikoi and, to save time, had asked Veterinary-Surgeon Gloag of the 11th Hussars to pass the first one on to Lucan.[10]

It may well have been the receipt of this order that caused Lucan to move some of the Heavy Brigade in the direction of the camp. In any case, it was soon followed by another (known as the Second Order): 'Eight squadrons of Heavy Dragoons to be detached towards Balaclava to support the Turks.'[11]

From his elevated position, Raglan could see that the Turkish battalion supporting Campbell's Highlanders in front of Kadikoi was beginning to disintegrate. He could also see a huge force of Russian cavalry and artillery advancing up the North Valley, and feared that its objective was Kadikoi. He was right.

At this critical moment, William Russell looked across 'at the group of officers representing the military mind of England' and 'was not much impressed with confidence' by what he saw. 'Lord Raglan was by no means at ease,' he wrote. 'There was no trace of the divine calm attributed to him by his admirers as his characteristic in moments of trial. His anxious mien as he turned his glass from point to point, consulting with Generals Airey, Estcourt, and others of his staff, gave me a notion that he was in "trouble".'

Meanwhile, the Light Brigade beneath them seemed blissfully unaware of the danger. 'I could see the officers,' wrote Russell, 'flask in hand, munching whatever they had, and smoking, and the men, as they stood by their horses, were chatting as if they were off duty . . . Lord Cardigan was standing with two or three officers apart in front of the line near me, easily recognisable by his figure and bearing, and I could make out many others – Lord George Paget, Douglas, Shewell, De Salis, Morris, Lord Fitzgibbon . . . etc.'[12]

But long before Raglan's message could reach Lucan, four squadrons of Saxon-Viemarsky Hussars, about 400 sabres in all, had crossed the Causeway Heights and were riding directly towards Campbell's position on high ground to the left front of the village.

As well as six companies of 93rd Highlanders (550 men) in their red tunics, green and black kilts and black bonnets, Campbell also had 150 assorted soldiers from Balaclava and a Turkish battalion supplemented by some stragglers from the redoubts. To his right rear was the entrenched battery of naval guns, on his left a battery of field guns.

With his men still lying down behind a slight rise to protect them from artillery fire, Campbell rode along the line.

'Remember, there is no retreat from here,' he called. 'You must die where you stand.'

Then as the Russian hussars got nearer he ordered them to stand up, in two lines, with his bearded Highlanders in the centre. Some could hardly contain their excitement and seemed on the point of advancing. '93rd! 93rd! Damn all that eagerness!' he shouted.

Seeing the tall bonnets of the Highlanders, the Russians charged. 'The ground flew beneath their horses' feet,' wrote Russell, 'fathering speed at every stride, they dashed on towards that thin red streak topped with a line of steel. The Turks fired a volley at eight hundred yards and ran. As the

Russians came within six hundred yards, down went that line of steel in front, and out rang a rolling volley of Minié musketry.'

The Russians checked, wheeled to the left and came on. Calmly dressing the line to face the new direction of the charge, Campbell ordered another volley at 250 yards as his artillery supports fired roundshot and grape. This time the Russians turned and fled, leaving no dead although many horses and men were wounded and collapsed after regaining the Heights.

'Bravo! Well done, Sir Colin! Bravo 93rd!' cried the knot of spectators around Lord Raglan on the Sapouné Heights.[13] But the battle was far from over because the main body of Russian cavalry, about 2,000 lancers and hussars under the command of General Rykov, had continued its advance down the North Valley. With their black horses, dark grey overcoats and broad-topped shakos covered by black oilskins, they looked from a distance to be 'a black-looking mass'. Reaching the gap in the Heights between No. 5 and No. 6 Redoubts, they wheeled to the left and began to cross the slight rise into the South Valley.[14]

On his way to support Campbell, Scarlett was picking his way through the vines and orchards to the left of the cavalry camp when Lieutenant Alexander Elliot, one of his aides-de-camp, happened to glance 'towards the ridge on his left, and saw its top fretted with lances. Another moment and the sky-line was broken by evident squadrons of horse.' Short-sighted, Scarlett needed some convincing that they were indeed Russians.[15]

At almost the same time, Captain Shakespear's troop of horse artillery spotted the enemy horsemen and opened fire, as did some French artillery on the Sapouné Heights and the field battery near Kadikoi. This may well have caused the Russians to pause, giving Scarlett vital seconds to form his nearest squadrons into line for the charge. He was not helped by the fact that they had to pick their way through the broken ground of the vineyard – comprised of 'tangled roots and briars, swampy holes' – and over a dry ditch before they could come to grips with the enemy.

Lord George Paget, watching from the Light Brigade's position some 400 yards to the west, did not give the 'Heavies' much chance: 'The dense mass of Russian cavalry, animated and encouraged . . . by the successes of the morning . . . advancing at a rapid pace over ground most favourable, and appearing as if they must *annihilate* and *swallow* up all before them; on the other hand, the handful of redcoats, *floundering* in the vineyard, on their way to meet them. Suddenly . . . the Russians halt, look about, and appear bewildered.'[16]

In fact, the Russian commander was carrying out a textbook manoeuvre by extending his front two ranks into two pincer arms that would envelop the small British force. It was a fatal error. By now clear of the vineyard, Scarlett ordered the charge and set off towards the enemy, followed closely by Elliot, his trumpeter and his orderly. Pulling ahead of the Scots Greys and a squadron of the Inniskillings who were surprised by this unorthodox advance, the lone quartet was quickly swallowed by the centre of the immobile Russian horde.

Hacking about with his sword anyhow, Scarlett received five slight wounds and a dent in his brass helmet. Elliot, a more skilled swordsman who had seen distinguished service in India with the Bengal Light Cavalry, was less fortunate and was wounded 14 times, including a blow through his cocked hat that would have killed him but for a silk handkerchief he was using as padding.

Next into action were the Scots Greys and a squadron of the Inniskillings (Tennyson's 'three hundred'). Moving at little more than a trot, they forced their way into the main body 'partly between the files, dismounting some of the Russians, and partly at the angles formed by the Russian centre checking. They then spread out something like a fan . . . After the first crash our men knocked or pulled them off their horses in every conceivable way.' As the two Russian wings began to close in, the remaining squadrons came successively into action: first the 5th Dragoon Guards, to the left rear of the Scots Greys. 'We went in with a shout and a yell,' wrote Lieutenant Richard Temple Godman, the adjutant, 'and for about five minutes we were all hacking away at each other, pistols discharging, and the devil's own row.'

At the same time the remaining squadron of Inniskillings, which had been leading the brigade column, charged the inward-swinging left wing 'at a splendid pace, the men sitting well down, and in good dressing . . . and catching [the Russians] as they did obliquely and on the bridle arm, unhorsed whole troops of them'.

Lastly, the 4th Dragoon Guards led by Colonel Hodge charged into the Russian right wing and it was this impact, along with that of the Inniskillings on the left wing, that was probably decisive, although the Royals sent by Lucan had also joined the mêlée. 'In five minutes,' wrote William Russell, 'the Muscovy horse, beaten out of shape and formation, disintegrated and pierced by Greys and Inniskillings, reeling from the shock of the 4th and 5th Dragoon Guards and the Royals, retired in disorder. It was a marvellous sight! There arose a great shout from the spectators. Curzon was sent down by Lord Raglan with the condensed eulogy "Well done!".[17]

As the beaten foe neared the ridge, their officers managed to stop a number in an attempt to rally them. But C Troop of the Royal Horse Artillery, which had galloped down from the Chersonese Plateau, now opened up from 700 yards, forcing them to retire into the North Valley.

Years later, Ivan Ivanovitch, a young Russian hussar officer who was slightly wounded in the battle, described the charge of the Heavy Brigade as 'magnificent', but put its success down to the 'bad management' of the Russian commander. 'The fatal mistake we made in the morning was to receive the charge . . . standing instead of meeting it with a counter shock. We had so many more men than you that had we continued our charge downhill instead of calling a halt just at the critical moment, we should have carried everything before us.'

Lucan, who had caught up with the heavy cavalry shortly before the charge began, later claimed to have ordered the 4th Dragoon Guards' decisive action, much to the anger of Colonel Hodge. 'I do think that Lord Lucan might as well have given me the credit of our flank charge,' he wrote to his mother in December 1854, 'and not have told such a falsehood about it in saying that he ordered it, when he never gave any orders at all.'

Casualties were remarkably one-sided. 'I am happy to say our brigade lost but seven men dead, but had a considerable number wounded, some mortally,' wrote Lieutenant Godman on 26 October. 'The ground was strewn with swords, broken and whole, trumpets, helmets, carbines, etc, while a quantity of men were scattered all along as far as we pursued. There must have been some forty or fifty of the enemy dead, besides wounded, for I went over the ground today to look at it.'[18]

Godman's estimate was remarkably accurate: the Heavy Brigade lost 8 killed and 70 wounded; the Russians a total of 300. But considering the numbers involved – 700 British and 2,000 Russians – the fatalities were very light.

This was partly accounted for by reason of the fact that many of the Russians had failed to sharpen their curved swords. One private in the 4th Dragoon Guards had 15 head cuts, 'none of which was more than skin deep'. Elliot, too, had survived multiple cuts and the worst, behind his ear, was apparently inflicted by one of the Scots Greys. The British, on the other hand, complained that their sword points could not pierce the thick Russian overcoats; they were more effective in cutting than stabbing. 'The wounds our long straight swords made were terrible,' wrote Temple

Godman, 'heads nearly cut off apparently at a stroke, and a great number must have died who got away.'[19]

Oddly enough, the greatest controversy surrounding the charge concerns Lord Cardigan's failure to support the Heavy Brigade by attacking the Russians in the flank.

He was positioned with three of his regiments – the 11th, 13th and 17th – on rising ground at the end of the Causeway Heights with a clear view of the action less than 500 yards away. His remaining regiments – the 4th and 8th – were in a hollow a little to the rear, facing the lower ground leading to the North Valley.

Cardigan later justified his inaction with the following sworn statement: 'I had been ordered into a particular position by Lieutenant-General the Earl of Lucan, my superior officer, with orders on no account to leave it, and to defend it against any attack of Russians.'

Lucan, on the other hand, gave a slightly different version of his own words: 'I am going to leave you. Well, you remember that you are placed here by Lord Raglan himself for the defence of this position. My instructions to you are to attack anything and everything that shall come within reach of you, but you will be careful of columns or squares of infantry.'[20]

The different interpretation of the order was to prove crucial. Cardigan had formed the impression that his role was strictly defensive, to only fight if attacked, while Lucan expected him to go on the offensive if anything came 'within reach'. Consequently, when the Heavy Brigade engaged the Russian cavalry barely a quarter of a mile away, Lucan assumed that Cardigan would attack.

According to Kinglake (who claimed to have 'conclusive' proof), Lucan 'was bitterly vexed by the inaction of the Light Brigade, and at the close of the combat he sent one of his aides . . . with a message which enjoined Lord Cardigan, in future, to lose no opportunity of making a flank attack'. Lucan's own version of the message was that 'when he was attacking in front, it was his (Lord Cardigan's) duty to support him by a flank attack, and that Lord Cardigan might always depend upon receiving from him similar support'. Cardigan always denied ever receiving such a message.

But even if Cardigan's recollection of his instructions was accurate, he should still have used his initiative to take advantage of the opportunity that was presented to him, particularly after the Russians had begun to retreat. 'There was the occasion,' noted the Vicomte de Nöe, a member of Canrobert's staff watching from the ridge, 'there should have been exercised the initiative of the cavalry general [Cardigan], and later in the day it was made apparent that bravery is no sufficient substitute for initiative.'

His failure to do so can only be put down to his inexperience on the one hand, and his feud with Lucan on the other. Anxious not to give his superior a chance to criticise him, he followed his orders – as he saw them – to the letter. But his frustration and envy were obvious to all as he rode up and down the line, muttering: 'Damn those Heavies, they have the laugh of us this day.'[21]

Even Captain William Morris of the 17th Lancers, the most experienced officer in the Light Brigade, could not persuade him to act. Nicknamed the 'Pocket Hercules' on account of his short, stocky build, Morris, 34, had commanded a squadron of the 16th Lancers during the First Sikh War in 1846. Returning to Britain the following year, he joined the 17th Lancers, taking time off in 1851 to pass through the Senior Department of the Military College with a first-class certificate. Because of this he began the war on Lucan's staff, and was only appointed to the temporary command of the 17th Lancers after its colonel had fallen ill and the second-in-command had died. The latter event had taken place only a few days before, and Morris was still wearing his staff officer's blue frock-coat and matching forage cap with gold-edged peak.

According to the regimental trumpeter, John Brown, Morris spotted the Russian cavalry advancing over the ridge and immediately ordered the 17th Lancers to go 'threes right' so as to be in position to attack its right flank. Brown then sounded the trot, but this alerted Cardigan who quickly appeared on the scene. 'What are you doing, Captain Morris?' he asked indignantly. 'Front your regiment!'

'Look there, my lord,' Morris replied, pointing with his sword at the advancing enemy. 'Let me take the regiment on to the attack.'

'Remain where you are, sir, until you get orders!' said Cardigan firmly.

Minutes later, with the Russians in confused retreat, Morris tried again. Riding up to Cardigan, he said: 'My lord, are you not going to charge the flying enemy?'

'No,' said Cardigan, 'we have orders to remain here.'

'But, my lord, it is our positive duty to follow up this advantage.'

'No, we must remain here.'

'Do, my lord, do allow me to charge them with the 17th,' Morris pleaded. 'Sir, my lord, they are in disorder.'

'No, no, sir!' came the hoarse, sharp reply loud enough to be heard in the ranks behind.

At this, Morris angrily wheeled his horse back towards his right squadron and, slapping his sword against his leg, said: 'My God, my God, what a chance we are losing!'

Captain White, the adjutant, then rode up to him and said: 'If I were in command of the regiment, I would attack by myself and stand a court-martial. There is a C.B. staring you in the face as you cannot fail.'[22]

In a sworn statement made after the war, Cardigan vehemently denied that Morris ever 'gave any advice, or made any proposal of the sort', stressing that 'it was not his duty to do so' and he 'did not commit such an irregularity'.

He later contradicted himself, and there is no doubt that Morris made such a request – the question is, when? In a letter to the Horse Guards, Morris stated that he had 'asked Lord Cardigan to attack the Russian cavalry in flank at the time they were engaged with the Heavy Brigade'. Captain the Honourable Godfrey Morgan of the 17th Lancers confirmed this in an affidavit in 1863, but put the timing slightly later: 'I perfectly remember Captain . . . Morris, in a moment of excitement, suggesting to the Earl of Cardigan that he should attack the retreating enemy.'

Cardigan himself later admitted to Kinglake that Morris had 'sought to push forward with his regiment' and that he had 'stopped the attempt', but at a moment when it had 'become too late to act with effect'. Such a tardy confession, however, lacks conviction, particularly in the light of his earlier denial.[23]

In any case, Cardigan could see for himself the glorious opportunity for making a flank attack, particularly after the Russians were engaged by the Heavy Brigade. 'We then expected to be ordered to sweep down on their right flank,' wrote Sergeant-Major Loy Smith of the 11th:

> Had we done so at the proper moment, I feel that few of them would have escaped, being either killed or made prisoners. But, much to our chagrin, we were held as spectators of this unequal combat for more than ten minutes. We could distinctly hear the din and shouts of our people, being only a few hundred yards off. Our excitement became very great and I am of the opinion that nothing but the strict discipline under which we were held prevented us breaking loose to assist our comrades of the Heavies.

But, to our joy and relief, we saw this mass of Russian cavalry
retreat over the Causeway Heights the same way they came.

Initially, Lord George Paget sympathised with Cardigan, pointing out that
to 'have effectually cut off the retreat of the enemy, or to have even
harassed them in their flight, more than a quarter of a mile of ground to
our right front must have been gained, and that down a somewhat steep
and broken descent'. Consequently, the Light Brigade would have to have
'moved off its ground the moment the enemy first appeared', a step which
was 'unjustifiable, until the result of the combat was known'. Later, however, after speaking to a number of men who had been present with the
forward regiments, his confidence in this opinion was shaken. 'Certainly,'
he wrote, 'the contrary opinion is very general among those who, being in
the first line, were in a better position to judge than myself.'[24]

The time was now 9.30 a.m. and a curious lull ensued as the Russians consolidated their positions along three sides of the North Valley. Their beaten
cavalry had retired to the eastern end and re-formed behind a battery of
eight guns manned by Don Cossacks. But a powerful force of eleven
infantry battalions and 32 guns still occupied the Causeway Heights as far
as No. 3 Redoubt, while Colonel Jabrokritsky with eight battalions, four
squadrons and 14 guns was established on the slopes of the Fedioukine
Hills to the north.

Raglan could see all this from his elevated position, and was anxious to
follow up Scarlett's brilliant victory by retaking the Causeway Heights. But
there was still no sign of his infantry and the minutes were ticking by.
Finally, at 10.15, he decided he could wait no longer and sent Lucan the
following order (known as the Third Order): 'Cavalry to advance and
take advantage of any opportunity to recover the Heights. They will be
supported by the infantry which have been ordered. Advance on two
fronts.'

Lucan rightly understood the 'Heights' to mean the Causeway Heights,
but wrongly assumed that Raglan did not wish him to take any action until
the infantry had arrived. However, it was a reasonable assumption given
the rather imprecise wording of the order, Raglan's restraint of the cavalry
thus far in the campaign, and the fact that it was generally considered
unthinkable to launch cavalry without support against fixed positions of
infantry and artillery. In consequence, he ordered the Light Brigade to

move into the North Valley to a point facing east between No. 4 and No. 5 Redoubts, while the Heavy Brigade would remain on the other side of the ridge. They would then be in a position to attack on two fronts as soon as their supports were in place. 'No infantry had at this time arrived from the heights of Sebastopol,' stated Lucan. 'I remained myself between my two brigades, anxiously awaiting their arrival.'[25]

Cardigan, too, was nervous but for a different reason. From his new location facing directly down the North Valley, he could clearly see the whole of the Russian position. Perceiving, rightly, that his brigade would soon be ordered to advance, he sent Lieutenant Maxse to warn Lucan 'that the hills on both sides of the valley . . . were occupied by Russian riflemen and artillery'. Lucan later claimed that Cardigan went further than this and 'objected to his brigade being placed where it was, as there were batteries of the enemy on the left, which would open up on it'. His verbal response was: 'Tell Lord Cardigan that he is placed there by Lord Raglan's orders, but that I will take care of him.'[26]

By now, the Light Brigade was dismounted and drawn up in the same two lines as before, with the 11th Hussars on the left of the front line, the 17th Lancers in the middle and the 13th on the right. The second line was a short way off, with the 4th Light Dragoons on the left and the 8th Hussars on the right. As they waited, some men smoked, officers drank rum from flasks and others ate whatever food was available – mainly biscuits and boiled eggs.

Unfortunately for them, while Cambridge's 1st Division – with further to go – was making satisfactory progress, Cathcart's 4th Division was not. Its commander had needed to be persuaded that this was not another false alarm, and his men were tired from their exertions in the trenches. Also, instead of following the Woronzoff Road, the 4th had marched south-eastwards towards the Col and was therefore behind the 1st Division.

As the minutes ebbed away, Raglan became increasingly impatient. Suspecting that Russian morale had been dealt a major blow by the defeat of their cavalry, he was convinced that an assault along the Causeway Heights would cause them to withdraw from the redoubts. But Lucan would not move without support. Suddenly, an eagle-eyed member of Raglan's staff piped up: 'By Jove, they're going to take away the guns!'

Through field-glasses, the Russians could be seen bringing forward horses with lasso tackle to remove the captured naval 12-pounders. The great Duke of Wellington had reputedly never lost an artillery piece and Raglan, his devoted lieutenant, was anxious to retain the same proud record. Turning to Airey, his Quartermaster-General, he dictated an urgent order to Lucan (known as the Fourth Order): 'Lord Raglan wishes the cavalry to advance rapidly to the front – follow the enemy and try to prevent the enemy carrying away the guns. Troop Horse Artillery may accompany. French cavalry is on your left. Immediate.'

After checking the wording of the pencil-written order, Raglan handed it not to his own duty aide, Captain Leslie, but to Captain Nolan, Airey's aide-de-camp and the best horseman on the staff. It was an unfortunate choice given Nolan's volatile temper and his well-known contempt for the cavalry commanders. According to Brigadier-General Hugh Rose, the British liaison officer with the French Army, Nolan was 'much excited' and called out, 'I'll lead them myself, I'll lead them on', as he spurred down the precipitous slope.

Raglan's parting words to him were: 'Tell Lord Lucan the cavalry is to attack immediately.'[27]

Minutes later Nolan had reached the valley floor and galloped through the interval between the 13th Light Dragoons and the 17th Lancers. Spotting Captain Morris directly in front, he called out: 'Where is Lord Lucan?'

'There,' replied Morris, pointing, 'there, on the right front! What is it to be, Nolan, are we going to charge?'

'You will see! You will see!' shouted Nolan over his shoulder as he galloped away.

According to Lucan, by the time Nolan reached him 'the whole of the infantry had not arrived'. Those which had, 'instead of being formed for an attack, or to support an attack . . . were, the greater part of them, sitting or lying down with their arms piled'.

He read the order from Raglan with growing alarm. Now he was being asked to advance to recover the guns without even infantry support. It was madness. Hesitating, he impressed upon Nolan the 'uselessness' and 'dangers' of such an attack.

'Lord Raglan's orders are that the cavalry should attack immediately,' Nolan retorted.

Seven hundred feet lower than Raglan, his view obscured by rising ground, Lucan could not see the captured naval guns being towed away. Did Lord Raglan have a different objective in mind? 'Attack, sir! Attack what? What guns, sir?' he demanded.

Waving his hand vaguely westwards, where he remembered the redoubts to be, Nolan exclaimed: 'There, my lord, is your enemy! There are your guns!'

Lucan later claimed that from his position he could see 'neither enemy nor guns' and that Nolan's gesture was towards 'the further end of the valley'. There, clearly visible to Cardigan and the Light Brigade at least, was the Don Cossack battery of eight cannon, the sun glinting off their polished barrels.

At this crucial moment, according to the interpreter James Blunt (who claimed to be one of only three onlookers), Lucan 'appeared to be surprised and irritated at the impetuous and disrespectful attitude and tone of Captain Nolan, looked at him sternly but made no answer, and after some hesitation proceeded to give orders to Lord Cardigan to charge the enemy with the Light Brigade'.

Even accounting for Nolan's vague gesture, Lucan's misinterpretation of Raglan's order is an enigma – not least because two days later, in a report to Raglan, he wrote: 'The Division took up a position with a view of supporting an attack upon the Heights when being instructed to make a rapid advance to the front to prevent the enemy carrying away the guns lost by the Turkish troops in the morning. I ordered the Light Brigade to advance in 2 lines, and supported them with the Heavy Brigade.'

In other words, he was well aware that the objective of the attack was to recover the naval guns. Why, then, did he order the Light Brigade down the North Valley instead of along the Causeway Heights? The only possible explanation is that a combination of Nolan's insolent gesture and the absence of any mention of the 'Heights' in the Fourth Order had led him to believe that Raglan intended him to attempt to save the guns by attacking down the valley.

After all, Raglan's actual intention – an unsupported cavalry attack against positions on the Causeway Heights – was, on the surface, only marginally less hazardous. Russell later wrote:

> I do not understand, even at this moment, how the Light Cavalry could have succeeded in doing that which, it is said, Lord Raglan intended they should accomplish. The guns were in Redoubts Nos 1, 2 and 3. The first was plainly inaccessible to horsemen – to have charged 2 and 3 in the face of the force of Infantry, Artillery and Cavalry, the enemy had within supporting distance of it, would have been quixotic in the extreme.[28]

Lucan now made his final plans: the Light Brigade would lead the attack with the Heavy Brigade in support. For some inexplicable reason, however, he failed to order the two troops of horse artillery, 11 guns in all, to provide covering fire. 'It had been the custom on brigade field days for artillery fire to precede a cavalry attack,' wrote Sergeant-Major Loy. 'Had this simple rule been followed out on the Causeway Heights for a few minutes before we moved off, it would have been of the greatest advantage to us.'

Instead, Lucan simply sent orders for the cavalry to remount. But with only one aide-de-camp, Captain Charteris, at hand (according to Blunt), it is just possible that he asked Nolan to warn the Light Brigade. Certainly, Private Wightman of the 17th Lancers recalled seeing Nolan ride up to Cardigan for a 'momentary talk . . . at the close of which he drew his sword with a flourish as if greatly excited'. It has been suggested that, on hearing Cardigan's objections to attacking, Nolan taunted him by asking if the Light Brigade was afraid. Cardigan is said to have responded furiously: 'By God! If I come through this alive, I'll have you court-martialled for speaking to me in that manner!'[29]

At some stage, possibly after this exchange, Nolan received permission from Captain Morris to ride in the charge with the 17th Lancers, and he positioned himself in front of the right squadron.

Meanwhile Lucan, mindful of his brother-in-law's earlier doubts, had decided to give the unwelcome order in person. Trotting over to where Cardigan was waiting, mounted at the head of his brigade, he said: 'Lord Cardigan, you will attack the Russians in the valley.'

'Certainly, my lord,' Cardigan replied, dropping the point of his sword at the same time, 'but allow me to point out to you that there is a battery in front, a battery on each flank, and the ground is covered with Russian riflemen.'

'I cannot help that,' was the retort, 'it is Lord Raglan's positive order that the Light Brigade is to attack the enemy.'

Lucan then added that he wished him 'to advance very steadily and quietly', and that it would be better to narrow his front by moving the 11th Hussars into a supporting position just behind. Considering this an affront to his old regiment, Cardigan 'strenuously' objected, but Lucan insisted and gave the order to Colonel Douglas in person.

Resigned to his fate, Cardigan rode over to Lord George Paget, commanding the 4th Light Dragoons. There was little love lost between them, but Paget was to lead the support line in the attack and his cooperation might be crucial.

'Lord George, we are ordered to make an attack to the front. You will take command of the second line, and I expect your best support; *mind, your best support,'* said Cardigan pointedly, noting with irritation that his subordinate was languidly smoking a cigar.

'Of course, my lord,' Paget came back equally sharply, resenting the inference, 'you shall have my *best* support.'[30]

Cardigan then returned to his position at the head of the brigade and placed himself about two horses' lengths in front of his two aides-de-camp, Lieutenant Maxse and Cornet Sir George Wombwell, themselves three lengths ahead of Nolan and the officers commanding the first line, Captains Morris and Oldham. As Lucan had ordered the 11th Hussars to fall back, the brigade was now deployed in three lines, each two horses deep. The first line had the 17th Lancers on the left and the 13th Light Dragoons on the right. A hundred yards further back, and slightly to the left rear, the 11th Hussars made up the second line. The third line was the same distance still further back, with the 4th Light Dragoons on the left and the 8th Hussars on the right.

In the final seconds before the brigade hurtled to its fate, as an ominous silence fell upon the valley, disturbed only by the creak of leather and the jingle of harness, Cardigan cut an impressive figure astride his magnificent chestnut charger, Ronald. 'His long military seat was perfection,' noted Private Wightman from the front rank of the 17th. 'He was in the full uniform of his old corps, the 11th Hussars, and he wore the pelisse, not slung, but on like a patrol jacket, its front one blaze of gold lace. His drawn sword was in his hand at the slope, and never saw I man fitter to wield the weapon.'

'Here goes the last of the Brudenells,' Cardigan muttered as he turned his horse to face the massed ranks behind him.

'The brigade will advance,' he said in his strong, hoarse voice. 'First squadron of the 17th Lancers direct.'

Then, to his trumpeter Britten: 'Sound the advance!'

It was 11 o'clock.

Cardigan said later that even at this point he 'still thought that the order must be a mistake and, to give time for a reverse of it, put his men slowly into motion, first into a walk, then into a trot'.

Other witnesses confirm this, and the 676 riders were still at the trot after 200 yards when Captain Nolan surged ahead of the front line. 'That won't do, Nolan!' shouted Captain Morris. 'We've a long way to go, and must be steady'.

But Nolan ignored him and, shouting and waving his sword, began to veer across the front of the 17th Lancers in the direction of the Causeway

Heights. Suddenly aware that the brigade was not going to wheel to the right to attack the redoubts, Nolan had taken it upon himself to correct the awful error. To an infuriated Cardigan, however, it appeared as if the eccentric Nolan was hurrying the brigade along. A junior staff officer, with no business taking part in the charge, was daring to precede him at the head of the brigade! 'No, no!' Cardigan bellowed. 'Get back into line!'

But Nolan would not listen. Onward he galloped, across Cardigan's front, shouting as he went.

With less than 50 yards separating the pair, a shell burst between them and a fragment of shrapnel hit Nolan square in the chest, piercing his heart. 'From his raised sword-hand dropped the sword, but the arm remained erect,' noted Private Wightman. 'All the other limbs so curled in on the contorted trunk as by a spasm, that we wondered how for the moment the huddled form kept the saddle. It was the convulsive twitch of the bridle hand inward on the chest that caused the charger to wheel rearward so abruptly. The weird shriek and the awful face as rider and horse disappeared haunt me now to this day, the first horror of that ride of horrors.'

Cardigan, too, heard him 'utter a shriek & a wail more like a woman's than a man's' and saw 'him turn his horse to the right'. Unaware that Nolan had been wounded, he 'thought the shot had frightened him'. But his contempt for Nolan was soon replaced by fear for his own life as cannon fire from three directions began to fall in earnest. 'The shower of grape shot and round shot . . . was awful,' he recalled, 'besides the flash fire of artillery and the flames which swept down the ranks every moment . . . I considered it certain death, but I led straight and no man flinched.'

He was convinced that he '*must* be hit somewhere' and wondered whether it would 'be in the chest' or if his horse would be 'struck first'.

But as Cardigan rode on unscathed, others were not so lucky. 'A corporal who rode on the right was struck by a shot or shell full in the face, completely smashing it, his blood and brains bespattering us who rode near,' observed Private Mitchell of the 13th. Single shells brought down up to four men and horses at a time, causing the survivors to swear as they jostled in their attempts to close ranks.

'The round shot passed through us and the shells burst over and amongst us, causing great havoc,' recorded Sergeant-Major Loy Smith of the 11th. 'The first man of my troop that was struck was Private Young, a cannon ball taking off his right arm . . . He coolly fell back and asked me what he was to do. I replied, "Turn your horse about and get to the rear as fast as you can."'

Hell had opened up upon us from front and either flank [recalled Private Wightman], 'and it kept open upon us during the minutes – they seemed like hours – which passed while we traversed the mile and a quarter at the end of which was the enemy. The broken and fast-thinning ranks raised rugged peals of wild fierce cheering that only swelled the louder as the shot and shell from the battery tore gaps through us, and the enfilading musketry fire from the Infantry in both flanks brought down horses and men . . . "Close in! close in!" was the constant command of the squadron and troop officers as the casualties made gaps in the ragged line, but the order was scarcely needed, for of their own instance and, as it seemed, mechanically, men and horses alike sought to regain touch.'

Amidst the cacophony of battle, Cardigan ordered his trumpeter to sound the gallop, but he never had the chance to sound the charge because seconds later he was unhorsed. By now the leading squadron, the right of the 17th, was surging forward, anxious to be out of the deadly crossfire, causing Cardigan to shout hoarsely: 'Steady, steady, Captain Morris!'

Soon after, John Lee, the right-hand man of the regiment, received a mortal wound and, grasping the arm of Wightman, his neighbour, uttered, 'Domino, chum!' before toppling out of the saddle. His old grey mare, also hit, kept going for some distance, 'treading on and tearing out her entrails as she galloped, till at length she dropped with a strange shriek'.

Now it was the turn of Captain White, commanding the leading squadron, to 'force the pace'. As he later admitted, he was desperate 'to get out of such a murderous fire, and into the guns, as being the best of the two evils', and consequently pressed forward until he was almost level with his brigadier. Cardigan checked him by placing the flat of his sword against his chest and telling him not to ride before his chief. Then, turning to the whole regiment, he shouted: 'Steady! Steady! The 17th Lancers!'

The respite was only momentary and seconds later, to prevent himself from being swallowed up by the front rank of the 17th, Cardigan 'let his charger out from the gallop to the charge'.

Now just 80 yards distant, the battery of guns fired a point-blank salvo of grapeshot which brought down men and horses in heaps. Among the killed were Captains Oldham and Goad, and Cornet Montgomery, of the 13th, and Captain Winter and Lieutenant Thomson of the 17th. But

Cardigan remained strangely immune from injury as all around men were hit.

Sergeant Talbot had his head taken off by roundshot, 'yet for thirty yards further the headless body kept the saddle, the lance at the charge firmly gripped under the right arm'. Wightman was hit in the right knee and shin by musket balls, his horse wounded three times in the neck, but he refused to fall out. Within yards of the cloud of white smoke that now masked the eight-gun battery, he could see Cardigan, directly ahead of him and 'steady as a church', raise his sword in the air and turn to shout a final command: 'Steady! Steady! Close in!'

Then Cardigan disappeared into the smoke as a final volley of shells crashed into the front line from the flank, unseating Captain White and stunning Wightman. Cardigan rode on, temporarily blinded, when suddenly a huge explosion accompanied by a flash of flame announced the presence of a gun just six yards ahead. So close was the blast, causing his horse to veer to the left, that he thought his right leg had been smashed, though it had only been struck by the aftershock. Then he was through 'at a gallop between the limber-carriages and tumbrils, by a gangway so narrow as hardly to allow passage for two horsemen going abreast'.[31]

Lord Lucan, meanwhile, was leading the Heavy Brigade forward at a somewhat more leisurely pace when, shortly after passing No. 4 Redoubt, they were subjected to what Colonel Yorke of the Royals described as 'the hottest fire that was probably ever witnessed'. Yet the regiments 'were beautifully steady' and Yorke 'never had a better line in a Field Day, the only swerving was to let through the ranks the wounded & dead men & horses of the Light Brigade, which were even then thickly scattered over the plain'.

But the guns were soon finding their mark, and during the next few terrible minutes the Heavies suffered more casualties than they had during their victorious charge. The Royals alone lost 21 men, including Yorke whose left leg was shattered. Lucan was slightly wounded in the leg by a musket ball, while Captain Charteris, his aide-de-camp, was killed and a further two members of his staff were wounded.

When he had reached a point roughly level with No. 3 Redoubt, and the Light Brigade had disappeared into the distance, Lucan decided that enough was enough. Remarking to Lord William Paulet that the Heavies 'were already sufficiently close to protect the Light Cavalry should they be pursued by the enemy', and that he 'could not allow them to be sacrificed as had been the Light Brigade', he ordered them to be halted. Only after two subsequent withdrawals were the leading regiments, the Royals and the Scots Greys, finally moved out of danger. There the brigade waited.

Writing later, Lucan pointed out that the Heavy Brigade 'would have been destroyed' had not the 'Chasseurs d'Afrique at this time silenced one of these batteries'. He might have added that this timely charge by French cavalry also greatly assisted the retiring remnants of the Light Brigade.[32]

The charge was undertaken by two squadrons of the 4th Chasseurs d'Afrique, a regiment only recently arrived in the Crimea, and part of the brigade of French cavalry which had been ordered down into the plain earlier in the day. Mounted on Algerian horses, these French irregulars had a formidable record in North African colonial wars.

They were sent against the nearest Russian battery of eight guns on the slopes of the Fedioukine Heights by their divisional commander, General Morris, in an attempt to assist the Light Brigade. Attacking the gun positions from the flank over broken and scrubby ground, these 150 horsemen under Major Abdelal managed to break through the line of skirmishers and force the hurried withdrawal of all eight guns. Counter-attacked by infantry, they themselves withdrew. At a cost of ten dead and 28 wounded, they had effectively neutralised most of the fire from one flank of the valley.

As Cardigan emerged at the gallop from the smoke behind the battery, he found himself alone and bearing down on a large body of slowly retiring Russian cavalry. Seeing the single horseman, however, they stopped and fronted. Cardigan was within 20 yards of them when he finally managed to halt Ronald. 'All along the confronting ranks of grey-coated horsemen,' wrote Kinglake, 'he found himself hungrily eyed by a breed of the human race whose numberless cages of teeth stared out with a wonderful clearness from between the writhed lips, and seemed all to be gnashing or clenched.'

Cardigan assumed that they were greedily eyeing the gold front of his pelisse. In fact, a noble officer by the name of Radzivill, an acquaintance from before the war, had recognised him and offered some Cossacks a reward for his capture unharmed. Two of them moved forward menacingly to take his surrender.

As this was happening, Private Wightman rode clear of the smoke and almost bumped into Lieutenant Maxse, Cardigan's aide-de-camp, who had been unseated and badly wounded.

'For God's sake, Lancer, don't ride over me!' shouted Maxse, before pointing towards Cardigan and saying: 'See where Lord Cardigan is, rally on him!'

Wightman at once set off in support of his chief, but was attacked by a Cossack who speared him in the right thigh. Retaliating, he chased the Cossack and finally unhorsed him by driving a lance into his back in front of two Russian guns which by this time were in the possession of two sergeant-majors from the 13th Light Dragoons. Having lost sight of Cardigan, Wightman did not see him again.

One man who did, Captain Percy Smith of the 13th, noticed that Cardigan, although being approached by Cossacks, kept his 'sword at the slope and did not seem to take any trouble to defend himself'. At the same time, he refused to surrender, at which the Cossacks jabbed at him with their lances. This attack was observed by two other men from the 13th, Lieutenant Johnson and Private John Keely, but their horses were badly wounded as they tried to intervene. One lance thrust had lightly wounded Cardigan in the hip, and now Johnson saw another Cossack jab at him 'with his lance resting on his right arm, his back half turned towards his Lordship, and thrusting with his left hand'. It seemed to Johnson as if the point had gone through Cardigan, but in fact it had caught his pelisse and nearly forced him from the saddle. Fortunately this last thrust, the 'right rear point', was made as the Cossack was about to join his comrades, who were retreating as the remnants of the Light Brigade advanced. Seconds later, Johnson saw Cardigan 'cantering quietly' away in the opposite direction.

According to his own account, Cardigan then returned to the battery but 'found no part of the brigade'. In the distance, however, he could see men of the 13th Light Dragoons and 17th Lancers 'retreating in knots up the valley' and, assuming that they 'constituted the entire remnants of the first line', he decided to follow them. In Kinglake's words, 'he satisfied himself that, so far as concerned the business of rallying or otherwise interfering with the shattered fragments of his first line, there was nothing he could usefully do, without first following their retreat'.

In fact, as Kinglake points out, the men 'Cardigan saw retreating were, all of them, men disabled . . . either by their own wounds, or else by the wounds of their chargers'. The formed remnants of the first line, on the other hand, were at that moment engaged with the vastly superior force of

Russian cavalry, while the second and third lines were in the process of joining them.

Later, Cardigan tried to justify his premature withdrawal by saying that his 'primary duty was with the first line' and that he 'could nowhere see his supports'. Neither argument is convincing: his duty was clearly the well-being of his whole brigade and, in any case, he made no effort to ascertain whether any significant part of his first line was still behind the guns; furthermore, it seems strange that he could not see his 'supports' when many survivors of the third line later claimed in sworn statements to have seen him:

> Lieutenant Edward Phillips, 8th Hussars: 'While the regiment was still advancing down the valley, I saw the Earl of Cardigan coming back. He passed the left flank of the regiment.'
>
> Trumpeter James Donaghue, 8th Hussars: 'I saw the Earl of Cardigan galloping past us towards the rear, coming from the position of the Russian guns in front of us . . . He was mounted on a chestnut horse, and wore the uniform of the 11th Hussars.'
>
> Private Daniel Deeran, 4th Light Dragoons: 'When we were charging up to the battery and within 300 yards of it, we met Lord Cardigan alone, returning to the rear on a chestnut horse; he was cantering back, and was on the left of [us].'
>
> Private John Ford, 4th Light Dragoons: 'My horse was shot as we were advancing to the Russian guns, and fell with me, my leg being under him. This was about 300 yards from the battery. While lying on the ground looking for some one to assist me . . ., I saw Lord Cardigan to the left of where I was lying, cantering to the rear. He was quite alone.'

In all, one officer and six men of both regiments were prepared to swear that they had seen Cardigan retiring *before* they had even reached the guns.

Cornet Hunt of the 4th Light Dragoons, on the other hand, recognised an officer who retired past his regiment on a chestnut horse as Cornet Houghton of the 11th Hussars. Hunt was convinced that Houghton was 'taken for Lord Cardigan by the men of the 4th and 8th'. Houghton did indeed retire early, having been mortally wounded in the forehead by a piece of shell during the early stages of the advance. But it would have been almost impossible to mistake him for Cardigan, given the latter's well-known appearance, their disparity in age, and the fact that Houghton's face was covered in blood from his wound.

Kinglake, therefore, seems justified in his comment that while Cardigan 'was magnanimously regardless of his mere personal safety, yet in other respects, he much remembered himself and all but forgot his brigade'.[33]

At the head of his left squadron, Captain Morris and about 20 men passed by the extreme right of the battery and, emerging from the smoke, found themselves confronted by at least two squadrons of regular hussars. Without pausing Morris charged, shouting: 'Now remember what I have told you, men, and keep together.'

Many of the Russians fled, unaware that their assailants were so few, but others held their ground and were soon joined by hordes of Cossacks. Temporarily defenceless, his sword buried in the body of a Russian officer, Morris suffered terrible wounds to his head from two sabre cuts and a lance thrust, and was eventually taken prisoner (later, like Sir George Wombwell, he escaped and managed to reach the safety of British lines before collapsing). Most of his men were either killed or captured.

As the rest of the front line entered the smoke-laden battery, some artillerymen sought safety under their carriages and limbers, while others tried to hitch up and tow away their guns. They were ruthlessly sabred and speared for their troubles. Many of the attackers were then rallied by Colonel Mayow, the Brigade-Major who had been ill and off-duty but who had charged anyway. He could see the Russian cavalry nearby, and realised that their only hope was to charge before the enemy did the same. Again the Russians broke, and Mayow and his small force chased them for 500 yards into a narrow gorge whose only exit was a bridge over an aqueduct.

Sergeant O'Hara and another fragment of the 17th tried to join them, but mistook Mayow's signal and charged to the left, where they met with the remnants of Morris's band and eventually cut their way free to safety.

Ivan Ivanovitch, the Russian hussar officer who had been wounded in the clash with the Heavy Brigade, was watching from a distance:

> It was the maddest thing that was ever done . . . They broke through our lines, took our artillery, and then, instead of capturing our guns and making off with them, they went for us . . . They came on magnificently. We thought they were drunk from the way they held their lances. Instead of holding them under their armpits they waved them in the air, and of course they were easier to guard

against like that. The men were mad, sir . . . They dashed in among us, shouting, cheering and cursing. I never saw anything like it. They seemed perfectly irresistible, and our fellows were quite demoralised.

By now the surviving 60 men of the 11th Hussars had passed by and through the right of the battery. They were halted by Colonel Douglas when 100 yards in the rear and ordered to 'Come in on the centre', so that the squadron interval was closed. Then, seeing Russian hussars and Cossacks, they charged.

'Waving our swords over our heads on we galloped,' recalled Sergeant-Major Loy Smith, 'expecting the next moment to be amongst these Russians but, to our surprise, when no more than 20 yards off, they wheeled about and galloped away in front of us.'

Eventually, however, the Russians reached the aqueduct at the extreme end of the valley and were forced to halt and face their pursuers. Douglas and his men now had no option but to retire, closely followed by the Russians, and as they did so they met with the 4th Light Dragoons under Lord George Paget, who had come forward after disabling a number of guns. Fearing they would be cut down as they tried to escape, Paget shouted: 'Half front; if you don't front, my boys, we are done!'

At this the 11th Hussars turned, and together with the 4th Light Dragoons presented a united front. Then someone shouted: 'They are attacking us, my lord, in our rear!'

Turning, Paget could see a large body of Russian lancers formed up in front of the guns some way to their rear, blocking off their retreat. Two squadrons strong, they had debouched from a gap in the Fedioukine Heights leading to the Traktir Bridge. 'We are in a desperate scrape; what the devil shall we do?' he asked Major Low. 'Where is Lord Cardigan?'

'Lord Cardigan has gone back some time,' replied Low.

There was only one option. 'Threes about!' shouted Paget. 'We must do the best we can for ourselves.'

They then charged the Russian lancers. Paget recalled:

Well, as we neared them, down they came upon us at a sort of trot (their advance not being more than twenty or thirty yards), they stopped . . . and evinced [an] air of bewilderment . . .

·A few of the men on the right flank of their leading squadrons . . . came into momentary collision with the right flank of our fellows, but beyond this, strange as it may sound, they did nothing, and actually allowed us to shuffle, to edge away, by them, at a distance of hardly a horse's.

Well, we got by them without, I believe, the loss of a single man. How I know not! . . . Had that force been composed of English *ladies*, I don't think one of us could have escaped.

Meanwhile Colonel Mayow, now with just 15 men, had also decided to retire, and as he did so he came upon Colonel Shewell and about 55 men of the 8th Hussars who had passed to the left of the Russian battery. Shewell, according to Cornet George Clowes, then asked Mayow if he knew 'where Lord Cardigan was' and Mayow replied 'that he did not know'.

Someone now pointed out that Russian lancers had formed in their rear (after debouching from the Causeway Heights) and Shewell, the senior officer, made the same instant decision as Paget had done. 'Right about wheel!' he shouted, before leading his 70 men against a force four times their number. Luckily the Russians had not finished their deployment and Shewell and his men were able to scatter them, thereby creating a gap through which Captain Jenyns and a number of survivors from the 13th Light Dragoons followed.

Whilst riding back up the valley, Colonel Mayow 'looked in every direction for Lord Cardigan' without success and was forced to conclude that he had been 'either killed or taken prisoner'.[34]

Cardigan later insisted that he had retreated 'gradually and slowly in rear of the broken parties of the first line up the hill'. Eyewitnesses tell a different story. Private Mitchell was making his way back up the valley on foot when Cardigan 'came galloping up from the direction of the guns'. Pulling up beside Mitchell, he asked: 'Where is your horse?'

'Killed, my lord,' came the reply.

'You had better make the best of your way back as fast as you can, or you will be taken prisoner,' said Cardigan sternly. He then rode a short distance towards the guns, but thought better of it and returned past Mitchell at the gallop in the direction of the British lines.

Lord Lucan was waiting in advance of the Heavy Brigade as Cardigan galloped up from the guns. 'When within a short distance of my front he brought his horse to a walk, and passed me going up the valley towards

Sebastopol,' recalled Lucan. 'He was at a distance of about 200 yards from me.'

Soon after, Captain Lockwood rode up. Cardigan's principal aide-de-camp, Lockwood had not charged with the other staff officers and Kinglake later claimed to have evidence that Cardigan had sent him to request infantry support from one of the divisional commanders.

'My lord, can you tell me where is Lord Cardigan?' asked Lockwood.

Lucan replied that Cardigan had passed him some time ago, but Lockwood must have thought that he meant in the direction of the guns because he rode off that way and was never seen again.

Only 'when all was over', according to Lucan, 'and the whole of the troops, heavy and light, had fallen back' did Cardigan ride up 'from the direction of Sebastopol' and speak to him.

'He at once,' wrote Lucan, 'in a very vehement manner, said that he must report the insubordination of Captain Nolan in placing himself in front of one of his squadrons, and his gross misconduct in shrieking and turning away. I had some difficulty in making him understand that Captain Nolan had been killed, and that his shrieks had been occasioned by his being shot through the heart.'

Cardigan's own version of events is that after riding 'slowly up the hill' he met Scarlett and, in Lucan's hearing, asked him what he thought of Nolan 'riding to the rear and screaming like a woman'.

'Do not say any more,' Scarlett is said to have replied, 'for I have ridden over his body.'

In a letter to Cardigan after the war, Scarlett confirmed this conversation but said that it had occurred after the remnants of the Light Brigade had gone past in a compact body. 'Whether you came from the Brigade on our left front or from any other quarter I did not see,' added Scarlett, 'but you joined us at a moderate pace and not till after I had seen the retiring Brigade.'

Given that Cardigan had, in Lord George Paget's words, 'been seen by many in retreat a very considerable time before' the formed remnants of the brigade retired, there is only one possible explanation for Scarlett's statement. He had not noticed Cardigan's initial withdrawal – assuming instead, when Cardigan eventually did ride up to speak to him and Lucan, that he had come straight from the guns.[35]

Cardigan then rode over to where the battered and weary survivors of the Light Brigade were gathering on a slope facing south towards Balaclava. Seeing their commander, they raised three cheers.

'This is a great blunder,' he responded somewhat defensively, 'but no fault of mine.'

'My lord,' replied one, 'we are ready to go back again.'

'No,' said Cardigan, 'you have done enough today, my men.'

Spotting Lord George Paget, one of the last to return on his wounded horse, Cardigan rode over to greet him.

'Holloa, Lord Cardigan!' said Paget dismissively. 'Were you not there?'

'Oh, wasn't I, though!' exclaimed Cardigan, turning to Captain Jenyns of the 13th Light Dragoons. 'Here, Jenyns, did not you see me at the guns?'

Jenyns replied that Cardigan had been 'two or three horses lengths in front of the 13th going into the guns'.

Changing tack, Paget said: 'I am afraid there are no such regiments left as the 13th and 17th, for I can give no account of them.'

To his relief, however, he then saw survivors from both regiments 'standing by their horses, on the brow of the hill' to his front.

Cardigan next sought out d'Allonville, the commander of the French cavalry brigade, to thank him for his timely assistance, and lastly he went to report to Raglan who, with his staff, had ridden down into the valley.

'What do you mean, sir,' asked a furious Raglan, 'by attacking a battery in front, contrary to all the usages of warfare and the custom of the service?'

'My lord,' came the plaintive response, 'I hope you will not blame me, for I received the order to attack from my superior officer in front of the troops.'

William Russell, who had also ridden down from the ridge, could see from the way that Raglan 'shook his head as he spoke, and jerked the armless sleeve of his coat' that he was 'much moved with anger'. Yet, when Cardigan turned to rejoin his brigade, 'he seemed in no degree depressed, and as he cantered away on the charger . . . he bore himself proudly'.

Cardigan went to check on the health of Lieutenant Maxse, his wounded aide-de-camp, and for a time fell asleep wrapped in his cloak beside Maxse's camp fire. Later still, however, he is said to have returned to his yacht.[36]

When the bloodied remnants of the Light Brigade formed up near the same ground they had charged from 25 minutes or so earlier, only 195 men out of 676 were still mounted. Even with the return of dismounted stragglers and riderless horses, the losses were crippling, although no two sources seem able to agree on the exact number.

Kinglake put the total number of casualties at 247 officers and men, with 113 killed and 134 wounded. In addition, he said, 475 horses were killed or shot on account of their wounds.

A more reliable source, however, is the Official Return of Adjutant-General Estcourt, which gives the total losses as 21 officers and 257 other ranks. Of these, 11 officers and 147 men were killed or captured; the rest returned wounded. The number of horses that were killed or had to be destroyed is given as 335.

Another source still – Nominal Returns of 25 October signed by Cardigan himself – gives a total of 21 officers and 273 other ranks. Of these, 107 are listed as killed and 187 as wounded and missing (although many would later die of their wounds). Most of the 50 or so men captured were also wounded. Casualties for horses are put at 397 killed, wounded or afterwards shot in consequence of their wounds.[37]

Among the prisoners-of-war was Private Samuel Parkes, Paget's orderly, who was later awarded the newly instituted Victoria Cross for defending an unarmed comrade, Trumpet-Major Crawford, against a number of mounted Cossacks. Crawford eventually escaped, but the selfless Parkes was captured when his sword was shot away. Similarly honoured were one officer – Lieutenant Alexander Dunn of the 11th Hussars, who during the retreat saved the lives of two men by personally killing their four assailants – and four N.C.O.s.

That evening, Parkes was taken before General Liprandi and asked whether he and his comrades had 'been made drunk before the charge'. Parkes' denial astonished Liprandi, who seemed to think that inebriation was the only logical explanation for such a suicidal charge. The Russian then asked if Lord Cardigan was the officer 'who went to the rear on the chestnut horse with white legs'.

'Yes,' replied Parkes.

'If he had not had a good horse, he would never have got back,' remarked Liprandi.[38]

The immortal status of all who had taken part was guaranteed when Alfred Tennyson, Poet Laureate, penned 'The Charge of the Light Brigade' on 2 December 1854, three weeks after reading Russell's report in *The Times*

describing it as 'some hideous blunder'. It is still one of the best-known
poems about war ever written:

I

Half a league, half a league,
Half a league onward,
All in the valley of Death
Rode the six hundred.
'Forward, the Light Brigade!
Charge for the guns!' he said:
Into the valley of Death
Rode the six hundred.

II

'Forward, the Light Brigade!'
Was there a man dismayed?
Not though the soldiers knew
Some one had blundered:
Their's not to make reply
Their's not to reason why,
Their's but to do and die:
Into the valley of Death
Rode the six hundred.

III

Cannon to right of them,
Cannon to left of them,
Cannon in front of them
Volleyed and thundered:
Stormed at with shot and shell,
Boldly they rode and well,
Into the jaws of Death,
Into the mouth of Hell
Rode the six hundred.

IV

Flashed all their sabres bare,
Flashed as they turned in air
Sabring the gunners there,

'Charge!'

Charging an army, while
All the world wondered:
Plunged in the battery-smoke
Right through the line they broke;
Cossack and Russian
Reeled from the sabre-stroke
Shattered and sundered.
Then they rode back, but not
Not the six hundred.

V

Cannon to right of them,
Cannon to left of them,
Cannon behind them
Volleyed and thundered;
Stormed at with shot and shell,
While horse and hero fell,
They that had fought so well
Came through the jaws of Death,
Back from the mouth of Hell,
All that was left of them,
Left of six hundred.

VI

When can their glory fade?
O the wild charge they made!
All the world wondered.
Honour the charge they made!
Honour the Light Brigade,
Noble six hundred![39]

15

———◆———

'See! The Conquering Hero Comes!'

If anyone had the better of the inconclusive battle of Balaclava, it was the Russians. Even after the fatal charge, Raglan had been keen to use his infantry to retake the three captured redoubts, but Canrobert dissuaded him by pointing out that troops would have to be removed from the siege lines to garrison them.

So the Russians remained ensconced on the Causeway Heights until the end of the year, and thereby denied the British the use of the Woronzoff Road for transporting supplies between Balaclava and the Chersonese Plateau. In fine weather this was not a problem, as the shorter route via the Col was preferred; but as winter set in it became increasingly difficult to supply the troops at the front.

And yet, as Sergeant-Major Loy was right to point out, the day could so easily have ended with a great victory for the British:

> We cut their Army completely in two, taking their principal battery and driving their cavalry far to the rear. What more could 670 men do? A glorious affair might have been made of it, had our infantry been pushed along the Causeway Heights with the Heavy Cavalry, and the French infantry with the Chasseurs d'Afrique along the Fedioukine Hills. The enemy was so panic-stricken that I feel convinced that the greater part of this army of 24,000 would have been annihilated or taken prisoners – they having only two small bridges to retreat over: the Traktir and the Aqueduct.[1]

316

Lord Raglan inevitably blamed Lucan, although in truth he himself had been rash in ordering the cavalry to advance without infantry support in the first place.

'You have lost the Light Brigade,' said Raglan bitterly when Lucan reported to him on the evening of the charge.

'I at once denied [this],' recalled Lucan, 'as I had only carried out the orders conveyed to me, written and verbal, by Captain Nolan. He then said that I was a lieutenant-general, and should, therefore, have exercised my discretion, and not approving of the charge, should not have made it.'

In his tent, two days after the charge, Lucan told Airey that he had given the order to charge under what he 'considered a most imperious necessity'. Airey then tried to argue that the order was 'not imperative'.

'Now be careful, General Airey,' threatened Lucan, 'that no responsibility is placed upon me in this light cavalry affair, as I will not bear any.'

'You may rest satisfied, Lord Lucan,' said Airey, 'you will be pleased with Lord Raglan's report.'

Taking Airey at his word, Lucan dropped the matter.[2]

Predictably, Cardigan was in no doubt as to who was to blame. 'My opinion is that the Lieutenant-General ought to have had the moral courage to disobey the order till further instructions were issued,' he wrote to his brother-in-law, Earl Howe, on 27 October.[3]

There is some truth in this. Yet the blunder could not have happened without all three principals – Lucan, Raglan and Nolan – in some way failing in their duty. Even interpreted accurately, Raglan's Fourth Order was both unnecessary and irresponsible. After all, the guns had been spiked and could not be fired, the infantry had nearly arrived, and an attack by cavalry alone along the Heights was bound to have been costly if not disastrous. In addition, Raglan should have taken into account the fact that Lucan's view of the battlefield was much more limited than his and made the Fourth Order more precise (by specifically mentioning the 'Heights', for example).

By allowing his personal contempt for Lucan to get the better of him, Nolan failed in the one essential duty of a staff galloper: to provide the officer in receipt of the message with any additional information necessary. If the written order was imprecise, then how much more was Nolan's insolent gesture: 'There, my lord, is your enemy! There are your guns!'

Even so, Lucan must bear the greatest burden of responsibility. By failing to insist on clarification from Nolan, he seems to have come to the inexplicable conclusion that Raglan expected him to save the naval guns by sending his division down the North Valley rather than along the Causeway Heights. He also failed to support them with horse artillery and to request the cooperation of the French cavalry.

Cardigan, on the other hand, can shoulder no blame, although his premature withdrawal was freely criticised by those in the know. According to Private John Edden of the 4th Light Dragoons, and others, the 'fact of Lord Cardigan's returning was immediately after talked of among the regiment'. Lieutenant the Honourable Somerset Calthorpe, one of Raglan's aides-de-camp, claimed to have been told about this by officers 'immediately after the charge'. They also told him 'that when the 2nd and 3rd lines had become engaged with an overwhelming force of the enemy, the officers in command of these lines, after inquiring in vain for the Earl of Cardigan, were obliged to take upon themselves the very serious responsibility of ordering a retreat'.[4]

Officially, however, Cardigan received nothing but praise. 'Major General the Earl of Cardigan led this attack in the most gallant and intrepid manner,' wrote Lucan in his report of the action to Raglan on 27 October.[5]

In General Orders of 29 October, Raglan congratulated Cardigan and his men for 'the gallantry they displayed and the coolness . . . with which they executed one of the most arduous attacks that was ever witnessed, under the heaviest fire'. In a private letter to the Duke of Newcastle, he noted: 'Lord Cardigan acted throughout with the greatest steadiness and gallantry, as well as perseverance.'[6]

Certainly, Cardigan's behaviour in the days immediately following the charge did nothing to tarnish his new heroic status. Mrs Farrel, a nurse at Balaclava, noted that twice in one day Cardigan came to visit those wounded in the charge, spending half an hour 'soothing' his trumpeter, Britten, 'a most pitiful case'. There 'never was any chance for him,' she wrote, 'though his lordship sees he has everything he wants.'

Fanny Duberly, who had watched the charge from high ground, had a long talk with Cardigan on 28 October and noted in her journal that he had 'distinguished himself by the rapidity with which he rode'. Her friendship with such a notorious roué had for some time been the subject of much gossip in the cavalry camp, although there is no proof that Cardigan's attentions were anything more than paternal.[7]

★

In late October, the remnants of the Light Brigade were moved up to the Chersonese Plateau to support the extreme right of the British line on the Inkerman Heights. Now with 7 miles separating his yacht and his men, Cardigan's pretensions to command became even more tenuous. On 4 November, accompanied by Hubert De Burgh, he was making his leisurely way towards the brigade when he heard the sound of firing. William Russell met them going in the opposite direction and later wrote:

> As I rode dawn the path between the hillside and the beach, into Balaclava, I encountered two horsemen – one in hussar uniform; the other, an unlovely gentleman, in a flat-brimmed bell-topper, frock-coat, and overalls strapped over patent-leather boots. The first was Lord Cardigan; the second, his friend, Mr de Burgh, known to the London world as 'the Squire'. They had just landed from the yacht whence the General commanded the Light Cavalry Brigade. 'Haw! Haw! Well! Mr William Russell! What are they doing? What was the firing for last night? And this morning?' I confessed ignorance. 'You hear, Squire? This Mister William Russell knows nothing of the reason of that firing! I daresay no one does! Good morning!'

When the Russians launched a massive attack at Inkerman in the early hours of 5 November, Lord George Paget was again Acting Brigadier.

At first, as the battle ebbed and flowed, there was nothing for the cavalry to do. Then, at 9.30 a.m., the order came to advance in support of the Chasseurs d'Afrique who were going to the assistance of French reinforcements – themselves in trouble on the extreme right of the British line.

But they were halted 200 yards below a ridge and never actually went into action; instead, for 30 pointless minutes they were subjected to an artillery bombardment. 'The enemy must have known we were there,' wrote Sergeant-Major Loy Smith of the 11th, 'for they dropped their cannonballs just over the brow of the hill so that they passed through us about breast high. One struck a horse's head, knocking it to pieces, then took off Sergeant Breese's arm, taking the three bars and leaving the crown. It then struck Private Wright, who was riding a Russian horse, full in the chest, passing through him.'

When Cardigan eventually arrived to take command, he 'at once ordered us to retire and take up a position a few hundred yards to rear,' wrote Loy Smith. 'The battle all this time was raging close in our front; the

wounded infantry frequently passing through us, some saying they thought
we should be beaten.'

Here they remained until the Russians, defeated, began to stream across
the Tchernaya in the early afternoon. They had lost an incredible 10,729
men killed, wounded and taken prisoner, although the British casualties
were also heavy at 2,357 with 597 killed, among them Sir George
Cathcart, commander of the 4th Division.[8]

Paget, who was particularly annoyed when Cardigan criticised him for
not mounting all the camp guards that morning, put his arrival with De
Burgh as late as noon. He also put Raglan's failure to mention the Light
Brigade in the despatch of the battle of Inkerman down to the fact that
Cardigan was absent when the brigade was ordered to advance. 'Either he
must mention my name, as being in command of the brigade,' wrote
Paget, 'in which case an explanation and justification of Lord Cardigan's
absence would have been necessary, or he must give the name of Lord
Cardigan, which was simply an impossibility.'

The day after the battle, an Allied Council of War decided to strengthen
the defences on the Inkerman Heights; this would enable the siege to be
continued into the new year, when reinforcements would make a spring
assault possible. Realising that the cavalry could have no active role in this
strategy, Lord George Paget received permission from Raglan to send in his
papers and return home. He had recently married and was intending to
retire anyway, but war had intervened.

On being told by his second-in-command that he had obtained his
leave, Cardigan replied generously: 'Have you really? Well I am very glad
to hear it, it does not surprise me, and I had anticipated it, your case being
quite different from that of all the others. I think you are quite right, and
were I in your position I should do just the same.'[9] Paget's was a timely
departure because winter soon set in, one of the worst in memory, with
rain and sleet turning the huge tented camps into a freezing quagmire. On
12 November, Lieutenant Temple Godman wrote:

> The horses are up to their fetlocks in mud and slush, through
> which one must paddle to get at them; the saddles soaked; the
> tents so crowded that the men have no room in them for their
> arms, which must therefore lie in the rain. In our tents everything
> is wet, except what one can wrap up in waterproof; mud outside
> and mud within. The men of course are worse off, having no
> change or only one of clothes – of course their clothes get wet in

the daytime, and their cloaks, and these they must sleep in as also their boots, for if they pulled them off they would never get them on again, no wonder we had 22 cases of sickness this morning. Dysentery is on the increase. If we are left like this the horses must soon die, and the men be knocked up.

That same day, Sergeant-Major Loy Smith noted in his diary: 'The nights are getting so cold that we can scarcely sleep, having but one blanket each and our cloaks . . . My jacket that was new when we left home is now nearly worn out and in rags and I have not had my overalls off since we landed, nor a change of any underclothing these seven weeks.' Next day, he wrote that 'through starvation and cold' the horses had 'changed so much in appearance that we scarcely knew them'.[10]

One of the biggest headaches for the Commissariat Department was how to transport enough forage from stores at Balaclava to the light cavalry camp on the plateau. On about 7 November, when the supply of hay began to fail, and later when that of barley began to fall off, the Commissariat suggested that the Light Brigade should send down horses each day to carry its own forage. Cardigan refused because Raglan had impressed upon him the importance of guarding the right flank of the British army; to have detached more than a third of his strength – 120 out of 330 horses – would, in his opinion, have made his task impossible. Furthermore, he felt, more horses would be lost travelling heavily laden over such difficult terrain than from lack of food.

There may have been some truth in this, although Cardigan was certainly remiss not to look for alternatives, such as offering to transport the forage half the distance or requesting the assistance of the Heavy Brigade, then relatively unemployed in the centre of the plateau.

Instead, he simply wrote to Lucan on 16 November, describing the hardships suffered by the horses and enclosing a number of letters of complaint from regimental commanders, with a request that they be forwarded to Raglan. When Lucan demurred, Cardigan wrote privately to Raglan on the 19th, enclosing copies of two of the letters. Raglan replied coldly that the 'state of the Light Cavalry could not be such as it is represented to be if the Comdg Officers had attended to their duty, & had taken such steps as were within their power to provide for their deficiencies'.[11]

The result was that *nothing* was done and when the Light Brigade was finally ordered down into the south valley on 2 December, its horses were so frail they had to be led. Many were left to die on the plateau, while a further 17 collapsed and died on the road down.

Incensed by what they saw as neglect, some cavalry officers were quick to blame their superiors. 'We are commanded by one of the greatest old women in the British Army, called the Earl of Cardigan,' wrote Captain Portal in a letter of 25 November. 'He has as much brains as my boot. He is only to be equalled in want of intellect by his relation the Earl of Lucan . . . Without mincing matters two such *fools* could not be picked out of the British Army to take command. But they are Earls!'[12]

By now, however, Cardigan's own health was a matter for concern. As well as diarrhoea, which he had now had for two months, he was also afflicted by a chronic inflammation of the mucus membrane of the bladder, a complaint that had been bothering him for many years. The staff surgeon had examined him on 10 November and recommended leave in Malta, and nine days later Cardigan wrote to Raglan to inform him that he would shortly be obliged to ask 'for leave of absence on sick certificate'. He continued: 'Were it not for bad health, I assure you I should have no wish to go, for you know you have no keener soldier in your army.'

He could, he suggested, get a certificate from the Principal Medical Officer without having to explain his 'ailments in detail before a Medical Board'. This would enable him to go on leave as soon as possible to a warm climate, possibly Naples. 'But I will follow your wishes and advice, even to the detriment of my heath.'

Raglan replied that if Cardigan wanted leave he had to go before a medical board in the usual way. Made up of the three staff surgeons of the expeditionary force, the board was convened on the *Dryad* on 3 December. Its verdict was that Cardigan was 'much reduced in strength' and that owing to 'the serious character of his complaints' he should be 'allowed to proceed to England for the recovery of his health'.

To Fanny Duberly he said sadly: 'My health is broken down, I have no brigade. If I had a brigade I am not allowed to command it. My heart and health are broken. I must go home.'

She was moved to write: 'Ever since he has been in the Crimea he has behaved very well, and I'm sincerely sorry for him.'[13]

On 5 December, Cardigan left the Crimea for good, consoled to some extent by a 'highly complimentary' letter from Prince Albert about the charge that had arrived the day before. He certainly was not sorry to see the back of Balaclava, with its ruined houses full of dying soldiers, streets ankle-deep in mud, and harbour a stinking mess of offal, driftwood and the occasional human corpse.

But instead of heading straight for home, he spent a few weeks recovering his health in Constantinople, and from there he sent Raglan two final letters of complaint about Lucan. The first was relatively selfless; in it he pointed out that in the list of officers who had distinguished themselves on 25 October, Lucan had named all the commanding officers and staff officers bar three, one of whom was his aide-de-camp, Lieutenant Maxse, who was wounded on arriving at the battery. He therefore asked Raglan if Maxse's name could be included in General Orders.

The second letter was a reiteration of his earlier complaints. 'I cannot,' Cardigan wrote, 'leave the country without affording you an opportunity of knowing how the duties of the command are carried on.' Lucan had persistently interfered in the running of the brigade and had thereby robbed Cardigan of his rightful authority. 'Can it be believed,' he concluded, 'that any other General Officers commanding Brigades can be so treated in the Army except those who have the misfortune to serve in the Cavalry Division?'[14]

For once, Raglan might have sympathised with Cardigan, because by this time he was locked in a feud of his own with Lucan over the responsibility for the charge. This had blown up at the end of November when Lucan finally saw a copy of Raglan's despatch to Newcastle, dated 28 October, in a newspaper report. Lucan's main objection was to Raglan's statement that 'from some misconception of the instruction to advance, the Lieutenant-General considered that he was bound to attack at all hazards'. In fairness, Raglan could hardly have said less, but Lucan was determined not to shoulder any of the blame.

On 30 November, Lucan responded to this 'grave charge and imputation reflecting seriously' on his 'professional character' by stating, in a letter to Raglan, 'those facts which I cannot doubt must clear me from what I respectfully submit is altogether unmerited'.

After reading the Fourth Order, he had 'urged the uselessness of such an attack' and the 'dangers attending it', to which Nolan had replied 'in a most authoritative tone' that Raglan's orders were 'that the cavalry should attack immediately'. On being asked where, 'as neither enemy nor guns being in sight', he responded 'in a most disrespectful manner, pointing to the end of the valley'. So 'distinct' was the 'written instruction' and 'so positive and urgent were the orders delivered by the aide-de-camp' that Lucan had 'felt it was imperative . . . to obey'. Although a lieutenant-general, he did not have the 'discretionary power' to ignore a written order from his Commander-in-Chief – to do so would have 'been nothing less than direct disobedience of orders'.

Through Airey, Raglan tried without success to get Lucan to withdraw this letter. Finally, and reluctantly, it was forwarded to Newcastle on 16 December. Raglan added in a covering letter: 'I am prepared to declare that not only did the lieutenant-general misconceive the written instructions . . . but that there was nothing in that instruction which called upon him to attack at all hazards.'

Furthermore, 'having decided against his conviction to make the movement', Lucan failed 'to render it as little perilous as possible':

> He was told that the Horse Artillery might accompany the cavalry, yet he did not bring it up; he was informed that the French cavalry was on his left, yet he did not invite their cooperation; he had the whole of the Heavy Cavalry at his disposal, yet he mentions having brought up only two regiments in support, and he omits all other precautions.[15]

While these letters were still in transit, Cardigan and Lucan came face to face at a grand New Year's Ball given by Lord Stratford at the British Embassy in Constantinople. Also attending were Sir Colin Campbell, on leave from the front, and Lord George Paget, who had been driven by the uninformed criticism of the clubs and journals at home to return with his wife to the Crimea as Cardigan's replacement.

Observing the ball from the Minstrel's Gallery was 15-year-old Bessie Carew who, with her mother, Lady Carew, and her aunt, Mrs William Morris, had accompanied the Pagets to Constantinople. Bessie noted in her diary:

> As Lord and Lady Stratford led the way into the ballroom the Rifle Band played 'God Save the Queen'. They were followed by Lord Lucan, or Lord Look-on as Lord George calls him, and Lord Cardigan, both looking very grumpy. Lord George told me that they were being sent home because of the 'mistake' at Balaklava, and he said a good thing too . . . Mama danced a quadrille with Lord Cardigan. She told me that he danced tolerably but smelt of

wine. There was quite a sensation when Omar Pasha, the Turkish General, entered in a most gorgeous uniform.[16]

In the New Year, Cardigan left Constantinople for Marseilles, retracing his steps through France and once again stopping for an audience with an admiring Napoleon III. But nothing could have prepared him for the rapturous welcome he received at Folkstone on 13 January 1855, as a gathering crowd cheered him and a band struck up 'See! The Conquering Hero Comes!' From a war that had degenerated into a costly and contro-versial stalemate, he was seen as a shining exception, a quintessentially British hero who had done the impossible and survived. It was a far cry from his departure, eight months before, as one of the most unpopular men in England.

Pictures of him appeared in shops everywhere, many showing him leap-ing the Russian battery as he cut down the gunners; *Punch* depicted him charging the guns amidst a storm of fire with the caption 'A Trump Card(igan)'; music halls reverberated to heroic ballads in his honour; even the novel woollen jacket that he had worn in the Crimea took his name and became a national institution.[17]

A vote of thanks was passed by both Houses of Parliament and Lord Aberdeen, the embattled Prime Minister, even turned down the Queen's offer of the Order of the Garter in favour of the man who had led the Light Brigade. 'Lord Cardigan's great gallantry and personal sacrifices seemed to afford him a just claim to your Majesty's favourable considera-tion,' wrote Aberdeen on 11 January.

But impressed as she was with reports of Cardigan's heroism, the Queen was not to be swayed. In her reply she pointed out that neither Lord Hardinge nor Lord Raglan had been so honoured, and that 'Lord Cardigan's personal character does not stand very high in the country'. Aberdeen was forced to concede and it was he, and not Cardigan, who was honoured with the Garter.[18]

Would the Queen have responded differently if Aberdeen had made his suggestion *after* Cardigan had returned to a hero's welcome? It is just pos-sible. For she was willing to invite him to stay at Windsor on 16 January – just three days after his return. That evening, she wrote in her journal:

> After dinner talked for some time with Ld. Cardigan, who is grown
> thinner & older though he does not look ill otherwise. He seemed
> quite touched when I told him that he had gone so brilliantly

through such great dangers. He said that the sickness & sufferings were great, but that the want of food & various other difficulties had arisen *since* he left . . . He spoke of the unfortunate murderous Charge, for which, he told the Duke of Newcastle plainly, Ld. Lucan was entirely to blame, by misconceiving Ld. Raglan's orders, not obeying them, & not *exposing* himself. Ld. Cardigan said that not one of the officers who went into that action, he believed, ever thought they would return out of it alive! He was slightly wounded by 2 Cossacks, but thought it of too little consequence to mention.

Cardigan's harsh criticism of Lucan was well-timed, because the following day the Queen had a long discussion with Newcastle – who had just received Lucan's letter and Raglan's covering note – 'about the Army & the state of affairs concerning it . . . [and] the advisability of recalling Ld. Lucan, who had shown himself unfit, & putting Ld. Cardigan in his place, for which he is quite fit!'

At dinner that evening, with Lord Hardinge the guest, Cardigan sat next to the Queen and expounded on the problems of supply in the Crimea. The Commissariat was 'very bad', but he had not told Lord Raglan, 'not thinking it was his duty'. Doctors were 'deficient', medicines and medicaments scarce, but the 'real mischief', he said, arose 'from the order to embark in light marching order'. Because of this 'the poor men had been without their kits or any of the necessaries quite essential to a soldier'. Furthermore, the lack of hammers, nails and billhooks meant that shelters could not be constructed. 'Hence, all the misery & suffering,' recorded the Queen. 'This is really unpardonable.'

After dinner, Cardigan recounted the story of the charge from a watercolour that had been sent to the Queen by the artist William Simpson. He described it, the Queen wrote, 'very simply and graphically – very modestly, as to his own wonderful heroism – but with evident & very natural satisfaction'.

Next morning, after breakfast, he again told the story of the charge – this time with the aid of a map – to the royal children and their parents assembled in the Long Corridor. The scene was later commemorated in a painting by James Sant which still hangs in the White Hall at Deene. Cardigan, sporting a magnificent moustache and whiskers, is standing next to Prince Albert, but the Queen is conspicuously absent. She is said to have insisted on being removed from the original picture after discovering some unpleasant detail about Cardigan's private life.[19]

From Windsor, Cardigan went straight to the Horse Guards, where he was told by Lord Hardinge that as of 1 February he would be the new Inspector-General of Cavalry. In approving the appointment, the Queen had not given up hope that he would still replace Lucan as commander of the Cavalry Division in the Crimea.

On 27 January, in one of his last acts in office, Newcastle replied to Raglan's letter of the previous month. 'Apart from any consideration of the merits of the question raised by Lord Lucan,' wrote Newcastle, 'the position in which he has now placed himself towards your lordship, renders his withdrawal from the army under your command in all respects advisable.' It was, therefore, 'Her Majesty's pleasure that he should resign the command of the Cavalry Division and return forthwith to England.'[20]

With Newcastle's letter still in transit, Cardigan was the talk of the Crimea. 'We hear that Lord Cardigan has been received in triumph in England,' wrote Colonel Hodge of the 4th Dragoon Guards on 31 January, 'and that all the shops are full of prints of him jumping a gun, and sticking a Russian en passant in mid-air. I do not think that he ever intends returning here, and better that he should not. He does not get on with Lord Lucan, and they are better parted.'

The bad news finally reached Lucan on 12 February and the following day he said goodbye to Colonel Hodge, who noted in his diary: 'He seemed much cut up about his recall . . . I pity him. He has been uniformly kind and civil to me, and though I think he is not the man to command, being obstinate and headstrong, he will be better than Lord Cardigan, should he come out here.'

Cornet Fisher of the same regiment was blunter: 'It is quite a relief to get rid of Lord Lucan . . . he was a horrid old fellow.'[21]

Lucan left immediately, determined to clear his name, but his cause was complicated by the fact that the government which had sacked him was no longer in existence. Through the months of December and January the newspapers had been remorseless in their criticism of the supply difficulties in the Crimea. The lack of adequate clothing, shelter and sustenance had brought on cholera, dysentery and malarial fever, with the result that almost 14,000 British troops were in hospital by the end of January. There were no ambulances to transport the men from the camp to the harbour, and the hospital ships were so crowded and ill-equipped that one in ten of the sick and wounded died en route to Scutari. Until the influence of Florence Nightingale and her nurses led to a dramatic improvement in hospital conditions, thousands more died there.

The result of all this was that when Parliament reconvened in late January, John Roebuck, the Radical Member for Sheffield, proposed a Commons select committee to inquire into 'the condition of our army before Sebastopol'. Despite government opposition, causing Russell to resign in protest, this was passed on 29 January by 305 votes to 148. Aberdeen now stood down and the Queen sent for Derby and the Conservatives, the largest group in opposition. But Palmerston would not pledge his support, and Derby would not serve without him. Russell was approached, but he too was unable to secure a working majority. Palmerston therefore became Prime Minister. In addition to Roebuck's select committee, which began a two-month inquiry on 5 March, he agreed to send two Commissioners, Sir John McNeill and Colonel Alexander Tulloch, to inquire into the failure of supply in the Crimea. His Peelite ministers, Gladstone, Graham and Herbert, resigned in protest.

Meanwhile Cardigan's charger, Ronald, had landed at Liverpool to a welcome normally reserved for bipeds. Visiting Deene shortly after, Lord Maidstone was told that 'the crowds were so anxious to have a remembrance of him that they pulled out hairs from his tail & mane'.[22]

The scenes were repeated on 6 February when Cardigan, in the uniform he had worn during the charge, rode Ronald through cheering crowds to Mansion House for a banquet given in his honour by the Lord Mayor of London. There he delighted the diners by giving a graphic if somewhat inaccurate account of the campaign and the charge. They were particularly moved when, describing the terrible number of casualties, 'his voice faltered, and he spoke with very evident emotion'. It was a 'modest' speech, pronounced the *United Service Gazette*, his long-time critic, 'as becomes a good Soldier, and in excellent taste'.[23]

If more proof was needed that the mainstream military establishment had forgiven Cardigan's past misdemeanours, it was provided when the United Service Club – which had blackballed him 46 times in the 1840s – convened an extraordinary general meeting to elect him as an honorary member.[24]

On 8 February, he left London by train for a civic reception in Northampton. As he alighted, the town band struck up and a large crowd, unperturbed by the falling snow, waved their hats and cheered. After the town crier had delivered a message of welcome from the mayor, Cardigan climbed into his carriage and was drawn by hand through streets lined with people anxious to get a glimpse of the hero of Balaclava. Once inside the assembly rooms of the George Hotel, he was hailed with deafening applause and presented with an address of congratulation signed by the residents of the town. Then he delighted the town worthies present by again recounting the story of the charge with even more poetic licence than hitherto.

'After riding through the Russian cavalry, we came upon the Tchernaya river,' he explained. 'There we stopped, and we had to retire by the same route by which we came, destroying as many of the enemy as we could . . . The scene of retiring, was lamentable in the extreme; still, nothing could be accomplished more regularly, or with greater order; there was no confusion, no hurry, no galloping about, no desire to retire too hastily, but the whole thing was conducted as coolly and systematically as upon parade.'[25]

A more misleading account of his own exploits could hardly have been given. By making liberal use of the word 'we' he deliberately gave the impression that he had been personally involved in all he described, almost as if it was he and not Colonel Mayow who had rallied the survivors of the first line. The fact is that he never got as far as the Tchernaya River, choosing instead to retire at the gallop before the last of his supports had even reached the guns. Although only a handful of officers and men in the Crimea were aware of this, his immodest attempt to claim credit for other men's deeds was bound to lead to a backlash.

For the moment, though, Cardigan was enjoying every minute of the public's adulation. On 9 February, at Deene, tenants from all three counties in which he had estates presented him with their own addresses of congratulation, and he responded with a grand dinner and, a few days later, a ball. On 19 February, he was back at the George Hotel to receive an address from the county of Northamptonshire which was over 40 yards long and contained several thousand signatures. That evening he dined with the Lord-Lieutenant, the Marquess of Exeter, and again could not resist giving a partial account of the campaign.

He had, he told his admiring listeners, 'lived the whole time in a common tent', although 'when the weather grew bad' he would go on board his yacht 'every night to sleep, get up very early in the morning, and ride along the shocking mud road up to the camp to be in time for the turning out of the men'.

Conveniently, his recollection of the charge after he had reached the guns was hazy. 'He remembers two Cossacks attacking him with their lances & wounding his horse – but does not know how he got clear of them,' wrote Lady Mary Cecil, who had withdrawn with the ladies and later heard the account from her father, Lord Exeter. 'Somehow or other he collected the remnant of his men. Ld G. Paget did the same & they rode back the same way, the guns sending shot after them the whole way home.'[26]

For the moment there was no one to put the record straight, and anything printed tended to be complimentary. None more so than George Ryan's *Our Heroes of the Crimea*, a mass-produced pamphlet published in the spring of 1855 and sold for a shilling. 'In this glorious and bloody encounter,' wrote Ryan of the charge, 'Cardigan cut down the enemy right and left.'

'It may be said,' Ryan concluded, 'without fear of contradiction, that the Earl of Cardigan is now the most popular soldier in England. As a gallant chevalier he won his golden spurs in a tilt with giants. All salute him as the lion of the British army; and a clasp to the Crimean medal will tell how he led heroes to fight on that bloody field, which gives to the world an example of devoted valour unequalled in warfare.'[27]

The public perception of Lord Lucan, who arrived in Britain on 1 March, could not have been more of a contrast. No cheering crowds, no brass bands, no dinners in his honour. Just stony silence. On reaching London he immediately sent his son, Lord Bingham, to demand a court-martial to give him the chance to clear his name, but this was refused on the grounds that he had not committed a military offence. Rather, he had been recalled because he could not get on with his Commander-in-Chief.

Over the next eight days, Lucan addressed the House of Lords three times on the subject of his recall, reading out his and Raglan's letters to Newcastle, and again demanding a court-martial. Lord Panmure, the new Secretary of State for War, wrote to Raglan on the 9th and said that the effect of reading out his letter had 'been completely to floor Lucan in public opinion, and even the *Times* confesses that your victory over him is complete'. He also told him that a court-martial 'would be a scandal to the Army, and must be avoided if possible'. He added: 'We have so far succeeded in preventing him and Cardigan from coming into collision.'[28]

On 14 March, Cardigan appeared before Roebuck's select committee and was asked a number of questions concerning the care of the horses during their time on the plateau. Why had sheds not been built to protect them from the cold? Because, Cardigan replied, there was no wood available and, in any case, many of the small number which were housed caught the contagious disease of glanders and died.

Why had there been a severe shortage of forage during November? Because the hills were so steep and the roads so impassable that no animals could be found to bring it up from Balaclava.

Why had he not used cavalry horses to transport it? 'I had no orders to do so,' Cardigan replied lamely, 'it was understood at the headquarters of the army that the Commissariat were to supply the forage, and I think that our horses, in the month of November, had been so exhausted from hard work by pickets, patrols, and exposure to the weather . . . that they would not have been capable of going six miles into Balaclava to be heavily laden with hay, and to bring it back again.'

Even without orders, might he not have considered it his duty to send his horses for provisions? 'No,' came the arrogant reply, 'I think not.'[29]

Three days later, Lucan again addressed the House of Lords on the subject of his recall and Cardigan, ignoring advice from Panmure to stay away, was present. In a long, rambling speech Lucan recounted the events of 25 October and after, quoting at one point from a letter that Sir George Cathcart had written to his wife three days before his death at Inkerman: 'You will read about the affair at Balaklava, in which the light cavalry brigade suffered so severely . . . Neither Lord Lucan nor Lord Cardigan were to blame, but on the contrary, for they obeyed orders. But *those* who gave the orders are much to blame for ordering the impossible.'

Lucan concluded the speech with a dramatic appeal to the government: 'You have wronged, grievously wronged, as zealous a soldier as Her Majesty has in the army. If . . . you are in any way doubtful that you have done an injustice, I ask you this, and no more: reconsider my case, and give me a court-martial and a fair trial!'

But before Panmure could reply for the government, Cardigan leapt up to 'correct' a remark made by Lucan that before the charge he had sent his aide-de-camp 'to state that the force of the enemy was so numerous in front of the Light Brigade that I felt it difficult to hold my ground'.

'No!' interjected Lucan.

'Yes,' insisted Cardigan, 'those were his very words. I sent no such message whatever. In the message I sent I said, that as I perceived a movement was going to be made, I begged to point out that the hills on both sides of the valley . . . were occupied by Russian riflemen and artillery.'

When Panmure was finally allowed to speak, he explained that Lucan had been recalled because 'although personal civilities might have continued, the confidence which ought to exist between the Commander-in-Chief and an officer commanding a division in his army had, to a certain extent, been shaken'.

By the close of the debate, no one had brought forward a motion supporting Lucan's demand for a court-martial. Instead, the Lords agreed to his original motion that a copy of his own account of the battle, as well as Raglan's despatch, be presented to the Queen by the House.[30]

But Lucan was not satisfied and within a few days had published a pamphlet containing a full account of his speech in the Lords, including an appendix repeating his claim that before the charge Cardigan had 'objected to his brigade being placed where it was, as there were batteries of the enemy on the left, which would open upon it'. He also stated that after the charge of the Heavy Brigade, he had chastised Cardigan for not making a flank attack.[31]

Cardigan refuted both accusations in a letter to *The Times* of 7 April. He had, he wrote, been 'personally placed by the Lieutenant-General in a particular position . . . with positive orders to remain there, and to watch a certain line of ground over which the Russians might have attacked . . ., and in the event of such being the case I had permission . . . to attack anything that might approach, except close columns of infantry'. In response to the first charge, he simply repeated the answer that he had given to the Lords.

By this time Lucan had returned to his estate in Ireland. Nevertheless, he replied on 13 April, insisting that his account was 'generally correct – certainly not less so than the description given in his Lordship's present letter, and in the speeches in which his Lordship has, at such length and on different occasions, brought his services before the public'.

When these reports reached the Crimea, Colonel Hodge wrote ominously: 'I think Lords Lucan and Cardigan had better not expose themselves before the public. Cardigan will get the worst of this if matters come to be looked into. There are some curious stories afloat about him here.'

As if on cue, *The Times* published a leading article on 5 May under the speculative heading: 'Our cavalry is sacrificed to the discord of two noblemen.' The two brothers-in-law promptly forgot their petty bickering in favour of defending themselves against this new charge.

It seems that only the inhabitants of his native Mayo were sympathetic to Lucan's cause. Their address on his return stated: 'The manner in which on every occasion you so zealously discharged your duties, and in particular the ability and gallantry with which you commanded in the cavalry action of Balaklava on the 25th . . . have been viewed by us with admiration. Such valuable services were indeed ill-requited by the Government who so unjustly recalled you from your command.'[32]

16

'Was Lord Cardigan a Hero?'

Cardigan never did return to the Crimea, although for a time it seemed as though he might. 'Lord Cardigan talks of leaving about the middle of March,' Panmure wrote to Raglan on 26 February.

The papers were quick to pick up on the story, and soon the Crimea was rife with speculation. 'A visit to the trenches today, and an alarming story that Cardigan is coming out to command the cavalry,' noted Lord George Paget on 14 March. 'I hope not,' was Lieutenant Temple Godman's reaction to the same rumour a day later, 'I doubt his discretion.'

They need not have worried, because Panmure had belatedly come to the conclusion that Cardigan was not the right man for the job. 'I shall . . . endeavour to convince Cardigan that his health is not sufficiently reinstated,' wrote Panmure to Raglan on 19 March, 'for his temperament is not such as to make him looked up to as a CO should be.'

Much to the delight of the cavalry, Scarlett remained in command until his wife fell dangerously ill and he was forced to return home in April. 'I am sorry he is gone,' wrote Lieutenant Temple Godman to his sister, 'we lost the services of the best man in the Division,' adding: 'Everyone here is disgusted with Lord Lucan . . .; he deserves what he got. Cardigan, too, is thought very little of, everyone was sorry to hear of his return, indeed it is said he took more care of himself on October 25th than was becoming.'[1]

Oblivious to this bad feeling, Cardigan was going about his new job as Inspector-General of Cavalry with the same minute attention to detail he

333

had displayed as a regimental commander. Within two months of his appointment he had reviewed every cavalry regiment in the British Isles – his arrival feared as much as his praise was valued.

On 18 June, the 40th anniversary of the Battle of Waterloo, Roebuck's select committee presented its fifth and final report. A number of highly critical draft resolutions proposed by its chairman had been excluded, resulting in a general tone that was remarkably restrained. 'An army encamped in a hostile country, at a distance of 3,000 miles from England, and engaged during a severe winter in besieging a fortress which, from want of numbers, it could not invest, was necessarily placed in a situation where unremitting fatigue and hardship had to be endured,' it stated.

Such 'unavoidable suffering' was 'aggravated' by 'dilatory and insufficient arrangements for the supply of this army with necessities indispensable to its healthy and effective condition'. The result was 'fatigue, exposure, want of clothing, insufficient supplies for the healthy, and insufficient accommodation for the sick'.

Largely exonerated, the government was taken to task for failing 'to augment the ranks of the army beyond the ordinary recruiting' at the outset of the war. The 'excessive fatigue necessarily resulted from the inadequacy of the force for the task assigned to it'. This was a far cry from Roebuck's highly critical draft resolution that was omitted from the report: 'What was planned and undertaken without sufficient information was conducted without sufficient care or forethought. This conduct on the part of the Administration was the first and chief cause of the calamities which befell our army.'

Instead of blaming individuals, the report concentrated on the administrative failings of various military branches, particularly the Commissariat and Medical Departments. The troops, on the other hand, deserved only praise: 'Their heroic valour, and equally heroic patience under sufferings and privations, have given them claims upon their country which will be long remembered and gratefully acknowledged.'[2]

On the same day that the report was presented, the Allies launched their long-awaited assault on the south-east defences of Sebastopol, known to the British as the first battle of the Redan. But General Pélissier, who had replaced Canrobert in May, had decided at the last minute to advance at dawn with no preliminary bombardment, and the attack failed. For Raglan this was the last straw. Denied his Waterloo, some say heartbroken, he fell ill and within ten days was dead. In a letter home, Colonel Hodge put the cause as 'exhaustion from dysentery, added to, I hear, by worry of mind, poor fellow'.[3]

It was not until 8 September that the Allies attacked again, this time after a three-day bombardment and timed, at noon, to coincide with the changing of the Russian garrison. Once more the Redan held out against the British, but the French succeeded in taking the strong Malakoff redoubt. With their defences breached, the Russians evacuated Sebastopol during the night and withdrew to the north. It had taken almost exactly a year, and 21,000 British lives, to complete a task which had been expected to take just a matter of weeks.

Nicholas II had died in March 1855 and it was left to his son, Alexander II, to agree to the terms demanded by the Allies at the Congress of Paris in 1856: the neutralisation of the Black Sea; the surrender of southern Bessarabia (and therefore control of the mouths of the Danube); the re-enactment of the Convention of 1841 closing the Dardanelles to warships in time of peace; the removal of Russian claims to an exclusive protectorate over Turkish subjects.

On 7 July 1855, Cardigan's service in the Crimea was officially recognised when the Queen made him a Knight Commander of the Bath (Lucan was similarly honoured, as were Quartermaster-General Airey and Commissary-General Filder). He would also be appointed a Commander of the *Légion d'Honneur* and a Knight (2nd Class) of the Order of the Medjidieh, and receive the Turkish and Crimean Medals. When the latter award arrived in the Crimea in September for distribution to all ranks, Paget dubbed it a 'vulgar looking thing' and likened its clasps for the various battles to decanter labels. 'They call them here "Port", "Sherry", and "Claret",' he wrote.[4]

While Cardigan remained ever popular with the general public, rumours that his conduct had been less than heroic were beginning to circulate. Reporting a rowdy demonstration against the war in Hyde Park on 8 July, *The Times* commented: 'Cabs and omnibuses were permitted to go by unmolested, but the only exception otherwise made was in favour of Lord Cardigan, who was recognised as he drove past, and who seems to enjoy a degree of popularity among the London mob, *which those who know the real nature of his services in the East, may be excused for wondering at!*'[5]

The first concrete seeds of doubt were sown in the public mind by the publication of George Ryan's pamphlet, *Was Lord Cardigan a Hero at Balaclava?*, in the late summer of 1855. Explaining in the preface this volte-face from his earlier work, *Our Heroes of the Crimea*, Ryan said that he had been put straight by an official at the Horse Guards who had heard at first hand from a number of officers involved. 'Let it not be said that I have dealt either unfairly or harshly with the Earl of Cardigan,' Ryan added ominously. 'His lordship and his friends who were with him in his yacht, on the 5th of November last, will admit that in maintaining silence as to what took place on board, when news of the attack on our position before Sebastopol was communicated, is downright merciful.'

Instead, the criticism was confined to Cardigan's actions during the Battle of Balaclava, particularly his failure to make a flank attack against the broken Russian cavalry and his premature withdrawal from the Russian guns during the charge of the Light Brigade. 'It was his duty,' wrote Ryan, 'as the general of the brigade, to have seen the remnant of his troops out of that dreadful affair, wholly irrespective of self.' Yet, contrary to claims he had made in various speeches, he had retreated past his supports 'before his time' and in a far from orderly manner which 'must have been occasioned by some sudden bewilderment, for it is said that his lordship galloped back as though the very devil pursued him'.

Unlike *The Times*, however, the military journals were not convinced. The *United Service Gazette* accused Ryan of being in Lord Lucan's pocket, and rejected the claim that Cardigan had retired prematurely: 'Retreating in order was out of the question. *Everybody* cut his way back when he found into what a trap the Light Cavalry had fallen and he was right.'[6]

Cardigan simply dismissed the pamphlet as vindictive hearsay, but it was soon followed by censure from official quarters. On 20 January 1856, the two Commissioners, Sir John McNeill and Colonel Tulloch, submitted their final report on the failure of Army supplies in the Crimea. Most of the criticism was directed towards Quartermaster-General Airey and Commissary-General Filder, but both Lucan and Cardigan were blamed for the unnecessary suffering of the horses and men of the Cavalry Division during the winter of 1854: Lucan for failing to provide hutted shelter; Cardigan for ignoring the Commissariat's suggestion to use cavalry horses to transport forage from Balaclava to the Light Brigade's camp on the plateau.

Both earls angrily refuted the charges – in letters to Lord Panmure and in speeches to the Lords – as did Airey and Filder, with the result that the government eventually agreed to institute a court of inquiry. The press anticipated a cover-up – particularly after the names of the seven members of the Board of General Officers had been announced, and it was learnt that all were of a Conservative persuasion and not one had been in the Crimea. They were not to be proved wrong.

The inquiry opened on 7 April in the Pensioners' Dining Hall of Chelsea Hospital, and dragged on until 19 May. The first thirteen days alone were mostly taken up with Lucan's complaints and his cross-examination of other witnesses, including Tulloch whom he accused of exaggerating the mortality rate of cavalry horses.

On 29 April, the fourteenth day, Lord Cardigan made his appearance. Responding to the Commissioners' charge that he had refused to send cavalry horses into Balaclava for supplies, he said that Raglan had forbidden such an expedient because it had previously resulted in the injury of too many horses. Furthermore, both Raglan and Canrobert had made it clear to him that to move the Light Brigade from the Inkerman Heights would be to leave the flank of the Allied position open to attack. Therefore, to have used a large portion of the brigade for supply duties would have left it too weak to carry out its main purpose. In any case, he said, more horses would have been lost carrying supplies over 12 miles of difficult ground than were actually lost from lack of food.

In conclusion, Cardigan demanded that the Board throw out the 'charge that I neglected to use every precaution to maintain the efficiency of the Brigade – a charge which I venture to hope is inconsistent with my whole professional career'. He then sat down to great applause from the public gallery.[7]

The Chelsea Board submitted its report in July and was immediately dubbed the 'Whitewashing Board'. As the press had feared, it seemed to exonerate both those blamed by the Commissioners, and the Commissioners themselves. Only Lord Raglan was accorded additional criticism, and he was no longer alive to defend himself.

The section concerning Cardigan noted that by the second half of November 'the greater number of horses in the encampment of the Light Brigade was 330, of which, owing to so many men being sick and absent, only 286 could be mounted'. Yet 'it would have required 120 horses to have brought up forage from Balaklava, and to have detached so large a proportion of the force would have diminished it to such an extent as to have rendered it virtually useless for the purpose for which it had been placed'.

Raglan, the report continued, had been made aware of 'the hardships the Cavalry were suffering' by Cardigan, Lucan and Commissary-General Filder, but there was no evidence that his 'attention was particularly called to the proposal of the Assistant Commissary-General, that the horses should be sent to bring forage from Balaklava'. What steps he might have taken had he been so informed could 'only be a matter of conjecture'. In any case, Cardigan's point that to have sent the horses to Balaclava 'would only have augmented the losses of the Brigade, although not in entire accordance with some of the opinions offered in evidence', appeared to 'be supported by a reference to the difficulties experienced in the Royal Artillery at the same period'.

The report concluded with the rather obvious statement that Raglan's military reasons for keeping the cavalry on the plateau appeared 'in some degree to have been irrespective of considerations of forage'.

Colonel Tulloch, who had attended every day of the Chelsea Board until a nervous breakdown forced him to retire on 5 May, responded to these points in a book published the following year:

> The conclusions of the Board on this subject appear necessarily to resolve themselves into this: that because Lord Cardigan might have had some difficulty in carrying up *all the barley* to which his corps was entitled, he was, therefore, justified in bringing up *none*. A half or even a quarter of the regulated allowance, in addition to what was supplied by the Commissariat, might, for a few days at least, have preserved life and health; but, forgetting apparently the homely adage, that 'half a loaf is better than no bread,' his lordship and the Board seem alike to have evaded all such middle courses.[8]

As more officers came back from the Crimea, Cardigan's heroic reputation came under increasing challenge. Now recovered from his wounds, Lieutenant-Colonel (formerly Captain) Morris of the 17th Lancers took Cardigan to task for denying that he had requested permission to charge the Russian cavalry in the flank. But despite an acrimonious exchange of letters, Cardigan was not put off from attending the society wedding of Eliza Taylor, Morris's sister-in-law, and Captain Robert Portal (one of his fiercest critics), held on 3 May at the Devonshire home of Sir Walter and Lady Carew (Eliza's other sister).

Miss Bessie Carew captured the mood perfectly in her diary:

> There were a lot of old Crimean friends at the [wedding] break-fast. Lord Cardigan, who no-one particularly wanted to see, he probably came to atone for the 'mistake' at Balaklava; Sir Colin Campbell, who everyone was delighted to see . . . Funnily enough, Papa and Lord Cardigan seemed to get on very well, I

think mostly because they both liked champagne. At the end of the breakfast, Lord Palmerston proposed a toast to the bride and bridegroom, making a very nice little speech. He wished them happiness and told Aunt Eliza that she was fortunate in her choice of one of the heroes of the Light Brigade of whom England is proud. Lord Cardigan said, 'Hear, hear,' as if Lord Palmerston was including him . . .[9]

In June 1856, it was the turn of Lord George Paget to cross swords with Cardigan on the subject of Paget's claim, in a letter to the *Morning Post*, that he had rallied the 4th Light Dragoons and the 11th Hussars behind the Russian guns before leading them to safety. Cardigan was of course worried that if Paget's version of events was accepted – that he had withdrawn in an orderly fashion at the head of a formed body of men, the remnants of the supporting regiments – the circumstances of his own retirement would come under closer scrutiny. He therefore set out to belittle Paget's achievement.

'Colonel Douglas,' he wrote to Paget on 18 June, 'frequently told me that he led the attack of his own regiment, and acted quite independently of any superior officer throughout the affair . . . I think you will on reflection admit that the momentary conduct of two regiments under such circumstances could not invest any one officer with the command of the whole.'

On 19 June, Paget replied that he could not 'perceive any error' in his statement, and that he 'had charge of the 11th Hussars, at a moment when that regiment and the 4th Light Dragoons found themselves in a position of most remarkable difficulty – cut off from the rest of the Brigade'. More letters flew between Portman Square and Albemarle Street, but still Paget would not back down, even when Cardigan threatened to send the entire correspondence to the *Morning Post*.

There was then a lull; but it was not long before criticism was being directed at Cardigan from other directions. In early September, he attended a banquet in his honour at Leeds and was presented with a silver-gilt sword and an address from the people of Yorkshire. As usual, he gave his own carefully edited version of the campaign to rapturous applause. *The Times* dubbed the speech a 'falsification of history'.

A week later a similar, if smaller-scale, dinner was given in honour of Colonel Morris in the Devonshire town of Torrington. Colonel George Buck, the local M.P., was reported by the *Daily News* as saying in his speech that their 'gallant guest was not placed in the same position as Lord Cardigan, who, it was said, had paid £40,000 for the present position he held in the army, and who when he met his friends at Leeds the other day was obliged to "try back" and first explain his conduct in the charge of Balaklava'. There had been nothing 'in the conduct of their guest as equivocal as to require such an explanation'.[10]

Cardigan was outraged, and wrote to Buck on the 18th demanding to know if the report was true. Buck replied that the report was 'very incorrect' and that he had simply stated that Cardigan's speech at Leeds 'was unsatisfactory to me'.

Writing from Dublin on 26 September, Cardigan pronounced Buck's letter as 'evasive' and pointed out that Morris had been made a Commander of the Bath and promoted to lieutenant-colonel without purchase, and was proof 'that officers in our service do not obtain promotion by money alone'. Such a man, 'never having been attacked by anonymous libellers, had no ground for entering into a defence of his conduct'.

For some reason, he then felt the need to defend his conduct by recounting the charge in some detail – something he could not do without distorting the truth: 'The survivors of the brigade all went about as they came upon the masses of the Russian cavalry and retreated. The whole of the remnant of the brigade was retreating at the same time.'

He concluded by chastising Buck, 'a country gentleman' and 'a Conservative member of a large borough', for uttering a 'slanderous insinuation' which he was 'unable or unwilling to account for'.

When he did not receive an immediate reply – Buck was away from home – Cardigan sent copies of all the correspondence to the *Morning Post*. But Buck would not be intimidated and on 2 October he wrote a lengthy response, noting that Cardigan's promotion to lieutenant-colonel 'was by far the most rapid' of all the staff officers who had served in the Crimea. Switching to the charge, he challenged Cardigan to provide 'details of the skill, judgment, and coolness with which you rallied and drew off your men from that terrible encounter'. A copy of this letter was sent to *The Times*.

With the war of words now public, others intervened. Lieutenant-Colonel J.G. Robinson, writing from the United Service Club to the *Morning Post* on 4 October, agreed with Buck that something was missing from Cardigan's account: 'He tells us a great deal about what he did going *into* the fight, but nothing as to his coming *out*. Where was he? Did he make any attempt to rally, or bring his men out in a soldier-like manner?'

Robinson had another point: 'Orders are, and always must be, *conditional*. A great deal must of course be left to the *discretion* of the general in command. When Lord Cardigan saw the *nature* of the force he was ordered to act against, would he not have been justified in not merely *hesitating*, but in *declining altogether* to obey the order?'

The Editor of the *Morning Post*, however, would not be swayed. He would not be surprised, he wrote derisively, if on account of riding so far ahead of his brigade they now accused Cardigan of 'an intention to desert to the enemy'.[11]

There the dispute seems to have ended – possibly because, on 24 October, Lord George Paget again took the offensive. In a letter to the Duke of Cambridge, now Commander-in-Chief, he complained that Cardigan was trying to belittle 'the heroic gallantry . . . of the two Regiments that formed the second or supporting line'.

Cambridge responded by having a copy of Paget's complaint sent to Cardigan for his comments. Cardigan replied on 10 November, stating that Paget 'claims a higher part than that which he really held in the attack; for I never can admit that he led a second line into action on that day'.

This letter was in turn forwarded to Paget, who responded from Brighton on 29 November. His 'sole object' in writing to Cambridge 'was that the services of the 4th Dragoons and 11th Hussars on that day should appear in their true light'. To back up this point, he quoted from a letter written to him by Colonel Douglas of the 11th Hussars: 'The real point of your letter, and that for which I came forward . . . was the severe crisis from which we extricated ourselves by the rallies of which you made mention, and for which we were never given credit by Lord Cardigan.'

Having seen a copy, Cardigan wrote to Cambridge on 16 December, complaining about the 'tone and tenor of Lord G. Paget's remarks upon his superior officer' and insisting that it was 'most unreasonable and even improbable that either of those regiments can really think that I have not done them justice'.[12]

Before he could take the matter any further, however, he was confronted with yet another threat to his status as national hero. On 13 December 1856, a two-volume work entitled *Letters from Head-Quarters: By an Officer on the Staff* was published by John Murray. Its author was Major (formerly Lieutenant) the Honourable Somerset Calthorpe, a member of Raglan's staff in the Crimea who was now serving as aide-de-camp to another relative, Lord Carlisle, Lord-Lieutenant of Ireland. The work contained five major criticisms of Cardigan's conduct:

During the reconnaissance in the Dobrudscha, Cardigan had 'most unnecessarily harassed the men'.

During the Battle of the Alma, when the cavalry went in front of the infantry, 'from some misconception of orders' Cardigan 'would not allow any prisoners to be taken'.

When the Heavy Brigade was engaged with Russian cavalry, Captain Morris 'begged to be allowed to charge with his regiment alone' but Cardigan 'would not give permission'.

When the Light Brigade reached the Russian guns, this 'was the moment when a General was most required, but unfortunately Lord Cardigan was not then present. On coming up to the battery . . . a gun was fired close to him . . . his horse took fright, swerved round, and galloped off with him to the rear, passing on the way by the 4th Light Dragoons and 8th Hussars, before those regiments got up to the battery'.

After Cardigan 'had sent in his resignation to Lord Raglan on the score of illness', a medical board decided that he was 'totally unfit to continue in command of the light cavalry'.[13]

Fortunately for Cardigan, genuine criticisms were mixed up with inaccuracies and half-truths – enabling him to refute them *en bloc*. On 26 December, he wrote to Cambridge asking permission 'to prefer charges, before a General Court-Martial, against Major the Honourable Somerset Calthorpe, for scandalous and disgraceful conduct, unbecoming the character of an Officer and a Gentleman, in publishing false and malicious statements against a General Officer'. Cambridge replied that Calthorpe had not committed a military offence, and that Cardigan would therefore have to seek redress in the civil courts.[14]

For obvious reasons, Cardigan was unwilling to wash his dirty linen in public. Instead, he asked Lord Burghersh – a friend who was related to Calthorpe and who had also served on Raglan's staff in the Crimea – to pass on his written objections to the offensive passages with a request to withdraw them. 'I cannot let his slanders pass unnoticed,' he added.

Calthorpe's begrudging response was to agree to only minor alterations: to retract the statements relating to Cardigan's order to release prisoners at the Alma, and the description that the Medical Board had found him 'totally unfit' to continue commanding the Light Brigade; and to remove the impression that Cardigan's horse 'ran away with him' at the Russian guns. Yet even these alterations could not be included in the second edition of the work because it had already been printed.[15]

In any case, Calthorpe was still standing by the central allegations that Cardigan had unnecessarily harassed his men during the Dobrudscha reconnaissance (debatable), that he had refused Morris permission to make a flank attack against the retreating Russian cavalry (true), and that during the charge he had never actually entered the Russian battery (false), but had retired before his third line had even reached the guns (true).

Cardigan now felt he had no option but to go public with his objections. On 5 February, he made a violent speech against Calthorpe in the House of Lords, demanding to know whether 'an officer who had thus disgraced himself, by publishing a statement containing allegations so gross, and so utterly devoid of a vestige of truth, should be allowed longer to draw even half-pay from the public purse'. Lord Panmure replied that Cambridge had no intention of court-martialling Calthorpe, and that if he wanted to pursue the case Cardigan could apply to the civil courts.[16]

But still Cardigan shrank from that option; choosing instead to ask Lord Carlisle to dismiss Calthorpe from his staff. Carlisle replied from Dublin on 7 March: to save him from embarrassment, Calthorpe had offered to resign after the House of Lords speech, but he had refused to accept. 'I cannot,' he wrote, 'consent to dismiss a friend, a relation, and a young officer who has lost the Chief and Patron in defending whom he may have shown himself too little scrupulous in attacking others, from the very humble and purely honorary post he holds in my own service.'[17]

The third edition of *Letters from Head-Quarters* – now condensed into a single volume – was published in December 1857 with the promised amendments, and for a time Cardigan let the matter rest there. He was perhaps content in the knowledge that the general public and the Horse Guards had largely dismissed the allegations that remained. But when Calthorpe arranged to exchange from half-pay into the 5th Dragoon Guards in the autumn of 1859, Cardigan did not feel he could stand idly by. The reason: three months earlier he had been appointed honorary Colonel of the same regiment.

On 12 November 1859, he went to see the Duke of Cambridge at the Horse Guards to ask him to intervene with the Queen to prevent Calthorpe's appointment. Cambridge refused, as the quarrel was a non-military matter, and instead asked an astonished Cardigan why – if he considered himself 'aggrieved' – he had not 'called-out' Major Calthorpe.

Recounting this conversation in a letter to Prince Albert on 14 November, Cardigan explained 'that having taken a similar step on a former occasion, I was tried in the House of Lords on a charge of felony, & the military laws against fighting duels have since become more stringent'. Albert's terse reply was that only the Commander-in-Chief could bring such an appeal to the Queen's notice.

Privately, however, Albert sympathised with Cardigan. On 15 November, he wrote to Cambridge, noting that the appointment 'would be rather an indignity offered to Lord Cardigan, & one which, if he possessed any good feeling, Major Calthorpe ought not to covet'. He added: 'There can be no doubt that the indiscretion of his work was very great, whatever faults Lord Cardigan may be answerable for, I feel that it will be difficult for you . . . to maintain the discipline of the Army, if an implied sanction is given to it by the Authorities. What is Lord Cardigan to do? He must not call him out, or a Court Martial demanded upon him would, even if granted, lead to general scandal.'

Cambridge, however, would not be swayed. Writing to the Queen on 17 November, he pointed out that the colonelcy of a regiment was 'an honorary appointment, which would not bring the General Officer holding it in any way into contact with the Major'. Furthermore, Calthorpe, 'hearing of what had occurred, has in a very proper spirit written a letter . . . in which he disclaims any feeling . . . which would be painful or improper to His Lordship as his superior officer'. In her reply of 19 November, the Queen agreed with Cambridge's points and said that she would not oppose Calthorpe's appointment. 'The Queen trusts,' she concluded, 'Lord Cardigan will see the propriety of letting now this matter drop.'[18]

Calthorpe was duly gazetted to the 5th Dragoon Guards on 2 December. But fortunately Cardigan's humiliation did not last long. In August 1860, General Sir Henry Wyndham, Colonel of the 11th Hussars, died and Cardigan was named as his successor. However, he had neither forgotten nor forgiven Calthorpe for *Letters from Head-Quarters* and in 1860 he instructed his solicitors, Ward and Mills of Gray's Inn Square, to seek counsel's opinion as to the possibility of bringing a case against Calthorpe for criminal libel. Bovill, the Q.C. consulted, advised that such action would 'not be expedient' and that it might be 'a more dignified course for his lordship not to come into a court of law on the subject'.[19]

Once again there was a lull until Calthorpe and Hubert De Burgh, Cardigan's brother-in-law, met by chance in Cadogan Place in May 1861. Under the assumption that a new edition was coming out, De Burgh told Calthorpe that Cardigan 'was most anxious' for him to 'withdraw certain statements, or at any rate modify them'. When Calthorpe said that no new edition was planned, De Burgh asked if he could 'publish some statement that might soothe Lord Cardigan'. Calthorpe initially refused, but agreed to a compromise after various arguments from De Burgh.

'I will undertake to say that but few more copies shall be issued from my publishers,' he conceded, 'but I cannot recall those in circulation; if Lord Cardigan likes to pay for the few copies that may be in circulation, of course he can do so.'

The following day, Calthorpe went to see Mr Murray who agreed to sell only the few remaining bound copies; the rest, unbound and numbering in the hundreds, would be destroyed. Soon after, Calthorpe met De Burgh riding in Hyde Park and told him what he had done. De Burgh replied (according to Calthorpe): 'Well, I think Lord Cardigan ought to be satisfied now.'[20]

For a time he was; at least until the first volume of Alexander Kinglake's definitive *Invasion of the Crimea* appeared in early 1863. This had the effect of reviving interest in the Crimean War which, in turn, led to Calthorpe's criticisms being re-aired. Cardigan's solicitors pointed this out in a letter to the recently promoted Lieutenant-Colonel Calthorpe on 4 February 1863, and said that they had reason to believe that there were still many copies of his book unsold. They therefore demanded an apology, the retraction of all statements 'derogatory' to Cardigan's 'character and conduct as an officer', and either a halt to the sale of any further copies or the insertion of an amendment 'satisfactory to his lordship'. Otherwise, Cardigan would make an application for criminal information in the Court of Queen's Bench.

When Calthorpe replied the following day, refusing 'to withdraw any one assertion' made in the last edition of his book, Cardigan's lawyers immediately carried out their threat. They based their application on Calthorpe's single most damaging statement: that during the charge Cardigan never entered the battery but instead turned his horse and galloped to the rear, thereby abandoning his men.[21]

To support their case, both sides hastily collected and filed witness affidavits. Lord Lucan, among others, provided one for Calthorpe, stating that during the charge, when 'no part of the Light Brigade' was in sight, he had seen Cardigan 'gallop up from the direction of the enemy' before slowing to a walk as he realised he was being watched. Only later, 'when all was over', did Cardigan reappear from the direction of Sebastopol. After reading this, Cardigan is said to have challenged his brother-in-law to a duel in

Paris. Lucan accepted and made his way across the Channel, but Cardigan was delayed and, when he did finally set off, Lucan had already returned.[22]

Nevertheless, Lucan's evidence did not affect the central issue of whether or not Cardigan had entered the battery. Cardigan, on the other hand, had gathered a number of affidavits from members of the leading regiments – including Colonel (former Captain) Jenyns, Percy Smith and the Honourable Godfrey Morgan – who had either seen him entering the guns or beyond them. On the strength of this evidence, a Rule was granted in Cardigan's favour at a preliminary hearing on 29 April.

The case was eventually heard in Westminster Hall on 9 June 1863, before the Lord Chief Justice, Sir Alexander Cockburn, and three other judges of the Queen's Bench. In his own evidence, presented in the form of an affidavit so that he could not be cross-examined, Calthorpe conceded that he was now 'satisfied that the Earl of Cardigan entered the Russian battery'. But 'in all other respects' he believed that the statements made in the third edition of his book were 'true' – particularly the one that read: 'This was the moment when a general was most required, but, unfortunately, Lord Cardigan was not then present.'

He continued: 'In consequence of the lapse of time, I have found great difficulty in obtaining evidence. Some of my most important witnesses are dead, some are serving in India and in the colonies, and some object to give positive evidence on events which happened so long ago. A still more serious difficulty . . . is the reluctance of military men of all ranks to give voluntary evidence affecting the character of an officer in the high and influential position of the Earl of Cardigan.'[23]

Despite these problems, Calthorpe still managed to present some impressive evidence in support of his contention that Cardigan had retreated prematurely. As well as Lucan's, he had affidavits from three officers – Colonel Mayow, Lieutenant Clutterbuck and Cornet Clowes – who had advanced past the guns and noted Cardigan's absence. He also had affidavits from one officer, Lieutenant Phillips, and six N.C.O.s and men from the 4th Light Dragoons and 8th Hussars who claimed to have seen Cardigan galloping to the rear before they even reached the guns.

Cardigan, on the other hand, not only had affidavits proving that he had entered the battery, but also one from Scarlett claiming (erroneously) that he was among the last of the first line to reach safety.

Having heard all the evidence and the arguments of the two barristers, Lord Chief Justice Cockburn gave his verdict: 'I can entertain no doubt that the passage in Colonel Calthorpe's work on which the present application has been made for a criminal information contains a most serious libel on the Earl of Cardigan.' Furthermore, the note in the third edition – that the idea that Cardigan's horse had run away with him was 'doubtless erroneous' – was 'the bitterest sarcasm' and 'an imputation on my Lord Cardigan having been wanting in personal courage in the discharge of his duty'.

However, Cockburn and his fellow judges could not reject the defence's argument that Cardigan had waited too long – five years since the publication of the third edition – to bring criminal proceedings against Calthorpe, particularly as the defendant had agreed to destroy the remaining copies in 1861. The case was therefore dismissed.

But not before Cockburn had sweetened the pill for Cardigan in his closing speech:

> There may be those who will say, Lord Cardigan, as a general, is open to criticism, but it should be a generous and liberal criticism, not one that should seek to cast a stain upon his courage and personal honour as an officer. I cannot help, therefore, rejoicing, feeling as I said before, that the reputation and honour of every man who took part in that great scene should be dear to us all, and that this opportunity has been afforded of setting Lord Cardigan right in the estimation, not only of his own profession, but of the public generally.[24]

In a sense Cockburn was right: Cardigan had obtained a moral victory. Even the normally critical *Times* conceded: 'The Battle of Balaclava has been fought over again in the Court of Queen's Bench, and this time Lord Cardigan remains master of the field.'[25]

Others were of the opinion that he had done his reputation more harm than good, however. In the fourth volume of his epic history, *The Invasion of the Crimea*, published after Cardigan's death in 1868, Alexander Kinglake wrote:

> On the one hand it had become clear from the proofs . . . that Lord Cardigan rode into the battery; and the highly favourable comments of the Lord Chief Justice added largely to the advantage thus gained by the plaintiff; but, on the other hand, the substance of the charge which had been brought against Lord Cardigan – the charge of having prematurely retreated – remained still upheld

against him as a charge deliberately persisted in by his adversary, and one which now rested no longer upon the mere assertion of an author narrating what he had heard from others, but – upon the testimony of numbers of men who (having at the time of the battle held various ranks in the army from that of Lieutenant-General commanding the cavalry down to the private soldier) declared upon oath that they had seen with their own eyes, and heard with their own ears, the things to which they bore witness.[26]

17

One Last Scandal

Somerset Calthorpe's book was not the only controversy to bedevil Cardigan's later years, for in early 1858 he became embroiled in a quite separate, personal scandal.

Having returned from the Crimea a national hero, he was even more desirable to members of the opposite sex; not least because his estranged wife, Elizabeth, had an incurable disease and was unlikely to live long. Chief among his pursuers was his long-time mistress, Lady Ailesbury, particularly after the death of her elderly husband, the 1st Marquess, in early 1856. She was anxious to gain an inheritance for her only son, Charles, as her stepson, George, had succeeded to the marquessate and the Ailesbury fortune. That July, Cardigan wrote to invite her to join a week-long house-party at Deene, signing the letter 'Yours affectionately, Cardigan'. Again in December, Lady Ailesbury was part of a shooting party that included Lord Burghersh, Sir George Wombwell, Hubert De Burgh and the Russian Ambassador.[1]

But Lady Ailesbury's matrimonial aspirations were dashed in January 1857 when Spencer de Horsey, an old friend of Cardigan's, arrived at Deene for yet another house-party with his 32-year-old daughter, Adeline. Cardigan knew her well – from visits to the de Horsey house and the great parties that he gave during the Season in Portman Square – but had always treated her 'quite like a *jeune fille*'. This time it was different.

'I can picture Lord Cardigan as I saw him then, surrounded by the Duchess of Montrose, Lady Villiers and Mrs Dudley Ward, who all

349

regarded me with none too friendly eyes,' wrote Adeline years later. 'Cardigan told me afterwards that, when I entered the room, he realised at once I was the one woman in the world for him. He was an impulsive character and he lost no time in letting me see the impression I had made.'[2]

With her long dark hair, sparkling brown eyes, vivaciously pretty face and elegant figure, Adeline could not fail to provoke the admiration of a man twice her age. But her physical attributes were only part of her attraction. She was an expert pianist, could sing in a beautiful mezzo-soprano voice and specialised in dancing the cachucha with castanets. She was said to have written the score for an opera at the age of 15, and could repeat even the lengthiest pieces on the piano after just one hearing. In addition, and thanks to her mother, she had received a remarkably broad education for a woman of her class, having studied Latin and Greek as well as Spanish, Italian and French.

Adeline was also impeccably bred; for the de Horseys traced their descent to the Normans, while her mother was Lady Louisa, daughter of the 1st Earl of Stradbroke. As a child she had attended a party given in the young Princess Victoria's honour by William IV at St James's Palace; exhausted by the excitement, she fell asleep in what proved to be the old monarch's special chair – much to his amusement. A constant visitor to the family house in Upper Grosvenor Street was the Duke of Wellington. 'He delighted to see us act little French plays,' Adeline recalled, 'and what an event those theatricals were! How we revelled in seeing the drawing-room turned into a theatre!'[3]

Adeline first met Cardigan when she visited Deene with her mother in 1842, shortly after being presented at Court; Lady Cardigan marked the occasion by giving her some 'beautiful Northampton lace'. When her mother tragically died of scarlet fever the following year, she took over the running of the family house and became her father's hostess. Forced to grow up fast, Adeline did not feel bound by the usual restrictions that applied to a young lady; when a 'rather risqué' play was showing at the Princess's Theatre, she asked her father to take her.

'Quite impossible, Adeline,' he replied. 'I am dining tonight with General Cavendish at the Club, a long-standing engagement, and even if I were disengaged, I should not think of taking my daughter to see such a play. Nothing, my dear, is so degrading as the public display of lax morals.'

Unperturbed by such sanctimoniousness, Adeline decided to go anyway and instructed her maid to book a box. For the sake of propriety, she then wrote to Lord Cardigan, her father's good friend, to ask him to join her. The overture had just begun when Cardigan entered the box. 'Miss de Horsey,' he said urgently, 'you must leave the theatre at once.'

'I'll do no such thing,' she replied. 'What on earth is the matter?'

'Well,' said a reluctant Cardigan, 'your father and General Cavendish are in the box opposite with – with their mistresses. It will never do for you to be seen. Do, I implore you, permit me to escort you home before the performance begins.'

More amused than annoyed at her father's duplicity, Adeline peeped out of the curtains of the box. There opposite was her father and the general, with two pretty women she had not seen before.

'I *shall* see the play,' she said, laughing, 'and you shall put me into a cab before it is over. I shall be home before papa returns from the "club".'

Not wanting to cause a scene, Cardigan agreed and, after a 'most enjoyable evening hidden behind the curtains', they left in the middle of the last act. Having hailed a hackney-carriage, Cardigan put Adeline and her maid into it and gave the driver instructions to take them home. Unfortunately, the driver was drunk and lost his way in the fog, and they did not reach Upper Grosvenor Street until gone midnight. Her father opened the door.

'Adeline, explain yourself. Where have you been? Is this the hour for a young lady to be out of doors? How dare you conduct yourself in this manner?'

'I've been to the Princess's Theatre, papa,' she replied demurely, noticing him start, 'and I saw you and General Cavendish there; I thought you were dining at the Club . . . and I saw . . .'

'Go to bed at once, Adeline,' interrupted her sheepish-looking father, 'we'll talk about your behaviour later.'

The subject was never mentioned again.[4]

With all her accomplishments, Adeline had no shortage of suitors. In 1849, she became engaged to the Count de Montemolin, the Carlist pretender to the Spanish throne, who shared her passion for music. But she did not love him, rather had she been dazzled by his royal rank, and when he abandoned the struggle in Spain so as to be with her she broke off the engagement. 'I . . . naturally concluded,' she later wrote, 'that after so lightly renouncing his obligations to those who trusted him . . . I, too, might one day be as easily forgotten.'[5]

★

With the house-party over, Adeline and her father returned to London, followed closely by a lovestruck Cardigan. It was not long before his 'marked attentions' towards Adeline became 'the topic of much spiteful and jealous gossip'. To try to put an end to it, Mr de Horsey forbade his daughter to communicate with Cardigan, but she ignored him. One way round the ban was to lower from her bedroom window, 'at the hour when Lord Cardigan rode past', a length of string weighted by coal. Her elderly suitor would then attach his *billets-doux* to the coal and she would haul it up.[6]

No one was more horrified at such behaviour than the Queen. 'Those early Victorian days were exceptionally conventional,' recalled Adeline, 'and the court was still as narrow-minded as when poor Lady Flora Hastings had been the victim of its lying slander. If Lord Cardigan and I had met in 1909 instead of 1857, no particular comment would have been made on our friendship, but in 1857 Society was scandalised because I had the courage to ride and drive with a married man who had an unfaithful wife.'

The gossip was given added malice, according to Adeline, because Lady Cardigan was known to be dangerously unwell. 'Once free, Lord Cardigan would be a prize well worth winning by match-making matrons with marriageable daughters, and his openly avowed affection for me had put an end to these hopes.'

Spencer de Horsey was conscious only of the disgrace that Adeline was bringing down upon her family, and as a last resort he threatened to quit London for good and take her with him. She responded by leaving home and putting up in a quiet hotel in Hyde Park Square. Not long after, she moved into 'a charming little furnished house in Norfolk Street, Park Lane', where she was attended by her father's former valet, Mathews, and three other servants. Cardigan was an almost daily visitor and together they would ride in Hyde Park, Adeline dressed in fetching riding-habits of violet, black or bright green, utterly 'regardless of the averted glances of those who had once called themselves my friends'.[7]

Adeline had been living openly as Cardigan's mistress for more than a year when, in the early morning of 12 July 1858, she was woken by a loud knocking at the front door. There was just enough time to pull on her dressing-gown before Cardigan burst into the room, took her in his arms and said: 'My dearest, she's dead . . . let's get married at once!'

When he had calmed down, he told Adeline that he had come straight from his wife's deathbed, and that she had urged him to marry her in preference to Lady Ailesbury, 'the extent of whose love affairs, it appears, was only known to Lady Cardigan, who told his Lordship the unvarnished truth about them'. But even with his late wife's blessing, Adeline insisted on waiting until a decent length of time had elapsed after her funeral.

Finally, in September, she joined Cardigan and a party of their friends at Cowes aboard his new yacht, *Airedale*, and they immediately set sail for Gibraltar. On the 28th, they were married there in the Military Chapel with Hubert De Burgh and Algernon de Horsey, Adeline's brother, as witnesses. The bride, the first Countess of Cardigan to be married on foreign soil, wore a typically unconventional outfit: white silk gown draped with a blue scarf, and a large hat adorned with feathers. That evening a ball was held aboard the *Airedale*, and after a 'very gay week' at Gibraltar they sailed to Cadiz, and from there took the train to Madrid. They arrived on 16 October, Cardigan's 61st birthday, to witness a review of 30,000 troops in honour of Queen Isabella whose birthday it also was.[8]

Rejoining the *Airedale* at Barcelona, they sailed to Italy, putting in at Leghorn and Elba before disembarking at Civitavecchia for a coach journey to Rome escorted by the Papal Guard. During their stay they were granted a private audience with the Pope, Pius IX, who blessed their marriage; Cardigan, however, was struck by the Romans' lack of enthusiasm for the papal government. Subsequently when, during the *Risorgimento*, Napoleon III sent troops to Rome in early 1860 to protect the Pope, Cardigan told the House of Lords that the measure was necessary. The Pope's rule, he said, 'was of so hateful, arbitrary, and intolerable a nature, that there was none more unpopular, and that to leave it without the support of the French troops would be to endanger the safety of all the authorities there'.[9]

Having returned overland from Italy, via Paris, the new mistress of Deene was welcomed on 14 December 'with a royal reception, six hundred tenants on horseback escorting our carriage from the station to the house'.

The following month, Adeline was listening to a debate in the House of Lords from the Peeresses' Gallery, sitting close to Princess Mary and the Duchess of Cambridge, when Lady Ailesbury appeared. Anticipating that her former rival would ignore her, Adeline spoke up: 'Oh, Lady Ailesbury, you may like to know that before Lady Cardigan died she told my lord all about you and your love affairs!'

'Hush, hush, my dear!' Lady Ailesbury whispered nervously. 'I'm coming to lunch with you tomorrow.'

From that day, Adeline recalled, 'We were outwardly the best of friends'.[10]

★

However, much of society was unwilling to forgive Adeline's behaviour before the death of Lord Cardigan's first wife. It was a time when, according to Lady Augusta Fane, Adeline's first cousin, 'the moral code for women was very strict and could not be transgressed with impunity'. She added: 'In Adeline's case envy and jealousy at her capture of so great a prize added fuel to the fire of the just anger of the virtuous.'[11]

The practical upshot of this was that Adeline became a social outcast: Queen Victoria refused to receive her at Court, and she was not welcome in the houses of the great families of the realm – including members of the Brudenell clan. Cardigan still received invitations, as if his behaviour had been any less reprehensible, but he invariably refused them. In May 1863, after four years of this torture, Cardigan tried to get his family, at least, to remove the ban. To Lady Emily Kingscote, a relative, he wrote that while he was happy to hear she wished to speak to him, he would not be 'satisfied with such a reconciliation unless at the same time you consented to recognise and visit my wife'.

On the same day he wrote to another kinswoman, Mrs Curzon, chiding her for not carrying out her promise the previous year to call on Adeline. 'I hope,' he concluded, 'that we may all be in future on the terms of friendship which ought to exist between those related to each other.'

Four days later, he wrote to Lord Hardwicke, apologising for declining an invitation 'to meet Royalty'. Even if he had not been indisposed, he explained, he would have found the experience 'very painful' given the fact that the invitation had not been extended to his wife. 'I never go out to evening parties,' he continued. 'The world is very severe – the difference between being married in England on the 29th of August or at Gibraltar on the 28th of September is utter ruin for ever in the eyes of the world. When I look at all the flagrant acts that are going on in the world, the details of which are known to all the Clubs in London, and yet those people are cherished and fêted.'[12]

Cardigan's only other misgiving was that Adeline (like his first wife) failed to produce children. Given that he was also childless from his first marriage to a woman who had had a daughter by her previous husband, it is tempting to conclude that Cardigan was infertile. Certainly, it was something he could never bring himself to admit. Visiting the church at Deene one Christmas Eve, as the villagers were hanging decorations, he noticed a large illuminated text on the wall:

UNTO US A CHILD IS BORN, UNTO US A SON IS GIVEN.

'Take that down,' he shouted angrily, 'it is a reflection upon her ladyship.'[13]

In almost every other way their marriage was perfect, however. 'I was ideally happy,' wrote Adeline after his death, 'and I do not believe any one could be a more devoted husband than Lord Cardigan was. There seemed no disparity in our ages, for he was full of the joy of life and entered into everything with the zest of a young man, and he appeared to have quite forgotten his unhappy life with his first wife.'

He was besotted with Adeline, and for a time refused to allow anyone else to escort her in to dinner; only after three years did she manage to persuade him 'to give up this very flattering habit'. Gradually, Adeline adjusted her own lifestyle to suit her husband. As he cared little for painting and books, she dutifully put these interests aside and instead 'entered into all his favourite pursuits': walking, driving, yachting and particularly riding.[14]

Not everything was as straightforward, though. One evening, when the Duke of Buccleuch had come to dinner, Adeline made a less than complimentary remark about the venison they were eating. Cardigan immediately ordered the servants to leave the room before saying to his wife: 'I would have you know that this is the first time that a Lady Cardigan has ever criticised the venison in this house! Let it be the last.'

Also, notwithstanding his age, Cardigan retained a hearty sexual appetite that could not be entirely assuaged by his young wife. 'That's where dear Cardigan used to go with his ladies,' remarked Adeline to her agent after his death, pointing to a tower in the garden. 'There's a room upstairs with windows where you can see people coming. He thought I didn't know, but I never interfered with him.'[15]

Despite her own headstrong nature, Adeline had quickly realised that the secret to good relations with her husband was to avoid unnecessary confrontation. He, in turn, remained devoted to her – despite the occasional dalliance – until his death. 'She is a very good little wife to me, and no two people could be better suited,' he wrote to his sister, Lady Charlotte Sturt, in May 1866. 'We are never apart, even for one hour in the twenty-four.'[16]

Cardigan spent enormous sums making Deene a residence fit for his adored second wife. One of the first warm-air central heating systems was installed (and upgraded a few years later by a hot-water version), as was a huge marble sunken bath in one of the turrets. As Adeline loved dancing, a large ballroom was added to the western end of the house; 70 feet long and 40 feet high, it was decorated in the Victorian Gothic style with stained-glass windows and a minstrels' gallery. A private band was recruited locally and led by a French bandmaster, Monsieur Holstein. It would play during balls and dinners, and beneath Adeline's window on the morning of her birthday, Christmas Eve.

Despite the social restrictions, the Cardigans still spent the Season in London in great style before proceeding to Cowes where they had a house, Rose Cottage, and a luxurious steam yacht: *Sea Horse* replacing *Airedale* in 1867 at a cost of more than £8,500.

Not surprisingly, Cardigan's income was unable to keep pace with such lavish expenditure, and in 1864 he was forced to raise £150,000 by mortgaging part of his estates. More loans were needed the following year, and after his death Adeline claimed to have paid off debts of £365,000.

During his time as Inspector-General of Cavalry, Cardigan was not above using his position to gain favours for personal friends. On 19 November 1857, he wrote to Colonel Edward Hodge, commanding the 4th Dragoon Guards at Manchester:

> My dear Colonel Hodge,
>   A friend of mine, Hubert de Burgh, is interested about Miss Reynolds, one of the principal actresses at the Haymarket Theatre, and one who is going to act immediately at the Manchester Theatre, and he has requested me to ask you and your officers to patronize her.
>   Believe me yours very truly,
>
> Cardigan.[17]

It is probably fair to assume, given the importance of the Inspector-General's half-yearly review, that Hodge and his officers did indeed patronise De Burgh's mistress.

When Cardigan's five-year tenure as Inspector-General ended in February 1860, he was effectively retired from the regular Army. But his military enthusiasm remained undimmed, particularly after his appointment as Colonel of the 11th Hussars in August 1860 and his promotion to Lieutenant-General six months later.

Also in early 1861, Cardigan was chosen to accompany Bertie, the 19-year-old Prince of Wales, to the Prussian army's annual manoeuvres. Unfortunately, his overbearing manner did not go down well with his hosts, themselves no amateurs in the art of conceit. 'The behaviour of this

Englishman was intolerably arrogant,' remarked Prince Kraft zu Hohenlohe-Ingelfingen, 'and his attitude towards Prussian officers was of a kind which he possibly could expect English officers to put up with – or which, perhaps, he thought was justified in an Englishman in his relations with Germans. As a result he was soon called out from many sides; but he preferred to follow the instructions of the Prince of Wales to leave the manoeuvres immediately and depart for England.'[18]

No angel himself, Bertie was soon immersed in a scandal of his own. Having returned from Prussia, he was sent to Ireland for ten weeks of intensive military training; the plan was for him to learn the duties of each officer rank – with a promotion every fortnight – so that he would be able to command a full battalion when the Queen and Prince Albert visited the Curragh in August. In the event, he made such poor progress that he was restricted to marching past at the head of a mere company.

This setback, however, was insignificant when set against his subsequent behaviour. After his parents had returned to England, his brother officers presented him with a young woman of dubious virtue called Nellie Clifden whom he promptly slept with. The Queen never forgave Bertie and partially blamed him for the death of her beloved Albert on 14 December 1861, aged just 42. He had fallen ill in late November after travelling to Cambridge in cold and wet weather to confront his errant son during his first term at university. In fact, Albert had almost certainly been suffering from stomach cancer for nearly four years and this latest illness – either pneumonia or typhoid – was simply the final straw.

Cardigan, meanwhile, had been keeping himself busy by writing and then publishing a drill manual entitled *Cavalry Brigade Movements*. The timing was unfortunate, because a year later the Horse Guards changed the long-established cavalry movement of three horses abreast to four. Cardigan immediately protested in a letter to the Duke of Cambridge, pointing out the practical difficulty of 'crossing a bridge, or passing through a narrow street'. His objections were acknowledged but ignored.[19]

A man like Cardigan, who had thrown himself so wholeheartedly into his career, was not someone who found retirement easy. It was still a surprise to the Horse Guards, however, when in September 1864, aged 66, he applied for the vacant post of Commander-in-Chief in Ireland. The rejection was polite but unequivocal.[20]

His final military act took place on 5 May 1866, when he reviewed his beloved 11th Hussars for the last time at the Middlewick drill-ground in Colchester. The regiment that had been his life would shortly sail for

India, and he had come to say goodbye. Fittingly, he was dressed in the uniform of his old corps and astride Ronald, the charger which had carried him through the hell of Balaclava. Although 68, his seat was still perfect, his back ramrod straight, his eyes still piercingly blue; only his white hair and moustache indicated the passing of the years.

'His Lordship,' reported the regimental journal, 'was accompanied by the Countess of Cardigan, a prepossessing young lady, attired in a blue riding-habit on a handsome charger, and several officers of distinction.' These included Colonel John Douglas, who had commanded the regiment at the charge, Colonel John 'Black Bottle' Reynolds, who had finally made his peace with Cardigan the previous year, and Baron von Brock of the Prussian Embassy.

After the parade inspection and the march past, the 11th Hussars put on a display of mock charges which was so realistic that two riders were unhorsed though not seriously injured. The regiment was then drawn up in close column for an emotional Cardigan to address them:

> Eleventh Hussars, [he began] it is with great pleasure that I come to take farewell of you. You have turned out well today, and you have worked well in the field. You were always a smart regiment, and you have not fallen off in any one thing. It was in Cawnpore my acquaintance with you commenced. You are going back to that land, and I am sure you will do very well, and I wish you every success and prosperity. If you should be called upon for active service I know you will always maintain that character that commenced with Salamanca and ended with Balaclava. You have my hearty farewell and best wishes. Goodbye.

Led by their commander, Lieutenant-Colonel Fraser V.C., the troops responded with three rousing cheers before marching back to their barracks.[21]

Both during his years as Inspector-General of Cavalry based in London, and after his retirement from the Army, Cardigan regularly attended the House of Lords. Most, but not all, of the debates he contributed to were about the military.

In July 1857, he spoke on the subject of transporting cavalry and infantry reinforcements to India, where a mutiny of native troops at

Meerut two months earlier had developed into a national rebellion. Was it true, he asked Lord Panmure, that the reinforcements 'about to be despatched to India for the purpose of suppressing the serious insurrection . . . were to be sent out in sailing vessels instead of steamers?' Surely, he said, the government would be failing to profit from the experience of the Crimea if, 'when they had so many war and merchant steamers at their command, they sent out these troops, whose speedy presence was required to meet a critical emergency, by sailing vessels'.

Panmure replied that 'the most attentive consideration of the Government had been given to this question'. The difficulty with steamers 'was the delay necessarily caused by coaling'. Several ports would have to be visited, 'whereas sailing vessels were able to shorten the course by keeping further from shore'. The result was that they would arrive at their destination 'as soon, if not sooner, than steam vessels'. For this reason, the government had given 'the preference to sailing vessels'.[22]

This was, of course, wishful thinking, and it was fortunate for the government that their troops in or near India had the rebellion well in hand by the time the first reinforcements arrived from Britain in August.

The following March, Cardigan defended the government against criticism that conditions for soldiers in barracks were inhumane. 'Of late years,' he told his peers, 'many arrangements had been made in the barracks with the view to the convenience and comfort of the soldiers.' Married men and their families 'had been removed from the rooms in which single men lived'; the 'rooms were better ventilated than formerly, and were not overcrowded, and the soldiers had in many instances comforts as far as it was possible to provide them'. And there was no truth in the claim that soldiers 'were fed entirely on boiled beef', for 'there was scarcely a regiment in the service in which the men had not three or four times a week good baked meat and potatoes'.[23]

Three months later, he spoke in opposition to Lord John Russell's Jewish Emancipation Bill. The Bill proposed the removal of the words 'on the true faith of a Christian' from the parliamentary oath, thereby enabling practising Jews to enter Parliament.

Since Catholic emancipation in 1829, Jews had been the only influential minority group still barred from politics on the grounds of religion. Ethnic Jews who had converted to Christianity – such as Sampson Gideon, David Ricardo and Benjamin Disraeli – were not affected, and they had been sitting in Parliament since 1770. In 1830, and again in 1833, the House of Lords rejected emancipation Bills sent up by the Commons. Seventeen years later, Baron Lionel de Rothschild, a member of the Jewish faith, was elected Liberal M.P. for the City of London but was unable to take his seat. This prompted his close friend Lord John Russell, the Prime Minister, to sponsor yet another Bill, but again it was defeated in the Lords. The pattern was repeated a number of times in the 1850s.

Opposition to Jewish emancipation before 1858 had come mainly from the Tory squirearchy and nobility. As defenders of the established Church, they saw themselves as duty bound to resist the admittance of M.P.s who, though they denied the divinity of Christ, would have the power to legislate on the organisation and doctrine of that church. Yet they were far from being anti-semitic in the modern sense of the term, although many may have felt a subconscious antipathy to the 'murderers of Christ'. Cardigan was very much a part of this tradition, and previously had always voted against emancipation.

On 1 July 1858, as the House of Lords debated the second reading of Russell's Bill, it became clear that many peers were uncomfortable with the prospect of removing from the oath the words 'on the true faith of a Christian'. It was the Earl of Lucan, Cardigan's arch-enemy, who found a way through the impasse by proposing a clause that would enable each House to make its own rules about the form of the oath.

Although it was supported by Lord Derby's minority Conservative government (which had replaced Palmerston's Whig administration in February), Cardigan spoke against the measure. The form of oath was irrelevant; he was simply not prepared to concede the principle of admitting Jews to Parliament. Such a question had, he said, 'been frequently discussed and decided in the House, and no reasons had been assigned why their Lordships should now change their course, and he for one was not ready to stultify the votes he had given on all former occasions'.

It had been argued, he continued, that unless such a measure was approved, 'a collision between the House of Commons and the courts of law would be the result'. He, however, 'was under no apprehension that any such consequence would flow from the rejection of the Bill'. The Conservative party had a duty 'to consider whether that large number of Liberal measures which were daily coming up from the other House . . . should or should not be at once assented to'. He could not help thinking, he said facetiously, that it 'would be much better that they should gracefully receive the sanction' of the Conservatives 'than that noble Lords should be brought down Session after Session for the next ten years to vote against them, and then at the end of that period be called upon to give them their support'.[24]

His words had some merit, but they failed – as they had so many times in the past – to acknowledge the increasingly liberal atmosphere of mid-Victorian Britain. It was simply no longer possible to prevent Jews or any other influential minority from participating in politics, any more than it had been feasible to block parliamentary reform in 1832. The inevitability of change was something Cardigan understood only at the very end of his life.

Russell's Bill, with Lucan's amendment, was passed by 143 votes to 97.

In an attempt to gain credit for a measure which many saw as unavoidable, Lord Derby's government introduced a moderate parliamentary Reform Bill in early 1859. Its rejection was followed by a General Election at which the Conservatives increased their seats by 30; but they were still ten shy of an overall majority, and were quickly defeated over a motion of no confidence. This allowed Palmerston – now 74 – and the Whigs to regain the helm, albeit with the support of the Radicals. Lord John Russell became Foreign Secretary, and William Gladstone Chancellor of the Exchequer.

For the next six years, Palmerston effectively vetoed any further parliamentary reform. But when he died suddenly on 18 October 1865, two days before his 81st birthday, and was replaced by his Foreign Secretary (now Earl Russell), parliamentary reform became the number one priority. Since 1832, the population of England and Wales had increased by a third from 14 to 21 million, yet only one million adult men – less than one in five – had the vote. Towns and cities had grown dramatically, yet one half of the borough population had 300 seats, the other half just 34. It was generally felt, therefore, that an extension of the franchise and a redistribution of seats were measures which were long overdue.[25]

Russell's Reform Bill was introduced to the Commons by Gladstone in March 1866. It ignored a redistribution of seats – a measure which would be introduced later – in favour of a moderate extension of the franchise: to householders of £7 rental in the boroughs and £14 rental in the counties. This would have given an extra 400,000 men the vote – half of them working class – increasing the total franchise to one in four of the adult male population in England and Wales.[26]

But seeing an opportunity to bring down the Whigs, Disraeli persuaded the Conservatives to vote with Robert Lowe and the right-wing Whigs (the 'Adullamites') who opposed any kind of parliamentary reform. Together, they defeated the government in June over an amendment to substitute rating value for rental in the counties. Lord Derby once again became Prime Minister of a minority government, with Disraeli as Chancellor of the Exchequer.

Popular pressure for reform was growing, with orators like John Bright addressing huge audiences, and when one in Hyde Park was banned in late July the crowd rioted and broke down the railings. 'I am coming reluctantly to the conclusion that we shall have to deal with the question of Reform,' Derby told Disraeli on 16 September.[27]

Ironically, the Representation of the People Act which finally became law on 15 August 1867, was far more sweeping than the measure the Conservatives had helped to defeat the previous year. The boroughs received universal household suffrage in that all occupiers became ratepayers, and all ratepayers became voters; in the counties, all householders of a rental value of £12 got the vote. Of 45 seats taken from small boroughs, 25 were given to the counties, 15 to the towns, a third member to Liverpool, Manchester, Birmingham and Leeds, and one to the University of London. The number of voters in England and Wales was thus increased by 938,000 voters to almost two million; about 40 per cent of the adult male population.

This had come about partly as a result of the popular demand for reform, partly because of the determination of Derby and Disraeli to stay in office by passing legislation of some description. In a minority, they needed the support of the Radicals, and this made the Act more far-reaching than they might have wished. Hence Derby's description of the reform as 'a leap in the dark'.[28]

Incredibly, Cardigan supported the Bill, and gave his reasons for doing so during its passage through the committee stage in the House of Lords on 1 August:

> My Lords . . . I have been in Parliament nearly fifty years, in this House and the House of Commons, during the whole of which time I have firmly supported a Conservative Government, and I confess that I have been much surprised at the Radical and Liberal course which the present Government have adopted with regard to the Reform Bill. To such an extent has this gone that for some time I considered I could not support the Bill. But the question of

Reform stands now in a peculiar position; it has been argued and discussed during a long Session in the House of Commons, and it does seem most desirable that the measure should be passed. The tide of Reform was stemmed for a long time by that great man, Lord Palmerston, but since his death the feeling for Reform has greatly increased, and I question whether now it would not be very dangerous to stop its progress; and I say, my Lords, we may hope for luck in this case which has before occurred in others. The question of the repeal of the Corn Laws was greatly objected to and opposed; but I believe that in the results there never was a measure more thoroughly successful, and that it was one of the best measures which ever passed through the Parliament of this country, conferring a great benefit upon every class of the community. Hoping that we may have the same good luck with regard to the Reform Bill, I shall give my vote in favour of the Bill as it now stands, firmly believing that if this Bill were not successful we should only obtain a more Radical and a more dangerous one from the party opposed to us in Parliament.[29]

Cardigan, the arch-conservative – the man who had opposed the Great Reform Act of 1832, the repeal of the Corn Laws in 1846, the admittance of Jews to Parliament in 1858, and who had supported Catholic emancipation in 1829 only out of loyalty to Wellington and his party – had finally, aged 69, accepted the inevitability and even desirability of change.

It is unlikely that he would have been disappointed with the results if he had lived to see them. Working-class voters were now in a majority in towns, but most of the new county voters came from the middle class. Overall, the composition of Parliament changed little, and if anything the Conservatives were the long-term beneficiaries of reform. The Liberals might have gained a majority of 112 at the General Election of 1868, but Disraeli and the Conservatives were able to turn this into a healthy majority of their own in 1874. It was the first time since the Repeal of the Corn Laws in 1846 that the Conservatives had had a stable majority government.

It was perhaps fitting that, given his own ability to cause chaos, Cardigan's final contribution to Parliament, on 6 March 1868, was to present a petition 'praying that some National Reward may be conferred on the family of the late Lieutenant-General Henry Shrapnel,' the inventor of the exploding shell. The question of remuneration had been mooted as long ago as 1837, but nothing had been done during Shrapnel's lifetime and by his will he had 'expressed a wish that some tangible reward should be conferred upon his son'. Cardigan 'now begged to propose that those services should be recompensed, or to refer the matter to a Committee to ascertain whether some honour, reward, or advantage should not be conferred upon the petitioner'.

Lord Longford, replying for the War Office, said that 'he could hold out no encouragement whatever to the petitioner that his prayer would be granted'. In consideration of his invention, the late General 'had received a special pension of £1,200 a year, which he had enjoyed for 28 years, and had received £10,000 from the East India Company'.[30]

With his military career over, Cardigan spent more and more time at Deene. One of the sports to which he turned increasingly was shooting. The old muzzle-loading twin-barrel shotgun – with which the great sportsman, 'Squire' Osbaldeston, was reputed to have killed 100 pheasants with 100 shots in the 1820s – had been replaced by the breech loader in the 1850s. But shotguns still had twin hammers and used black-powder cartridges; firing-pins, choke bores, self-ejectors and smokeless powders would not appear until the 1870s.

Cardigan's shoots were typical in that they still operated in a semi-formal way, with rabbits and hares often making up as much of the bag as pheasants. During one occasion, Cardigan told his gamekeeper to send the beaters through a nearby wood. The keeper tried to protest, but was cut short. After a number of pheasants had been killed, Cardigan called the keeper over and said: 'Why did you wish to prevent me shooting through that covert?'

'Well, my lord,' came the reply, 'that wood does not belong to you, and the gentleman as owns it is shooting there tomorrow.'

Another time, Cardigan was invited to shoot with the Duke of Buccleuch at Geddington Chase. During lunch at the Keeper's Lodge, Buccleuch showed his guest a hat which had been hanging on an iron rod in the cottage wall when the iron was struck by lightning, making a hole in the hat. Examining it, Cardigan exclaimed: 'Just how I shot Tuckett.'[31]

Although not a deeply religious man, Cardigan always attended church on Sunday and expected his servants to do likewise. Dressed in a frock-coat and carrying a tall chimney-pot hat, he would sit with Adeline and their guests in the family pew; the housemaids, in black dresses and regulation bonnets, sat in force behind.

As death approached, he dwelled increasingly on the question of his salvation. 'I hope, my dear Brudenell,' wrote his sister Charlotte in 1866 after the death of her husband, 'that you are thinking seriously of the great change which we must (at our age) expect, and flee for refuge to the only hope set before us – the Gospel of Christ.'

'I assure you,' he replied, 'I think much more seriously on those important subjects to which you allude than I formerly did.'[33]

When he did travel down to London, Cardigan would often take the night mail train from Leicester, which involved a 25-mile carriage ride from Deene with a change of horses on the way. But as he was not in the habit of leaving until the last possible moment, his postilion had to make up the time by furious riding. After the first change of horses, there was a steep hill a mile long with a sharp curve half-way down and a brook at its base. 'What about Warley Hill, my lord?' asked young Bob the postilion, the first time he made that journey.

'Gallop down it, you damn fool,' Cardigan replied. 'If I am not afraid to risk my neck, you need not mind breaking your damn thing.'

There was never any time to stop at the turnpike gates and the postilion would be forced to shout ahead for them to be opened, adding, 'Pay on the way back!' as the carriage thundered past. At Leicester Station, the train would always be ready to leave, and as he boarded it Cardigan would throw Bob a sovereign to pay the toll and share the change with the other postilion.[32]

One last opportunity to become Lord-Lieutenant of Northamptonshire presented itself to Cardigan when the Marquess of Exeter died on 15 January 1867. Having already suggested himself as a replacement during Exeter's illness, he now made a formal application to Lord Derby, the Prime Minister. The day after receiving Cardigan's letter, an exasperated Derby wrote to General Grey, the Queen's Private Secretary:

> The evening papers yesterday announced the long expected death of Lord Exeter, and half an hour later I received from Lord Cardigan a letter, dated from Devon the same morning, and

evidently sent up by messenger, formally renewing his application for the Lord Lieutenancy for which I had already privately told him that I could not submit his name to the Queen. I have disposed of the question and probably made an enemy of him.

Lord Southampton was duly appointed instead, but Derby was anxious to make amends. In February, the colonelcy of one of the Household regiments of cavalry fell vacant and Derby intimated to the Queen, through Grey, 'a wish to give it to Lord Cardigan, already furious at not getting the Lord Lieutenancy of Northamptonshire'. The reply came back that the Queen 'did not at all like the idea of Lord Cardigan's appointment to one of the Household regiments of cavalry, as it would bring him constantly in contact with the Court' and 'that the appointment would be disagreeable to her'.[34]

The monarch who had invited Cardigan to Windsor three days after his return from the Crimea, who had listened spellbound to his description of the charge, and who had recommended him as Lucan's replacement as commander of the Cavalry Division, had been unable to forgive his immoral behaviour before his first wife's death. The revelations from the Calthorpe case cannot have made her any more sympathetic. Lucan, by contrast, had lived quietly since the Crimea and was rewarded by being made Gold Stick and Colonel of the 1st Life Guards in 1865. A year before his death in 1888, he would be promoted to Field-Marshal.

In early March 1868, the Pytchley Hunt met at Rockingham Castle. As the Master, John Anstruther Thomson, was moving off with the hounds, Cardigan rode up to him. 'You have known me many years,' he said.

'Yes, sir,' replied Thomson.

'I have always been a very healthy man.'

'Yes, sir.'

'Just now I got a fit of giddiness. I'm not well; I'm going home – goodbye,' said Cardigan, before setting off at a walk down the broad avenue leading to Deene. But an hour later, with the hunt now near Deene, Cardigan reappeared wearing a mackintosh. 'I felt better,' he told Thomson, 'so I thought I would come out for a little while.'[35]

On Wednesday, 26 March, a fine spring morning, Cardigan was out riding a young horse he had recently bought – with Adeline and a guest, Sir Henry Edwards – when a groom met them with the news that William

Bell, one of his gamekeepers, had been killed by an exploding gun. On reaching Bell's lodge three miles away, Cardigan sent Adeline and Sir Henry home before entering. 'He was much affected by the sight of his unfortunate servant,' reported the *Northampton Mercury*, 'though he observed he had seen gun-shot injuries of a more ghastly character in the Crimea. He spoke with great kindness to Miss Bell, the sister and house-keeper of the deceased, and after telling her that everything that he could do to console the family should be done, and that she must not give way to incessant grief, he bid her good morning, and rode away at a gentle trot.'

About a quarter of a mile from home he met William Siddons, the assis-tant road-surveyor, on his way to Gretton. Having remarked that the roads were much improved and did not shake the carriage as they used to, Cardigan bid Siddons 'Good day' and continued on his way.

Soon afterwards, some children who were playing at the side of the road noticed Cardigan's horse rear and plunge before throwing its rider. One of them called to the surveyor, who ran down the road and found Cardigan lying on the ground, his face ashen and foaming at the mouth. Sending some women from cottages nearby to raise the alarm, he lifted Cardigan to his feet and partly carried him about 200 yards towards the house until a carriage arrived to take him the rest of the way.

For two days Cardigan lay unconscious, gasping for breath. Doctors were called from Weldon, King's Cliffe, Stamford and London, but noth-ing could be done. 'The knowledge that he could not speak to me and did not recognise me intensified my grief a thousandfold,' wrote Adeline. 'But mercifully his suffering was not prolonged.' In the late evening of Friday, 28 March 1868, the last of the Brudenells died.

The post-mortem, carried out the following evening, found an effusion of blood and water on the brain and 'led to the conclusion that death had arisen from concussion'. On the other hand, it is just possible that he fell from his horse as the result of a stroke; according to his wife, a blood clot had formed on his brain after a serious fall while hunting in 1862, causing him to have periodic seizures for the rest of his life.[36]

Over the weekend, Cardigan's body lay in the ballroom at Deene, the coffin covered with a crimson velvet pall emblazoned with his coat of arms, resting on a dais in the middle of the room. Upon the pall lay his peer's robes and the uniform he had worn at Balaclava, along with his sabre and orders of knighthood. With the shutters closed and the walls hung with black, the only light provided was from four huge candlesticks, one in each corner. In two days, nearly 2,000 people filed past the coffin in silence.

On Monday, 31 March, the funeral procession set out from the court-yard of the great house to the village church. At its head walked Mathews, Adeline's faithful servant who had become Cardigan's valet, carrying his coronet on a crimson cushion. Then came the coffin, draped with crim-son velvet and borne by four brother officers of the 11th Hussars. Immediately behind followed Ronald, his charger, between two grooms; then the family mourners, their tall hats wrapped with black crêpe; and next, two by two, 62 tenants from three counties. Bringing up the rear were the gamekeepers in green liveries, and the private band. Following tradition, no women were present.

The church was already packed with neighbours, relations and friends, and villagers from Deene and Deenethorpe. Others stood silently in the churchyard. After the service Cardigan was laid to rest above ground, as he had insisted, in a specially built tomb in the Brudenell Chapel. His family then returned to the house to hear the terms of his will. Subject to vari-ous legacies, all Cardigan's possessions, including 25,000 acres of land, were left to his wife for life with remainder on her death to Lord Robert Brudenell-Bruce, the fourth and youngest son of Ernest, later the 3rd Marquess of Ailesbury. His titles automatically reverted to his senior living relative, George, the 2nd Marquess of Ailesbury. Henceforth, the Earldom of Cardigan would be a courtesy title held by the eldest son of the Marquess.

Bequests of £7,000 and £5,000 were made to Hubert De Burgh and Lord Westmorland (formerly Lord Burghersh) respectively. De Burgh's wife Marianne, sister of the first Lady Cardigan, was left an annuity of £100, as were Cardigan's groom, coachman and gardener. His French butler, Gallant, received £150 a year.

After the will had been read, Lord Ernest Bruce went for a walk in the park with Adeline's younger brother, Colonel William de Horsey. 'Well, it's a good thing for Robert, as Lady Cardigan won't last long!' said Lord Ernest.

'Look here, my lord,' came the icy reply, 'you seem to forget that you are talking about my sister.'[37]

On learning of the conversation, Adeline was furious and, from that moment, she determined to outlive her 22-year-old kinsman, then serving as a naval officer in Jamaica. She managed this with three years to spare: Lord Robert dying in 1912; she, aged 90, in 1915. According to her cousin, Lady Augusta Fane, a regular visitor at Deene, her later years were marked by increasingly eccentric behaviour:

> Some neighbours, calling on her at Deene, found her dressed in Lord Cardigan's red military riding trousers and cuirass with a leopard skin thrown over her shoulders. Her visitors looked rather surprised at this get up, and were still more astonished when she told them it was her bicycling costume! Sometimes she would come down attired as a Spanish dancer, with a coloured skirt covered with lace and a mantilla and high comb, when she would dance the cachucha, playing the castanets with great skill and verve. Another evening she would flit round the great hall dressed like the Grey Nun who was supposed to haunt the place, when it behoved her guests to show alarm by hiding under the tables and chairs. In every-day life she wore a wig composed of golden curls with a scarlet geranium fixed behind her ear . . . For several years before her death she kept her coffin in the inner hall and would order her butler, Knighton, to lift her into it so that she might be certain that it was comfortable.[38]

'The kindest thing one can say about [Cardigan] is that he was a very stupid man, who tried to hide his stupidity by a display of arrogance and bluster,' wrote Guy Paget, author of *The History of the Althorp and Pytchley Hunt*.[39]

This is a typical and in some ways understandable assessment of a man whose life was dogged by so much self-inflicted controversy. It is also untrue. No idiot could have come top of his class at Harrow at a time when the school was educating future Prime Ministers of the calibre of Sir Robert Peel and Lord Palmerston; no idiot could have displayed such an increasingly confident performance on the floor of both Houses of Parliament.

At the same time, Cardigan could never be described as an intellectual, nor would he have wished to. With little interest in books and art, his exposure to culture was confined to music and plays – not least because attending the theatre was so much a part of society life. But such 'philistinism' in no way set him apart from his contemporaries, particularly military men who tended to view learning for its own sake with great suspicion. Little more was expected of a cavalry officer than for him to know his duty, ride well, shoot straight and at all times behave like a gentleman.

The popular image of Cardigan today (most recently propagated by the *Flashman* books) is of the archetypal early-Victorian Army officer: an arrogant, homicidal snob with too much money and too few brains, as likely to be found aboard a woman as a horse. Like all caricatures, it is a distortion of the truth, but based on fact nonetheless. What made Cardigan so easy to ridicule was that everything about him was excessive: his wealth, his good looks, his libido, his pride, his arrogance.

This last character trait can, in part, be put down to the fact that he was an adored only son used to getting his way. The one chance to reverse this trend was lost when he was removed from Harrow – an environment which might well have tempered his overbearing nature – after just two and a half years.

But the full reason may be more complicated still. Outward bravado is often the result of fundamental insecurity, which in Cardigan may have come about through the contradictions and uncertainties of his early years. His father was the heir to one of the richest earldoms in the kingdom, yet his uncle's late marriage had put this succession in doubt and Cardigan's youth was spent in the relatively modest confines of a small country manor. His father was related to many of the oldest and most powerful noble families in the kingdom, yet his mother's origins were comparatively humble. The legacy of this was his preoccupation with rank and social position, illustrated by his continual demand for marks of royal favour.

It did not help that his parents were unexceptional, unprepossessing people, and that his father's one act of self-assertion was to marry beneath himself. Deep down, Cardigan may not have respected his parents and, as a result, they were unable to provide him with either the emotional security or the moral boundaries that he needed to be able to develop into a well-rounded young man. All this was compounded when he chose as his first wife a woman equally as vain and self-obsessed as he was himself.

How much different his life might have been if Adeline had been his first wife is difficult to assess. He certainly became less temperamental once he was able to give, and receive, genuine affection. It is probably no coincidence that the most liberal gesture of his life – voting for the Reform Bill of 1867 – took place during the relatively harmonious years of his second marriage.

Cardigan always had a sensitive, generous side to his nature, but it was reserved on the whole for people he did not feel threatened by: most women, tenants, servants and ordinary soldiers. Gentlemen were a different proposition, particularly members of the gentry whom he identified as his social inferiors (partly a repudiation of his mother's background). Because of his own social and military rank, he felt that he could berate them for not living up to his high standards of military duty. Conversely they, as officers and gentlemen, thought themselves his equal and were not used to such high-handed treatment. Only Lord George Paget discovered the secret to serving under Cardigan without either constantly giving in to him or living in a state of permanent disharmony: managing him 'with calmness and firmness, and when one is in the right'.[40]

The great irony of Cardigan's life is that he deserved neither the level of opprobrium directed at him before the Crimean War, nor the adulation afterwards (albeit tempered as the truth became known). In his desire to produce the finest cavalry regiment in the British Army – an ambition he seems to have achieved – he undoubtedly overstepped the mark with his domineering treatment of junior officers. But a number of them must also bear a share of the responsibility for the collisions that took place. Objecting to the extra work needed to satisfy his high standards, many responded by deliberately provoking him.

Radical politicians and much of the press were only too happy to portray Cardigan as the villain – a prime example of the dangers of the purchase system whereby any man, whatever his character defects, could attain a position of authority simply by virtue of his wealth and rank. Their ends were invariably political, with Cardigan portrayed as the archetypal Tory, an inbred aristocrat who opposed all change and rode roughshod over his social inferiors. But they only ever told half the story.

He was indeed a staunch Tory, anxious to retain the established order, and to this end he voted against the Reform Bill of 1832 and the Repeal of the Corn Laws in 1846. But he also voted for parliamentary reform in 1867, and his support of Catholic emancipation cost him the goodwill of his political patron and kinsman, Lord Ailesbury. His long affair with Lady Ailesbury may have been an act of revenge.

To his troops he was undoubtedly a hard taskmaster, even a martinet. But despite the public perception, he did not insist on rigid discipline out of sadistic pleasure; he did so because he believed it was the only way to ensure efficiency – and he may have been right. At the same time he never shirked his own responsibilities, was always conscious of the welfare of his men, and in return was respected and even admired. The steadiness of the Light Brigade at Balaclava was thanks, at least in part, to his tireless preoccupation with drill.

Cardigan is, of course, best remembered for leading the charge of the Light Brigade. It was this single event that for a time wiped out, in the minds of the public and the press, all the shame and scandal of the previous 20 years. But, in truth, his actions that day were somewhat less than glorious – particularly his hasty and undignified withdrawal from the guns. This is not necessarily to impugn his courage – his boxing, hard riding and willingness to duel are evidence of that – rather to emphasise his military naïvety. Having reached the guns, he quickly convinced himself that he had fulfilled his duty and was at liberty to make his way to safety.

'That he believed himself to be a hero, and that he also believed his conduct as leader of the famous charge to have been from first to last irreproachable, there can be no doubt whatever,' wrote 'Thormanby', the respected hunting correspondent.[41]

But this self-delusion ultimately proved counter-productive. As more and more officers returned from the Crimea, rumours of his alleged misconduct began to spread. Instead of treating them with lofty disdain, he made the mistake of challenging the most damaging – contained in Calthorpe's book – in court. Despite gaining a moral victory, he failed to undermine the central allegation that he had retreated prematurely from the charge. On the contrary, Calthorpe produced a number of witness affidavits in support of this claim and thereby dealt a mortal blow to Cardigan's military reputation.

Even as ardent an admirer of Cardigan as 'Thormanby' – who described him in *The Kings of the Hunting-Field* as the 'most charitable and kindly of men' – was under no illusions when it came to his conduct at the charge:[42]

> He was the first to dash in at a gallop among the Russian guns, but, unfortunately for his reputation, he was not the last to come out. Beyond all question, he left the men, whom he had so gallantly led to their goal, to find their way out of the tangle in which they were involved, as best they could. From the moment he got among the Russian cavalry he effaced himself as a leader, and simply fought, like Hal-o'-the-Wynd, 'for his own hand'. Why he should so strangely have forgotten or ignored the duties of a leader is an enigma to which no one has offered a satisfactory solution. He was not the sort of man to lose his head in a crisis, yet unless he did so on that occasion, his conduct is inexplicable.[43]

The charge of the Light Brigade was a heaven-sent opportunity for Cardigan to put the endless controversy of his life behind him. Instead, his conduct during the action generated yet more controversy, and ensured that his rehabilitation in the minds of the public would never be truly complete.

Chapter Notes

Abbreviations: principal archives

British Library: BL
The Correspondence of Sir Robert Peel (PEEL)

Northamptonshire Record Office, Northampton: NRO
The Brudenell Papers (BRUD)

National Army Museum, London: NAM
The Crimean Papers of Field Marshal Lord Raglan (RAGLAN)
The Diary of the 3rd Countess Harrowby (HARROWBY)
The Letters of General Sir William Forrest (FORREST)
The Typescript documents of James Blunt (BLUNT)

National Library of Scotland, Edinburgh: NLS
The Letters of General Sir George Brown (BROWN)

University of Nottingham: NU
The Diary of W.D.N. Drury Lowe (DRURY)

Public Record Office, Kew, London: PRO
War Office Records (WO)

The Royal Archives, Windsor Castle: RA
Queen Victoria's Journal (QVJ)

Wiltshire Record Office, Trowbridge: WRO
The Ailesbury Papers (AILES)

As the following sources are frequently used, they are abbreviated as shown. Full descriptions are contained in the bibliography.

Adeline: Adeline, Countess of Cardigan, *My Recollections*.
Anglesey: Marquess of Anglesey, *A History of British Cavalry: Vol. II 1851–71*.
Affidavits: Hon. Somerset Calthorpe, *Cardigan v. Calthorpe: Affidavits filed by the Respondent*.
Baldick: Robert Baldick, *The Duel*.
Court Martial: *Proceedings of the General Court Martial upon the Trial of Captain Wathen*.
Duberly: Mrs Henry Duberly, *Journal Kept during the Russian War*.
Eight Months: 7th Earl of Cardigan, *Eight Months on Active Service*.
Gronow: Rees Howell Gronow, *Captain Gronow*.
Hodge: Edward Hodge, *Little Hodge*.
Kinglake: Alexander Kinglake, *The Invasion of the Crimea*.

Loy Smith: George Loy Smith, *A Victorian RSM*.
Mitchell: Albert Mitchell, *Recollections of One of the Light Brigade*.
Russell: W.H. Russell, *The Great War with Russia*.
Paget: General Lord George Paget, *The Light Cavalry Brigade in the Crimea*.
Speech: *Speech of Major-General the Earl of Lucan in the House of Lords, Monday, March 19, 1855*.
Sweetman: John Sweetman, *Raglan*.
Thomas: Donald Thomas, *Charge! Hurrah! Hurrah!*
Trial: *The Trial of James Thomas Earl of Cardigan*.
Wake: Joan Wake, *The Brudenells of Deene*.
Woodham-Smith: Cecil Woodham-Smith, *The Reason Why*.

To avoid cluttering up the text with footnotes, sources are often grouped together under one note.

Chapter One – A Chequered History

1 Pepys, *The Shorter Pepys*, p. 866.
2 Wake, p. 177.
3 Ibid., p. 282.
4 Ibid., p. 341.
5 Ibid.
6 Ibid.; Robert Brudenell to Ailesbury, 6 March 1795, AILES, 9/35/266, WRO.
7 Stanton, *On Chiltern Slopes*, p. 126; Ibid., p. 51.

Chapter Two – Early Promise

1 Woodham-Smith, p. 15; Letter to author from Alasdair Hawkyard, Archivist, Harrow School, 27 April 1995.
2 Collins, *The Public Schools*, p. 286.
3 Ibid., pp. 288–9.

4 C.J. Tyerman, 'Byron's Harrow', in Hunter, *The Harrow Collection*, p. 29.
5 Hawkyard, *William Henry Fox Talbot*, p. 19.
6 Charles Torlese, 'A Hundred Years Ago', *The Harrovian*, Vol. XXIV (1911), p. 56.
7 Letter to author from Hawkyard, op. cit.
8 Chandos, *Boys Together*, pp. 138–9.
9 Torlese, 'A Hundred Years Ago', op. cit.
10 W.H. Fox Talbot to his mother, 7 May 1812, 'Letters from Harrow School: 1811–1815', Talbot Papers, Lacock Abbey.
11 'Thormanby', *Kings of the Hunting-Field*, pp. 247–8.
12 Gronow, pp. 213–14.
13 Cardigan, *Autobiographical Account of his Military Career*, 20 Aug., 1863, BRUD, N/IV/1, NRO.
14 *The History of the University of Oxford*, V, p. 316.
15 Letter to author from Judith Cuthoys, Assistant Archivist, Christ Church, Oxford, 28 March 1995.
16 Gash, *Aristocracy and People*, p. 13.
17 Hibbert, *George IV*, pp. 132, 137–8.
18 Gronow, p. 30.
19 Ibid., p. 18.
20 *The History of White's*, I, p. 175.
21 Longford, *Wellington*, p. 62.
22 W. R. Cartright to Lord Brudenell, 10 and 12 Nov. 1819, BRUD, F/III/288, NRO.

Chapter Three – Mrs Johnstone

1 Gronow, p. 17.
2 *The History of White's*, II, pp. 163–4, 180.
3 *The Times*, 24 June 1824.
4 Ibid.; Tollemache, *The Tollemaches of Helmingham and Ham*, pp. 136–7.
5 *The Times*, 24 June 1824.
6 Tollemache, op. cit., pp. 139–40.
7 Gronow, pp. 167–8.
8 *The Creevey Papers*, p. 75.
9 *The Times*, 24 June 1824.
10 Woodham-Smith, p. 21.
11 Brudenell to Ailesbury, 21 Sept. 1825, AILES, 9/35/229, WRO.
12 Adeline, p. 92.
13 Cardigan, *Autobiographical Account*, op. cit.
14 Ibid.
15 Murray, *The History of the VIII Hussars*, I, pp. 386–7, 389–90.
16 Cardigan, *Autobiographical Account*, op. cit.
17 Apperley, *The Chase*, p. 54.
18 *The Army Purchase Question*, p. 22.
19 Longford, op. cit., p. 184.
20 Cardigan to Peel, 23 Dec. 1841, PEEL, Add. MSS. 404998/f/130, BL.
21 *Hansard's Parliamentary Debates*, 3rd Series, Vol. 86, pp. 1222–4.
22 Longford, op. cit., pp. 184–9.
23 *Morning Chronicle*, 23 March 1829.45–8.

Chapter Four – The Arch-Conservative

1   Pocock, *Sailor King*, p. 212.
2   Woodward, *The Age of Reform*, p. 25.
3   Longford, op. cit., p. 227.
4   Ibid., p. 269; Woodward, op. cit., p. 78.
5   *Hansard's*, 3rd Series, Vol. 3, pp. 1150–65.
6   Ibid., Vol. 5, pp. 187–92.
7   Ibid., pp. 1296–7.
8   Gronow, p. XV.
9   *Northampton Mercury*, 7 July 1832.
10 Ibid., 22 Sept. 1832.
11 *Northampton Herald*, 15 Dec. 1830.
12 *The Times*, 26 Nov. 1832.
13 *Northampton Mercury*, 22 Dec. 1832.
14 Woodham-Smith, p. 39.

Chapter Five – Court-Martial

1   Wylly, *XVth Hussars,* pp. 275–8.
2   Ibid., p. 280.
3   *Court Martial*, p. 220.
4   Ibid., pp. 59, 223–4.
5   *New Weekly Despatch*, 2 Feb. 1834.
6   *Court Martial,* pp. 66–7, 76–8.
7   Ibid., pp. 150–52, 159–61, 241–2.
8   Ibid., p. 163.
9   Ibid., pp. 52, 56, 164–6, 245–6.
10 Ibid., pp. 48, 167–8.
11 Ibid., pp. 8–11, 84–6, 169–74.
12 Ibid., p. 175.
13 Ibid., pp. 106–7, 128–31, 138–41, 147–8, 176–9.
14 Ibid., pp. 2–4, 284–5.
15 Ibid., pp. 8–12.
16 Ibid., pp. 13–32.
17 Ibid., pp. 33, 39, 45.
18 Ibid., pp. 53, 61, 63, 66.
19 Ibid., pp. 67–70.
20 Ibid., pp. 72–4, 77–80.
21 Ibid., pp. 88–9, 96.
22 Ibid., pp. 108–9, 113–16.
23 Ibid., pp. 117, 123, 127.
24 Ibid., pp. 148–51, 154.
25 Ibid., pp. 154–218.
26 Ibid., pp. 219–21.
27 Ibid., pp. 223–4, 229.
28 Ibid., pp. 239–64.
29 *The Times*, 30 Jan. 1834.
30 *United Service Gazette*, 11 Jan. 1834.

Chapter Six – A Change of Fortune

1 General Order, 1 Feb. 1834, *Court Martial*, pp. 269–80.
2 *New Weekly Despatch,* 2 Feb. 1834.
3 Cardigan, *Autobiographical Account,* op. cit.; *Return of Copies or Extracts of Correspondence respecting Lord Brudenell,* BRUD, N/XVII/6, NRO; Sweetman, p. 94.
4 *Drakard's Stamford News,* 11 Feb. 1834.
5 *The Greville Memoirs,* II, p. 338.
6 Thomas, p. 58.
7 Nethercote, *The Pytchley Hunt,* p. 86.
8 *Naval and Military Gazette,* 6 June 1835.
9 Somerset to Hill, 16 Sept. 1835, quoted in Sweetman, p. 94.
10 Woodham-Smith, pp. 50–51.
11 Somerset to Hill, 14 Oct. 1835, quoted in Sweetman, pp. 94–5.
12 *Historical Record of the Eleventh Hussars,* p. 77.
13 *Morning Chronicle,* 24 Sept. 1840.
14 *The Times,* 1 April 1836.
15 *Morning Post,* 2 April 1836.
16 *Morning Chronicle,* 7 April 1836.
17 *Hansard's,* 3rd Series, Vol. 33, pp. 534–83.
18 Brudenell to Peel, 10 May 1836, PEEL, Add. MSS. 40422/f/86, BL.
19 *United Service Gazette,* 7 May 1836.
20 Cardigan, *Autobiographical Account,* op. cit.
21 Dunbar, *Golden Interlude,* pp. 118, 122.
22 Loy Smith, pp. 37–43.
23 Cardigan, *Autobiographical Account,* op. cit.
24 *Historical Record of the Eleventh Hussars,* pp. 78–80.
25 Loy Smith, pp. 44–6.
26 Woodham-Smith, p. 59.
27 Cardigan, *Autobiographical Account,* op. cit.
28 Loy Smith, p. 48; *United Service Gazette,* 16 June 1838.
29 Thomas, p. 74.
30 Weintraub, *Victoria,* pp. 112–13.

Chapter Seven – The 'Black Bottle Affair'

1 Loy Smith, p. 53.
2 *Morning Herald,* 14 and 20 Aug. 1838.
3 Nethercote, op. cit., pp. 99, 104.
4 *Naval and Military Gazette,* 20 Oct. 1838.
5 PEEL, Add. MSS. 40426/f/342 and f/390, BL.
6 *Historical Record of the Eleventh Hussars,* pp. 81–2.
7 Loy Smith, pp. 55–6.
8 *Morning Chronicle,* 12 Aug. 1839.
9 Ibid., 22 Aug. 1839.
10 Ibid., 12 Aug. 1839.
11 Ibid., 12 & 16 Aug. 1839.
12 Ibid., 22 and 23 Aug. 1839.
13 *Morning Herald,* 21 Aug. 1839.

14 Thomas, pp. 80–81.
15 Cardigan, *Autobiographical Account*, op. cit.; RA QVJ: 15 Oct. 1839.
16 Loy Smith, pp. 56–7.
17 RA QVJ: 7 March 1840.
18 *Historical Record of the Eleventh Hussars,* pp. 85–6.
19 *Northampton Herald,* 21 March 1840.
20 *Bell's Life in London,* 29 March 1840; *Northampton Herald,* 28 March 1840.
21 *The Globe,* 16 Sept. 1840.
22 *United Service Gazette,* 31 Oct. 1840.
23 *The Globe,* 16 and 17 Sept. 1840; *Morning Chronicle,* 6 Oct. 1840.
24 *Morning Chronicle,* 6 and 16 Oct. 1840.
25 *United Service Gazette,* 31 Oct. 1840.
26 *The Times,* 6 Oct. 1840.
27 *Historical Record of the Eleventh Hussars,* pp. 87–8.
28 Dale, *Fashionable Brighton,* pp. 13–18, 135, 138–9.
29 Wake, pp. 372–3.
30 *Brighton Herald,* 26 Sept. and 3 Oct. 1840.
31 Ibid.

Chapter Eight – Intent to Murder

1   *Morning Chronicle,* 4 Sept. 1840.
2   Cardigan's Handwritten Account of the Duel, BRUD, N/VIII/1, NRO.
3   *Trial,* pp. 28–45, 80–82.
4   *The Times,* 16 Sept. 1840; *The Globe,* 16 Sept. 1840.
5   *Morning Chronicle,* 9 Oct. 1840.
6   FORREST, 5804/32, NAM.
7   Sweetman, pp. 95–6.
8   Baldick, p. 42; *The Globe,* 21 Oct. 1840; *The Times,* 21 Oct. 1840.
9   *The Times,* 29 Sept. 1840.
10 *Morning Chronicle,* 2 and 5 Oct. 1840.
11 *The Sun,* 26 Sept. 1840; *Brighton Herald,* 26 Sept. and 6 Oct. 1840; *The Times,* ibid.; *Morning Chronicle,* 6 Oct. 1840.
12 *Morning Chronicle,* 12 Oct. 1840.
13 *The Times,* 15 and 22 Oct. 1840.
14 General Order No. 538, Horse Guards, 20 Oct. 1840, BRUD, N/VII/2, NRO.
15 RA QVJ: 12 and 16 Oct. 1840.
16 Woodham-Smith, pp. 73–4.
17 *Brighton Herald,* 24 Oct. 1840.
18 *The Times,* 24 and 26 Oct. 1840; *United Service Gazette,* 31 Oct. 1840.
19 *The Globe,* 3 Nov. 1840.
20 *The Examiner,* 8 Nov. 1840.
21 Loy Smith, p. 58.
22 *Naval and Military Gazette,* 16 Jan. 1841.
23 *Morning Chronicle,* 30 Oct. 1840; Woodham-Smith, pp. 75–6; *The Times,* 30 Jan. 1841.
24 RA QVJ: 31 Jan. 1841.
25 *Naval and Military Gazette,* 5 Dec. 1840 and 20 Feb. 1841.

26 Ryan, *Was Lord Cardigan a Hero at Balaklava?*, pp. 19–20.
27 Paget, *The History of the Pytchley Hunt*, pp. 163–4; Nethercote, op. cit., pp. 112-13.
28 *Morning Chronicle*, 7 Jan. 1841.
29 *Alligator*, 16 Jan. 1841.

Chapter Nine – 'Plague-spot of the Army'

1   *Morning Chronicle*, 25 Jan. 1841.
2   RA QVJ: 31 Jan. 1841; Townsend, *Modern State Trials*, I, p. 212.
3   Baldick, pp. 109–10.
4   *The Times*, 29 Sept. 1840.
5   RA QVJ: 28 Jan. 1841.
6   *Trial*, pp. 2–9.
7   Ibid., pp. 10–27.
8   Ibid., p. 32.
9   Ibid., p. 35.
10 Ibid., p. 81
11 Ibid., pp. 93–6.
12· Ibid., pp. 97–8.
13 Ibid., pp. 98–9.
14 Ibid., pp. 99–101.
15 Ibid., pp. 106–9.
16 Ibid., pp. 110–16.
17 Ibid., pp. 116–23.
18 RA QVJ: 16 Feb. 1841.
19 *Morning Post*, 19 Feb. 1841.
20 Wake, p. 388.
21 *Morning Chronicle*, 18 Feb. 1841; *The Times*, 17 and 18 Feb. 1841.
22 Baldick, pp. 113–14.
23 *Hansard's*, 3rd Series, Vol. 56, pp. 1394–1410.
24 Loy Smith, pp. 58–9.
25 *Morning Chronicle*, 14 April 1841; *Morning Post*, 19 April 1841.
26 *Hansard's*, 3rd Series, Vol. 57, pp. 956–8.
27 General Order, 22 April 1841, quoted in Thomas, p. 146.
28 *The Times*, 24 April 1841.
29 *The Letters of Queen Victoria*, I, pp. 330–31.
30 RA QVJ: 25 April 1841.
31 *The Letters of Queen Victoria*, I, pp. 331–2.
32 RA QVJ: 25, 26 and 29 April 1841.
33 RA QVJ: 6 May 1841.
34 *Hansard's*, 3rd Series, 1841, Vol. 58, pp. 338–49.
35 *Historical Record of the Eleventh Hussars*, pp. 89–91.
36 *United Service Gazette*, 10 July 1841 and 18 March 1848.
37 Ibid., 2 Dec. 1848, 6 Nov. 1852 and 10 Dec. 1853.
38 PEEL, Add. MSS. 40489/f/343 and f/345, 40498/f/130, BL.
39 Ibid., 40446/f/247, 40498/f/134 and f/138.
40 *Historical Record of the Eleventh Hussars*, p. 91.
41 Anstruther Thomson, *Eighty Years' Reminiscences*, I, pp. 85–90.
42 Jackson, *History of the United Service Club*, p. 35.
43 *United Service Gazette*, 8 Oct. 1842 and 25 Dec. 1847.

Chapter Ten – Criminal Conversation

1 Cardigan to Peel, 3 March 1842, PEEL, Add. MSS.40503.f.194, BL.
2 Peel to Cardigan, 7 March 1842, ibid., f.200; *The Letters of Queen Victoria*, I, p. 386.
3 Brialmont, *Wellington*, IV, pp. 112–13; Adeline, p. 10.
4 RA QVJ: 20 and 21 April 1842; *The Letters of Queen Victoria*, I, pp. 393–4.
5 Sweetman, p. 97.
6 RA QVJ: 27 April 1842.
7 Hill to Queen Victoria, 15 April 1842, RA B4/76.
8 Stockmar to Queen Victoria, 20 July 1842, RA Y152.
9 *Halifax Guardian*, 20 Aug. 1842.
10 Woodham-Smith, pp. 97–8.
11 FORREST, 5804/32, NAM.
12 Woodham-Smith, p. 98.
13 Ibid., p. 99.
14 Ibid., p. 100.
15 *Freeman's Journal*, 17 Oct. 1843.
16 Loy Smith, p. 64.
17 *Freeman's Journal*, 21 Oct. 1843; Anglesey, *One-Leg*, pp. 235–6, 292–4, 313–15.
18 *The Times*, 28 Feb. 1844.
19 Fraser, *Flashman and the Angel of the Lord*, p. 21.
20 *Freeman's Journal*, 8 Sept. and 21 Oct. 1843; *The Age*, 24 Sept. 1843.
21 Anglesey, *One-Leg*, p. 316.
22 *The Times*, 22 and 23 Dec. 1843; *The Age*, 23 Dec. 1843.
23 *United Service Gazette*, 1 Feb. 1844.
24 Anglesey, *One-Leg*, p. 315.
25 *The Times*, 28 Feb. 1841.
26 Tollemache, op. cit., p. 126.
27 Adeline, pp. 26–7.
28 Thomas, p. 174.
29 Adeline, pp. 93–4.
30 Fraser, op. cit., p. 21.
31 Adeline, p. 92.

Chapter Eleven – The Sick Man of Europe

1 Loy Smith, p. 65.
2 Ibid., p. 68.
3 Ibid., p. 65.
4 Wellington to Ellenborough, 18 Feb. 1846 (copy sent to author by Lord Colville).
5 Loy Smith, p. 67.
6 Blake, *Disraeli*, p. 221.
7 Woodward, op. cit., p. 122.
8 Blake, *Disraeli*, p. 227; *Hansard's*, 3rd Series, Vol. 83, pp. 111–23.
9 Ibid., Vol. 86, pp. 1222–4.
10 Blake, *Disraeli*, p. 241.
11 *The History of White's*, p. 223.
12 Nethercote, op. cit., p. 353; Paget, *The Flying Parson*, p. 276.

13 Fane, *Chit-Chat*, p. 41.
14 Loy Smith, p. 69.
15 *John Bull,* 11 Nov. 1848.
16 *Historical Record of the Eleventh Hussars*, p. 176.
17 BROWN, MS. 1848/f/24, 1859/f/8, 2847/f/428, NLS; Longford, op. cit., p. 372.
18 *Hansard's*, 3rd Series, Vol. 111, pp. 1362–5.
19 Woodward, op. cit., p. 247n.
20 BROWN, MS. 1848/f/39 and f/53, NLS.
21 Ibid., MS. 1848/ff/61–4.
22 *The Letters of Queen Victoria*, II, pp. 476, 478.
23 Blake, *Disraeli*, pp. 328–48.
24 Palmer, *The Banner of Battle*, pp. 6–7.
25 Ibid., p. 14.
26 Ibid., p. 20.
27 *The Times*, 12 Dec. 1853; *Morning Chronicle,* 20 Dec. 1853; Loy Smith, p. 77.
28 *The Letters of Queen Victoria*, III, p. 16.
29 Hodge, pp. 3–4.
30 Woodham-Smith, pp. 33–4.
31 Russell, p. 118.
32 Ibid., pp. 315–16.
33 Sweetman, pp. 172–3.
34 Hodge, p. 6.

Chapter Twelve – Off to War

1 Hibbert, *Raglan,* p. 3.
2 Sweetman, p. 170.
3 Hibbert, *Raglan,* p. 8.
5 *The Times*, 4 May 1854.
5 Ibid., 22 and 25 April 1854.
6 Loy Smith, p. 89.
7 Duberly, pp. 2–19.
8 Loy Smith, p. 80.
9 Temple Godman, *The Fields of* War, pp. 11–12.
10 Hodge, p. 14.
11 Woodham-Smith, p. 145.
12 Ibid., p. 147.
13 Duberly, pp. 19–21.
14 Palmer, op. cit., p. 56.
15 Duberly, p. 29.
16 BROWN, MS. 1859/f/133, NLS.
17 Duberly, pp. 31–4; Temple Godman, op. cit., p. 26.
18 Woodham-Smith, p. 149.
19 Ibid., pp. 149–50, 152, 153.
20 Palmer, op. cit., p. 59.
21 BRUD, N/IV/2 and 3, NRO.
22 Anstruther Thomson, op. cit., I, p. 165.
23 *Eight Months*, pp. 36, 48.
24 Cardigan to Raglan, 30 June 1854, RAGLAN, 6807/292/6, NAM.

25   Anstruther Thomson, op. cit., I, p. 165.
26   Raglan to Cardigan, 3 July 1854, BRUD, N/IV/5, NRO.
27   Hodge, p. 17.
28   Anstruther Thomson, op. cit., I, p. 165.
29   Ryan, *Was Lord Cardigan a Hero?*, p. 23; Duberly, pp. 46–7.
30   Mitchell, p. 24; Temple Godman, op. cit., p. 33.
31   Forrest to his brother, 17 July 1854, FORREST, 5804/32, NAM; Paget, p. 7.
32   Russell, pp. 115–16.
33   Ryan, *Was Lord Cardigan a Hero?*, p. 20.
34   *United Service Gazette*, 5 Aug. 1854.
35   Anstruther Thomson, op. cit., I, p. 166.
36   *Affidavits*, pp. 8–9.
37   RAGLAN, 6807/292/6, NAM.
38   Graham to Clarendon, 1 March 1854, quoted in Palmer, op. cit., p. 61.
39   Quoted in Sweetman, p. 195.
40   Newcastle to Raglan, 29 June 1854, WO 6/74/5, PRO.
41   Temple Godman, op. cit., p. 35.
42   FORREST, 5804/32, NAM.
43   Hodge, pp. 18, 20.
44   Anglesey, p. 37.
45   Duberly, p. 53.
46   Mitchell, pp. 28–9.
47   Duberly, p. 58.
48   Mitchell, p. 29.
49   Loy Smith, p. 94; RAGLAN, 6807/292/6, NAM.
50   Mitchell, p. 29.
51   Cardigan to Raglan, 7, 12 and 19 Aug. 1854; Raglan to Cardigan, 18 and 20
     Aug. 1854, RAGLAN, 6807/292/6, NAM; Mitchell, p. 29.
52   Ibid., p. 30; Shakespear, quoted in Anglesey, p. 37; Loy Smith, p. 94.
53   RAGLAN, 6807/292-6, NAM.
54   Mitchell, p. 33; Duberly, p. 66.
55   Mitchell, pp. 35–6.
56   Duberly, p. 71.
57   Forrest to his brother, 27 Aug. 1854, FORREST, 5804/32, NAM.
58   Paget, p. 9.
59   Quoted in Woodham-Smith, pp. 163–4.
60   *Eight Months*, pp. 69–70.

Chapter Thirteen – Crimea

1   Duberly, p. 73.
2   Mitchell, p. 37.
3   Woodham-Smith, pp. 168–9.
4   Duberly, p. 78.
5   Mitchell, p. 40; Loy Smith, p. 96.
6   Duberly, p. 80.
7   Mitchell, p. 42.
8   Loy Smith, p. 98.
9   Paget, p. 18.
10 Loy Smith, p. 99; Mitchell, p. 49.

11 *Eight Months*, p. 75; Russell, p. 47; Mitchell, p. 50; Williams, *XI Hussars,* p. 190.
12 Anglesey, p. 47; Mitchell, pp. 51–2; Forrest to his brother, 12 Oct. 1854, FORREST, 5804/32, NAM.
13 Loy Smith, p. 102.
14 Mitchell, p. 55.
15 Kinglake, III, p. 286.
16 Loy Smith, p. 106; Anglesey, p. 49.
17 BLUNT, 5610–47, NAM; Woodham-Smith, p. 192.
18 Paget, p. 29; Anglesey; 49; Loy Smith, p. 106.
19 Russell, p. 116; BLUNT, 5610/47, NAM.
20 Mitchell, pp. 56–7.
21 Palmer, op. cit., p. 105; Russell, p. 75.
22 Cardigan to Raglan, 21 Sept. 1854, quoted in Woodham-Smith, p. 194; Lucan to Raglan, 22 Sept. 1854, Raglan to Lucan, 28 Sept. 1854, quoted in Russell, pp. 319-20.
23 Ibid., pp. 320–21.
24 Paget, p. 32.
25 Loy Smith, p. 113.
26 Ibid., pp. 113–14; Mitchell, p. 66; Pennington, *Sea, Camp and Stage*, p. 51.
27 Loy Smith, p. 115; HARROWBY, 19 Feb. 1855, 7712/46, NAM.
28 Anglesey, pp. 52–3.
29 Mitchell, p. 64.
30 HARROWBY, 19 Feb. 1855, 7712/46, NAM.
31 Calthorpe, *Head-Quarters*, I, pp. 217–18; Loy Smith, p. 118; Mitchell, p. 65.
32 Ibid., p. 68.
33 Paget, p. 50.
34 Woodham-Smith, p. 203.
35 Hodge, p. 33.
36 *Extracts from Letters of ER Fisher-Rowe*, p. 19; Anglesey, p. 58; Duberly, p. 100; Paget, p. 64.
37 Ibid., p. 57.
38 FORREST, 5804/32, NAM.
39 Paget, p. 58.
40 Duberly, p. 103.
41 Hodge, p. 33.
42 Paget, p. 59.
43 Woodham-Smith, p. 207.
44 Paget, pp. 63–6.
45 BLUNT, 5610/47, NAM; Russell, pp. 130–31.
46 BLUNT, 5610/47, NAM.
47 Russell, pp. 127–8.

Chapter Fourteen – 'Charge!'

1 Paget, pp. 161–2.
2 Anglesey, p. 63.
3 Paget, p. 162.
4 Mitchell, p. 79.
5 Loy Smith, pp. 125–6.
6 Paget, p. 165.

7   *Speech of Major General the Earl of Lucan in the House of Lords,* p. 7.
8   Russell, pp. 138–40.
9   Mitchell, p. 80; Russell, pp. 140–41; Loy Smith, pp. 125–6; Duberly, pp. 117–18.
10 Loy Smith, p. 127; Anglesey, p. 67n.
11 Sweetman, p. 247.
12 Russell, pp. 144–6.
13 Kinglake, IV, pp. 124–5; *Russell's Despatches from the Crimea,* p. 122; Barker, *The Vainglorious War,* p. 156n; Russell, p. 147.
14 Lt Strangways, quoted in Anglesey, p. 65.
15 Kinglake, IV, p. 133.
16 Paget, pp. 174–5.
17 Lt Strangways, quoted in Anglesey, pp. 70–71; Temple Godman, op. cit., p. 78; Russell, p. 151.
18 Ivanovitch, quoted in Anstruther Thomson, op. cit., I, p. 177; Hodge, p. 49; Temple Godman, op. cit., p. 76.
19 Anglesey, p. 73; Temple Godman, p. 102.
20 Kinglake, IV, pp. 209–10n.
21 Ibid., pp. 208, 209n, 219–20; *Speech,* p. 29.
22 Carew, *Combat and Carnival,* pp. 210–11; Hibbert, *Raglan,* p. 141; Wightman, *Nineteenth Century,* p. 851.
23 *Affidavits,* pp. 9, 21; Kinglake, IV, p. 217n.
24 Loy Smith, p. 130; Paget, p. 176.
25 *Speech,* pp. 8–9.
26 *Hansard's,* 3rd Series, Vol. 137, p. 736; *Speech,* pp. 30–31.
27 Calthorpe, *Head-Quarters,* I, p. 313; *Speech,* p. 9; Palmer, op. cit., p. 129.
28 Wightman, op. cit., p. 852; *Speech,* p. 9; Kinglake, IV, pp. 238–41; BLUNT, 5610–47, NAM; Lucan to Raglan, 27 Oct. 1854, RAGLAN, 6807–288-2, NAM; Russell, pp. 154–5.
29 Loy Smith, p. 131: Wightman, op. cit., p. 852; Thomas, p. 242; Fane, *Chit-Chat,* p. 42.
30 Kinglake, IV, p. 401; Paget, p. 170.
31 Wightman, op. cit., pp. 852–4; Russell, p. 165; HARROWBY, 19 Feb. 1855, 7712/46, NAM; Kinglake, IV, pp. 256, 266, 292; Cardigan to Howe, 28 Oct. 1854, quoted in Wake, p. 408; Mitchell, p. 84; Loy Smith, p. 132.
32 Yorke, quoted in Anglesey, p. 94; Kinglake, IV, p. 400.
33 Ibid., pp. 291–2; Wightman, op. cit., p. 855; Smith, quoted in Anglesey, p. 96; Kinglake, IV, pp. 292, 295–8, 402; Johnson to Cardigan, 17 Dec. 1859, BRUD, N/XV/8, NRO; *Affidavits,* pp. 22–7; Hunt to Calthorpe, quoted in Cardigan, *Statement and Remarks,* p. 22; Loy Smith, p. 132.
34 Anstruther Thomson, op. cit., I, pp. 176–7; Loy Smith, p. 134; Paget, pp. 188–92; Parkes's affidavit, *Affidavits,* p. 31; Kinglake, IV, pp. 329–33; Clowes' and Mayow's affidavits, *Affidavits,* pp. 19, 21.
35 Cardigan to Kinglake, undated, BRUD, N/XV/1, NRO; Mitchell, p. 85; Lucan's affidavit, *Affidavits,* pp. 17–18; Kinglake, IV, p. 359; Cardigan's Statement, Kinglake, IV, p. 402; Scarlett to Cardigan, 4 Sept. 1855, BRUD, N/XV/9, NRO; Paget to General Yorke, 29 Nov. 1856, BRUD, N/XV/8, NRO.
36 Ferguson's affidavit, *Affidavits,* p. 28; Paget, pp. 193–4; Jenyns to Cardigan, 2 Sept. 1855, BRUD, N/XV/8, NRO; Cardigan's Statement, Kinglake, IV, pp. 402; Russell, p. 160.

37 Kinglake, IV, p. 357; Official Return of the Adjutant-General, 26 Oct. 1854, quoted in Loy Smith, pp. 213–15; Nominal Returns, 25 Oct. 1854, BRUD, N/XV/9, NRO.
38 Parkes' affidavit, *Affidavits*, p. 31.
39 *The Oxford Book of War Poetry*, pp. 115–16.

Chapter Fifteen – 'See! The Conquering Hero Comes!'

1 Loy Smith, p. 148.
2 *Speech,* pp. 11–12.
3 Wake, p. 408.
4 *Affidavits,* pp. 6, 25.
5 RAGLAN, 6807–288-2, NAM.
6 General Orders, 29 Oct. 1854, BRUD, N/XV/9, NRO; Anglesey, p. 105.
7 Thomas, pp. 252–3; Duberly, p. 124.
8 Loy Smith, pp. 153–4; Russell, p. 177; Sweetman, p. 259.
9 Paget, pp. 230, 253.
10 Temple Godman, op. cit., pp. 86–7; Loy Smith, pp. 158–9.
11 Tulloch, *The Crimean Commission*, pp. 25–30; Thomas, p. 256.
12 Portal, *Letters from the Crimea*, p. 71.
13 Cardigan to Raglan, 19 Nov. 1854, quoted in Woodham-Smith, pp. 264–5; *Affidavits*, p. 10; Thomas, pp. 257–8.
14 *Eight Months,* p. 104; Cardigan to Raglan (two letters), 12 Dec. 1854, RAGLAN, 6807/288/2.
15 Speech, pp. 11–16; Sweetman, pp. 264, 271–2.
16 Carew, *Combat and Carnival*, p. 188.
17 *Punch*, 25 Nov. 1854.
18 *The Letters of Queen Victoria,* III, p. 67; Thomas, pp. 262–3.
19 RA QVJ: 16–18 Jan. 1855.
20 Quoted in Woodham-Smith, pp. 262–3.
21 Hodge, pp. 83, 86–7.
22 HARROWBY, 7 Feb. 1855, 7712/46, NAM.
23 *The Times,* 7 Feb. 1855; *United Service Gazette*, 10 Feb. 1855.
24 *Northampton Mercury,* 10 Feb. 1855.
25 Ryan, *Was Lord Cardigan a Hero?*, pp. 35–6.
26 HARROWBY, 19 Feb. 1855, 7712/46, NAM.
27 Ryan, *Our Heroes of the Crimea*, pp. 48, 58.
28 *The Panmure Papers,* I, pp. 99–100.
29 *Report of the Select Committee on the Army before Sebastopol*, Parliamentary Papers, 1854–55, IX, Part 1, pp. 259–77.
30 *Hansard's*, 3rd Series, Vol. 137, pp. 731–73.
31 *Speech*, pp. 29–30.
32 *The Times,* 7 and 13 April, 5 May 1856: Hodge, p. 102.

Chapter Sixteen – 'Was Lord Cardigan a Hero?'

1 *The Panmure Papers,* pp. 80, 112; Paget, p. 88; Temple Godman, op. cit., pp. 142–3.
2 *Report of the Select Committee on the Army before Sebastopol*, op. cit., Part 3, pp. 367–87.

3   Hodge, p. 116.
4   Paget, p. 117.
5   *The Times*, 9 July 1855.
6   Ryan, *Was Lord Cardigan a Hero?*, pp. IX, 52; *United Service Gazette*, 15 Sept. 1855.
7   Ibid., 3 May 1856.
8   Tulloch, *The Crimean Commission and the Chelsea Board*, pp. 26–30.
9   Carew, *Combat and Carnival*, p. 209.
10 *The Times*, 4 Sept. 1856; *Daily News*, 11 Sept. 1856.
11 *Morning Post*, 30 Sept., 7, 11 and 14 Oct. 1856.
12 Correspondence between Cardigan, Paget and Cambridge, June–Dec. 1856, BRUD, N/VIII/1, NRO.
13 Calthorpe, Head-Quarters, I, pp. 86, 184, 310, 317; II, p, 5.
14 BRUD, N/XV/8, NRO.
15 *Affidavits*, pp. 7–12.
15 Ibid., pp. 12–13.
17 BRUD, N/IV/28, NRO.
18 RA Ell/34, 35, 36, 38 and 42.
19 Thomas, p. 295.
20 *Affidavits*, pp. 14–15.
21 BRUD, N/XV/8, NRO.
22 *Affidavits*, pp. 17–18.
23 Ibid., p. 16.
24 Ibid., pp. 211, 219.
25 *The Times*, 11 June 1863.
26 Kinglake, IV, pp. 426–7.

Chapter Seventeen – One Last Scandal

1   Cardigan to Lady Ailesbury, 4 July 1856, AILES, 1300/5233, WRO; DRURY, 11 Dec. 1856, Dr/F/109, UN.
2   Adeline, pp. 94–5.
3   Ibid., p. 7.
4   Ibid., pp. 39–44.
5   Ibid., p. 82.
6   Stirling, *William de Morgan,* p. 149.
7   Adeline, pp. 94, 95, 97.
8   Ibid., pp. 98–101.
9   *Hansard's*, 3rd Series, Vol. 156, p. 1028.
10 Adeline, pp. 102–4.
11 Fane, *Chit-Chat*, pp. 44–5.
12 Wake, pp. 435–6.
13 Ibid., pp. 437–8.
14 Adeline, pp. 104–6.
15 Wake, p. 432.
16 Ibid., p. 431.
17 Hodge, p. 147.
18 Wake, p. 429.
19 Cardigan to Cambridge, 9 Aug. 1862, BRUD, N/XV/9, NRO.
20 Military Secretary to Cardigan, 30 Sept. 1864, ibid.

21 *XI Hussar Journal*, 1911, pp. 14–15.
22 *Hansard's*, 3rd Series, Vol. 146, p. 949.
23 Ibid., Vol. 149, pp. 802–3.
24 Ibid., Vol. 151, p. 726.
25 Woodward, op. cit., pp. 182, 600.
26 Blake, *Disraeli*, pp. 439–40.
27 Ibid., p. 450.
28 Woodward, op. cit., pp. 187–8.
29 *Hansard's*, 3rd Series, Vol. 189, p. 571.
30 Ibid., Vol. 190, pp. 1147–8.
31 Fane, *Chit-Chat*, p. 43; Geddington News Letter, undated, Brudenell Papers, Deene Park.
32 Wake, p. 439.
33 Ibid.
34 Ibid., p. 437.
35 Anstruther Thomson, op. cit., p. 382.
36 *Northampton Mercury*, 4 April 1868; Adeline, p. 108.
37 Wake, pp. 442–5; Adeline, pp. 109–10.
38 Fane, *Chit-Chat*, pp. 46–7.
39 Paget, *The Pytchley Hunt,* p. 261.
40 Paget, p. 66.
41 'Thormanby', op. cit., p. 247.
42 Ibid., p. 250.
43 Ibid., p. 244.

Bibliography

Anglesey, Marquess of, *History of the British Cavalry: Vol. II 1851–1871* (Leo Cooper, 1975).
———, *One-Leg: The Life and Letters of Henry William Paget, First Marquess of Anglesey, 1768–1854* (Jonathan Cape, 1961).
Anstruther Thomson, John, *Eighty Years' Reminiscences*, Vol. 1 (Longmans, 1904).
Apperley, Charles James, *My Life and Times* by 'Nimrod', ed. E.D. Cuming (1927).
———, *Nimrod's Hunting Reminiscences* (Bodley Head, 1926).
———, *Nimrod's Hunting Tours* (Bodley Head, 1926).
———, *The Chase, the Road, and the Turf* (Edward Arnold, 1898).
Army Purchase Question, The (London, 1858).
Barker, A.J., *The Vainglorious War: 1854–56* (Weidenfeld & Nicholson, 1970).
Barthorp, Michael, *Heroes of the Crimea: The Battles of Balaclava and Inkerman* (Blandford, 1991).
Baldick, Robert, *The Duel: A History of Duelling* (Chapman & Hall, 1965).
Blake, Robert, *Disraeli* (Methuen, 1969).
Brialmont, M., and Gleig, Rev. M.A., *History of the Life of Arthur Duke of Wellington*, 4 Vols (Longman, 1860).
Brooksbank, Arthur, *Letters from the Crimea by a Subaltern Officer* (privately printed, 1873).
Brown, Gen. Sir George, *Memoranda and Observations on the Crimean War, 1854–5* (privately printed, 1879).
Burke Peerage and Baronetage (London, 1826).
Calthorpe, Hon. Somerset, *Cardigan v. Calthorpe: Affidavits filed by the Respondent* (John Murray, 1863).
———, *Letters from Head-Quarters*, 2 Vols (John Murray, 1856).
Cardigan, Adeline, Countess of, *My Recollections* (Eveleigh Nash, 1909).
Cardigan, James Thomas Brudenell, 7th Earl of, *Eight Months on Active Service* (1855).
———, *Statement and Remarks upon the Affidavits filed by Lieutenant-Colonel Calthorpe* (1863).

Cardigan, James Thomas Brudenell, 7th Earl of, *The Cavalry Brigade Movements* (1861).
Cardigan, Earl of, *The Wardens of Savernake Forest* (Routledge, 1949).
Carew, Peter, *Combat and Carnival* (Constable, 1954).
Chandos, John, *Boys Together: English Public Schools 1800–1864* (Hutchinson, 1984).
Cokayne, G.E., *The Complete Peerage:* Vol. 3 (London, 1913).
Collins, William L., *The Public Schools* (Blackwood, 1867).
Compton, Piers, *Cardigan of Balaclava* (Robert Hale, 1972).
Creevey Papers, The, ed. Sir Herbert Maxwell (John Murray, 1903).
Dale, Antony, *Fashionable Brighton* (Country Life, 1947).
Duberly, Mrs Henry, *Journal Kept during the Russian War* (Longman, 1855).
Dunbar, Janet, *Golden Interlude: The Edens in India 1836–1842* (John Murray, 1955).
Eden, Emily, *Up the Country,* 2 Vols (Bentley, 1866).
Extracts from Letters of E.R. Fisher-Rowe during the Crimean War, 1854–55, ed. Major L.R. Fisher-Rowe (privately printed, 1907).
Fane, Lady Augusta, *Chit Chat* (Thornton, 1926).
Fraser, George Macdonald, *Flashman and the Angel of the Lord* (Harvill, 1994).
Gash, Norman, *Aristocracy and People: Britain 1815–1865* (Edward Arnold, 1979).
Goldfrank, David M., *The Origins of the Crimean War* (Longman, 1994).
Greville Memoirs, The, 3 Vols, ed. H. Reeve (1875).
Gronow, Rees Howell, *Captain Gronow: His Reminiscences of Regency and Victorian Life 1810–60,* ed. Christopher Hibbert (Kyle Cathie, 1991).
Harrow School Register, The, 1801–1893, ed. R. Courtenay Welch, (Longmans, 1894).
Hawkyard, Alasdair, *William Henry Fox Talbot* (privately printed, 1989).
Hearder, Harry, *Europe in the Nineteenth Century 1830–1880* (Longman, 1988).
Hibbert, Christopher, *George IV: Regent and King 1811–1830* (Allen Lane, 1973).
———, *The Destruction of Lord Raglan* (Longman, 1961).
———, *The Great Mutiny: India 1857* (Penguin, 1980).
Hinde, Thomas, *Courtiers: 900 Years of Court Life* (Victor Gollanz, 1986).
Historical Record of the Eleventh or Prince Albert's Own Hussars (London, 1843).
History of the University of Oxford, The, V, The Eighteenth Century, ed. L.S. Sutherland and L.G. Mitchell (Clarendon, 1986).
History of White's, The, 2 Vols (London, 1892).
Hodge, Edward, *Little Hodge,* ed. Marquess of Anglesey (Leo Cooper, 1971).
Hopkirk, Mary, *Queen Adelaide* (John Murray, 1946).
Hunter, P.D., *The Harrow Collection* (1994).
Jackson, Maj.-Gen. Sir Louis, *History of the United Service Club* (London, 1937).
James, Robert Rhodes, *Albert, Prince Consort* (Hamish Hamilton, 1983).
Judd, Denis, *The Crimean War* (Granada, 1975).
Kinglake, Alexander, *The Invasion of the Crimea,* 8 Vols (Blackwood, 1863–87).
Letters of Queen Victoria, The, 1837–1861, 3 Vols (John Murray, 1907).
Lockhart, J.G., *Memoirs of the Life of Sir Walter Scott, Bart* (John Murray, 1837).
Longford, Elizabeth, *Wellington: Pillar of State* (Weidenfeld & Nicholson, 1972).
Loy Smith, George, *A Victorian RSM* (Costello, 1987).
Moyse-Bartlett, Lt.-Col. H., *Louis Edward Nolan and his influence on the British Cavalry* (Leo Cooper, 1971).
Murray, R.H., *The History of the VIII King's Royal Irish Hussars 1693–1927,* 2 Vols (Heffer, 1928).
Nevill, Lady Dorothy, *Under Five Reigns* (Methuen, 1910).
Nethercote, H.O., *The Pytchley Hunt: Past and Present* (London, 1888).

Oxford Book of War Poetry, The, ed. John Stallworthy (Oxford, 1984).

Oxford Dictionary of Quotations, The, Second Edition (Oxford, 1968).

Paget, General Lord George, *The Light Cavalry Brigade in the Crimea* (John Murray, 1881).

Paget, Guy, *The History of the Althorp and Pytchley Hunt 1634–1920* (Collins, 1937).

———, *The Flying Parson and Dick Christian* (Leicester, 1934).

Palmer, Alan, *The Banner of Battle: The Story of the Crimean War* (Weidenfeld & Nicholson, 1987).

Panmure, Lord, *The Panmure Papers* (Hodder & Stoughton, 1908).

Pennington, W.H., *Sea, Camp and Stage* (1906).

Pepys, Samuel, *The Shorter Pepys*, ed. Robert Latham (Penguin, 1987).

Pocock, Tom, *Sailor King: The Life of King William IV* (Sinclair-Stevenson, 1991).

Portal, Captain Robert, *Letters from the Crimea: 1854–1855* (privately printed, 1900).

Proceedings of the General Court Martial upon the Trial of Captain Wathen, 15th Kings Hussars (Roake & Varty, 1834).

Report of the Select Committee on the Army before Sebastopol, House of Commons Parliamentary Papers, 1854–55, IX, Parts 1–3.

Return of Copies or Extracts of Correspondence respecting Lord Brudenell (printed by order of the House of Commons, 13 April 1836).

Russell, William H., *Russell's Despatches from the Crimea*, ed. Nicolas Bentley (Panther, 1970).

———, *The Great War with Russia* (Routledge, 1895).

Ryan, George, *Our Heroes of the Crimea* (1855).

———, *Was Lord Cardigan a Hero at Balaklava?* (1855).

Sanders, Mary, *The Life and Times of Queen Adelaide* (Stanley Paul, 1915).

Speech of Major-General the Earl of Lucan in the House of Lords, Monday, March 19, 1855 (Hatchard, 1855).

Stanton, A.H., *On Chiltern Slopes* (Blackwell, 1927).

Stirling, A.M.W., *William de Morgan and his Wife* (London, 1922).

Stocqueler, J.H., *A Personal History of the Horse-Guards from 1750 to 1872* (London, 1873).

Sweetman, John, *Raglan: From the Peninsula to the Crimea* (Arms & Armour, 1993).

Temple Godman, Richard, *The Fields of War: A Young Cavalryman's Crimea Campaign*, ed. Philip Warner (John Murray, 1977).

Trial of James Thomas Earl of Cardigan before the Right Honourable the House of Peers, The (Gurney, 1841).

Thomas, Donald, *Charge! Hurrah! Hurrah! A Life of Cardigan of Balaclava* (Futura, 1976).

'Thormanby' [W. Willmott Dixon], *Kings of the Hunting Field* (Hutchinson, 1899).

Tollemache, Maj-Gen E.D.H., *The Tollemaches of Helmingham and Ham* (Cowell, 1949).

Townsend, William C., *Modern State Trials*, I (Longmans, 1850).

Tulloch, Colonel Alexander, *The Crimean Commission and the Chelsea Board* (London, 1857).

Weintraub, Stanley, *Victoria* (Unwin Hyman, 1987).

Wake, Joan, *The Brudenells of Deene* (1959).

Wightman, J.W., 'One of the "Six Hundred" on the Balaclava Charge', *Nineteenth Century*, Vol. 31, 1892.

Wilkinson-Latham, Robert, *Uniforms & Weapons of the Crimean War* (Batsford, 1977).

Williams, Godfrey, *The Historical Records of the Eleventh Hussars* (George Newnes, 1908).

Williams, Major G.T., *Regimental History of the 11th Hussars* (Gale & Polden, 1925). Abridged edition.

Woodham-Smith, Cecil, *The Reason Why* (Penguin, 1958).

———, *Queen Victoria: Her Life and Times 1819–1861* (Hamish Hamilton, 1972).

Woodward, Llewellyn, *The Age of Reform: England 1815–1870* (Oxford, 1962).

Wylly, Col. H.C., *XVth (The King's) Hussars 1759–1913* (Caxton, 1914).

PERIODICALS

The Age
Alligator
Bell's Life in London
Brighton Herald
Daily News
Drakard's Stamford News
The Examiner
Freeman's Journal
The Globe
Halifax Guardian
The Harrovian
John Bull
Morning Chronicle
Morning Herald
Morning Post
Naval and Military Gazette
New Weekly Despatch
Nineteenth Century
Northampton Herald
Northampton Mercury
Punch
The Sun
The Times
United Service Gazette

Index

Lennox, Lord George, 96, 176
Letters from Head-Quarters (Calthorpe), 341–3, 345, 346, 372
Light Brigade, 232, 321–2; advance on Sebastopol, 265, 266; camped in Devna, 244–5; charge of *see* Charge of the Light Brigade; and cholera, 255; embarkation for Crimea, 257–8, 259, 261; inaction over Heavy Brigade's flank attack on Russian cavalry, 293–6; regiment composition, 253; reigning in by Raglan after battle of Kourgane Hill, 268, 269; and Russian attack on Causeway Heights, 286
Lincoln, Lord, 215
Liprandi, General, 285, 313
Liverpool, Lord, 27, 28
Lockwood, Captain, 311
London, 23–4
Londonderry, Marquess of, 184–5
Louis XVIII, King, 30
Lovett, William, 188
Loy Smith, George, 192–3, 212; on Cardigan's regime, 108, 111, 210, 211; and charge of Light Brigade, 302, 309; and Crimea, 241, 263, 264, 265, 269, 275, 276, 286, 295–6, 316, 321; and escorting Prince Albert on landing, 116–17; and Inkerman battle, 319–20; on Prince Albert's review of 11th Hussars, 217–18; on 'Richard Reynolds Affair', 149; stationed in India, 100, 101, 102, 103, 104, 106
Lucan, Earl of (Bingham), 232–3, 254, 275; background, 232–3; command of Cavalry division in Crimea, 232, 233–4; camped at Varna, 259–60; and Sebastopol advance, 265; and Raglan's reigning in of troops after battle of Kourgane Hill, 268, 268; disputes with Cardigan, 233, 243, 245–7, 262, 266, 270, 271–3, 278, 279–80, 294, 323, 331–2; refusal to attack Russian cavalry, 279; and charge of Heavy Brigade, 292, 293; and Third Order, 296–7; and Fourth Order, 298–300; and charge of Light Brigade, 304–5, 317; and Cardigan's premature withdrawal, 310–11, 345–6; blamed for failure of charge of Light Brigade, 317–18, 323–4, 326; recall from Crimea, 330, 331, 327; attempts at clearing name after Balaclava, 331–2; and Jewish Emancipation Bill, 360; post Crimea, 366

Macaulay, Thomas, 170, 172, 176
Matrimonial Causes Act (1857), 36
Maude, Captain, 286

Maxse, Lieutenant, 257, 323
Mayne, Richard, 158
Mayow, Colonel, 265, 282, 308, 310
Melbourne, Lord, 89, 91, 110, 117, 174, 175, 176
Menschikoff, Prince, 229
Miguel, Don, 63
Military and County Club, 179
Milton, Lord, 56, 57, 58
Mirfin, Mr, 157
Mitchell, Private Albert, 255, 256, 261–2, 264–5, 266, 268, 302, 310
Molesworth, Sir William, 93, 94–5, 96, 227
Molyneux, George, 40–1
Morning Chronicle, 168, 230; and 'Brent Affair', 112, 113–14; and Cardigan, 93, 125; and flogging of Rogers, 171–2; letter criticising Cardigan, 132; and 'Richard Reynolds Affair', 144, 147
Morning Herald, 47, 109, 115
Morning Post, 93, 147, 167, 168, 172
Morris, Lieutenant-Colonel William, 294–5, 308, 338, 339, 340
Morse Cooper, Major, 143
Moysey, Henry, 128
Muntz, Mr, 176

Napoleon I, 19–20
Napoleon III, 223, 228
Naval and Military Gazette, 91, 109, 147, 149, 168
Nesselrode, Count, 228
Nethercote, H.O., 216
Newcastle, Duke of, 231, 234, 236, 327
Nicholas I, Tsar, 227–8, 228–9, 230, 247
Noël, the Hon. Gerard, 218
Nolan, Captain Louis, 270, 284; background, 251; on Cardigan, 252; and charge of Light Brigade, 2, 3–4, 298, 299, 300, 301–2, 317, 323

O'Connell, Daniel, 44, 190, 192
O'Connor, Feargus, 188
Omar Pasha, 243
Ottoman Empire, 227–31
Oxford, Edward, 178

Pacifico, Don, 221
Packenham, Major-General Sir Hercules, 140, 143
Page, Captain, 138, 139
Paget, Lord George, 259, 265, 273, 286–7, 290; and battle of Inkerman, 319, 320; and Cardigan, 279, 281, 282, 296, 339, 341, 371; and charge of Light Brigade, 3, 300–1,

Smith, Tom, 153
Smyth, Major Carmichael, 190
Somerset, Lord Fitzroy (later Lord Raglan),
    88, 114, 137, 154, 186, 225; and Cardigan's
    re-appointment, 91, 92; in Spain, 30–1;
    and Wathen Trial, 86–7; see also Raglan,
    Lord
Spain, 30–1
St Arnaud, Marshal, 238, 242, 244, 267, 270,
    271
St James's Military Club, 179
Stanley, Lord, 216, 221
Stockmar, Baron, 187
Straits Convention, 227
Sun, The, 140, 141, 149
Surret, Private, 67
Sweetman, John, 234

Temple Godman, Lieutenant Richard, 245,
    254, 291, 292, 320–1, 333
Tennyson, Alfred, 313–15
Thackwell, Lieutenant-Colonel (later General
    Sir) Joseph, 60–1, 62, 254
Thistlewood, Arthur, 29
Thom, Sergeant-Major James, 64, 78, 79–80
Thomson, John Anstruther, 182, 203–4, 366
'Thormanby', 372
Times, The, 93, 230, 238, 335; and 'Black
    Bottle Affair', 126; and Paget case, 199,
    204–5 ; and 'Richard Reynolds Affair', 147;
    and Roger's flogging, 173; and Tuckett
    Trial, 157, 168, 169; and Wathen Trial, 83
Tollemache, Admiral John, 32, 34, 35
Tollemache, Wilbrahim, 19
Tories, 26, 50, 51 see also Conservative Party
Torlese, Charles, 15, 16
Traveller's Club, 30
Tresham, Mary, 6
Tuckett, Lieutenant Harvey, 105, 109, 119;
    duel with Cardigan, 132–5; hearing over
    duel, 137–40, 144; trial, 156–7, 158–66;
    reaction to Cardigan's acquittal, 167–70
Tulloch, Colonel, 336, 337, 338
Turkey see Ottoman Empire
Turner, Colonel Charles, 77

United Service Club, 178, 328
United Service Gazette, 83–4, 97, 125, 147,
    178, 179, 183, 252, 328, 336
Uxbridge, Earl of, 20; see also Anglesey,
    Marquess of

Victoria, Queen, 102, 110, 151; assassination
    attempt, 177–8; and Cardigan, 145, 157,

174–5, 186–7, 325–6, 366; Coronation,
    106–7; and 11th Hussars, 185–6; and
    Prince Albert, 116, 357; and Tuckett duel,
    135, 157, 158; and Wellington, 225
Vienna Congress, 229–30
Vivian, General Sir Hussey, 38, 92

Waddington, Mr, 161–2
Wainwright, Captain, 138
Wales, Prince of (later King Edward VII),
    356–7
Walker, Captain, 275
Walthew, Mr, 163
Waterloo, Battle of, 19–21, 160
Wathen, Captain Augustus, 182; Cardigan's
    criticism of, 62–3, 66–7; first arrest, 64–5;
    request of leave, 65–6; addressing of men,
    72–4, 74–5, 76–7, 79–80; clothing issue
    debt, 64, 68–9, 75, 76, 77, 78, 79; second
    arrest, 74; charges brought against, 75–6;
    trial, 76–84; acquittal, 85–6, 95–6
Weguelin, Lieutenant, 191
Wellington, Duke of, 2, 29, 40, 110, 170,
    178; attacks on house, 51, 53–4; and
    Battle of Waterloo, 19, 20–1; and
    Cardigan, 91–2, 111, 190, 191, 218, 224,
    225; and Catholic Emancipation, 43–4,
    45; duel with Winchilsea, 46–7, 156; and
    Lady Ailesbury, 207; and parliamentary
    reform, 49–50, 53; on purchasing of
    commissions, 42–3; reaction to Sabbath
    flogging, 175; resignation as Prime
    Minister, 50; and Reynolds court-martial,
    145–6; death, 225
Westenra, Henry, 38
Westmorland, Lord, 179, 180
Whigs, 26
White, Captain, 303
White's, 30
Whyte-Melville, W.H., 18–19
Wightman, Private, 300, 302, 303, 304,
    305–6
Wilde, Sir Thomas, 201–2, 203
William IV, King, 48, 54, 87, 89, 102
Wilton, Lord, 21, 207, 208
Winchilsea, Lord, 46–7, 156
Winter, Frederik, 195, 196, 197, 199–200,
    202–3
Wombwell, Lieutenant Sir George, 269
Woodham-Smith, Cecil, 12
Wrangham, Serjeant, 140
Wyndham, Sir Henry, 191, 344

York, Duke of, 37, 40